AF560063

Commemoration of the 75th Year of Independence

INDIAN ARMED FORCES IN 2047 AT THE CENTENARY OF INDEPENDENCE

Commemoration of the 75th Year of Independence

INDIAN ARMED FORCES IN 2047

AT THE CENTENARY OF INDEPENDENCE

Edited by

Lt Gen Gautam Banerjee

Vivekananda International Foundation
New Delhi

PENTAGON PRESS LLP

First published in 2023 by

PENTAGON PRESS LLP
206, Peacock Lane, Shahpur Jat
New Delhi-110049, India
Contact: 011-64706243

Typeset in Adobe Garamond, 11.5 Point
Printed by Aegean Offset Printers, Greater Noida, U.P.

ISBN 978-93-90095-80-3 (HB)

www.pentagonpress.in

Contents

General N C Vij
PVSM, UYSM, AVSM (Retd)
Hony Col of the DOGRA Regt & DOGRA Scouts

Former -

- Chief of the Army Staff
- Founder Vice Chairman
  National Disaster Management Authority
- Director
  Vivekanand International Foundation
  Author of the Book - The Kashmir Conundrum
  The Quest for Peace in a Troubled Land

SADODYAMI

House No - 4500A, Sector-23A
Gurgaon (Haryana)
PIN-122017
Ph: 0124-4364500
E-mail: gncvij@gmail.com

Foreword

75th Anniversary of India's emergence as an independent, sovereign nation-state is a landmark event for India. Salience of that event is further signified by the unification of her diverse administrative units into a singular democratic dispensation. Thus, for the first time in nearly twelve centuries, the people of India earned the authority to chart the nation's destiny themselves. For a nation ruthlessly persecuted, trampled and plundered over the centuries, the journey towards that destiny has been fraught with humungous difficulties and challenges. The singular reason behind such a long period of suffering is that the Indians never stood united and allowed themselves to lose their strategic insight.

A united, well-endowed and democratic India instantly became an eye sore for her militarist, autocratic neighbours and their overt and covert associates, whereas the Indian military came to be her foremost saviour against their incessant aggressions. That notwithstanding, the fact is that it has taken many decades for our polity to appreciate, the difference between a colonial and a nationalist military institution and the latter's contribution to sovereign nation building.

In the recent years, the situation is apparently on the mend. The state is well sensitised to the possession of a strong military that must be a feature of a prosperous nation. Many path-breaking military modernisation and empowerment schemes stand initiated, including an emphasis on "Atam Nirbhar" campaign (self depend once). But there are fiscal and technological constrains which could divert us from the solemn purpose. That enjoins the nation's military professionals to envision our future military goals and propagate the achievable guidelines for India's military empowerment. The time frame considered is the coming 25 years, that is, at the Centenary of our Independence. This volume is an attempt to envision that journey.

I hope these essays would be read with great analytical interest and the spirit would be imbibed.

General N C Vij, PVSM, UYSM, AVSM (Retd)
- Former Chief of the Army Staff &
- Founder Vice Chairman, National Disaster Management Authority

New Delhi
March 2023

Preface

There is considerable hope and optimism in the country as India celebrates 75 years of Independence and enters what the Prime Minister has termed as 'Amrit Kaal', a golden era when we will emerge as a developed country. India has become the fifth-largest economy globally and is likely to emerge as the third largest in the not too distant future.

As India aspires to attain global prominence in the remaining 25 years of the Centenary, the national security challenges have become more complex. The reconfiguration of the global power equation, the rise of China, China-Pak nexus, militarisation of the Indian Ocean, arms race in outer space, weaponisation of sanctions, instability in the neighbourhood, rising threat of weapons of mass destruction, terrorism and radicalisation, salience of climate change for security, food, energy and water security issues, illegal migrations, and internal security issues are some of the numerous challenges that India has to deal with urgently.

As India becomes a leading economic power, it will also have to address the onerous task of modernisation and transformation of its armed forces. This will require political will, strategic thinking, resources, adoption of technology and holistic approach to national security. Military capability will remain an indispensable component of the comprehensive national strength along with the economy, diplomacy, technology, human resources, energy, and soft power.

How do leading military thinkers view the state of the Indian armed forces in the 75th year of Independence and what is their vision of India's armed forces of the future? The VIF is delighted to publish this volume of essays titled '*Indian Armed Forces in 2047 at the Centenary of Independence*'. Distinguished thinkers, experts and practitioners, who have devoted their lifetime to the service of the nation as members of our armed forces share their perspectives on these issues.

The essays provide a 360-degree view of India's security environment, armed forces' transformational imperative, security architecture, resource availability, and the need for developing jointness among the armed forces. There are also considered views on the Indian army, navy, air force, and special forces. The essays take a close look at information warfare, defence intelligence, the emergence of aerospace, capability development, future of wars, emerging technologies, and range of inter-connected issues. The experts provide a range of suggestions for policymakers.

I am grateful to General N.C. Vij (retd.) for writing a foreword to the book. My gratitude to Lt-General Gautam Banerjee (retd.), a leading expert on military affairs, who has edited the book. Last, but not the least, I would like to thank the eminent writers for their thoughtful contributions.

New Delhi
2 March 2023

Dr. Arvind Gupta
Director, VIF

Editor's Note

The current decade has witnessed far-reaching strategic, societal, and economic developments in India's progressive journey towards her deserved place in the world order. These developments are distinguished by the state's confident policy-making, adoption of pioneering initiatives and committed implementation of them—rise of a new India, so to say. As the nation continues to break free of pre-colonial inflictions and post-independence liabilities, both in material and cognitive terms, to secure its sovereign disposition along a vista of freedom, peace and prosperity, the 75th Year of Independence is a remarkable landmark indeed—a *celebration of the elixir of independence.*

There have been, and continue to be, formidable hurdles for the nation to negotiate on that journey. Among such hurdles, preservation of territorial sanctity, economic sovereignty and political relevance in competitive intra- and inter-regional dispensations are tedious ones. The rigours of such tests are determined by India's geographic situation between two compulsively revisionist, aggressive and militarist neighbours, the rising burden of economic compulsions and the ruthless dynamics of global politics. Political wisdom states that as a rising India proceeds to secure her benign aspirations of peace and prosperity, it would be mandatory to sustain the journey with possession of robust military prowess. That indeed is a hoary concept of a nation's 'military security'.

The purpose of this Vivekananda International Foundation publication is to visualise, candidly, for readers, a futuristic construct of India's military prowess. In that, the 75th Year of Independence is adopted as the base year and its centenary, 2047, as the first destination. Authored by prominent military thinkers of the time, this book is made of 20 essays, each discussing one aspect of the nation's military security. Notably, the visualisations conform to our strategically non-aggressive ideals of military security, while the discussions are consciously tethered to the nation's affordable defence economics.

New Delhi
28 February 2023

Gautam Banerjee, Lieutenant General (retd.)
Vivekananda International Foundation

Contributors

Lieutenant General (Dr.) J.S. Bajwa, PVSM, UYSM, SM superannuated after over 39 years of distinguished military service in diverse operational environments. A former commandant of the Officers' Training Academy, Chennai, and Chief of Staff Eastern Command, the General has authored three books on China's military. Currently, he is the Editor of the prestigious quarterly magazine, *Indian Defence Review.*

Major General Ajay Chaturvedi, AVSM, VSM (retd.) is a veteran engineer officer of the Indian Army who has held the appointments of Deputy Director General Financial Planning, Assistant Chief of Integrated Defence Staff in the Defence Intelligence Agency, Chief Engineer Northern Command and Chief of Staff of a tri-service command. A prolific author, he has been writing and lecturing extensively on national security, disaster management, and value-based leadership besides being a regular speaker on strategic issues in various universities. Presently, he is Vice-Chairman of the Lucknow-based think tank, 'STRIVE' and the Executive Director of another think tank, the 'Eco Development Foundation' for UP and Uttarakhand.

Brigadier Rahul K. Bhonsle (retd.) is an army veteran with over three decades of active service. He is an independent consultant on research and knowledge management in defence and security issues in the Indo-Asia-Pacific. He is the Director of the much regarded 'Security Risks Asia', a risk and knowledge management consultancy based in Delhi since 2006.

Sujit Dutta, former Professor of Peace and Conflict Studies at the Jamia Millia Islamia Central University and a Senior Fellow at the Institute for Defence Studies and Analyses, New Delhi, Prof. Sujit Dutta is Editor of the '*National Security*' Journal and a Distinguished Fellow, Vivekananda International Foundation (VIF), New Delhi.

Lieutenant-General Anil Ahuja (retd.), PVSM, UYSM, AVSM, SM, VSM & Bar, is a Distinguished Fellow at the VIF. He is the former Deputy Chief of the Integrated Defence Staff for Policy Planning and Force Development. He commanded a Corps along the northern borders in Arunachal Pradesh and Assam. Having been Secretary of the Defence Acquisition Council, Co-Chair of India-USA DTTI Inter-Agency Task Force, and Additional Director-General of Military Operations, he has hands-on experience of India's operational capability development.

Lt-Gen (Dr.) Rakesh Sharma, PVSM, UYSM, AVSM, VSM, commanded the Fire and Fury Corps in Ladakh responsible for Kargil, Siachen Glacier and Eastern Ladakh facing both Pakistan and China. The General was the Adjutant-General of the Indian Army responsible for Human Resource Management and superannuated in 2017. He is currently a Distinguished Fellow at the Vivekananda International Foundation (VIF) and Centre for Land Warfare Studies (CLAWS), and on the Executive Council of The Institute for Defence Studies and Analyses (IDSA) and Global Counter Terrorism Council (GCTC). He is a regular participant in seminars, delivers lectures in various institutions, and writes regularly for newspapers and military journals.

Vice-Admiral A. K. Chawla, PVSM, AVSM, NM, VSM, Ph.D. (retd.) is a former Flag Officer Commanding-in-Chief of the Navy's Southern Command and a former Captain of the aircraft carrier, INS *Viraat.* Highly experienced in maritime operations, defence acquisition, military diplomacy, human resource management and training, he is an accomplished maritime thinker and author. A regular contributor to various defence journals, he is currently an Eminent Resource Faculty for the Rashtriya Raksha University and a Council Member of the United Services Institute, as also several other think tanks. As an environmentalist, he was conferred the prestigious 'Golden Peacock Environment Management Award' in 2020.

Air Marshal Anil Chopra, PVSM, AVSM, VM, VSM (retd.) is a fighter pilot, test pilot, and a pioneer of the Mirage-2000 fleet. He commanded operational air bases in both the western and eastern sectors. Post superannuation, he has been a member of the Armed Forces Tribunal, and a member of the executive council of Jawaharlal Nehru University. An avid writer having more than 650 published articles and authored or edited seven books, the Air Marshal is the Director-General of the Centre for Air Power Studies.

Lieutenant-General (Dr.) Kamal Davar, PVSM, AVSM (retd.) a former corps commander and head of the Mechanised Forces, raised the Defence Intelligence Agency and served as its first Director-General. General Davar is a well regarded military thinker, and a prolific writer and speaker on strategic matters. He has also been a participant in Track 2 diplomacy.

Air Vice-Marshal Rajesh Isser, AVSM, VM (Gallantry) (retd.) has combat exposure in Sri Lanka (IPKF), Congo, the Kargil War and the Siachen Glacier. He has authored four books and written more than 70 articles in national and international journals. Presently, he is a Distinguished Fellow at the Centre for Air Power Studies.

Maj-Gen. Dhruv C. Katoch, SM, VSM is an alumnus of Sherwood College, Naini Tal, the National Defence Academy, Khadakvasla, the Defence Services Staff College, Wellington, the Higher Command Course, Mhow, and the National Defence College, New Delhi. He has an M.Phil. degree in Defence Studies from Madras University and has been awarded the degree of Doctor of Philosophy (*honoris causa*) from the Indira Gandhi University, Rewari, in 2016. The General has edited/co-edited eight books and writes and speaks on defence and security related issues. He also frequently appears on news channels as a discussant. He has served as the Director of the Indian Army's premier think tank, the Centre for Land Warfare Studies (CLAWS) and is presently Director, India Foundation, a leading think tank of India.

Major-General (Dr.) Prabir Kumar Chakravorty is a former Defence Attaché to Vietnam and a former Additional Director-General (Artillery) at the Integrated HQ of Defence (Army). He is a prolific writer and has authored many books dealing with Military Strategy. Currently, he is a Senior Fellow (veteran) at the Centre for Land Warfare Studies, New Delhi.

Lieutenant-General P.C. Katoch, PVSM, UYSM, AVSM, SC (retd.) is a Special Forces officer, and a former DG Information Systems of the Indian Army. He holds a Master's degree in Defence and is a graduate from the National Defence College, New Delhi. He writes regularly on international affairs, geopolitics, military, security, and technical and topical issues for Indian and foreign publications He has spoken at various security institutions in Afghanistan, China, Japan, the Maldives, South Korea, Taiwan and the USA, and has published three books on topics of national security.

One of the foremost experts on electronics and communications, **Maj-Gen P.K. Mallick,** VSM (retd.) is a graduate of Defence Services Staff College and an M. Tech from IIT, Kharagpur. Besides wide experience in command, staff, and instructional appointments in the Indian Army, he has also been a Senior Directing Staff (SDS) at National Defence College, New Delhi. A former Consultant with the Vivekananda International Foundation, New Delhi, Gen Mallick is a prolific and well-read writer on security matters.

Air Marshal Diptendu Choudhury, PVSM, AVSM, VM, VSM (retd.), a former Commandant of the National Defence College, New Delhi, is an alumnus of the Royal College of Defence Studies UK, a Post-Graduate in Strategy and International Security from King's College, London, a Master of Philosophy on Defence and Strategic Studies, and a Ph.D. on Air Power. He is an avid air power scholar, regular writer and speaker on strategy, air power and national security. Actively associated with various strategic think tanks, the Air Marshal is also a Distinguished Fellow at the VIF and the Centre for Air Power Studies.

Lt-Gen (Dr.) V.K, Saxena is a former Director-General of the Corps of Army Air Defence. He is a Distinguished Fellow at the VIF and a Visiting Fellow at the CLAWS. The General is a UN scholar and a prolific writer with five books to his credit. He is also a frequent face on TV contributing on multiple subjects in his domain of core competency.

Major-General (Dr.) Bipin Bakshi, AVSM, VSM (retd.), a Sword of Honour recipient and a Gold Medallist from the Indian Military Academy and Gold Medallist from the College of Military Engineering, is a paratrooper-engineer, scholar, warrior and sportsman, with singular achievements in youth empowerment, sailing, and national security. He has commanded an Infantry Division and was the IG Training at the NSG. He has been awarded the *Vishisht Seva Medal* (*VSM*) and *Ati Vishisht Seva Medal* (*AVSM*) in recognition of his dedicated service to the nation.

Lieutenant-General N.B. Singh, PVSM, AVSM, VSM, ADC is a former DGEME, DGIS and Member, Armed Forces Tribunal. He had been Deputy Military Attaché (Technical) at Moscow and had an opportunity to get an insight into the military industrial complex. He is presently a Director at Munitions Technology Pvt. Ltd., a Hyderabad-based technology think tank.

Brig. Vinod Anand is a Senior Fellow at the VIF, New Delhi. He holds a post-graduate degree in Defence and Strategic Studies and is an alumnus of the Defence Services and Staff College and College of Defence Management. He has earlier been a Senior Fellow at the Institute for Defence Studies and Analyses and the United Service Institution, New Delhi. He is the author of many publications on military and strategic issues including regional and international security; he coordinates various research activities besides focusing on India's Act East Policy, situations in the Asia Pacific and development in South East Asia, particularly China and Myanmar.

Lt-Gen Gautam Banerjee, PVSM, AVSM, YSM (retd.) is a former Commandant of the Officers Training Academy, Chennai, and former Chief of Staff Central Command. A well-regarded thinker and author of a score of books, papers and articles on military strategy and administration, he is a Distinguished Fellow and Editor at the Vivekananda International Foundation, New Delhi.

1

Future Wars, Nations, and its Militaries

J. S. Bajwa

"People always make war when they say they love peace."

—D.H. Lawrence

Approach

As India prepares to step forward beyond 75 years of its independence into the final quarter for its centenary, there is a need to pause and introspect what it has achieved in the security domain and where does it need to go from here.

When confronted with such a critical issue, it is best to go back to the basics and develop a concept from it. Through a series of questions an argument is hereby presented.

What is a Nation?

Although France after the French Revolution (1787–99), is often cited as the first nation-state, some scholars consider the establishment of the English Commonwealth in 1649 as the earliest instance of nation-state creation. Today a nation is identified by a defined and demarcated geographical boundary, and variously by its people who are of common descent, ethnicity, race, religion, history, language(s) and its culture and tradition. It has a national symbol and a national flag. Citizenship is based on a principle of *jus sanguinis* ("right of blood") based on organic ties through family descent to national community and homeland or on a principle of *jus soli* ("right of the soil")wherein there is the individuals' loyalty to state institutions and acceptance of a shared political culture.[1]

India is a multi-ethnic, multi-religious, multilingual and multi-cultural sovereign state (a political entity on a territory) that is guided by a nation (a cultural entity).

What is the Responsibility of a Nation-State?

A nation-state is responsible to protect its core values, territory, resources, declared national interests, undertake measures to pursue its national interests without external hindrance, protect its people from foreign interference and subversion, protect the individual's right to freedom, create an environment for the people to secure a livelihood. Ipso facto, the nation-state is thus responsible to protect the country from external aggression and internal strife. In addition, through a swathe of measures of good governance it should ensure the safety and stability of the lives of the common people.

How does a Nation safeguard its Values and pursue its National Interests?

> *"The meaning of national interest is survival—the protection of physical, political and cultural identity against encroachments by other nation-states."*—**Morgenthau.**

In describing the national interests that nations seek to secure, a two-fold classification is generally made: necessary or vital components, something nations are prepared to go to war for; and variable or non-vital components of national interests, something that nations would like to see fulfilled but will not resort to go to war for them.[2]

In order to be more precise in examining the interests which a nation seeks to secure, Thomas W. Robinson presents a six-fold classification of interests which nations try to secure, as follows:[3]

Primary Interests: These are those interests in respect of which no nation can compromise. It includes the preservation of physical, political and cultural identity against possible encroachments by other states. A state has to defend these at all costs.

Secondary Interests: These are less important but quite vital for the existence of the state. This includes the protection of its citizens abroad and ensuring diplomatic immunity for its diplomatic staff.

Permanent Interests: These refer to relatively long-term interests of the state.

Variable Interests: These interests are those that are considered vital for the national good in a given situation. India's neutral stance in the Ukrainian war could be considered as such.

General Interests: This entails common interests of various nations, e.g., maintaining international peace; preserving the sanctity of global commons, arms control and nuclear disarmament could be in this category.

Specific Interests: These grow out of the category of general interests. Securing the economic rights of developing countries through the New International Economic Order is a specific interest of India and other developing countries.

What are India's Core Values and National Interests?

Core values are traits or qualities that are not just worthwhile but also represent a nation's highest priorities, deeply-held beliefs, and fundamental driving forces. They are the heart of what the country and its citizens stand for in the world. India's core values could be described as sovereign autonomy, universal brotherhood (*Vasudhaiva Kutumbakum*) and non-violence, representative democracy, tolerance and accommodation, social equality, plurality, socialism and collective wellbeing, and upholding the spirit of the Constitution.[4]

National interests can be defined as the claims, objectives, goals, demands and interests which a nation always tries to preserve, protect, defend and secure in relations with other nations. These can be described as a nation's cultural, economic, political, religious and military goals. The nation takes concerted measures in pursuit of these goals. Within the field of international relations, national interest has frequently been assumed to comprise the pursuit of power, security and wealth; this is the most crucial concept in international relations. This is the key concept in foreign policy as it provides the material based on which foreign policy is made. Thus while formulating foreign policy, governments are guided by their respective national interests.

India's national interests could be identified as: territorial integrity, protection from coercion and external interference, peaceful relations with neighbours and extended neighbourhood, regional leadership and net security provider in the extended region, freedom to pursue economic development, commerce and trade, internal harmony, unity in diversity and religious freedom, and assistance in economic development of neighbours.

How does a Nation secure its National Interests?

In order to secure its place in the comity of nations, the state should be prepared to undertake any measure to secure and pursue its interests including the use of hard power. In fact, if the various measures are supported with hard power in the background, there is more chance of the outcome being favourable. Generally accepted methods or instruments to further the country's national interests in international relations are brought out in the succeeding paragraphs.

Diplomacy: Undoubtedly, in international relations, the foremost tool available to a nation is diplomacy. Diplomatic negotiations, through a process of persuasion, threats, rewards or denial of rewards is employed to meet the goals and objectives of the nation and for conflict-resolution and reconciling divergent interests of the state. Morgenthau regards diplomacy as the most primary means.

Propaganda: The next important instrument is propaganda. It is about salesmanship and selling the nation's political ideas. "Propaganda is a systemic attempt to affect the minds, emotions and actions of a given group for a specific public purpose".—Frankel.[5] China's 'Three Warfare' strategy is an official political and information pre-kinetic warfare strategy employing media or public opinion warfare, psychological warfare, and legal warfare.[6] In the era of social media an adversary will invariably resort to generating 'fake news' or 'alternate truth' and subvert the population through these insidious tactics resulting in communal disaffection and internal turmoil.

Economic Means: Economic stability and wealth have enabled developed nations to dictate terms in furthering their interests. Their stranglehold on international institutions allows them to coerce the lesser-economies to do their bidding. The sanctions regimes are a powerful tool to do so.

Alliances and Treaties: Alliances and treaties are generally concluded by two or more states for a common interest. These have a binding legal obligation. The old adage, "My enemy's enemy is my friend", brings out an underlying reason for alliances and the China-Pakistan relations aptly exemplifies this. Chinese aggression in Eastern Ladakh in 2020 came about despite there being numerous treaties on maintaining peace and tranquillity on the Line of Actual Control (LAC). That kind of trust deficit between nations is anathema in bilateral relations.

Coercion: Hard power used in means short of war and posturing is an unwritten law of international relations. Intervention, lowering the level of diplomatic interaction, embargoes, blockades, economic and social boycotts, reprisals, retribution and retaliation are measures taken by nations as means of coercion. One or more of these measures in concert may be undertaken by a nation to force the other to accept a particular course of behaviour or desist from an action considered harmful to the nation using such coercive measures.

War and Aggression: War and aggression do not have explicit sanction as a means to secure a nation's interests, but neither is it banned. Military power is an integral and paramount element of national power. While *Jus ad bellum* refers to the conditions under which nations may resort to war or to the use of armed force in general, an act or a set of threatening conditions considered detrimental to the nation's wellbeing can be interpreted as *casus belli* and be reason enough to actually resort to commence a war.

What is the Role of the Military in Securing/furthering National Interests?

Peace is the first and most important condition for continued prosperity and freedom. For a state, power means wealth, resources, security, and dominance. Many are uncomfortable with the notions of power politics, great powers and power balances. This discomfort has, in the past, led to hopeful appeals to notions of international law and norms, and the pacifist belief that the support of major powers or of institutions like the United Nations will alleviate the threat. This notion would *ipso facto* imply mortgaging the nation's security to these institutions! Yes, power is not just complex, it is also problematic. Some worry that a 'national interest' view of the world ignores the role of values, particularly the human rights and collective good of humanity. In fact, there are those who would draw a sharp line between power politics and a principled foreign policy based on values.[7] Military power is intended to project superiority; it therefore matters in international relations.

In a period of peace, a nation, more often than not, targets the defence budget. At the end of the Cold War in 1991, the Bush administration somewhat reduced the defence spending. However, the Clinton administration witlessly accelerated and deepened these cuts. The results were devastating; military readiness declined, training suffered, military pay slipped 15 per cent below civilian equivalents, morale plummeted, and the services cannibalised existing equipment to keep airplanes flying, ships afloat and tanks moving. The increased difficulty in recruiting people for the armed forces or retaining them was hardly surprising.[8]

The Realist School, the dominant approach in international relations, assumes that states not only struggle for power but also seek to maximise it. Therefore, it is necessary to ensure that India's military can deter war, project power, and fight in defence of its interests if deterrence fails.

War

Unlike in the past when wars were fought for religion, labour, resources or living space, war in the current era is waged against an enemy of the nation and its people. Thus, an enemy can be defined as a nation, group of nations or non-state actors whom the government perceives are inclined to harm the interests of the nation and its people. Many theories claim or imply that wars result ultimately from the allegiance of men to nations. A state is ultimately governed in its behaviour by what is loosely summed up as the 'national interest', which occasionally clashes directly with the national interests of other states.[9] National interest drums up nationalism which not only induces wars but, through the severity of its influence, makes compromise and acceptance of defeat more difficult.[10] Indeed, relations between states and peoples have been regularly accompanied by mutual misunderstanding, tension, suspicion and hostility. It is the responsibility of the government to prepare its people psychologically to hate the enemy so that there is no remorse when fighting him. Therefore, nations invariably project themselves as trustworthy, peace-loving, honourable, and humanitarian, while the enemy is treacherous, belligerent, expansionist and cruel.

For Clausewitz, "war is not merely a political act but a real political instrument, a continuation of political intercourse, a carrying out of the same by other means" (*On War* (1943), p. 280). He defines it as a rational instrument of foreign policy: "*an act of violence intended to compel our opponent to fulfil our will*". That is to say, war is one means of political intercourse, characterized by military force, to accomplish political ends.[11] War has an enduring nature that demonstrates four continuities: a *political dimension*, a *human dimension*, the existence of *uncertainty* and that it is a *contest of wills*.[12] Clausewitz further argues that war is a phenomenon consisting of three central elements or dominant tendencies. This triad, or trinity, is a paradoxical relationship "composed of primordial violence, hatred, and enmity.[13] To view war as a contest between two militaries is missing the forest for the trees. As war consumes immense human, financial and material resources of a nation its end state must conform to the political aim that is set. Non-military and uninitiated minds do not comprehend this vital aspect.

In essence war is a political instrument of a government using its military power to subdue a belligerent opponent. Thus, de facto, war targets the opponent's government. The military is the instrument used to psychologically force the opponent's government to submit to the demands placed by the government which has a superior force. Military power is supreme and the sole guarantor of success in diplomacy and commerce.

Nature and Character of Future Wars

It is an accepted fact that the nature of war remains unchanged—violent application of military force. However, the character of war is determined by the political objectives that are set as an aim and the means adopted in the application of the scale of violence. Thus, the character of war in various forms could be a *clash of conventional forces, limited war, regional war, guerrilla war, proxy war, hybrid war, non-contact war, cyber war, 4G warfare, 5G warfare, even going up to 7G warfare* (paralysing a country by targeting their network-based critical assets—banking, electricity, nuclear facilities, etc., or Domain-Specific Vulnerabilities—The 'Assassin's Mace') and *8G warfare* (where no one dies on either side of the conflict. That suggests that we need the capability to temporarily incapacitate our enemy's forces and their population, similar to the effects of the movie *Star Trek*). There will be no declaration of war, and attribution to a specific adversary will be extremely difficult due to the character of a non-contact war. Future wars are thus going to be a 'whole-of-government' war.

Transforming the Military for Future Wars

Post World War II conventional wars have resulted in a stalemate, be it the Korean War, Indo-Pak wars of 1947-48 and 1965, Sino-Soviet war of 1969, and Iran-Iraq war 1980-88. Decisive victories resulted in the India-China war of 1962, Indo-Pak war of 1971 for liberation of Bangladesh, Arab-Israel war of 1973, the USA in the Persian Gulf against Iraq, the USA in Vietnam, the Soviet Union in Afghanistan, the USA in Afghanistan, and the International

Coalition in the breakup of Yugoslavia were wars between conventional forces and unconventional groups and non-state actors which saw the defeat of conventional well-equipped military forces at the hands of *lightly armed, highly trained and mobile bands of religious-ethnic mercenaries exploiting their intimate knowledge of terrain and local resources with support of the local population.*

The recent conflict between Armenia and Azerbaijan over the disputed Nagorno-Karabakh region included extensive use of missiles, drones, and rocket artillery. The 44-day war featured a diverse array of legacy and advanced air and missile strikes as well as defence platforms. The ballistic missiles used spanned generations, from the older Soviet-era Scud and Rocha missiles to the newer and more advanced Islander and the Israeli-made LORA (Long Range Attack) missiles. Drones of Russian, Turkish, Israeli, and indigenous designs performed both reconnaissance missions and supported artillery use and strike missions. Unmanned aerial vehicles (UAV) and loitering munitions attacks were able to destroy heavy ground units, including T-72 tanks and advanced S-300 air defences. The conflict's use of these various weapons provides important information and insights into how modern wars will employ the *growing spectrum of missiles, drones, and artillery.*[14]

The ongoing war in Ukraine has seen large-scale employment of surface-to-surface conventional warhead missiles, cruise missiles, ship-to-shore missiles, hypersonic missiles, heavy artillery, highly mobile counter-artillery radars, shoulder-fired anti-aircraft missiles, air surveillance radars, fourth generation anti-tank missiles, drones, UAVs and even man-pack 'kamikaze' drones. Most of the missiles are guided for precision strikes. With all this man-portable weapon systems, Ukraine has relied on small teams of soldiers operating in a non-linear battlefield who are familiar with the local terrain to stall the advance of Russian mechanised columns. A *small team with aggressive leadership and good communications is the new-found formidable force.*

There is an invisible battle that the West is losing to Russia in Ukraine. Russia is currently dominating the arena of *ground-based electronic warfare*—the discipline dedicated to detecting and interfering with enemy radar and communication signals while protecting friendly forces from similar effects. This realm is essential to the modern battleground because militaries increasingly rely on radar, radio signals, and satellites to track and relay the position of friendly and enemy forces, coordinate attacks between headquarters and those in the field across long distances, operate drone systems and guide weapons to targets.

Perhaps Russia's most successful deployment of this ability is in its ongoing conflict with Ukraine, where a 2017 army study detailed the devastating effectiveness of its electronic warfare capabilities in shutting down Ukrainian FM radio and cellular networks. Jammers, which disrupt command signals, brought down over 100 Ukrainian drones, while signals intelligence was used to target deadly artillery strikes. In other cases, the Russian systems emitted signals that caused artillery and missiles to prematurely detonate or veer off course. In one particular operation, soldiers' families received hoax texts stating, "Your son is killed in action", prompting calls and texts to the soldiers. Minutes later, artillery struck the location where a large number of cell phones was detected.[15]

A future war which India will have to fight will include many of the characters of war mentioned above. Another factor in a war India will have to fight is defending its territory which is claimed by China and Pakistan and re-establish India's control over the territories of Aksai Chin and Pakistan-Occupied Kashmir (POK). This will remain a long-term political goal of the country.

One of the lessons emanating from the Ukraine war is that the defender has inherent advantages vis-a-vis the attacker. However, defence will not achieve victory; it will lead to protracted war and stalemate. For victory, offensive operations are necessary. The ability to launch a formidable counter-offensive or riposte in the same theatre will compel the attacker to recoil at the operational level. Also, the capability to threaten or actually launch a *quid pro quo* in another theatre of operation will force the enemy to rebound at the strategic level. Thus, *the Indian 'Joint Doctrine of the Armed Forces–2017' that says the character of future wars is likely to be "ambiguous, uncertain, short, swift, and lethal" needs rethink.*

India's Military Imperatives

The future Indian military needs to focus its emphasis on fighting dispersed in high and super-altitude areas. The following should be given due consideration:

- Induction of drones and UAV's of all types for the three Services.
- Multi-barrel rocket launchers of various calibres.
- Ground, air and ship launched BrahMos missiles.

- Defensive and offensive electronic warfare capabilities require a quantum jump.
- Mobile counter-artillery and counter-mortar radars.
- Ground, air and space based surveillance systems.
- Portable shoulder-fired anti-air missiles.
- Portable four and five-generation anti-tank/bunker bursting missiles.
- Conversion of maximum heavy artillery and air force ammunition to be precision enabled.
- Light tanks for Ladakh and North Sikkim should be a priority.
- Early production of futuristic infantry combat vehicles (FICV) and light armoured multipurpose vehicles (LAMV) for mechanised infantry units operating in high-altitude areas of Ladakh and North Sikkim.

Two and four-men all-terrain vehicles (Quad Bikes) for small team operations in the high-altitude terrain of Ladakh and North Sikkim for the infantry.

- Attack helicopters should be exclusively with Army Aviation, not the Air Force.
- Increase the staying power of the Special Forces of the Armed Forces Special Operations Division for protracted operations behind enemy lines.
- Immediate introduction of digital maps of the LAC and Line of Control (LoC).
- Shift from GPS to indigenous navigation with Indian constellation on priority.
- Ammunition depots should be moved well forward and built in secure shelters in the mountains.
- Road infrastructure will require unwavering emphasis. Work on tunnel under Se La in West Kameng sector of Arunachal Pradesh, and tunnels on the road from Manali to Leh to make it an all-weather road need to be speeded up.
- Construct and operationalise advance landing grounds and forward area rearm and refuelling points (FAARP) for quick replenishment and induction of reinforcements all along the LAC.
- Revival of the concept of the future infantry soldier as a system (F-INSAS) and make it happen.

The reorganisation of infantry, armoured, mechanised infantry, artillery, combat support and logistics support units need serious consideration to fight future wars in complex conditions in the dispersed non-linear tactical battle areas and in depth areas. All these tiers would be under constant threat of being targeted by long-range precision guided vectors, be they surface-to-surface missiles, rockets in concentrated salvos, armed drones, kamikaze drones or directed energy weapons. Electronic warfare offensive by the adversary will be unrelenting.

Linked to the exercise of transformation is the creation of theatre commands (TCs). How will TCs contribute to more effective responses to a 'one front' and 'two front' threat is debatable. With paucity in resources of air assets, attack helicopters, utility and heavy lift helicopters, armed drones, long-range heavy artillery, multi-barrel rocket launchers, surface-to-surface missiles, air defence artillery, precision guided munitions, radars of all types, engineering resources, electronic warfare assets, surveillance assets—the list goes on—it seems that TCs are merely being looked at from an financial angle and administrative point of view to reduce manpower numbers of headquarters as they presently exist. The Air Force Chief is on record saying that Air Defence Command is not a viable proposition with the present state of air resources. It will be more prudent to dispassionately reconsider the very idea of TCs and not impose it on the military just because the USA has them and China has undertaken to implement theirs. It has been six years since China reorganised its seven military regions to five theatre commands but the operational doctrines are still in a flux. India cannot match the USA and China in their defence R&D, technological edge and defence budgets. Militaries that are dependent on weapons, equipment, and ammunition through imports should refrain from building castles in the air.

Induction of hi-tech weapons and equipment into the military without substantial modification to the organisation of units and formations would be futile. It will amount to these units merely having hi-tech systems in their midst and yet being employed as hitherto.

Ratiocination

The Ministry of Defence should get over the aversion and skewed mindset against senior serving military officers in the Defence Minister's entourage in his security-related dialogues with foreign governments. It would also not be a bad idea to have the defence minister don a military uniform to convey synergy. Russian and Chinese defence ministers are always attired in military uniforms, while other Western delegations are invariably accompanied by senior serving military officers. The government also does not need to create a parallel khaki-uniform army with its armed police forces due to some equivocal notion of creating a counter to a possible military coup!!

Linked to building a credible military capability is the concept of '*Agnipath*' which could turn out to be deeply flawed. Considering the emerging complexity of future wars, seasoned experts are needed, not 'raw youthful'; soldiers who will not run around the battlefield like jack rabbits. Inexperienced, not fully trained and integrated manpower will only provide cannon fodder to the adversary. Is India relying on Desiderius Erasmus' statement that "War is delightful to those who have no experience of it"? The Ukraine war has brought to the fore that lightly armed seasoned veterans can do a fairly good job of fending off the heavily armed offensive of the Russians. That this scheme will save much needed money required for modernisation is also an irrational notion, while it is touted as the basic reason behind this step to be readily swallowed by all. The truth is that the government will have to continue to bear the pension bill till 2037 after which the savings on account of *Agnipath* scheme will begin to show.

What needs serious discussion is as to how the military can best achieve the aim of forcing the opponent' government to accept own government's demand or writ, whether it is by posturing, coercion, signalling, military brinkmanship, demonstration of force, capture of territory, infliction of heavy losses on its military, destruction of vital infrastructure or threatening to overthrow the regime in power. The structure of the military should be based on a priority from amongst these factors before the transformation is undertaken. With the mosaic in all hues outlined above, *India will have to seriously debate and deliberate on how to fight, with what to fight and how much to fight in a future war.*

The famed US military war-fighting concept of 'Air-Land Battle' took 10 years (1973-1984) of theoretical grounding by a team of the training and doctrine command (TRADOC) of the USA. There were hundreds of presentations, debates and discussions with maximum number of units with the team before it was accepted. It was then followed by the 'transformation of forces' when technology, weapons and equipment were dictated by the accepted concept. That concept has since been replaced by the concept of 'Full Spectrum War'. If the Indian military is to transform, it cannot be based on a theoretical concept emanating from behind the closed doors of perspective planning directorates or the training command. It should involve those younger officers and commanders who will fight the future wars and the scientific community which will be required to develop and deliver the whole range of war wherewithal. It is an onerous undertaking that needs fullest government support.

ENDNOTES

1. Nation-state: Definition, Characteristics and Facts; https://www.britannica.com/topic/nation-state
2. Article shared by Dinesh; National Interest: Meaning, Components and Methods; https://www.yourarticlelibrary.com/international-politics/national-interest-meaning-components-and-methods/48487
3. Ibid.
4. Ibid.
5. Op cit.
6. https://en.wikipedia.org>Three_warfares
7. Condoleezza Rice, "How to Pursue the National Interest"; https://www.hoover.org/research/how-pursue-national-interest
8. Ibid.
9. Joseph Frankel, "War", https://www.britannica.com/topic/war/International-law
10. Ibid.
11. Francis Miyata, "The Grand Strategy of Carl von Clausewitz", https://warroom.armywarcollege.edu/articles/grand-strategy-clausewitz/
12. Manoeuvre Self-Study Program, https://www.benning.army.mil/mssp/Nature%20and%20Character/
13. Brian Cole, "Clausewitz's Wondrous Yet Paradoxical Trinity", https://ndupress. ndu.edu/Portals/68/Documents/jfq/jfq-96/JFQ-96_42-49_Cole.pdf?ver=2020-02-07-150502-163.
14. Shaan Shaikh and Wes Rumbaugh, "The Air and Missile War in Nagorno-Karabakh: Lessons for the Future of Strike and Defence", https://www.csis.org/analysis/air-and-missile-war-nagorno-karabakh-lessons-future-strike-and-defense
15. Sebastien Roblin, "Electronic Warfare: Where US is Losing the Invisible Fight to Russia's Dominant Capabilities", https://www.nbcnews.com/think/opinion/russia-winning-electronic-warfare-fight-against-ukraine-united-states-ncna1091101

2

SEEDS OF CONFLICT IN THE 2050S

Ajay Chaturvedi

> *"Difficulties are meant to rouse, not discourage. The human spirit is to grow strong by conflict."*
>
> **—William Ellery Channing**

Introduction

Conflict can be defined as an outcome of perceptual incongruence between two adversaries (these could be states or organisations or individuals), different aspirations of those who have conflict at hand (they could be states, organisations or individuals), arrogance of power of one of them and differences in the value systems of states, individuals or groups. Important contributory factors are place, time, and circumstances. However, of the three, time is the most important factor, because it is dynamic and has a bearing on the other two. It is therefore essential that in any relationship a time perspective is taken into consideration because technology, values, aspirations, and interests continue to change with time.

From a very wide canvas on the philosophical plane, there is a need to come down to what in this paper are plans to analyze. Here, an attempt will be made to identify the areas which will impact India's growth in the next three decades and if the fallouts of conflicts on account of these factors could possibly be resolved.

India's Uniqueness

The Indian subcontinent is located between high mountains in the north and sea in the south. In the north-west, in ancient times, there was Persia whose legacy state is modern Iran. Across the Himalayas, in the north- east, was

Tibet which is now a part of China. In the east, China was always present. Over a period, however, the Indian subcontinent has got split into a few independent sovereign states. The latest picture is that India has Pakistan in its north-west and west, China in the north, north-east and east, Bangladesh in the east and Myanmar further east. Nepal is sandwiched between India and China. In the south, Sri Lanka is separated by the Palk Strait. Indonesia is separated by sea from the Indian island territory of Great Nicobar. In the south-west across the sea lies the Maldives.

Here, it also needs to be appreciated that India has only 2.4 per cent of the world's surface area and 4 per cent of the total sweet water available worldwide but supports a population of 17.7 per cent. In absolute terms, this population is likely to grow to 166.8 crore by 2050 CE, whereas China at that point in time will have a population of just 131.7 crore. These are the potential sources of competition and conflict.

Likely Scenarios in 2050

India in 2050

India's population is likely to touch 1.668 billion.[1] After peaking in 2050, it is likely to start declining thereafter. India's Muslim community will expand faster than its Hindu population, rising from 14.4 per cent in 2010 to 18.4 per cent in 2050. Christians are expected to make up 2.2 per cent of India's population in 2050. The combined strength of other religious denominations would be 46 million.[2] The median age in India was 26.8 years in 2015; this figure is projected to increase to 38.1 by 2050.[3] India will be a country having the largest working age population in the world and possibly the youngest population too.[4] However, the skill level may not be what would be required at that point in time. Whether indigenous resources, which appear to be already over-stretched, water in particular, would be a major factor to cause social conflicts in the country is a matter of concern and needs further analysis.

India will be the second largest economy after the People's Republic of China (PRC) and ahead of the United States of America (USA). In terms of purchasing power parity (PPP) and in absolute terms, the size of the economy will be to the tune of $ 35-40 trillion.[5] A large part of it will be the digital economy. Manufacturing in the telecom sector will increase substantially. The literacy rate would be in the range of 90-99 per cent.[6] By 2050, under a high emission scenario, average temperature could rise to 2°C and over 1.3°C if there is a marginal reduction in emissions or a medium emission pathway. Such a rise in temperature will result in a number of coastal areas and islands going under the sea. This is where India's commitment during COP-26 (Conference of Parties) at Glasgow to zero emission will come handy. India will also experience a decline in rice and wheat yields due to climate change, which, in economic terms will be 1.8-3.4 per cent of the GDP.[7] This will impact India's food security and as such be a source of conflicts.

India will meet 75 per cent of its energy requirement from renewables and 25 per cent from nuclear. This transformation of energy sourcing will result in major expenditure on re-engineering the systems and also on research and development of materials and equipment to enhance the efficiency of the systems. In defence production, India would be substantially self-sufficient, especially in the domain of electronics, communications, and related fields.

Geo-politics and Warfare

Apart from powers such as China, India, USA and possibly Europe and Russia, the neo geo-political dynamos by 2050 would be Indonesia, Brazil, Mexico, Nigeria, Kenya, Turkey, Egypt, the Philippines, Colombia, Iran, and Vietnam. Technological, ecological, social, and cultural soft-power would likely compete with economics and military hard power as the deciding factors in the power matrices in the geo-political sphere. The world will be highly networked and technologically driven. Artificial Intelligence (AI), Internet of Things (IoT) and big data analytics will be the drivers for decision making. Climate change will adversely impact the availability of resources. Rising population with depleting resources will be a source of widespread unease and consequent conflicts.

More than territory, conflicts will arise over spheres of influence, water, resources, and supply-lines. China, with its expansionist policies, will be a source of tension where her sphere of influence will clash with the sphere of influence of other countries. Finally, it can be concluded that the outcome of an engagement will be decided on effective application of the comprehensive national power of the adversaries.

Weaknesses of effective transnational capacities highlight a need to upgrade the United Nations. To address the issues of a changing world order, the United Nations Organisation (UNO) will have to reform and privileges of past, like the 'veto power' of Permanent Members of the UN Security Council, will have to be dispensed with. India and China will assume centrality because of their economic heft as well as large working population. This will accentuate tensions between India and Pakistan or whatever that would be left of it, which, by that time will be substantially under Chinese influence. China will also try to use her deep pockets to influence Nepal, Sri Lanka and even Iran and Russia, which will be detrimental to Indian interests. Unease with China will result in conflicts in the Indo-Pacific Region (IPR) and Indian Ocean Region (IOR).

There is a possibility that in the domain of warfare, armies might accommodate freelance contractors (though this system miserably failed in Afghanistan) and militias, special robotic and space-based weapon systems, long-range high-speed missiles and cyber forces to shape battle fields of the future. Artificial Intelligence (AI)-based intelligence, surveillance and reconnaissance (ISR) systems and more powerful AI-based drones will add to the degree of complexity in future battle fields. Such changes are likely to lead to restructuring the nations' traditional military organisations. Even in future battle fields, the Ukraine war has once again flagged the centrality of boots on the ground. It is possible that countries like India where serving in the armed forces is a matter of pride will continue to have large standing armies.

Some Existing and Potential International Conflicts

Boundary Disputes

India has boundary disputes with China, Pakistan, and Nepal. With Nepal, the dispute is because of the incongruence in perception about the Treaty of Sugauli-1816.[8] With China, it is another case of incongruence in perception regarding the Simla Treaty of 1914[9] in the east, and China's claimed suzerainty over Tibet (which she annexed in 1950-51) based on which she claims territories in the west all along the entire Line of Actual Control (LAC).[10]

With Pakistan, India has two disputes. First is about the illegal occupation of a portion of the erstwhile State of Jammu & Kashmir (J&K), which had acceded to India on 26 October 1947 in accordance with the provisions of the Indian Independence Act of 1947.[11] Pakistan has mainly two interests in J&K. One, she demands that J&K being a Muslim majority state should be a part of Pakistan. This demand, however, is illegal because the Instrument of

Accession to India signed by the then Maharaja of J&K was in accordance with the provisions of the Indian Independence Act-1947. Pakistan's second interest is her religion-based 'Two-nation Theory' which lies conclusively debunked once Bangladesh seceded to gain independence. Pakistan does not honour the UN Security Council Resolution of 1947 adopted on 21 April 1948, which stipulates that Pakistan should withdraw all its forces from J&K, and demands a jump to step three—a plebiscite—without taking the mandatory preceding steps. In any case, lots of water has flowed down the Jhelum since then and now the issue is that they have to vacate that illegally occupied portion of J&K territory.

The second dispute with Pakistan is in the maritime domain, about the terrain of Sir Creek.[12] This issue, a legacy of the past, is not that complex, and by a bit of give-and–take, could be promptly resolved if there is such an inclination.

Water Disputes

The source of conflict between India and Pakistan is also on account of a need for equitable distribution of water resources which are otherwise monolithic in nature. Although India and Pakistan have the Indus Water Treaty-1960 (IWT) in place for equitable distribution of the waters of the Indus river system as brokered by the World Bank, but both countries feel that the treaty no more meets their respective aspirations and interests. While India wants a review based on new realities, Pakistan wants more rights on the waters of the river system based on legacy. It is unlikely that this issue would ever get resolved because despite having the lion's share of the waters of the Indus River Basin, Pakistan's new demands are not going to be satiated. She wants rights over the waters of the eastern rivers also, while actually, her water problem is due to wastefulness in utilization of the waters allocated to her, and not due to the IWT. Allocation of water will continue to remain a source of conflict between the two countries.

A similar dispute exists between India and Bangladesh about their shares in the Teesta water, wherein India is the upper and Bangladesh is the lower riparian. India and Bangladesh had a similar issue with respect to the Ganga water but that was resolved in 1996.[13] However, even that accord is being questioned by both India and Bangladesh.

There is a water-related dispute between India and China also. China is attempting to divert water from the Brahmaputra River. Among the 40 dams China intends to build in the Tibetan portion of the Brahmaputra basin, 20 expected to generate 60,000 MW of power, will be on the Yarlung Tsangpo itself. It is proposed to build a vast tunnel under the ridge that separates the two arms of the river's 'Big Bend' and divert 50 billion cu mtrs of water a year to the south-eastern slope where it will fall over nine cascading hydropower dams to generate 40,000 MW of peak power. These dams will be only a few kilometres upstream of the India-China border and the water will fall precipitously from 3,500 mtrs on the Tibetan plateau to 700 mtrs in Arunachal Pradesh. These dams were proposed to be built during the period 2010-15. Although China claims that the dams will not infringe on the rights of the lower riparian states of India and Bangladesh as they would be 'run-off the river' projects, but this claim has been contested by many analysts who have pointed out that the storage created behind the 11 existing dams is already sufficient to deny much-needed water to Bangladesh and India during a drought. Here, it needs to be noted that by 2015, China already had 300,000 MW of new generating capacity, which she did not need.[14] Therefore such a plan, besides depriving the rights of lower riparian states as enshrined in the UN Convention of 1997[15] on trans-national water channels, could also be used by China as a weapon to cause disaster in the lower reaches at will, as indeed she had done in the Parechu incident.[16]

Chinese Ambitions in the IPR and the IOR

The PRC, with its growing economic muscle, is becoming aggressively assertive. Disconcertingly, her aggressive actions are impacting India in more than one way. China is creating a 'String of Pearls' which refers to the network of Chinese military and commercial facilities and political relationships along its sea lanes of communication (SLOC), which extend from the Chinese mainland to Port Sudan in the Horn of Africa.[17] The sea lanes run through several major maritime choke points like the Bab el Mandeb, Strait of Hormuz, Straits of Malacca, and the Lombok Strait. Along this SLOC, China has created her own strategic maritime centres in Djibouti, Pakistan (Gwadar), Sri Lanka (Hambantota), Bangladesh (Sonaldia and Chittagong), Myanmar (Sittwe and Kyaukpyu), the Maldives, and Somalia. This indicates Chinese intentions to have a permanent presence of the PLA navy in the IOR. Obviously, such a 'string' system would encircle India and threaten her power projection capability as well as maritime trade, poach in her exclusive economic zone (EEZ) and so present a threat to her territorial integrity. Besides, the Vladivostok-Chennai sea link[18] which is vital for energy transportation from the Russian Far East to India would pass through the South China Sea and as such will be vulnerable to China's coercive action. As Indian trade in this region increases, conflict with China's attempts to dominate the IOR and IPR would be inevitable and India will have to find ways to deal with it.

Potential Flash Points of Internal Conflicts in India

Widening Gap: Needs and Availability of Resources

The mismatch between the growing population, defined space, and shrinking water availability would have serious adverse implications for life and livelihood in India. To make matters worse, climate changes resulting in changing rainfall patterns is a cause of concern for planners in India.[19] Such changes have already started having a significant impact on availability of water, both direct and indirect. Some of the possible outcomes are fast diminishing reliable water storage reservoirs which as it is are smaller than the world average; large-scale wetland degradation and contamination of existing water resources (surface as well as sub-surface); depleting ground water; excessive deforestation due to lack of awareness as well as needs for habitat for the teeming millions; and, smaller storage capacity.[20] These aspects have already started making the task of water management extremely challenging. Further, growing scarcity of water coupled with low adaptive capability due to existing utilisation practices are having serious adverse social and economic implications for millions of poor.

A recent study by the International Food Policy Research Institute (IFPRI) found that more than half the world's population and approximately half the global grain production will be at risk due to water stress by 2050. It is projected by IFPRI that India's food production could drop 16 per cent and the number of those at risk of hunger could increase 23 per cent by 2030 due to climate change.[21]

Besides agriculture, a possible water crisis in the inland fishery sector is also a threat to food security. Aquatic species are generally more sensitive to water temperatures, and the stratification of water bodies can be impacted by climate change to affect fish growth and its viability due to poor watershed management. By the late 21st century, climate change is likely to increase the frequency and intensity of droughts and a large part of the globe may experience famine. Disasters like floods and prolonged droughts will be quite common in the near to distant future. It needs to be appreciated that such instances of water crisis would have an impact on food security and industrial output of the country. Food scarcity or food quality issues can also cause anxiety-related responses as well as mental health disorders. The unfortunate incidents of suicides by farmers will be even more frequent. If this state of decreasing water availability is not addressed timely, it will be a major source of social conflicts because of the ever increasing demands of a rising population, industrial needs, and new water-intensive agricultural practices.

Global Connect: Conflict of Civilizational and Evolving Values

Threat of Divisiveness in Society

An important part of India's evolution as a nation is that this is an ancient civilisational state in which the two most unifying factors were common heritage and common culture. However, India has always been a promised land for invasions from the north-west (Islamist Central and West Asians) as well as the Western seaboard (Christian Europeans), besides being a destination for steady migrations from the East.[22, 23, 24] Though the invasions were initially meant for plunder, the invaders, after coming from the dry and parched lands of Arabia or Central Asia, settled here due to fertile land and abundance of resources. Certain migrations from seaboards also happened from as far as Africa and across the sea from Indonesia and Thailand. The new arrivals brought with them their own culture and traditions. Most got assimilated well in Indian society without losing their distinct identity and without causing any social disharmony like the Parsis and Jews. Certain others like those who came from Africa and Indonesia have maintained their distinct identity even today. Muslims and Christians who arrived from the north, northwest and west not only maintained their own identities but also believed in aggressive proselytization.

The British under their policy of 'Divide and Rule', kept creating an environment of distrust between the communities and their policy finally resulted in the partition of the country. Post partition also, the situation did not improve. In fact, it slowly started to become acute especially after the demolition of the disputed Babri Mosque at Ayodhya in 1992. One of the major reasons for the widening chasm has been the role of Pakistan which has always been trying to weaken India by alienating her Muslims based on their religious affinity. In recent times, with the Hindus becoming more assertive against what is viewed as the state's minority vote-bank appeasement politics, the situation is becoming quite explosive. In this connection the Minister of State of Home Affairs (MHA), Sri Nitya Nand Rai, informed the Lok Sabha on 29 March 2022 that in the five-year period from 2016 to 2020 there had been as many as 3,399 cases of communal or religious rioting in the country. He further added that in 2016 there were 869 communal riots. The number steadily reduced for the next three years but rose again in 2020 to 857.[25] The conflict is basically due to mutual distrust and corruption of the values associated with various cultures, religions and the spirit of the Indian Constitution.

Here, it needs to be appreciated that the diversity on account of language, culture, demography, and religion makes India unique, as in no other country such plurality is allowed to thrive. However, many a time such internal diversities are used by forces inimical to the country and certain myopic sections of the native society to weaken India. The impact of social media and globalization of mis-information has also a very profound effect on accentuating distance between the communities. It is a disconcerting fact that internal conflicts based on various kinds of perceptual incongruence are unlikely to be resolved any time soon. An analysis of past events leading to such societal distancing clearly brings out that unless addressed timely with due firmness, due sagacity and with a spirit of accommodation, the nation could reach a point where the probability of another societal vivisection cannot be discounted. India's national leadership and the governance model would have to handle such linguistic, cultural, and religious diversities and use it as strength rather than a weakness.

Impact of Social Discriminations

India has a very large population of dalits and tribals that works out to over 34 per cent of the total population.[26] This section of society has been exploited over a long past. With the promulgation of an egalitarian Constitution of independent India, there has been a continuous spread of social uplift, education, and related awareness. However, some among this section have started becoming quite assertive, even aggressive. This kind of social churning is resulting in a conflict between haves and have nots. Manifestation of these conflicts is being experienced in the form of what is known as the frequent occurrence of 'caste conflicts' across the country, persistence of the 'Naxalite movement' in the rural areas and rise of 'Urban Naxalism' as an anti-establishment movement in urban areas. The Naxalite movement which started in 1967 in the village of Naxalbari in North Bengal later spread across large tracts of rural India. Though contained to some extent in recent years, until 2021, nearly 46 districts in10 states still remained affected by it.[27]

Another reason for the discontent in the country has been the reservation policy. This policy is a cause of severe resentment among the people of the so-called 'upper castes' on the one hand, while, on the other hand, the aspirations among the real and perceived dalits and tribals continue to rise. Prejudice against the dalits and tribals in general, and denying them development opportunities is indeed a serious matter and conflicts based on such inequalities would need due diligence over a long period to reconcile. Similarly, dissatisfaction over this policy among the non-reservation classes also needs to be addressed. To make matters worse, new kinds of reservations are invented, like education and job reservations for the locals.

It is the responsibility of the national leadership, and more so that of society, to address these problems so that biases meted out to all the marginalised sections are controlled and reconciled. Unless attended to, these issues are likely to snowball into major internal conflicts.

The Way Ahead

By 2050 CE, India will be an economically strong country. However, so will be India's main adversary, the *People's Republic of China*. India's disputes with China are not likely to get resolved any time soon, and as such, India will have to be prepared to deal with a belligerent China on the LAC, in the maritime domain, in the economic arena and its persistent subversion in India's neighbourhood. The way to deal with China, which understands only the language of power, will be to create power alignments with like-minded friendly countries. That would be possible when India is able to create robust inter-dependencies with friendly countries based on mutual interests.

Pakistan is expected to become considerably weak, and possibly split into smaller parts. Meanwhile, it will continue to have the propensity to export cross-border terrorism and communal disharmony in India. Therefore, India will have to work out such policies, whereby religion-instigated anti-national influences are fully repudiated, and every section of Indian society, including the people from the Kashmir region of J&K as well as the religious minorities, is fully committed to India's territorial integrity.

With the *other neighbours*, models of inter-dependence would have to be strengthened to wean them away from the influence of China. Afghanistan is a highly unstable country due to its own ethnic configuration; if it remains unstable, its continuation of export of terror should be expected. Dealing with Afghanistan in the west and Myanmar in the east, both of which are geographically important for India to have connectivity with Central Asia and South-East Asia respectively, will remain a challenge for India. May be the use of India's soft power and helping them in their critical areas could help in dealing with them.

As far as internal issues are concerned, the *economy* has to become stronger. However, prosperity without equality will be a cause of social stresses which would lead to conflicts. Therefore, very consciously, the decision makers will have to apply themselves to work out a governance model wherein society as a whole becomes prosperous. One of the important areas which will need to be addressed is reduction of the high import bill on account of fossil fuels; that is where more and more dependence on *Renewable and Nuclear Energy* would have to be planned. Use of indigenous resources will definitely help in improving the economy. Additional emphasis on *research and development* will help India to tackle problems on its own, especially in the domain of frontier technologies like AI, IoT and Robotics. Space and cyber domains would have to be especially addressed. These steps would also help India to become self-reliant. A more resilient economy will help India to work out mitigation strategies to tackle the ill effects of *climate change*.

Social inequalities and disharmony will have to be addressed. In this regard, efforts will have to be made to improve the Human Development Index by paying more attention to social security, health, education, women empowerment and rise of gross national income. One area which causes major social resentment is the prevalence of corruption. This can be tackled on the one hand with firmness in dealing with the defaulters and on the other by paying more attention to the traditional values of India.

ENDNOTES

1. An internet upload: https://qz.com/india/2186917/un-says-indias-population-may-overtake-chinas-in-2023/

2. Conrad Hackett, 21 April 2015,"By 2050, India to have world's largest populations of Hindus and Muslims", published by Pew Research Centre, 21 April 2015, and uploaded on https://www.pewresearch.org/fact-tank/2015/04/21/by-2050-india-to-have-worlds-largest-populations-of-hindus-and-muslims/
3. An internet upload: https://www.statista.com/statistics/254469/median-age-of-the-population-in-india/
4. T. V. Mohandas Pai, "2050: India to have largest working population", *The Economic Times* 30 January 2011 and uploaded on https://economictimes.indiatimes.com/special-feature/2050-india-to-have-the-largest-working-age population/articleshow/7388225.cms?utm_source=contentofinterest&utm_medium=text&utm_ campaign=cppst
5. A PWC Report, "The Long View: How will the global economic order change by 2050?", February 2017 and available online: https://www.pwc.com/gx/en/world-2050/assets/pwc-the-world-in-2050-full-report-feb-2017.pdf
6. How will India be in 2050 – Einsty- An internet upload: https://einsty.com
7. *India News*, "India could lose 1.8 to 3.4% of GDP by 2050 due to decline in rice and wheat yields" *Hindustan Times* 28 October 2021, available online on https://www.hindustantimes.com/india-news/india-could-lose-1-8-to-3-4-of-gdp-by-2050-due-to-decline-in-rice-and-wheat-yields-101635360100658.html
8. The treaty of Sugauli established the boundary between India and Nepal. It was signed on 4 March 1816 between the East India Company and Guru Gajaraj Mishra following the Anglo-Nepalese War of 1814–16.
9. On 3 July 1914, the British, Tibetan and Chinese plenipotentiaries signed the Simla Convention without the Chinese's formal signature. They also signed an additional bilateral declaration with the claim that the Convention would be binding on them and that China would be denied any privileges under the agreement until it signed it.
10. The term "Line of Actual Control" is said to have been used by Chinese Premier Zhou Enlai in a 1959 note to Indian Prime Minister Jawaharlal Nehru. The boundary existed only as an informal cease-fire line between India and China after the 1962 Sino-Indian War.
11. The Indian Independence Act-1947 is an Act of the Parliament of the United Kingdom that partitioned British India into the two new independent dominions of India and Pakistan. As per the provisions of this Act, the rulers of the princely states (565 in numbers) existing in the British Indian Empire were given the right to join either Pakistan or India, considering two major factors: Geographical contiguity and the people's wishes.
12. Sir Creek is a 96 km strip of water in the marshes of the Rann of Kutch in Gujarat. It is a disputed region between India and Pakistan. The creek roughly separates the Kutch region in India and Pakistan's Sindh province. The dispute dates back to 1908 when the then Sindh Division and Kutch had a dispute about the boundary between them and their differences were whether Sindh's boundary lay to the east of Creek (interpretation of Sindh) or as per Thalweg (centre of the channel) principle. Despite a number of rounds of talks, the issue remains unresolved.
13. India and Bangladesh signed the Indo-Bangladesh Ganges Treaty-1996 to share the waters of the Ganga at Farakka. The treaty will come up for review in 2026. There are a total of 54 common rivers and not only does India need to resolve issues related to water sharing with Bangladesh, she also needs to make a common front against the PRC which is exploiting the water of the Brahmaputra (Yarlung Tsangpo) at the cost of the lower riparian states of India and Bangladesh.
14. Prem Shankar Jha, "Why Is China Reviving Its Plan to Build Dams on the Brahmaputra

Now?",*The Wire*, 10 March 2021 and uploaded on https://thewire.in/world/china-revive-dam-plan-brahmaputra-yarlung-tsangpo-india

15. The 1997 United Nations Convention on the Law of the Non-Navigational Uses of International Watercourses is the only treaty governing shared freshwater resources that is of universal applicability. The Convention was concluded on 21 May 1997, as an annexure to General Assembly Resolution 51/229. Article 5, contained in Part II, reflects the principle that is widely regarded as the cornerstone of the Convention, and indeed the law in the field: equitable and reasonable utilization and participation. It requires that a state sharing an international watercourse with other states utilize the watercourse, in its territory, in a manner that is equitable and reasonable vis-à-vis the other states sharing it.
16. In 2000 and 2004, across the border upstream of Parechu, a tributary of the Sutlej River, a lake was formed. It is suspected that it was deliberately breached to cause widespread devastation in the lower reaches in India. This confirms that the Chinese could use water as a weapon by virtue of being the Upper Riparian State.
17. The String of Pearls is a geopolitical hypothesis proposed by US political researchers in 2004. It refers to China's attempts to encircle India and more importantly safeguard her interests along her sea lanes of communication through the Indian Ocean Region by establishing a number of strategic bases/centres.
18. The proposed Chennai-Vladivostok maritime connectivity was crystallised at the policy level during Prime Minister Narendra Modi's visit to Vladivostok to attend the Eastern Economic Forum (EEF) in 2019. Although it will reduce travel time by 16 days, the safety and security of this route is vulnerable to Chinese domination in the South China Sea.
19. K. Shadananan, "Climate change and water: Ripple marks", *Down to Earth,* 25 May 2020 and uploaded on https://www.downtoearth.org.in/blog/water/climate-change-and-water-ripple-marks-69829
20. India currently stores only 6 per cent of its annual rainfall or 253 billion cubic metres, while developed nations strategically store 250 per cent of the annual rainfall in arid river basins. As such, India relies excessively on groundwater. Although, India has 5,000 major or medium dams, barrages, etc., to store the river waters and enhance ground water recharging but finally it has capacity to store only 6 per cent of rain water.
21. Global Food Policy Report: IFPRI, 14 May 2022 and uploaded on A Report on Global Food Policy Report: Climate Change & Food Systems, International Food Policy Research Institute (IFPRI), 14 May 2022.
22. K.M. Mohamed and K.M. Mohammad, "Arab relations with Malabar coast from 9th to 16th centuries", Indian History Congress in the Proceedings of the Indian History Congress, Vol. 60, Diamond Jubilee, pp-226-234.
23. R. Lusome and R.B. Bhagat, "Migration in Northeast India: Inflows, Outflows and Reverse Flows during Pandemic", *The Indian Journal of Labour Economics* and uploaded on https://doi.org/10.1007/s41027-020-00278-7 About three-fourths of international migrants in the North-east moved from Bangladesh, 6 per cent from Nepal, 4 per cent from Myanmar and the rest from other countries. Migration from Bangladesh constitutes the major contributor of international migration in the states of Tripura, Assam and Arunachal Pradesh. International migration in Nagaland, Arunachal Pradesh and Meghalaya is dominated by Nepali migrants, while migration from Myanmar dominates the international flow in Mizoram. The Meitei of Manipur trace their origins to Thailand.
24. Christianity was introduced to the Indian subcontinent by Thomas the Apostle in 52 AD when he sailed to the Malabar Coast (present-day Kerala). However, Christianity arrived in

the 15th century with the arrival of Vasco da Gama.

25. A *Wire* report, "India Witnessed 3,399 Cases of Communal or Religious Rioting Between 2016 and 2020", 29 March 2022 and uploaded on https://thewire.in/government/india-commuanl-religious-riots-2016-2020
26. A report from the Research Directorate, Immigration and Refugee Board, Canada, "India: The current situation of Dalits, especially in Punjab; and any protest rallies held by Dalits in Punjab in 1997 and 1998 and subsequent reaction by the authorities" dated 1 April 1999 and uploaded on https://www.refworld.org/docid/3ae6ad3914.html
27. A PTI report, "Maoist Influence down to just 46 districts in 2021 from 96 in 2010: MoS Home Nitya Nand Rai", *New Indian Express,* 9 February 2022.

3

Regional Politics in the Future: Strategic Salience of Non-Adversarial Neighbours

Rahul Bhonsle

A Look at the Past as the 'Future'

India's neighbourhood is characterised by positives of geostrategic location, electoral democracy, a youth bulge, harmonious diversity, and aspirational ambitions.[1] Decades after most states in the region gained independence from a common colonial master, Great Britain, harnessing this potential continues to be a work in progress. Conversely, multiple challenges are faced in terms of political and economic stability which has manifested in some cases into security threats in the form of militancy and terrorism. Geostrategic location particularly with ongoing competition in the Indian Ocean Region which has emerged as a subset of the greater Asia-Pacific known as Indo-Pacific has only increased the dilemma for states that have failed to gain economic sovereignty and continue to be dependent on aid, assistance, and investments. Inter and intra state differences have led to concerns of sustained instability in the region. Thus, the road ahead for states in the Indian neighbourhood is expected to be an attempt to overcome the substantial baggage of the past, and correct the structural imbalances within while adjusting to transformations occurring in the external space without having the ability to shape the same.

From India's perspective due to factors stated above, the neighbourhood is a source of strength as well as concern. India has the distinction of having common borders with all states, is the largest in terms of population, economy, as well as military potential, and wields substantial clout in the geopolitical arena. For countries in the region, relations with India thus assume salience. Importantly, in the past, those countries which have closely integrated with India have been able to prosper and are currently looking at entering the middle-income group of developing economies such as Bangladesh and Nepal. Bhutan, with an integrated politico-economic relation with India, has been able to achieve a high level of prosperity signified by the emphasis on Gross National Happiness or GNH. The Maldives is also increasingly benefiting with its "India First", policy. Neighbours such as Pakistan which have chosen an adversarial path against India are tottering on economic bankruptcy while Sri Lanka is in a similar predicament as circumstances forced Colombo to balance Indian influence with that of an extra–territorial power—China. The lesson is obvious—*India is the fulcrum of South or Southern Asia.* This recognition has come even to the *de facto* authority in Afghanistan which calls itself the Islamic Emirate of Afghanistan (IEA) or the Taliban, which is seeking a wider economic relationship with India despite concerns of the benefactor of the group in power—Pakistan.

Cognisant of these factors, India's foreign policy priority in terms of "Neighbourhood First", which is not a cliché, has been a driver for closer engagement in all spheres from the political to economy and security with countries in the neighbourhood. India's relations with Pakistan and China have received adequate prominence; however, there is a need for expanding understanding the linkages with non-adversarial neighbours ranging from Afghanistan, Nepal, Bhutan, Myanmar, Bangladesh, Sri Lanka, and the Maldives by examining the impact of vectors which have significance in the future. This is being attempted by examining geopolitical competition, geo-economic alternatives and opportunities, internal political fissures, governance and economic issues, energy dependency, climate change, pandemics and disaster resilience, universal human rights, and finally, defence and security. Strategic salience of neighbours has been discussed in tandem with these factors and summarised in the concluding segment.

Geopolitical Competition

As countries in India's neighbourhood remain aid, trade, investment, and remittance dependent, they will face the challenge of expanding geopolitical competition in the years ahead. This, in as much as South Asia is concerned, has multiple tracks, and is not restricted to the USA and China. The trajectory of competition and contestation between Washington and Beijing is on the rise and touches numerous spheres from politics, economy, and technology to security. There is unlikely to be any decrease in this dyad of adverse relations in the medium term and beyond. Thus, balancing between China and the USA is a sequitur for South Asian neighbours including, one could argue, India. Governments such as Bangladesh which can do so successfully will reap benefits while those that fail to do so are likely to fall into a debt or even a security trap.

Apart from China and the USA, Russia continues to wield considerable influence in the region, due to historical political, diplomatic and security presence; while this may weaken, there are long-term linkages in terms of defence, nuclear and energy which can extend to 2050 and beyond. The disputation between the USA and Russia will remain a factor in moving ahead. The European Union (EU) as a block also wields considerable economic influence in the region and is also expanding its security presence in the Indo-Pacific. The GSP Plus trade concessions offered by the EU are important benefits for trade by developing countries in South Asia. In a wider perspective, the USA, EU, and China are in an economic competition with the latter relatively isolated. Iran is another factor which has been causing disruptions with the historical antipathy against the USA and as an important energy producer.

From the Indian perspective, engagement with neighbours will have to factor in the influence of geopolitical stakeholders in the region. Towards this end, a calibrated approach is essential by laying down the 'red lines', an offensive term for 'concerns', over India's strategic interests in the neighbourhood which would have an impact over the country's security. These will expand to economic and political interests as well, thus implying that large projects in the neighbourhood such as the Chinese investment Hambantota port will no longer be welcomed. The China-Pakistan Economic Corridor (CPEC) is another example of the investments which India would require its neighbours to avoid without impinging on their sovereignty. While there is a well-worn maxim in the context of India and China that there is enough space in the region for accommodating the interests of both, where the sphere is contested, the scope narrows.

Geo-economic Alternatives and Opportunities

The flip side of geo-political competition is geo-economic alternatives and opportunities. To keep away from the malign influence of stakeholders which are hostile to Indian interests, geo-economic alternatives and opportunities have to be offered to nations in the region apart from India's own development aid and assistance. Towards this end, multilateral initiatives through the QUAD—Australia, India, Japan and the USA—or the Asia-Africa Growth Corridor (AAGC) planned by Japan and India need mention. India's Indo-Pacific Oceans Initiative (IPOI) is another integrating mechanism which can link neighbours. Clearly, at present, these arrangements are conceptual in nature and lack the degree of economic heft of China's Belt and Road Initiative (BRI). A positive correction is thus overdue to keep the neighbours glued to the India-led, 'bandwagon'. Such an approach cannot be seen as containing China but only to provide better alternatives to Beijing's more mercantilist and exclusivist approach. This is also intrinsic as India provides opportunities to neighbours of connectivity—infrastructure, communications, socio-political linkages, culture and people-to-people relations which need to be flagged in the bilateral dimension to gain confidence and comfort of the neighbours.

Internal Political Fissures

Ironically, while the South Asian region is marked by democracies minus Afghanistan and partially Myanmar, the systems have yet to develop some characteristics such as independence of institutions including the media, free and fair electoral process, equity in political parties with elected leadership, elimination of corruption and criminality in politics. On the other hand, democracies seem to have imbibed some of the worse characteristics of their older and more established counterparts such as the increasingly acrimonious personalised rivalries seen in the USA in the past few years.

The stability of the constitution is an issue in many countries ranging from Nepal to Myanmar, Sri Lanka, and the Maldives. The propensity to manipulate the constitution to benefit the ruling leadership or the party without projecting how this will impact the people is another major impediment to political stability. Towards this end, political stability will continue to be a concern in India's neighbourhood and constant state fractures are expected to cause disruptions which, in turn, will be manipulated by external stakeholders to advantage.

To manage this debility in the long-term, India will have to provide the lead in terms of a political culture that is inclusive, respects institutions and works for the benefit of the people and national interests. In the absence of India becoming the guiding light in this sphere, a transactional approach of supporting political parties which are supportive of India appears to be the alternative. Such alternatives have been exercised but have shown very clear infirmities. How far can India move from a transactional to a transformative approach, thus providing a beacon for others in the neighbourhood to change, remains to be seen.

On the outliers of democracy in the region, India will continue to face a dilemma of managing relations with Afghanistan. Afghanistan has an exclusive political architecture based on the Taliban's interpretation of the Sharia that is alien to the region. Myanmar will also pose a challenge, with the propensity of the army to seize power after experimenting with democracy from time to time. Presently, Myanmar is going through what has been characterised by analysts as a 'civil war'; thus what emerges from the armed confrontation between the people and the military remains to be seen. India is faced with a dilemma of principles versus pragmatism, and a concern that the gap will be exploited by Myanmar's other neighbour, China.

Governance and Economic Issues

Some countries in India's neighbourhood have governance issues, both administrative as well as economic. To obtain a credible overview, a data-based perspective is included by using the government Effectiveness Percentile Rank evolved by the World Bank Institute Worldwide Governance Indicators for the year 2020. The Governance Indicator[2] as a percentile rank is as low as 5.29 for Afghanistan, 15 for Nepal, 20 for Bangladesh, 49 for the Maldives, 50 for Sri Lanka and 65 for Bhutan.[3] Importantly, despite a higher percentile for Sri Lanka in 2020, in a span of under two years, the economic governance system in the country has collapsed leading to a people's revolution on the streets between May and July 2022, removing the president and the cabinet. This also indicates the fragility of governance in countries in the region. Afghanistan may also be a test case wherein if the percentile was as low as 5.29 in 2020, today it may be in the negative. The cases of Nepal and Bangladesh are also instructive as the two are to graduate to the middle-income status in the coming years and yet do not inspire confidence in government effectiveness as improvement can only be incremental in the future.

While India has been assisting these countries for improvement of economic governance, there could be a case for increasing level and quality in multiple domains, sectors, and organisations. The management of inflation is an example. India's Reserve Bank of India (RBI) and the government have agreed to keep inflation in a band of 2-6 per cent. If the RBI is unable to keep inflation within this band, an explanation is required to be given to the Ministry of Finance. The Monetary Policy Committee (MPC) of the RBI is thereafter required to take steps to rein in inflation. Such a measure was undertaken by the MPC on several occasions in 2022 to bring down inflation to 6 per cent. Had Sri Lanka or Pakistan established such a mechanism, the crisis faced by the latter country at present when inflation has crossed 40 per cent would not have occurred.

At the same time, there are concerns in the neighbourhood of overbearing influence of India with fears of loss of sovereignty. The 'India Out' campaign launched by the Progressive Party of Maldives (PPM) in that country in 2022 is instructive. Even though India's exposure in the Maldives is limited to raising canards, the PPM head and former President Abdulla Yameen have attempted to distort New Delhi's image. Some firm action by the present government under President Ibrahim Solih of the Maldives Democratic Party (MDP) prevented the issue spiralling out of control. Thus, apprehensions of India's role and fear of New Delhi's 'take over', so to say, remains a factor in the region which may be a constraint.

Energy Dependency

Energy dependency on oil and gas in countries in the region is expected to continue in the years ahead despite attempts at a transition to renewable energy resources, potential for which is adequate. Political, economic and infrastructural factors are preventing harnessing substantial hydropower resources in the region—Nepal and Bhutan. Investment is a major challenge as resources are limited. Thus, energy dependence on West Asia is expected to continue in the years ahead which will also be impacted by geopolitical disruptions.

Climate Change, Pandemics, and Disaster Resilience

The impact of climate change is being felt by the developed as well as the developing world every year. The heat wave that raged across South Asia in

March–April 2022 has singed Europe including the United Kingdom. Rains and floods wreak havoc in Nepal, Bangladesh, and even Bhutan every year. John Roome, Regional Director, South Asia Sustainable Development, writing in the World Bank blog on 10 February 2022, highlights that South Asia will be one of the regions where climate crisis is expected to have a major impact in going ahead. "*South Asia sits precariously on the front lines of the global climate crisis. As temperatures increase, the region – which is experiencing a 'new climate normal' – is predicted to see hotter weather, longer monsoon seasons, and increased droughts*".[4] Resilience against climate change is essential whereas resources will remain a major constraint.

Climate change-induced disasters are a linked factor and the vulnerability of the region is well established. As a report by USAID notes, South Asia is a multi-hazard belt facing, "cyclones, droughts, earthquakes, floods, landslides, and tsunamis".[5] A historical overview of the chronology of disasters in the region will be packed with several events occurring in a short span of time. Cyclones, for instance, occur on multiple occasions in a year; earthquakes are also not uncommon while landslides disrupt movement in the hilly terrain. Cloudbursts are also occurring increasingly which have been linked to climate change. Much has been done for mitigation of disasters; however frequent recurrence implies that rescue and relief remain a challenge. Rehabilitation of those impacted takes years, thus adding to the trauma of the people at large. The situation is expected to get worse in the future.

Pandemics such as COVID-19 which impacted the world, devastated South Asia as well. Purely from the perspective of data on COVID-19 cases and examining the number of cases and deaths per million population, South Asian countries have been able to manage the impact of virus reasonably well. Health systems which were expected to collapse did not. Yet, preparedness for another similar catastrophe that could occur is not assured and thus it will remain a critical factor in the years ahead.

Universal Human Rights

The significance of universal human rights is expected to increase in the years ahead and it will have much salience as is evident from the example of Afghanistan. The *de facto* authority or the Taliban government which seized power on 15 August 2021 has failed to gain recognition from any country even after a year due to lack of inclusiveness and denial of equal rights to women. Importantly, countries that had recognised the previous rule by the Taliban in the second half of the 1990s—Pakistan, the United Arab Emirates and Saudi Arabia—also have, two decades later, refused to do so even if the current regime is relatively less harsh than its previous avatar. On the other hand, despite the ingrained politics, a higher level of awareness is expected to place it on the watch list, if not as outright pariahs, with all those countries in the region who lack a basic degree of human rights concerns. Smaller states can be increasingly placed under greater pressure on human rights issues.

Defence and Security

State-on-state challenges in the dimension of defence and security are seen as unlikely in India's neighbourhood, apart from the adversarial relations between India and Pakistan and China which is not the subject of this paper. Non-traditional security threats, however, assume importance. These are substantial and include: militancy and terrorism, transnational crime, human and drug trafficking, inflow of refugees, disasters and pandemics (covered separately), maritime piracy and crime, energy security, disasters and famines, and so on. Added to these is the cyber and information medium which has gained salience in the past decade or so.

The criticality of the militancy and terrorism dimension remains acute in Afghanistan and Myanmar while other states such as Sri Lanka and Nepal seem to have crossed the hump for now. Bangladesh is vulnerable to the fanning of extremist Islamist violence which, though reasonably curbed, still has the potential for creating sustained challenges in the future. The Maldives, a mono-religious state, also faces a low-level challenge of religious extremism, and to avoid its extension necessitates capacity building for the future.

Summarising the Strategic Salience of Neighbours

The strategic salience of non-adversarial neighbours for India arises from deep and unique inter-linkages—physical, economic, socio-cultural, religious, and people-to-people. India is a common factor for countries in the neighbourhood. A friction in this natural association due to geo-politics and geo-economics is bound to create abrasions which cannot be in the interests of India as well as the neighbours. Conversely, linkages with India are known to invariably strengthen the states in the region as is evident by the events of the past decade. India's 'Neighbourhood Policy' will be required to invest considerable political, diplomatic, economic, and security capital for sustainable stability in the neighbourhood.

Overcoming the influence of a competing power such as China, and, to a lesser extent, Pakistan, will require providing alternatives such as the Bangladesh, Bhutan, India, Nepal (BBIN) sub-regional initiatives for infrastructure and trade connectivity. The Bay of Bengal Initiative for Multi-Sectoral Technical and Economic Cooperation (BIMSTEC) is another measure that has got all likeminded neighbours on board for mutual benefit. These need greater mobilisation of resources in various formats; collaboration through the QUAD (USA, India, Australia, and Japan) related groups are a *sine qua non.*

On the defence and security front, cooperative security architecture such as the one developed recently under the Colombo Security Conclave (CSC) with India, the Maldives, Sri Lanka, or the Coastal Surveillance Radar Systems, and Maritime Domain Awareness (MDA) platforms such as the Information Fusion Centre (IFC)–Indian Ocean Region (IOR) need strengthening and expansion. Bilateral security support to countries in the region for capacity building such as line of credit for acquisition of arms and munitions, grant of assets such as Dornier maritime surveillance aircraft, etc., need to be pursued with vigour.

At the same time, where the defence and security of India is intricately linked, as with Bhutan and Nepal, the appropriately crafted treaties need to be sustained through mutual consultations. Apprehensions among a section of leadership in India's neighbourhood countries who raise the factor of sovereignty from time to time should be handled with maturity to avoid adversarial fallouts.

ENDNOTES

1. India's neighbourhood is also referred to as South Asia or Southern Asia and includes Afghanistan, Pakistan in the west, Nepal and Bhutan in the north, Bangladesh and Myanmar in the east and Sri Lanka and Maldives in the Indian Ocean Region. Of these the adversarial neighbours, Pakistan are China are not a part of this article.
2. Government effectiveness captures perceptions of the quality of public services, the quality of the civil service and the degree of its independence from political pressures, the quality of policy formulation and implementation, and the credibility of the government's commitment to such policies. Available at file:///C:/Users/Dell/Downloads/ge.pdf
3. World Bank Institute Worldwide Governance Indicators. Available at https://info.worldbank.org/governance/wgi/Home/Reports
4. Roome John. World Bank. "South Asia Climate: Solutions to tackle climate change in South

Asia." 10 February 2022. https://blogs.worldbank.org/endpovertyinsouth asia/southasia4climate-solutions-tackle-climate-change-south-asia#:~:text=South%20Asia%20sits%20precariously%20on,vulnerability%20has%20long%20been%20apparent

5. USAID South Asia - Disaster Risk Reduction Fact Sheet, Fiscal Year (FY) 2018. https://reliefweb.int/report/afghanistan/south-asia-disaster-risk-reduction-fact-sheet-fiscal-year-fy-2018

4

A Troubled China and Asia's Growing Anxiety

Sujit Dutta

Two broad political trends distinguish the past decade of Xi Jinping's authoritarian rule in China. The trends appear mutually inconsistent but none the less have coexisted and define the current situation in China. The first is a triumphalism about China's relentless rise as a rival global power to the USA that has been prominently propagated by Communist Party General Secretary Xi Jinping and the party elite and has fed an increasingly ultra-nationalist ideology, coercive diplomacy, and expansionism that constitute the most serious threat to Asia. The triumphalism is based on large advances in Chinese GDP and several front-line technologies such as Artificial Intelligence, its manufacturing capacities and centrality in the global supply chain. Its rapid and massive military build-up with an intention to secure its expanding economic and strategic interests intimidates all its neighbours.

The essence of the message China has tried to convey is that it has arrived as a global power and must get the respect of other leading powers and obeisance from lesser powers in the international system. Specifically, China expects its 'core interests' —securing its expansive and unilateral territorial claims on land and sea—to be conceded. Both Hu Jintao and Xi Jinping formally—and in the end, unsuccessfully—proposed global power sharing with the USA where each would accept the other's 'core interests'—a flexible and expandable term—and result in a revamped, cooperative 'bipolar' imperial order. Thwarted, it has hit out in all directions, amid a global pandemic crisis when all states were struggling to save their people and their economies. Repression at home and military actions abroad—against India, Japan, the Philippines, Vietnam, and steady occupation of the South China Sea isles and waters, and threat to forcibly occupy Taiwan—have become China's markers of rise as a power.

The other trend, ironically, is a deep sense of brewing internal crisis and external setbacks—of a looming siege. The November 2021 party resolution adopted at its sixth plenum indicates an organisation that is not fully in unison behind its leader's stated mission and policies. A restive society facing multiple problems and challenges has come to characterise Xi Jinping's much-hyped 'new era'. The response has been a concentration of all power—political, military, economic—in the hands of Xi, enabling him to initiate a series of political 'struggles' against his perceived opponents, dissidents, political re-education and stabilisation campaigns, and establishment of a dystopian surveillance state that leaves no scope for individual rights, privacy, or security. In the name of ridding the party of corruption and enabling Xi to achieve the China Dream of national rejuvenation, the Communist Party leadership—with a majority in the Politburo Standing Committee handpicked by Xi himself—has, in fact, given him these powers. By setting aside the two-term and 70-year age limit on leadership posts, the CPC has not only paved the way for the exercise of untrammelled power by Xi, it has also severely negated the vital gains from the rules that Deng Xiaoping and the post-Mao reformers had enshrined in the constitution to ensure a regular and peaceful transition of power and prevent a perpetual one-man dictatorship as under Mao that had devastated China for three decades. The all-powerful party-state is no more certain that without such unrestrained political authority of its leader, the party's rule would be secure, and Xi's stated mission would be attained. Since he rose to power, the number of times Xi has reminded the People's Liberation Army (PLA) that its principal task is to protect the party rule, are a veritable testimony to the social disaffection and the party's fear of protests and turmoil.

Despite the huge expansion of the economy and rapid industrialisation through the past two decades, social tensions are growing. Many segments of society—intellectuals, professionals, lawyers, workers, and peasants—suffer from alienation and anxiety because of falling growth, job losses and growing restrictions on expression of genuine grievances. Limits on dissent, absence of basic freedoms of expression and collective action, and rule of party cadres rather than the rule of law have always been a feature of Communist rule in China, even in the post-reform period. But this has been acutely aggravated by the sweeping censorship of all printed and internet content, including social media, and the deep penetration of society by an all-encompassing surveillance state. As wages have risen, and labour-intensive manufacturing is becoming less profitable and competitive, the debt-fuelled investment strategy has reached its limits, as reflected in the collapse of real estate giants such as Rio Grande. A consumption-led 'dual circulation' economy is yet to take off, and the economic model has begun to lose its sheen. The impact of the COVID-19 pandemic that began in Wuhan—whose origins the party has deliberately suppressed—and an expansive lockdown strategy that China has pursued to contain it has further bruised the economy and society.

A Troubled Communist Party in its Centenary Year

The Xi-led party command recognised the problems and the challenges the country and the party face in the important 6th plenum document adopted in November 2021titled the "CCP Central Committee's Resolution on the major achievements and historical experience of the party's 100-year struggle",[1] It draws attention to key problems that need to be addressed by a strong, united, nationalist leadership. As is to be expected, it does not blame either the current or the previous leaders under whom many of these problems developed or analyse their causes; instead, it underlines them as the rationale for Xi's authoritarian leadership and term extension. Nonetheless, the resolution is important for understanding the party's concerns.

Among the crucial issues highlighted are a lack of party discipline, absence of effective governance at provincial and lower levels, and "weak, ineffective, diluted, and marginalized efforts in implementation" of the party's policies. The resolution says, "the central committee's major decisions and plans were not properly executed as some officials selectively implemented the party's policies or even feigned agreement or compliance and did things their own way." As China scholar Joseph Fewsmith points out: "Lower levels doing things their own way has been a long-standing issue because local officials either have their interests or need to deal with local problems that are very different from those envisioned by central leaders. Nevertheless, to raise this issue as sharply as the document does suggest that many leaders are passively resisting at least some of Xi Jinping's policies".[2]

The resolution further states that for some time after the reform and opening began, there has been "a blatant culture of formalism, bureaucratise, hedonism, and extravagance, and a prevalence of privilege-seeking attitudes and behaviour." It is clearly a reference to the two-decade period of Jiang Zemin and Hu Jintao following the 1992 reforms and opening up when corruption and abuse of power within the party, and social inequality had sharply grown even as China was rapidly modernising and recording high growth rates. The resolution further states that during the phase "some officials engaged in cronyism and ostracized those outside of their circle". It notes that "such misconduct, interwoven with political and economic issues, led to a startling level of corruption that damaged the party's image and prestige and severely undermined relations between the party and the people..." Yet, such acute problems, especially corruption, have clearly not gone away even under Xi for all the campaigns, arrests, sackings, and clean-ups. The resolution states, "Corruption is the greatest threat to the party's long-term governance." In other words, corruption persists within the Party at all levels.[3]

The problems of the differences and divide between central and local authorities, indiscipline, factionalism, institutionalization and corruption, that the resolution underlines have been persistent issues within the Communist party. The resolution states that the party is opposed to "the selection of officials solely on the basis of votes, assessment scores, GDP growth rates, or age, or through open popularity contests". The party's policy now is to select and promote honest and committed cadres that adhere to the party's organizational line. In the run-up to the 19th party congress many officials were retired or purged while two or more promotions were granted to some, mostly those with close ties to Xi Jinping. Such exercises are likely to worsen the tendencies that the resolution is criticizing. Just as finding honest and disciplined cadres favoured by the party leader does not address the issues of corruption or non-implementation of the party line, increasing centralisation in the selection of officials, politically favoured promotions and purges could further alienate, demoralise and marginalise many dynamic and effective local cadres that are seen as not toeing Xi's leftist line, as Fewsmith observes. The party's problems of factionalism, lack of local initiative and poor implementation can only grow.

Since purges, scrutiny of cadres, disciplining and selection of honest and politically loyal cadres, and more centralised control have not stemmed the tide of corruption and other problems, the reasons for what are clearly described as the 'greatest threat' and are deep rooted and to be found elsewhere. It is perhaps ingrained in the very authoritarian institutional structure of the party, its monopoly over power, the acute concentration of powers in the hands of the top leader and his handpicked loyalist cadres, the sycophancy that this promotes, and the absence of checks and balances, freedom of expression and the rule of law. However the party resolution does not and cannot discuss them.

Party-Military Relations

The Communist Party's control over the military has been significantly strengthened since Xi took over as the chairman of the central military commission (CMC) that heads the Chinese armed forces. Under Xi's direction, a sweeping restructuring of the PLA was carried out in 2015. It was the most significant overhaul of the PLA since 1949—the year the People's Republic was founded by the Communist party, and aimed to transform the military doctrine, organisation, and approach to meet the challenges of warfare in the 21st century. The organisational changes included the establishment of three new services; the merger of the seven military regions into five war zones; and an expansion of the CMC to include 15 departments, subordinate commissions, and offices. The allocations for the military have risen steadily, crossing over 200 billion dollars in 2021—second only to that of the USA, and significantly larger than those of Russia, India, and Japan.

The organisational changes and emphasis on modernization is only one dimension of Xi's work within the military. He has been deeply concerned about weak party leadership over the PLA, rampant corruption among high officers, and loyalty tithe party line. Since he came to power in 2012, Xi has repeatedly emphasised that the military should work under the party leadership and not as a separate entity of the government. In a striking observation that can only be deemed as a criticism of the party-military relationship under the former party general secretary and CMC chairman, Hu Jintao, the 2021 resolution says: "For a period of time, the party's leadership over the military was obviously lacking." It claims this problem has been resolved. The "solution" has been to bring the military under Xi's personal control, multiple purges of top officers, and promotion of loyal generals. The impact on the PLA's morale and organizational effectiveness is not known but they certainly do not address the underlying structural issues.

Between 2012 and 2019, it is estimated that over a hundred PLA officers have been retired or investigated. A growing list of top and senior PLA officers have been arrested, expelled from the party, and imprisoned on corruption charges. These included Gen. Guo Boxiong, Gen. Xu Caihou, both former vice-chairmen of the CMC, and Gen Fang Fenghui, senior member of the CMC, Gen Zhang Yang, and Gen Li Jinai, former heads of the PLA's political work department, Gen Liao Xilong, former head of the general logistics department. Gen Du Jincai, head of the CMC's discipline inspection commission, was also retired, on corruption charges. Many of the purged officers were seen to be close to Xi's predecessors—Jiang Zemin and Hu Jintao, and therefore were seen as untrustworthy. The extraordinary extent of the purges and churning of the highest rungs of the military is indicated by the fact that "perhaps 90 per cent of the PLA officers" that attended the 19th party congress were first-time participants.[4]

Shockingly, some of the most senior officers removed (Xu Caihou and Guo Boxiong) were accused at the 19th party congress of plotting a coup. Liu Shiyu, chairman of the China Securities Regulatory Commission, declared that Xu and Guo, along with Bo Xilai (former party secretary of Chongqing), Zhou Yongkang (former member of the Politburo and head of the Ministry of Public Security), and Ling Jihua (former head of the general office of the Chinese Communist party) had been planning "to usurp the party's leadership and seize power." "The other person, Liu, listed was Sun Zhengcai, party secretary for Chongqing until this past summer and rumoured to be among the short list for future leaders of China. The fall of Sun, his linkage to Bo Xilai, Gen Guo and Gen Xu raises questions about the extent of internal dissension, and how far that dissent might extend within the PLA.[5]

External Challenges Grow

China's internal problems and the domestic challenges confronting Xi are compounded by the external setbacks that his foreign and defence policies have brought about for China. For three decades after its rapprochement with the USA, the Western alliance, Soviet Union/Russia, Japan and India, the PRC had an extremely positive and peaceful external environment for its reforms and modernisation. The party under Deng and his chosen reformist leaders, Jiang Zemin and Hu Jintao, enjoyed global support, access to global markets, capital, technology, research institutes and academia, and low security costs. The 'peaceful rise' posture articulated by Zheng Bijian for this period flowed from Deng's instruction to the party: 'hide your strength, bide your time', and avoid conflict with the major powers, especially the USA.

That phase began to close as China's power grew, the USA and the West went into a financial crisis, Xi Jinping was elevated as s successor to Hu, and an ultra-nationalist, statist, and more conservative political line began to prevail within the top leadership. The party convinced itself that the USA was in decline and the time was ripe for a more assertive posture to advance China's 'core interests' and demand global power sharing with the USA. Indeed, the thesis of a 'window of opportunity' for China's assertive rise had begun to be articulated post-2001 when the USA faced an attack on New York and Washington from Islamic forces and was drawn into a deleterious 'war on terror'. However, an assertive stance and strategic competition with the USA was not seen as advisable by most reformers.

By2009, however, the assertive foreign policy posture was clearly visible as China stepped up its military actions in the South China and East China seas. An open declaration of China's great power ambitions and parity with the USA became the official line with Xi's coming to power in 2012. Xi and his backers were convinced that the USA was in decline and the moment for China to assert its 'core' interests and role as a great power had arrived.

Tensions with its neighbours have steadily grown since 2009-10 as China's occupation of islets in the South China Sea, and military actions against Taiwan, Bhutan, Japan's Senkaku, and India's Eastern Ladakh have been initiated. Following the election of Donald Trump as US president, the simmering frictions with the USA erupted into the open and have continued to prevail under Joe Biden. The USA has declared China as its strategic rival, even as Xi's policies have led to conflicts with India, Japan and Australia. The re-emergence of the QUAD is a strategic response to Xi's ultra nationalism, military actions and expansionism in the Indo-Pacific region. With the European Union too declaring China as a strategic competitor, and Southeast Asia increasingly worried about Chinese actions and intentions, Xi has lost most of the gains of the 'peaceful rise' line that dominated the reform era. He must now deal with a more inimical external environment.

Beijing University scholar Jia Qingguo's recent warning that the search for absolute security internally and externally through excessive expenditure on defence and national security can be highly destabilising as the Soviet

Communist party fatally learnt, can only be seen as an indirect critique of Xi's hard-line and search for total or comprehensive security.[6]

The Revival of *'Douzheng'* or Struggle

The seriousness of the challenges facing the country and the Communist party, and Xi's preferred way to deal with them is reflected in the return of the politically loaded phrase 'struggle' or *'douzheng'* in Xi's speeches and party writings since the 19th party congress. The phrase has a Maoist lineage in Chinese party politics and recalls the grievous political attacks on the 'enemy', or party members who either disagreed or opposed Mao's ultra-left political line. It invokes the violence and the vast persecutions that devastated the party and the country during the Cultural Revolution, which finally went out of Mao's control and the PLA had to be called in to restore a semblance of order. Xi's revival of the phrase does not seem to bode well for the party and the country. "For many, still, *douzheng* invokes not just the need for unity towards common goals, or a can-do attitude, but warns instead of deep and potentially traumatising division."[7]

By 2019, the frequency of the usage of *'douzheng'* had sharply risen. In a speech on 3 September 2019 to young communist cadres being trained at the central party school, Xi Jinping talked about the huge challenges confronting the Communist party and the country. According to the official *Xinhua News Agency*, Xi in that speech mentioned the word an astonishing 56 times. The phrase appeared in over 100 articles in the party organ, *People's Daily*, that year, and continues to be regularly invoked, underlining the nature of normal politics under Xi. In David Bandurski's words: "The Chinese Communist party is once again the party of struggle, turning on itself as much as on the problems the country faces."[8]

On an Uncertain, Disturbing Course

By the time of the party centenary in 2021, the China dream had conspicuously soured. The spread of the corona virus through China's industrial heartland had cast a pall of gloom over the economy and the polity and had soured Xi's plans for a smooth passage to perpetual rule and ambitions of a technology-led future path of glory that would cut through the middle-income trap. Before the virus broke out in December 2019, the break-up with its principal benefactor—the USA, the open defiance of the regime day after day by millions in what was considered an insignificant outpost of capitalism, Hong Kong, and the attendant economic slowdown had already set in and shaken Xi's absolutism and confidence. The 'black swan' event—the outbreak of COVID-19 that began in Wuhan and spread through China's global networks,—has also struck its blow, clouding the future and sapping Xi's image and energy.

China is facing a wide set of serious structural problems. The tensions can be felt all around and have gripped its economic model, inner-party politics, party-PLA relations, its large private sector that employs millions of workers, the Belt and Road Initiative, its banking and financial system and its foreign policy. And yet, Xi Jinping and his nationalist supporters in the Communist party have pursued for seven years now a calculated aggressive stance both at home and abroad in the hope that the emerging crisis can be beaten. Xi's solution has been increased centralisation, acute concentration of power in his own hands, expanding state control over the private sector, a crack-down on big tech companies, and a return to Maoist symbolisms, struggles and socialist rhetoric. Yet no solutions to the structural problems are visible. With economic performance found wanting, a nationalist patriotic campaign is being stepped up to rally the people behind Xi and the party, even as all-round surveillance, censorship, securitisation, and repression grow.

The 20th party congress later this year is expected to give Xi another term to set the troubled house in order, achieve the technological breakthroughs that would spur growth again, realise the goal of 'unification' with Taiwan and occupation of all claimed territories. In the changed domestic and external environment none of this is going to be easy. However, that may not prevent Xi, the CPC and the PLA from pursuing his dangerous and high-risk strategy that can escalate into a war. The anxieties can only grow for Asia and a world already under deep stress.

ENDNOTES

1. "CCP Central Committee's Resolution on the Major Achievements and Historical Experience of the Party's 100-Year Struggle", *Xinhua* in Chinese, 16 November 2021. https://china.usc.edu/ccp-central-committee-resolution-major-achievements-and-historical-experience-party-over-past
Find the official English translation here: "Full Text: Resolution of the CPC Central Committee on the Major Achievements and Historical Experience of the Party over the Past Century." *Xinhua*, 16 November 2021. https://english.www.gov.cn/policies/latestreleases/202111/ 16/ content_WS6193a935c6d0df57f98e50b0.html

2. Joseph Fewsmith, History as Patriotism: But Can Discipline Solve Structural Issues? In Anna Scott Bell (ed.) *Party Watch Annual Report*, 2021, pp. 20-26.
3. Ibid.
4. Cheng, Dean. "Xi Jinping and His Generals: Curiouser and Curiouser." War on the Rocks, 18 January 2018. https://warontherocks.com/2018/01/xi-jinping-generals-curiouser-curiouser/
5. Ibid.
6. Mai, Jun. "Remember the Soviet Union, Top Chinese Policy Adviser Says in Warning against Blind Pursuit of Absolute Security." *South China Morning Post*, 22 January 2022. https://www.scmp.com/news/china/diplomacy/article/3164103/remember-soviet-union-top-chinese-policy-adviser-says-warning
7. Bandurski, David. "Why China's Communist Party Is 'Struggling'." *Hong Kong Free Press*, 10 September 2019. https://www.hongkongfp.com/2019/09/10/chinas-communist-party-struggling/
8. Ibid.

5

Military Capability Development: Modernisation, Transformation and Indigenisation

Anil Ahuja

"*... the threats to national security have also (sic) become widespread, the methods of warfare are also changing. Earlier, we used to imagine our defence only till land, sea, and sky. Now the circle is moving towards space, moving towards cyberspace, moving towards economic, social space. In such a scenario, we have to move anticipating the future challenges and change ourselves accordingly. Self-reliance will help the country a great deal in this regard.*"

—Prime Minister Narendra Modi at 'Swavlamban', 18 July 2022.[1]

"*We appreciate India's role as a stabilizing force on the region's geographic frontlines. Your nation understands better than many: peace and prosperity are only attainable when all respect the principles of territorial integrity, freedom of navigation and freedom from coercion—all of these are fundamental to the rule-based international order. Only then, to borrow Prime Minister Modi's words, can "nations small and large prosper...free and fearless in their choices.*"

—James N. Mattis, Former US Secretary of Defence, Delhi, 6 September 2018[2]

Security Environment

The remarks quoted above sum up the changing geostrategic realities of India, where it has come to be on the geographic frontline of the region with China, a major power competing for primacy in the global power play with the USA. It also highlights the changing character of war, extending across multiple domains.

Military clashes and stand-off along the Line of Actual Control (LAC) in Eastern Ladakh since mid-2020 and augmented deployments all along the hitherto thinly-held northern borders are indicative of China's commitments and heightened threat potential against India's northern territories. Intensified Chinese infrastructure and habitat developments all along the LAC, in the area of Doklam (India-Bhutan–China tri-junction,[3]) north of the vital Siliguri Corridor, in Eastern Ladakh (bridge over Pangong Tso,[4] China's National Expressway G-695, improvement of air bases in Tibet), and intensified air exercises are clear indicators of that situation. Despite progressive disengagement from various flashpoints in Eastern Ladakh (Hot Springs, Gogra, Pangong Tso, Kailash Range, Demchok) during the period February 2021 to September 2022, effective de-escalation of forces from the military confrontation in the Ladakh sector does not seem to be in sight, yet.

The threat along the Western border also persists and has, in fact, intensified. Pakistan itself remains crisis-prone, hugely polarised due to internal politics, and continues to suffer from a serious economic meltdown with debt in excess of US$ 250 billion. Further west, Afghanistan, under the Taliban regime, remains infested with Islamic State Khorasan Province (ISKP) and Al-Qaeda in co-existence with the Tehreek-e-Taliban Pakistan (TTP) and the Haqqani Network. Linkages between Pakistan and the terrorist groups on one hand and the all-weather friendship between Pakistan and China on the other constitute a perpetual security concern for which the Indian armed forces need to remain prepared.

With increasing forays by the People's Liberation Army (PLA) Navy in the Indian Ocean, challenges also manifest in the maritime domain, particularly so over the last decade. As the former Chief of Naval Staff, Admiral Karambir Singh, speaking at the Raisina Dialogue (2021), said, "*China looks west for its energy, markets, and resources, so it won't be surprising that soon they would be coming into the Indian Ocean Region, because flag follows trade*".[5] This trend is evident from the increased PLA navy deployments of ships, submarines, survey, and other vessels in the region. On the western seaboard, despite economic constraints, the Pakistan navy is working towards becoming a 50-platform force by about 2030-2035,[6] thus adding to the challenges of the Indian Navy. The PLA navy and the Pakistan navy are also training to operate jointly in the maritime domain. The 'Guardian' series of naval exercises, being held since 2020 (the second edition was held in July 2022 off the Shanghai coast[7]) are aimed at honing their inter-operability.

These developments in India's immediate neighbourhood, as well as the changing global and regional security paradigm, suggest the growing need for comprehensive capability development of the Indian armed forces across conventional and emerging asymmetric domains. This is essential for a nation of India's stature which is looked upon as the region's net security provider and is expected to help maintain a rule-based order in contributing towards the idea of 'Security and Growth for all in the Region' (SAGAR).

The combat edge of the Indian armed forces continues to be strengthened through efforts of '*modernisation*', '*transformation*' and '*indigenisation*', terminologies often used interchangeably. However, *in the absence of a well-articulated vision and a defined end state, the results achieved from these efforts and the expenditure being incurred thereon remains sub-optimal.* Today, at $ 76.6 billion, India is the third highest military spender in the world.[8] It is also among the largest importers of arms, procuring nearly 11 per cent of arms sold globally.[9] Despite this, substantial capability voids continue to prevail, suggesting a need for a more nuanced conceptual planning.

Some issues to be addressed in this regard are: (a) Distinguishing between *modernisation* and *transformation*; (b) the *end* towards which these are being directed; (c) how to *dovetail* the two; (d) to what extent can *indigenisation* be a measure of operational readiness; and (e) can indigenisation in *defence* be an end in itself ?

Modernisation and Transformation

Modernisation

Military modernisation entails qualitative improvement of the existing family of weapon systems to enhance their operational capability, viz., *range, accuracy, mobility, speed of delivery, lethality, terminal effect, stealth, all-weather capability, etc.* It may also be aimed at enhancing battlefield transparency, securing networks or degrading an adversary's capabilities through cyber, electronic warfare (EW), space; enabling a more efficient battlefield (or platform) management system; improving information fusion; enhancing the span of control; optimisation of resources (including manpower) etc. In essence, it entails enhancement of combat potential largely by incorporating the latest advancements in technology into the existing systems.

To illustrate, the efficacy of India's armour fleet of T 72 and T 90 tanks is being progressively enhanced through '*modernisation*', incorporating improvements like explosive reactive armour, upgraded engines, and improved fire control, communication and navigation systems. Likewise, the range and lethality of India's indigenous Pinaka multi-barrel rocket launcher system are also being enhanced by modernisation of its munitions system, inducting enhanced range rocket system (EPRS), area denial munitions (ADM) rocket systems, etc.[10] Similar performance enhancement programmes are under implementation for various other systems.

For capability development of standing military forces within limited budgets, modernisation attains the highest priority, for it impacts the immediate war-fighting capability. It can also be absorbed without any significant changes in doctrines and organisational structures, and only by tweaking some tactics and operational procedures. An aspect to be noted is that induction of modern high technology weapons in itself does not constitute '*transformation*' which entails supplementing these with newer concepts of employment and doctrines.

Transformation

With critical and emerging technologies incrementally finding their way onto the battlefield, it is often stated that we are 'transforming', i.e. transiting from the '*industrial era war fighting*' to the '*digital era battlefield*'. Induction of just modern high-technology weapons, however, does not constitute *transformation*. That entails concurrently evolving or revolutionising the concepts of employment and war-fighting doctrine to most optimally employ advanced weapon systems to generate a higher state of conflict management. What good are AI-enabled swarm drones or unmanned armed aerial or underwater systems or batteries of hypersonic missiles, and such other disruptive weapon systems, unless they are optimally integrated to enhance the overall tempo of operations, and create unprecedented decision and response dilemmas for the enemy? In the absence of refined concepts, modernised inductions remain but marginal force multipliers, and will be utilised sub-optimally.

The concurrent evolution of concepts for orchestrating conflict escalation ladders across the domains is imperative to transcend from *modernisation* to *transformation*. This may entail conceptualising the conduct of *non-contact warfare*, creating *reverse linearity*, planning greater *dispersion*, focussing on *integrating fires* rather than just the formations, a review of *organisational structures* and *equipment tables*, optimisation of *manpower* and more. Today, technology has become the driver for formulating doctrines and concepts, a fact not adequately appreciated.

In planning the transformation of the armed forces, it is imperative to conceptualise the future battlefield, evolve concepts and a doctrine of integrated war-fighting and review organisational constructs 'before' embarking on transformation. Thereafter, the modernisation programmes must gradually be nudged in that direction to achieve transformation in the next 10-12 years. Transformation, which includes absorption of technology by the rank and file and training of individuals and formations, is 'evolutionary' rather than 'revolutionary' in implementation within limited defence budgets. It would be prudent not to compromise on the modernisation needs of today in favour of some futuristic 'gizmos' which do not fit into the pattern of war-fighting yet.

Besides the cardinal changes within the armed forces and in the war-fighting doctrine, as stated above, '*transformation*' would also substantially impact the country's defence industrial base. Emphasis should be on progressively shifting from funding research and development (R&D) and manufacturing of legacy systems to transformational technologies and weapon systems. A critical planning challenge before the Indian defence planners would be in appreciating that there would be existing and legacy technologies and weapon systems that may be good enough to meet current and near-future needs. The *transition*, therefore, needs to conform to emerging technological development levels and the financial resources available. This entails a rigorous internal exercise.

The services and the Ministry of Defence (MoD) need to diversify from dealing only with established defence public sector undertakings (DPSUs) and private defence majors to innovators and start-ups. These technology start-ups and micro, small, and medium enterprises (MSME) would need to be mainstreamed by hand-holding and funding to integrate them into the larger defence supply chains, domestically and globally. Consideration of this aspect is vital for the Indian defence sector today while we are at the threshold of transforming our war-fighting and venturing seriously into indigenisation for self-reliance.

Indigenisation

Building on lessons learnt from the challenges of yesteryears and the ongoing geostrategic contestations in the Indo-Pacific and Euro-Atlantic, the government has intensified its efforts to achieve self-reliance. The February 2022 Ukraine conflict, with related disruptions, has added urgency to the efforts in the defence sector. Emphasis is now being laid on innovation, indigenisation, and promotion of the defence industry, including the private sector, to make India a defence manufacturing hub. Ambitious targets of defence production of Rs. 1. 75 lakh crore (US$ 23 billion) and defence exports worth Rs. 35,000 crore (US$ 4.8 billion) by 2025 have been set.[11] Towards that end, the Union budget 2022-2023 earmarks nearly 70 per cent of the defence capital budget for the domestic defence industry; 25 per cent of the R&D budget for research by the private sector and academia; and Rs. 60 crore (US$ 8 million) for programmes under 'Innovation for Defence Excellence' (iDEX).[12]

Indigenisation in defence is a laudable and desirable objective and is neither isolationism, nor protectionism, nor autarky, as some global arms manufacturers suggest. At the same time, it is also not a measure of a nation's military capability or combat potential. It is an enabler for capability development through *modernisation* and *transformation* and a significant component of the country's 'Comprehensive National Power' (CNP).It is sought to be achieved through integration with global supply chains, rather than through insulation. Most significantly, it needs to be done *without diluting the operational preparedness* against active adversaries.

The foundation of *indigenisation* has to be laid on a clear visualisation of the future battlefield, defining the concept of operations across multiple domains and prioritising the capabilities required to be acquired for each domain (*land, sea, air, EW, cyber, space, strategic, etc*.). In the absence of such visualisation, the services would continue to acquire 'more of the same' assets with which they are fighting today, exhausting meagre budgets to choke their inventories for the next three to four decades with weapon systems which may not be the most appropriate for the transformed battlefields. Non-availability of this *road map* also denies appropriate guidance to the defence industry which may make huge investments in manufacturing weapons that have no domestic or global market in the future. It is one's apprehension that today the Indian private defence industry is making its perspective plans based either on weapons and equipment currently in service, or being sought under emergency procurement programmes, or in the perceived space created through promulgation of 'Positive Indigenisation (Negative Import) lists'. This is not necessarily appropriate and may turn out to be detrimental to the national effort of *Atmanirbharta,* as well as a bad business decision, besides future defence preparedness.

To be implementable, the road map of transformation has to be aligned to the financial allocations (defence budget) and a timeline, which itself should be related to the nation's larger geopolitical objectives. India's vision of becoming a US$ 5 trillion economy, a net security provider in the Indo-Pacific and a middle power of reckoning in the Indo-Pacific is predicated on building credible CNP, including substantial hard military power, indigenously. All these aspirations need to be aligned to a defined timeline and resourced accordingly. Towards that end, the services, based on their considered capability development plans, would need to prepare a year-wise prioritised acquisition list with yearly cash outgo for a time horizon of say 10 years—the stipulated time horizon of the integrated capability development plan in the defence planning process.[13] The total requirement would need to be compared with budget allocations expected in the normal course, indicating additional allotments sought. This alignment, which has remained elusive hitherto, is fundamental to the implementation of the indigenisation and capability development roadmap.

Another significant aspect is the sourcing of technology and acquiring Intellectual Property Rights (IPR) for the domestic industry. A realistic appraisal suggests that in India, we are reasonably self-reliant in *old and some current technologies.* We, however, have *voids in the cutting-edge current and critical emerging technologies.* Some of these need to be sourced globally against commercial and security barriers. Also, most defence technologies cannot be acquired in a stand-alone mode and come tied either to acquisitions or through arrangements with foreign governments and global private arms manufacturers owning the technologies and IPRs. Calibrated and well-planned global acquisitions are thus a route to achieving self-reliance in the long run as well as to fill up critical operational voids in the current and short term.

In this long journey of achieving self-reliance in major systems, the first step is to invite global players to collaboratively manufacture in India for the world market, as it is being done. For this to succeed more than it has so far, substantial financial investments would need to be made by the government or private players, or through public-private partnerships, to attract production facilities to India. Foreign manufacturers would move in only when they sense commercial advantages of scaling up production, reducing production costs, and accessing a greater market share in India than in other countries of the region or through India.

To acquire IPRs, initially, we may need to start with co-production and co-assembly. With this arrangement, some IPs will get shared. Thereafter, we could evolve to co-development of next-generation capability with shared IP. This, in turn, would set the stage for the transfer of some know-how for indigenous production of components of the platforms. Over a period of time, some modifications and upgrades to the platform could be carried out in India. Progressively, this will result in Indian production facilities becoming part of global supply chains. This seems a pragmatic road map, spread over a period of about a decade or decade-plus, through which the vision of *indigenisation*, including in high-end weapon systems, can be realised.

In the critical and emerging technologies, innovation and its application to defence capabilities can enable the creation of an ecosystem for bilateral defence cooperation with major defence partners. Countries like the USA are today domestically partnering more closely with start-ups and 'disruptive technology' companies. The arms majors in these countries are also looking around globally for next-generation technology to speedily bridge the lead taken by their peer competitors like China. It is important that the Indian talent pool of innovators and start-ups gets noticed so that they get intimately integrated with global arms manufacturers and get a portion of the huge defence spending being made by the USA and other countries, while furthering our own capability in the long run. It is heartening that this process has already commenced. Thirty-five per cent of India's defence exports in the last five years, amounting to approximately US$ 2.5 billion, constitute exports to the USA, as part of their supply chains.[14]

Finally, indigenisation is an expensive proposition. It requires immense investment in R&D, promoting innovation, acquiring IP, and setting up infrastructure and facilities. Allowance also has to be made for some inevitable initial failures. Amortising all these costs, domestic products will take time to materialise and would initially be expensive. This aspect merits consideration while allocating defence budgets. In India, in the last few years, nearly 1.6 per cent of the GDP is being allotted as the defence budget (minus pensions).[15] This has barely been adequate to meet the needs of sustaining the standing force levels and maintaining routine operational preparedness. Thus, the recent endeavours to sub-allocate these very allocations from the capital head to promote indigenous industry, start-ups, defence innovations, and R&D in the private sector, would continue to remain fund constrained. While the defence sector presents ample opportunities to promote the country's industrial base, this effort needs to be supported by the allocation of a 'defence budget plus', to accommodate core defence needs and for the promotion of indigenous capability.

Conclusion

Military capability is a significant component of CNP and building this capability against competing demands of financial resources remains a challenge. Another significant challenge, in the Indian context, is of balancing the competing needs of maintaining operational readiness to meet prevailing challenges, while concurrently creating an indigenous defence technological and industrial base—an imperative whose significance has grown with geopolitical contestation. This complex national effort requires a clear perception of the future battlefield environment, matching doctrines and concepts of operations and a clear integrated prioritisation of the requirements of military *modernisation* and a road map for *transformation.* This analysis is an endeavour to support that effort.

ENDNOTES

1. PM addresses NIIO seminar, 'Swavlamban'. 18 July 2022. https://www.narendramodi.in/prime-minister-narendra-modi-addresses-niio-seminar-swavlamban-in-new-delhi-563224
2. Secretary of Defence Mattis' Remarks at India 2+2 Joint Press Conference, post Inaugural 2+2 Dialogue. 6 September 2018. https://www.defense.gov/News/Transcripts/Transcript/Article/1621909/secretary-of-defense-mattis-remarks-at-india-22-joint-press-conference/
3. Press Trust of India. "New images of a Chinese village in Doklam plateau emerge, says report". *Business Standard.* 19 July 2022. https://www.business-standard.com/article/current-affairs/new-images-of-chinese-village-in-doklam-plateau-emerge-says-report-122071901549_1.html
4. Pradip R. Sagar. "China's new bridge on Pangong Tso forces India to rethink posture in Ladakh". *The Week.* 29 May 2022. https://www.theweek.in/theweek/cover/2022/05/27/chinas-new-bridge-on-pangong-tso-forces-india-to-rethink-posture-in-ladakh.html
5. Kaushik Krishn. "Regular Chinese Navy presence in Indian Ocean Region over past decade: Navy Chief". *The Indian Express.* 15 April 2021. https://indianexpress.com/article/india/regular-chinese-navy-presence-in-indian-ocean-region-over-past-decade-navy-chief-7274021/
6. "Formidable Challenge: Keeping A Close Watch on Chinese Forays into the Indian Ocean, Says Navy chief". *ABP Live.* 20 September 2022. https://news.abplive.com/news/indian-navy-chief-admiral-r-hari-kumar-india-naval-revolution-china-pakistan-security-challenges-military-1554392

7. PTI. "With eye on Indian Ocean, China and Pakistan kick off naval, air drills to jointly deal with maritime threats". *The Times of India.* 10 July 2022. https://timesofindia.indiatimes.com/india/with-eye-on-indian-ocean-china-and-pakistan-kick-off-naval-air-drills-to-jointly-deal-with-maritime-threats/articleshow/92786699.cms
8. "At $76.6 billion, India is the third highest military spender in the world". *The Indian Express.* 26 April 2022. https://indianexpress.com/article/india/global-military-spending-india-china-russia-7885931/#:~:text=India%20was%20the%20third%2Dhighest,Institute(SIPRI)%20said%20Monday
9. "India is amongst the world's largest arms importers, says SIPRI as it cites conflict with China". *The New Indian Express.* 14 March 2022. https://www.newindianexpress.com/nation/2022/mar/14/india-is-amongst-the-worlds-largest-arms-importers-sayssipri-as-it-cites-conflict-with-china-2429965.html
10. Ministry of Defence. Press Information Bureau (PIB). Pinaka Mk-I (Enhanced) Rocket System and Pinaka Area Denial Munitions Rocket Systems successfully flight-tested by DRDO & Indian Army. 9 April 2022. https://pib.gov.in/PressReleasePage.aspx?PRID=1815236
11. AIR News. Raksha Mantri Rajnath Singh says, India to achieve Aatmanirbharta in defence sector by 2025. 17 September 2022. https://newsonair.com/2022/09/17/raksha-mantri-rajnath-singh-says-india-to-achieve-aatmanirbharta-in-defence-sector-by-2025/#:~:text=Defence%20Minister%20Rajnath%20Singh%20has ,of%2035%20 thousand%20crore%20 rupees
12. Union Budget 2022-2023. Press Information Bureau, Government of India, Ministry of Defence. 1 February 2022. https://pib.gov.in/newsite/PrintRelease.aspx?relid=231242
13. Defence Acquisition Procedure 2020. Paras 24-25, Chapter 1, Page 7. https://www.mod.gov.in/sites/ default/files/DAP2030new_0.pdf
14. Press Release. Ministry of Defence India. 21 April 2022. https://pib.gov.in/PressReleaseIframePage.aspx? PRID=1818622
15. Ahuja Anil. Optimising Capability Building with the Defence Budget. Delhi Policy Group Policy Brief, Vol. VII, Issue 12. 9 February 2022. Pg 2. https://www.delhipolicygroup.org/uploads_dpg/publication_file/optimising-capability-building-with-the-defence-budget-3719.pdf

6

SHAPING INDIA'S MILITARY STRATEGY IN THE 2050S

Rakesh Sharma

Introduction

India is geographically located in a far-from-benign strategic environment, which normally argues for a strong and effective military force capable of defending territorial integrity and sovereignty from possible threats from several sources. The articulation of India's long-term military strategy will be based on judgment of the prevailing and prospective geo-strategic environment. It can be argued that in addition to domestic politics, bureaucratic tussles, organizational inertia, group think, psychological barriers and learning wrong lessons from history, failure of security strategies is also due to inappropriate assessment of the environment.[1]

The greatest challenge of our times is to be able to make correct and timely assessments of changes taking place and the nature and extent of challenges and opportunities they present.[2] To formulate a long-term military strategy for the 2050s, it is imperative to have a holistic visualisation of principal regional threats and challenges, including asymmetric ones, transnational threats, and even unanticipated ones! In a democratic dispensation like India, the conduct of any military campaign will ever remain conditioned to political ends. Prospectively, warfare will transcend beyond the three services—Army, Navy and Air Force. New and modern domains of warfare have emerged like cyber, space, electro-magnetic spectrum and informational, and they will introduce dramatic changes in warfare.

More fundamentally, warfare conducted in newer operational domains may not simply depend on kinetic warfare to achieve political ends. The lines between peace and war will stand overlapped or blurred. Since the domains of warfare would have largely proliferated, multiple agencies like the National Security Council Secretariat (NSCS), National Technical Research Organisation (NTRO), National Cyber Security Coordinator, Defence Research & Development Organisation (DRDO), Indian Space Research Organisation (ISRO), the Atomic Energy Commission and even the Central Armed Police Forces (CAPF) would be proportionately be involved in combat operations.

National Military Strategy

Military strategy cannot be viewed in isolation. In prosecution of national security policy, the military will be one instrument, a prominent one, along with other parameters of national power—diplomacy, economic leverages, political strength and 'will'—duly cumulated with soft power. It is thus argued that that in such a multi-domain and hybrid warfare environment, joint military strategy will become part and parcel of the mother document, the National Military Strategy, which by itself will draw from the National Security Strategy to bring all elements of national power together. That brings in the necessity for formulating a *National Security Strategy* and a *National Military Strategy*.

A national military strategy, hence, would envisage employment of all of the nation's military and civil capabilities at the highest levels, and long-term planning, developments and procurements to create the requisite capabilities for assured success and victory. This strategy will have to be enunciated by the politico-military establishment in peace, which would lead to force-restructuring and preparations for prosecution of modern wars. Strategic history is amply populated with cases of policy-makers assigning impossible tasks and soldiers being compelled to operate in the absence of clear political guidance. Such incongruities have to be avoided.

How will such a military strategy for the 2050s be formulated? Indeed, it will be an exacting process. To argue further, the national military strategy would be derived from political formulation of national aim, vision and interests as well as a national security strategy, thus implying the dominance of political ends. India's geographic strategy, which will change with time, will also have clear diktats and would lead to the appropriate strategic context for

India. In the oncoming era leading to the 2050s, India's strategic formulations would need to consider the security landscape as a systemic construct of political uncertainties, increasing relevance of globally intertwined geo-strategic environment, and the challenge of a rising China in collusion with Pakistan. By the 2050s, developments in the technological, operational, and political domains would have converged to create conditions that favour a transition to usage of 'discriminate force'—selective use of military power—attributed to the phenomenon of globalisation and the growing transparency of the battlefield.

The theme of this paper is to envision future wars which could be conducted with the aim of achieving a situation of political advantage, and not merely a military victory. Consequently, there is the need to instil a methodical and constructivist rigour in the discourse over the evolving determinants of shaping India's military strategy for the 2050s.

The South-Asian Strategic Geography by Mid-21st Century

The strategic geography of India is significant as it relates to the study of spatial areas of South Asia as a whole that affects India's national security and prosperity in the region. The critical aspect of strategic geography is that it has been changing with human needs, development of nations, their geo-political ambitions and strategic relations among them. In the context of South Asia, significant changes can be forecast for not too distant a future. South Asia comprises Afghanistan, Bangladesh, Bhutan, India, the Maldives, Nepal, Pakistan, and Sri Lanka, covering about 4,480,000 sq km or 10 per cent of the Asian landmass. South Asia also has a near-super power neighbour in the north, the People's Republic of China (PRC).

Geography matters immensely and strategically affect the South Asian region. The strategic geography of the region is undergoing intense transition due to China's Belt and Road Initiative (BRI) as well as the larger geo-strategies of the Indo-Pacific. The trends are certain and have to be accepted as inevitable. National policies of sovereign countries of the South-Asian region and the transitional socio-economic developmental processes that these policies would lead to would place them in starkly differing situations. The BRI is the most significant engine of China's geo-political ambitions, and South Asia is at the heart of it. In the coming decades, a number of projects will fructify, though some might get jettisoned. The geographic barrier of the Himalayan mountains between Nepal and China as well as the Pakistani and Nepalese landscapes would be changed by railways, roads, and tunnels. China will dig into its technology and deep pockets to ensure that such infrastructure developments render the South-Asian nations dependent on it for a long period.

It has been often stated that the BRI's flagship project, the *China-Pakistan Economic Corridor* (CPEC), may collapse under its own weight due to issues in Baluchistan, financing difficulties (especially the dire straits of the current Pakistan economy), ecological fragility of the region (especially in Gilgit Baltistan or GB), serious vagaries of terrain, altitude and weather, and geological apprehension of earthquakes/floods/landslides. Yet, because of the enormous advantages to China—geo-politically, economically and with prospects of resources—the plan should succeed in some measure. If that happens, the entire Pakistan Occupied Kashmir (PoK) and GB will be inundated with Chinese managers, supervisors, and workers, many of them ex-People's Liberation Army (PLA). Indeed, Chinese workers may establish a permanent presence by constructing their own administrative enclaves, as in Gwadar. The age-old socio-cultural character of GB will be largely subsumed in this economic invasion of the area.

China's investments under the *China Myanmar Economic Corridor* (CMEC) are part of China's geo-political ambitions. With the rise of the Rohingya crisis and refugee influx, the Chinese have literally become the largest supporter of Myanmar. Though the Myanmar government has not been too forthcoming on the CMEC, the Chinese government will eventually have its way. Simultaneously, the CMEC that envisages a 'Y-shaped' corridor connecting China's Kunming to Mandalay and then extending east and west, respectively to Yangon and Kyaukpyu, will come through. These trans-Himalayan economic corridors will link Nepal and Myanmar with China's Yunnan, Sichuan, and Gansu provinces as well as Tibet, and Pakistan with Xinjiang and Tibet, to allow intensive trade and interaction. Apparently, a new architecture is on the make. As part of the BRI, China has been building or upgrading ports all around India—in Kyaukpyu (Myanmar), Chittagong (Bangladesh), Hambantota (Sri Lanka), and Gwadar (Pakistan), besides many other countries in the Indian Ocean Rim (IOR). In all these countries, China is providing substantial military and economic aid and political support.

The *Indo-Pacific* will increasingly become a major geo-strategic focal point. With an approximate area of 73,556,000 sq km, the Indian Ocean has the most critical sea lanes and choke points connecting the Middle East, Africa, and South and East Asia with Europe. The Indian Ocean will become even more vital for securing movement of crude oil from the Persian Gulf and the large maritime trade within and through the cean. These economics and trade-transit needs are to be viewed within the context of the numerous, serious ongoing security challenges in the IOR that are likely to continue. It is no surprise that major naval powers and regional navies, especially the PLA navy, have placed the Indian Ocean as a priority theatre of current and future operations for strategic planning and maritime security activities which include counter-terrorism, counter-trafficking and counter-piracy missions. All major powers, such as the USA, Australia, Japan, the United Kingdom, France, India, and China have sought stakes in the security of the IOR. The Indian Ocean, lying at the crossroads of Africa, Asia, and Australia houses a number of littorals that also play critical roles in the region.

The Indo-Pacific's fortunes will be tied to the remarkable rise of China, unprecedented historically by its sheer scale and ambition. Its territorial claims in the South China Sea would have been firmed and extended by its belligerence into the East China Sea and its rapid advance into the IOR through ambitious strategic and economic initiatives. Its efforts to establish an order that favours China should be seeing some fruition. Militarily, the Indo-Pacific will continue to be full of flashpoints of potential sources of armed conflicts. The rise of China, India, and the ASEAN bloc, and their respective ambitions to create spheres of influence and balance adversaries, will invariably be the important features of the 2050s.

In sum, current changes in regional strategies are laying down the strategic context for the future. China's push in infrastructural construction in southern Asia has become extremely significant in that Robert Kaplan's terms of "flattening of Himalayas" and "defeat of distance" is becoming truer. The strategic geography between India and China has clear diktats. It is apparent that with increased economic stakes and a larger maritime presence, China will have to cover the IOR with its naval presence, thus increasing the possibilities of naval engagements in the region. The Indo-Pacific also presents new opportunities for India's great power ambitions as her priorities and significant investments will remain within the IOR. If India wants to be a major geo-political player in Asia, she will need to leverage strategic geography to her full advantage. In that context, strategic geography and the transition it is undergoing have increased the threats and challenges for India.

Strategic Threats and Challenges by Mid-21st Century

India, by virtue of its strategic geography and disputed borders, is placed in an adversarial strategic environment, which mandates a strong and effective military force to ensure her territorial integrity and sovereignty. Undeniably, India will be a leading power in the foreseeable future; it is assessed that the Indian economy would cross the thresholds of US$ 5, 10, 20 and 30 trillion in 2027, 2034, 2043, and 2048, respectively. With this would come extra-territorial responsibilities, which necessitates that India will have to quickly build up and consolidate her military strength, mark out a geo-strategic perimeter and choose options wisely in order to play key roles as a regional balancer and stabiliser.

China's military strategy documents highlight the direction for the PLA to be able to fight and win wars, deter potential adversaries, and secure Chinese national interests overseas. There is increased emphasis on the importance of the maritime and information domains, offensive air operations, long-distance mobility operations, long-range precision guided vectors, and space and cyber operations. China's sharpening of claws rapidly from restructuring, testing and exercising, and the concept of "informatisation" figures prominently in PLA writings. China will have a modern military capable of modern war in the near future.

China will reach the pinnacle as a global power with global aspirations, and attempt to re-create its primacy of previous times. Contemplating China's future course is 'an exercise in frustration.'[3] With a pending, intransigent boundary dispute with China, it is mandatory for India to explore how the relationship with China will unfold. Tensions in Eastern Ladakh predict a continuity of aggression and belligerent attitude of China in pursuance of its geo-political ambitions. Indeed with a focus on 2049, becoming a 'Great Power' by any and all means is imperative for China. It might give an impression of being a benign *status quo* power that largely supports multilateralism. However, its actions portray revisionism and expansionism to promote and shape an environment favourable to its ambitions. With increasing strength and a global presence, a stronger possibility exists of threats manifesting from China in the mid-and long-term.

Pakistan was born without a clear identity, and by the inability to create and nurture one; subsequently, maintaining its integrity itself is an onerous task. Pakistan suffers from a crisis of identity and an omnipresent threat of

Balkanisation. Animosity with India lends to Pakistan's credence of identity, which is its bedrock for retaining itself as a nation-state. It is obvious that the anti-Indian-ness that is in the Pakistan Army's DNA, which virtually controls the polity of the nation, is unlikely to be done away with in the foreseeable future. Pakistan, defines its security in tangible terms, as its military capability to thwart a military threat from India, and so provide legitimacy to the Pakistan army as the custodian of nationalism. The geo-strategic location of the nation, grave asymmetries in development among the provinces and the extraordinary role that the Pakistan army has played, compounds the anxieties over the state of Pakistan, presently and in the future. Its current poor economic condition and attempts to seek soft loans add fuel to the fire. Hence, any great socio-political change in Pakistan that would lead to an attitudinal change may not happen without attendant internal upheaval and instability. It is also obvious to any discerning analyst that a comprehensive strategic transition to a more benign thinking in Pakistan is most unlikely in the foreseeable future. That would keep India embroiled in combating an intransigent Pakistan army on the Line of Control and the international border, and in a proxy war, in the hinterland. Pakistan therefore will remain an adversary in perpetuity, and that mandates India's hard power considerations and war-winning strategy.

In contemplating Pakistan's grey zone strategy, its relevant approach can be described as "...to reap gains, whether territorial or otherwise, that are normally associated with victory in war".[4] Pakistan, without crossing established red lines and exposing itself to the penalties and risks of escalation to conventional war, will keep attempting to reap success by utilizing proxies.

In matters of *China-Pakistan collusion*, Pakistan has already upgraded its security calculus with China through the CPEC. The collusive nuclear warhead-ballistic missile-military hardware nexus between China and Pakistan, described by both as an 'all-weather friendship', has grown to menacing proportions. In a similar context, despite regular interactions at the highest level, little movement is evident on the India-China boundary question. With collusive support from China, Pakistan is also a testing ground for the latest Chinese technology in the next conflict or even in peacetime. It would employ a combination of different types of warfare—conventional, insurgency, terrorism, and information warfare (IW)—that is, a concoction of military and non-military, kinetic and non-kinetic kinds. The burgeoning nexus clearly indicates a unified anti-India front of the two adversaries in the north and the west.

The *IOR* has major sea lanes of communications (SLOC) connecting the Middle East/West Asia with Europe, East Asia, Africa and the USA. It is also the passage for more than 80 per cent of world's sea-borne oil trade-transits—40 per cent through the Strait of Hormuz and 35 per cent through the Straits of Malacca, to the west coast of USA, South-East Asian nations, Japan, China and Australia—making it a lifeline of international trade and economy. It also has the world's industrial hub to its east in Asia, while to its west lies the world's largest concentration of oil reserves (80 per cent) within the Persian Gulf region. China, having become the world's largest importer of raw materials and largest exporter of manufactured products, is becoming increasingly assertive in correspondingly enhancing its power, resources and market access. Through the maritime BRI, China is seeking to construct infrastructure in IOR ports to resupply and refit its naval assets. Its port facilities in Gwadar (Pakistan), Hambantota (Sri Lanka), Chittagong (Bangladesh), Kyaukpyu and Yangoon (Myanmar) are under creation. It has established increasing Chinese maritime ties with the Maldives, Seychelles and Mauritius.

China has been creating the world's largest and modern navy and will attempt to expand its blue-water navy capabilities into the IOR. All these point towards the Chinese intent of projecting power, protect its maritime interests and create a permanent naval profile in the IOR in another two decades. These activities are a portent of a future maritime arms race within the IOR and beyond. India, in all measures of contemplation, dominates the subcontinent and has the biggest role in the Arabian Sea, the Bay of Bengal and the IOR. Its central location in the IOR and proximity to the sea lanes emanating from the Persian Gulf, the Malacca Straits and the Red Sea/Gulf of Aden, makes it a natural naval power. The Indian Diaspora in the IOR nations also has its significant diktats. India therefore continues to be the dominant naval power, with vast responsibilities due to its extensive maritime trade, its island territories, vast coastline and geo-political expectations. India has strengthened strategic links with the IOR littoral states, and ties with USA and its allies through diplomacy, and is internally committed to build-up its own military power to complement its strategic outlook. That necessitates that India continues with the build-up and modernisation programs of its maritime prowess, including amphibious, maritime, air and naval joint warfare capabilities.

India can ill-afford to ignore China's increasing economic and military might, its assiduous efforts to create strategic bases in the IOR, its deliberate stalling of progress in the Sino-Indian border talks, and close economic and military affiliations with Pakistan. The interregnum era up to 2050, with its many intermediate milestones, will be of major tensions, with India being a major geo-political contender in the periphery.

Formulation of a National Military Strategy

The articulation of a national military strategy for the mid-21st century demands sufficient forethought and analysis. This is essential to achieve the ends with the means at hand and those likely to be available in implementation of India's strategised concepts and the manner of their execution. Paraphrasing it, the national military strategy becomes a plan that signifies utilisation of means and concepts of employment of national power and employment of the military to achieve political ends. If the prevention of war is the reigning theme of national power, then it has to be proved by enunciation of a national military strategy and concepts, and by creating requisite capabilities to operationalise the concepts, followed by training and exercises in a composite manner, to attain the military aims which would have been gleaned from political ends. The cherry on the cake is the perceptible political—and national—'will' and commitment to order the execution of military plans.

Politics creates war, so success or failure in war is ultimately the responsibility of the political leadership.[5] War-fighting strategies would have reasonable failure rates or might achieve less than the end-state if not envisaged with in-depth analyses. Military strategy in its operational execution is thus a military responsibility, while stating the end-state is a political task. Clausewitz insists that politicians must understand the military instrument that they intend to use, but in historical practice that has been an exceptional condition, not the norm.[6] The duty of military leaders is to see that political leaders do not fail because they had poor advice. Hence, evolution of military strategy is a two-way traffic between the political and military professionals, in which, in a democratic dispensation like ours, the final call will rest with the government.

India will remain in an uneasy neighbourhood, with a disputed active border with Pakistan and a disputed, un-demarcated one with China. It is unfortunate that even after four full-fledged wars, one border war and a plethora of counter-insurgency operations, where the armed forces have distinguished themselves with their valour and sacrifice, India has been unable to evolve comprehensive strategies for optimal use of its military and other components of national power to protect its interests.[7]

A *National Military Strategy* envisages employment of all the nation's military capabilities and capacities to undertake operations at the highest of levels in all domains including cyber, space and electronic warfare, and to assure victory or success through the processes of long-term planning, development and procurements. Just a military operational domain will not survive contact with the realities of future wars. Contextually, in India, the question arises whether the doctrines enunciated by the three services as well as the joint services have been prepared conjointly with the government and if they have the government's stamp of approval. *Au contraire* doctrines do not focus on the desired '*ends*', and are basically written concepts *sans* physical outcomes in the domain of strategies. The three services have distinct cultures, ideals, organisations and capabilities. They also tend to enhance their own tools and solutions and develop doctrines that promote their respective interests.

Shaping military strategy is a complex process involving bureaucracies and intellectuals, both civilian and military. Invariably, the civilian bureaucracy considers the military as too rigid, hawkish, a little too offensive minded and with unrealistic plans. The services obviously have not adjusted their philosophies in accordance with the political vision. One can train for the mastery of operational and tactical skills, but the imagination needed for a national strategy cannot be taught reliably. All decisions for war and peace akin to undeclared warfare but actually leaps in the dark means that even detailed analysis and honest judgements could well turn out to be wrong. A national military strategy is therefore an imperative as it would lead to conjoined creation of joint strategies, joint force-structures and organisations, and integrated plans to create the requisite capability.

What then is military strategy? In ancient Greece, it was the "art of the general". In the USA, it is defined as the art and science of employing the armed forces of a nation to secure the objectives of national policy by the application of force, or the threat of force.[8] It has also been defined as consisting of joint objectives, ways and means in the form of an equation: *Strategy = Ends + Ways + Means* broadly elaborated as:

- Ends: Objectives that the three services strive for;
- Ways: Joint courses of action to attain the objectives;
- Means: Optimal use of instruments by which ends can be achieved.

A *National Military Strategy* will include the establishment of military objectives, formulation of military strategic concepts to accomplish the objectives, and creation and use of military resources to implement the concepts. It is also imperative to mention that the political '*ends*' as contemplated by the political hierarchy will need translation to a military '*end-state*'—each of which would be different. A national military strategy would signify integrated utilisation of military means and concepts of employment of the military. If the achievement of *deterrence*, credible, punitive or dissuasive, is the national strategy, then it has to be proven by enunciation of joint military concepts, creation of requisite military capabilities to operationalise them and training and exercising in a composite manner to attain military aims. Certain significant issues in the formulation of a national military strategy for India are as enunciated below:

- As conventional wars may be conditional, the military hierarchy must *involve the polity at the highest of levels* to obtain guidance and direction.
- Some may say it is unwise, impossible, or even dangerous to enunciate a national military strategy openly. However, its *formal enunciation denotes the arrival of India at the international stage* as a nation in league with others who do so. Military strategy may however be fully or partially declaratory and/or classified or even deceptive.
- A national military strategy must be joint in all its formats as it is wont to be, *cumulating in holistic utilisation of national power*. It will subsequently be necessary to be translated into service-specific concepts and plans at strategic and operational levels; in the latter case corresponding to the tri-services echelons.
- Long-term strategies must be based on estimates of future threats, objectives and requirements, and therefore not be constrained or dominated by considerations of current force posture. The objectives and *strategic concepts of a joint military strategy would establish the essential requirements for the capabilities for the three services, individually and as an integrated whole*. The acquisition of such capabilities will, in turn, be influenced by the availability of resources, say the annual budgets and predictive allocations. We have to consider resources as an element of joint military strategy so as to avoid a mismatch of strategic capabilities for the future. A case in point is the requirement of the existing fourteen corps-level formations, plus additional strike corps for the Army, 42 squadrons for the Air Force and a 200-ship

Navy including a third aircraft carrier, within the finite resources, and with each service planning independent deterrence and concepts for winning wars. That is why operational strategies must be based on joint capabilities, and not on threats alone if threats are examined by each service autonomously.

- India will need more than one military strategy at a time: strategies for conventional warfare, insurgencies and terrorism, information warfare and cyber security, utilisation of special forces, nuclear war, net security provider's role in the region and the like, for instance, against known adversaries. Military strategy can change frequently since objectives can change on account of any shift in precepts of warfare. At the policy level downwards, the year 2020 is a pointer towards a rethink on the objectives related to China. A duly *empowered tri-service standing organisation, including academics and veterans, to contemplate over doctrines, strategies and concepts is imperative* in this fast-changing world.

Strategising for India—Building Capabilities

"In theory, foreign policy determines military strategy...Reality is rarely so simple."[9] However, India has ventured into new territory by moving ahead on the Quadrilateral Security Dialogue (QUAD) with the USA, Japan and Australia. Without entering into a formalised alliance system, the QUAD itself is a significant step forward, one that is looked upon with great consternation by our adversaries. With the agreements signed with the USA over the last few years, a different message is being conveyed by India, one that will have a bearing on the future of warfare and deterrence in South Asia.

India's adversaries have mastered the creation of adverse narratives and use of advanced technologies to embrace new forms of warfare. Hence it must be expected that in future the conflicts that India will have to face—or is facing presently—will necessarily and largely be with the adversaries utilising the psychological, economic, political and cyber realms in addition to contestations on the borders. Increased confusion and disorder will ensue when weaponised information, abetted externally against India, would create insecurities among the populace. The conventional Indian concepts of war have thus to be made compatible with the realities of warfare of the twenty-first century.

India, hence, must develop a framework of strategic deterrence against weaponised information, finance, cyber and other subversive forms of aggression from the adversaries. A 'one size fits all' national security policy would not be effective. While salience and preparations for a modern conventional, kinetic war cannot be put on the back-burner, accepting that a type of grey zone campaign against India may be ongoing is critical. Hence the enunciation of a national military strategy followed by joint multi-domain specialisation would indicate the right preparation for future warfare. That is a responsibility resting upon the shoulders of today's political and military leaders.

Seven Postulations

Seven key *postulations* for a *national military strategy* are proffered here:

- Non-kinetic warfare describes domains that can well be termed as largely quasi-military. Prosecution of aggressive actions by an adversary in the quasi-military domain would cause damage or destruction to the national infrastructure and the socio-economic foundations of the nation. *India must take such externally abetted actions as acts of war,* even if the adversary is unidentifiable, un-provable or resorts to plausible deniability.
- Cyberspace contributes to the blurring of the distinction between peace and war. Even the question of whether a cyber-attack constitutes an 'armed attack' is pivotal. Cases in point would be cyber-attacks on national infrastructure, power grid, banking system, and the like. War thus may be a permanent state, and must not be imagined merely as a territorial contest. *India needs to redefine war, even as manifestations of warfare in a quasi-military domain* that would hurt the foundations of the nation.
- Apparently, many such war-fighting methodologies will not be exclusive to the military domain. Defensive and law enforcement capabilities in India, as symbolised by the National Security Guard (NSG), the NTRO, the National Cyber Security Coordinator, intelligence agencies, CAPF and state police require parallel developments, which need to be skilfully fused in a specifically tailored *National Security Structure*, and be parts of national security as well as military strategies. A national counter-terrorism centre (NCTC), which has been on the anvil for some time, linked with the national

intelligence grid (NATGRID) and other law-enforcement and intelligence agencies is a necessity. Warfare necessitates intensive consolidation of all the resources and security assets available with various infrastructural agencies without resorting to a 'battle for the turf'. India, with its huge challenges, is ripe for an *apex internal security organisation having the requisite mechanisms for preparing databases and analyses.*

- If war is a continuation of politics "by other means" (Clausewitz), social networks tend to continue politics by additional means to influence susceptible people. Indoctrination or causing cleavages in society through social networks is not cyber-warfare which uses the internet to attack and disrupt networks. As has been seen in India, such means of influencing create new, dangerous predicaments that mandate astute preparations to counter. Herein, therefore, multi-prong and concerted efforts are necessary to deal with this ever-expanding stream of diatribe. *We need much better public-private cooperation, and ensure that social networks establish permanent monitoring systems.* There ought to be legal incentives and punitive *actions for social media networks* for compliance.
- Psychological warfare, fake news campaigns, propaganda, subversion, intimidation, demoralisation and the like affect military campaigns as well. State and non-state actors are weaponising information to their advantages. It is not that psychological warfare and propaganda is a new realm; however, the media, including social media, have multiplied manifold, their techniques are being made sophisticated, and the effects they are having on the populace is substantial. Psychological warfare is leading to increasing radicalisation and it needs to be addressed immediately by parallel streams of a well-planned counter-radicalisation and information management plan. 'Narrative Warfare' and 'Influence Operations' are other realms that India needs to venture into to generate long-term narratives for the nation. We also require duly focused *plans to counter adverse narratives—a continuous stream of adverse propaganda*—from our adversaries. For this, there is need of a conjoined team of experts like social psychologists and media/social media experts.
- India is a diverse and developing nation and an aspirational society that is prone to internal protestations. There is a need to build '*sentiment analysis systems*' to continually analyse our societal anxieties.

Sentiment analysis should be a process of extracting opinions from within the nation that have different schisms—positive, negative, or neutral. With the help of sentiment analysis, we will be able to collate the nature of opinions that are reflected in documents, websites, social media feed, etc. Sentiment analysis thence can be used *to monitor and analyse social phenomena and spot potentially dangerous situations to determine the general mood of society.*

- The likelihood of a strong conventional kinetic response to a hybrid non-kinetic attack or any protracted grey zone campaign must not be negated. *Quid pro quo* response to any form of grey zone operations may emanate in a totally different realm. The issue created by hybridization of threats opens new vistas in deterrence debate and response options, and mandates further analysis. Suffice it to say that just a strong conventional force will not be adequate to deter grey zone warfare. Hence, proportionate and disproportionate responses to such attacks cannot be predictable; they would be contingent on national 'will' and political intent at that juncture. India will therefore require an effective *bouquet of quid pro quo hybrid options, a quiver full of variable arrows that can be selectively employed as stronger deterrence.*
- The challenges of strategic cyber weaponry with an adversary's malware-embedded browser hacking or hardware trojans that export data unfettered, or are sleepers that can be activated on call, are dangerous portents for the national infrastructure. Such cyber challenges are growing exponentially. In a critical infrastructure, the equipment and software must be sanitized and detection systems for existing systems planned to thwart inimical designs against the nation, or we may face what is often termed a 'Cyber Pearl-Harbour'! India has the internal potential to *establish expertise for effective defensive cyber defence, and that must be undertaken on a war-footing.*

Conclusion

Twenty-first century warfare thus is metamorphosing without a distinct pattern, where conventional operations with increasing utilization of special forces, irregulars and terrorists are not dissimilar or fundamentally different approaches. There is an increasing blurring of distinctions between war and peace, between the different domains of conflict (land, maritime, air, space, cyber) and between kinetic and non-kinetic effects. The cyber domain contributes to this blurring by creating uncertainty as to what constitutes a conflict in cyberspace. These are then the means employed in combination by the adversary and conducted by both state and non-state actors.

Therefore, hybridity in warfare has evolved as a combination of more than two elements of power and components of a widely spread spectrum of conflict, both kinetic and non-kinetic. Kinetic in this consideration would imply a spectrum from space and chemical, biological, radiological and nuclear (CBRN) weapons, to land, air, and naval forces, and insurgents and terrorists. Non-kinetic power would encompass diplomacy, political activities, information warfare (IW) including social media, cyber disruption of critical infrastructure, subversion, criminal and economic activities and such like conflicting activities. Such evolved hybrid warfare can hence be examined as a combination of both kinetic and non-kinetic tools, used disaggregated or aggregated as and when needed!

In sum, therefore, clean drafting pads and a clutch of thoughts among the leaders, military and civilian alike, and a fresh contemplation of optimal utilisation of military power in strategising 21st-century war-fighting concepts are imperatives in planning capabilities that would abide with us till the mid-century. The national military strategy must be both practical and purposeful. War-fighting strategic transition must precede any force-restructuring.

Serious, methodical *ways* of strategic transition and internally generated substantial *means* will assuredly lead to well-analysed and credible right-sizing to create a 21st-century modern, forward-looking force, capable of achieving the necessary *ends*. Such a military war-fighting philosophy will also denote that we have *'arrived'* as a modern forward-looking force, with 21st-century credentials.

ENDNOTES

1. Tang Shiping, A Systemic Theory of the Security Environment. *The Journal of Strategic Studies*, Vol. 27, No. 1, March 2004, p. 1.
2. Jasjit Singh, "A Security Strategy for the 21st Century", in AVM Kapil Kak, (ed.), *Comprehensive Security for an Emerging India*, Centre for Air Power Studies, New Delhi, 2010, p. 1.
3. Harvey Nelson, "The Future of Chinese State", in *The Modern Chinese State,* (ed.) David Shanbaugh (Cambridge, UK: Cambridge University Press, 2000), p. 216.
4. Hal Brands, 'Paradoxes of the Grey Zone, Foreign Policy Research Institute, 5 February 2016, accessed at https://www.fpri.org/article/2016/02/paradoxes-grey-zone/ on 29 December 2019.

5. Christopher Bassford, *Policy, Politics, War, and Military Strategy, Maine Corps Doctrinal Publication 1-1, Strategy, 1997, available online at http://www.clausewitz.com/readings/Bassford/StrategyDraft/*
6. Ibid, Note 3, p. 7.
7. Vijay Oberoi, *Indian Defence Review*, Vol. 30, Issue 1 Jan-Mar 2015,dated 2 March 2015.
8. J.C.S. Pub. 1: *Dictionary of Military and Associated Terms.* Washington: U.S. Department of Defence, 1 June 1987, p. 232.

7

Indian Navy at the Centenary of Our Independence

A.K. Chawla

Introduction

This essay will attempt to forecast what the Indian Navy (*IN*) should look like at the centenary of our independence in 2047. Force-level forecasting traditionally starts with a 'net assessment', or comparative analysis of military, technological, political, economic and other factors governing the relative military capability of countries over a specific time period and potential response to an anticipated scenario.[1] As a thumb rule, forecasting of scenarios for a time period of five years is reasonably accurate; ten years can be done with some certainty; fifteen years being the maximum time period for any kind of long-term planning, with the caveat that course corrections be made at least every five years. Since, space here is insufficient for a detailed net assessment followed by platform-level bean-counting, it will instead abbreviate the process to focus on likely threats in the maritime theatre by the middle of the 21st century, and a broad overview of the desired force composition of the IN in the same time frame. However, before that, it is important to keep in mind seven macro issues that require to be taken into account while planning not just for the Indian Navy of 2047, but for India's national defence in general.

Necessity for Comprehensive Approach in Enunciation of National Strategies

For long-term defence planning, enunciation of national strategies needs to be the starting point, so that apex-level guidance is available for subordinate strategies. There is an *urgent need for India to articulate and develop its national strategies commencing with a national security strategy (NSS), and then a national military strategy (NMS)*, which should be linked with existing single service and joint strategies (such as the Navy's maritime strategy). This is especially important, as the next major step in India's military transformation, the formation of theatre commands, requires much greater coherence between joint and single service strategies. The NSS and NMS needs to be enunciated every time there is a new government at the centre after general elections, and definitely after five years, even if the government is re-elected. The NSS and NMS, as also other subordinate strategies, need to be made public, though there will always be certain sections that will have to remain classified. In this regard, the US model is the best one to follow.

The other issue is that *any strategy that we enunciate needs to be holistic*. A NSS, by its very definition, takes a holistic approach to national security, with internal and external security, national diplomacy, economic security, etc., being integral components of such a strategy. As an example, there is an urgent need for India to take a comprehensive national approach to the development of its maritime power, including downstream requirements to support that strategy. This implies that aspects of maritime infrastructure, ship-building and ship repair, technology, human resources, and development and coordination of all other national and state maritime agencies, such as the Coast Guard, maritime police, oceanographic research, fisheries, maritime archaeology, etc., need to be part of the maritime strategy in order to make it more than the sum of its individual parts.

China's maritime strategy offers a good example, as it encompasses the development strategy for the entire range of maritime issues that constitute a nation's maritime power and also encompasses global strategic-level maritime initiatives such as the maritime silk road (MSR), which, in turn, is an integral part of their belt and road initiative (BRI). In the same manner, the NMS should not just be an 'operational directive', but also encompass modernisation, indigenisation, defence industry, acquisition procedures, jointness, training, etc. It needs to be borne in mind that only holistic strategies will correctly drive force development, indigenisation, human resource development, training requirements, infrastructure, etc. Finally, each strategy should be accompanied by follow-on 'action plans' with broad targets and timelines under each head, so that progress can be measured in tangible terms. Without tangible goals, specific timelines and responsibility affixed to specific departments and authorities, strategies remain paper exercises.

Necessity for Assured, Predictable Defence Funding

The issue of defence funding would flow from the first recommendation and is the most important part of any strategy, as it allows plans to be translated into reality. *There needs to be assured long-term funding provided for approved acquisition plans for a five-year period, with the provision of rolling over funds in succeeding years.* This is important for two reasons: *firstly,* the fact that most capital procurement projects are spread over at least five years and can go up to 20 years for aircraft carriers and strategic submarines; and *secondly*, timelines for capital projects often slip for a variety of reasons causing funds to lapse and resulting in considerable effort to resurrect the spending in the following financial year.

The second and even more important aspect of defence funding is the quantum of funds required to uphold our national defence. There has always been a tussle between the armed forces and the civilian bureaucracy, as also between the three services, over the amount of funding necessary for backing India's national defence. This can easily be resolved once the NSS, NMS, and long-term integrated perspective plan (LTIPP) are in place, as then there would be a national consensus on our defence requirements, and their funding. Here, it needs to be remembered that expenditure on a country's defence is akin to an insurance policy—the better you are insured, the greater is the assurance of national security, stability, and well-being. Moreover, if a majority of the defence spending is invested within the country, as our indigenisation programmes seek to do, then it is a powerful force for a country's overall development.

Measures to Spur Defence Indigenisation to Major Defence Systems

This brings us to the next important issue of indigenisation. We should aim to be largely self-reliant in defence by 2047. While considerable effort has gone into *Atmanirbhar Bharat* and preceding indigenisation initiatives, there needs to be greater impetus towards making our indigenisation process simpler and facilitate the entry of large private vendors in the defence industry, if we are to truly make India self-reliant in defence. For this to happen, it is important to provide an avenue for *'single vendor approval' for the private sector*, which currently exists only for the public sector. First enunciated in the defence procurement procedure (DPP)-2006—after the recommendations made by the Kelkar committee were accepted by the MoD—in the form of the creation of *Rashtriya Udyog Ratnas (RURs)* in both public and private sectors, it was actualised only for the public sector, with the private sector *RURs* being dropped in 2013.

It is essential to resurrect the provision of private sector *RURs* (along with existing public sector *RURs*) for various cogent reasons. These include: the episodic nature of major defence purchases such as ships, submarines, aircraft, tanks, etc., because of their high cost and long life; and, the necessity for original equipment manufacturers (OEM) to maintain design teams and infrastructure, conduct research and development (R&D), and retain the requisite human resources over long periods of time. In the face of these realities flies the fact that it is not cost-effective for the private sector to maintain idle infrastructure or human expertise, and continue with the R&D necessary to either upgrade or build the next generation of weapon systems during the long intervals between successive orders. Multi-vendor competition, while necessary for commonly used items, is a disincentive for big ticket items for the private sector, which has to make a decent profit to survive. As a consequence, in all countries that have a mature defence industry, each segment of major weapons systems and platforms generally has only one or at the most two OEMs, mainly in the private sector.

The problems of having 'single vendor' approval, especially cost competitiveness, can be overcome with the creation of agencies similar to the defence contract audit agency (DCAA) and the defence contract maintenance agency (DCMA) in the USA. The DCAA's primary function is to conduct independent audits of defence contracts to determine whether the prices quoted by defence contractors are 'allowable, allocable and reasonable'. To do this, it is empowered to examine defence contractor accounts, records, and business systems to evaluate whether contractor business accounts and practices are in compliance with stipulated laws. In its annual report to the US Congress for 2019, it was stated that the DCAA had saved the US government US$ 3.7 billion in defence spending in 2019.[2] These mainly included big-ticket items, generally manufactured by single vendors. The DCAA works in concert with the DCMA, which is responsible to ensure that the government receives the highest quality and services on time and at the best value for each dollar that is spent.

The second, and equally important necessity, is to simplify the defence acquisition process. Despite various attempts to do so and periodic reviews of the DPP, this remains trapped in the morass of red tape, which not only delays the acquisition of defence equipment, resulting in capability voids, but also drives up the cost of defence acquisitions manifold. While this paper cannot go into details due to shortage of space, a few steps are essential. These include the need to fully integrate the defence acquisition organisation under the department of defence (DoD) with the acquisition goals defined in the LTIPP by the department of military affairs (DMA) and the staff requirement organisations of the individual service headquarters, and the need to make the defence acquisition organisation accountable to achieve targets within a defined time period.

Focus on Human Resources

As is well known, the provision of modern weapons systems alone is not sufficient to make a potent armed force. Qualified, trained, and motivated human resources are equally essential. Indeed, skilled and motivated human personnel with inferior weapon systems have often given a bloody nose to better equipped but poorly trained and motivated forces—the current war in Ukraine being the most recent example. In the case of the Indian armed forces, we have done very well thus far to have an all-volunteer force, which is well trained and motivated, and has proved itself in most major conflicts and crises since our independence.

However, this cannot be taken for granted. Changing socio-economic reasons have made a career in the armed forces less attractive. This was thus far only the case with the officer cadre, but in the last two years it has also started afflicting personnel below officer ranks (PBOR), who now have many better employment options in the civil sector. Though there is no shortage (as yet) of volunteers for PBOR, a growing majority of those who join the armed forces leave for civil employment after the minimum engagement period. The issue of retention, which was hitherto a 'Western' problem, is now with us. This bodes ill for retention of human expertise for the effective use and maintenance of hi-tech weapon systems, and is becoming an encumbrance to operational efficiency, especially at sea, where OEMs or civil expertise are not readily available.

Recent attempts to change the induction pattern of officers and sailors, such as the *Agnipath* scheme, the inevitable introduction of women officers and PBOR in all branches of the three services, proposed changes in the pension scheme, etc., have resulted in growing uncertainty in the human resources (HR) management and training of our personnel. We can ill-afford this at a juncture when defence modernisation is also going through a financially challenging period. Consequently, it is recommended that stability be ensured in HR policies and 'evolutionary' rather than 'revolutionary' changes are brought about. The HR aspect is one that generally receives short shrift. However, with most Indian families likely to be one-child and nuclear by 2047, *assured and easy availability of human resources can no longer be taken for granted.* India's population growth is already below the total fertility rate (TFR) replacement level of 2.1, being 2.0 in 2022, and predicted to dip to 1.94 by 2025.[3] India's higher defence organisation (HDO) will need to look at this issue closely and come up with the right solutions to ensure a duly motivated and professional armed forces in 2047 and beyond.

Need for an Indian Model of Military-Civil Fusion

By pooling infrastructure, human resources, industry, educational and research institutions, logistics support, etc., through its military-civil fusion (MCF) strategy, China has enabled economy of effort, development of dual-use technologies, and, in general, better harnessed national resources towards a common goal. The Chinese MCF has not only emulated the original model of the US 'Military-Industrial Complex', but has taken it much further. In China, there is a dedicated national-level organisation to progress MCF, which is replicated at the provincial and lower levels, and the coordination sections of various connected ministries. MCF departments also exist in every service in China. Specific goals and timelines are laid down by China's National Party Congress (NPC) and monitored by their central military commission (CMC), which is directly under the president. Selected extracts of progress in MCF are published under a separate section of China's defence white papers.

There are aspects of MCF that are worthy of emulation and need to be institutionalised in India as well. The fact that modern warfare tends to be 'hybrid' in nature, 'entailing an interplay or fusion of conventional as well as unconventional instruments of national power and tools for subversion', makes MCF even more urgent.

Importance of Jointness and Integration in Modern Warfare

The importance of jointness and integration in modern battlefields was clearly demonstrated during the first Gulf War. Since the 1990s, most of the world's militaries, including China's, have progressed steadily on this path. China had announced sweeping military reforms in 2015, whereby theatre and functional commands were created. This has synergised the PLA's military power and focussed their attention on new dimensions of warfare such as space, cyber and electro-magnetic, besides giving primacy to maritime power. Such reforms in India, though planned, have been moving at a glacial pace and need to be expedited.

It took India almost two decades to set up the office of the chief of defence staff (CDS) consequent to recommendations made by the Group of Ministers in 2001. It has also been over two decades since India's first joint command was established in the Andaman and Nicobar Islands in 2001, to serve as a 'crucible for jointness'. Discussions to establish theatre commands, mandated by the cabinet committee on security (CCS), have already gone on for over three years, but there does not seem to be any consensus emerging on the issue. Starting off with the establishment of theatre commands, *India should aim to have a totally integrated armed forces by 2047.*

Centrality of Technology in Modern Warfare

Technology is the key to modern warfare and software is everywhere on the modern battlefield. The Ministry of Defence has recognised this issue and has published a technology perspective and capability roadmap (TPCR).[4] Till now, the DRDO has been at the forefront of indigenising technological capability in the Indian armed forces, with limited involvement of the private sector. Apart from the single-vendor model discussed above, which would give an impetus to R&D expenditure by private players, India needs to exploit the large brains trust available through the virtuous triangle of government, academia, and the defence industry to grow indigenous technology for the defence sector in India.

Special focus needs to be given to defence software, especially as this is a core national strength. Software drives our weapon systems, sensors, command, control and communication systems, intelligence networks, logistics systems, and, indeed, the entire back-up of national infrastructure required to support military operations in war and in peace. This is evident from the fact that the percentage of dependence on software in modern weapon systems has increased from a negligible amount in the 1970s, to over 90 per cent in the latest combat aircraft, ships, and submarines. As our defence systems become fully networked, and as we move towards greater automation, our dependence on machine learning (ML) and artificial intelligence (AI) is also increasing, thereby increasing not just our efficiency and effectiveness in combat as well as during peacetime operations, but also our vulnerability to disruption through cyber warfare. In fact, our ability to respond against future threats of hypersonic weapons, directed energy weapons, and even biological warfare, will be based on our ability to generate reliable and safe software solutions for our systems. Therefore, the requirement of indigenous capability in software in defence systems is today inescapable and needs to be an area of special focus.

The Indian Navy's Force Structure in 2047

Having seen the macro issues that India's HDO needs to keep in mind while planning for the military structure of 2047, let us now think of a broad overview of the Indian Navy's force-structure that should exist by 2047. Over the next 25 years, it would be safe to assume that India's enemies are not likely to materially change their policies. Hence, China and Pakistan are likely to continue to remain our principal adversaries and the IN needs to be capable of taking them on in the maritime arena, both individually and in a two-front scenario. While a threat-based capability runs against Disraeli's dictum that, '*a nation has no permanent friends or enemies, only permanent interests*', preparedness against both China and Pakistan combined has the advantage of also catering for any other kind of future threats that are likely to confront India in the envisaged time period.

An exposition on the Indian Navy's force structure in 2047 needs to take into account both the threats that India will likely face in that period, and our maritime interests. The defence of our coastline, maritime zones and island territories is an unchangeable factor of our maritime interests. However, India's maritime interests have expanded over the past two decades to now encompass the maintenance of security and stability in our extended maritime neighbourhood, where smaller countries in the Indian Ocean Region (IOR) look upon the Indian Navy as a net security provider and preferred security partner. Over the past seven decades, the Indian Navy's benign presence has also ensured that the vital international sea lanes of oceanic commerce connecting the Suez Canal to the Malacca Strait, that pass close around the Indian peninsula and its island territories, remain free for international navigation, which has been acknowledged by the international community. With the international acceptance of the 'Indo-Pacific' concept over the past decade, India and the Indian Navy's role in ensuring peace and stability in the wider Indo-Pacific region will grow exponentially in the years ahead.

Almost 95 per cent of India's trade by volume and 70 per cent by value transits over the seas. Today, India also depends on the seas for importing over 85 per cent of its petroleum product needs, apart from the import of over 50 per cent of its needs for coal. India's energy needs are expected to double by 2040.[5] Despite our active push for alternative and greener energy sources, declining domestic production of oil and gas will more than double India's dependence on the seas for its trade and energy needs by 2047. It is also seldom realised that the seas are the conduit for over 99 per cent of the data required to feed today's information economy, which can be disrupted by an adversary.[6] With land-based resources depleting, the world is now turning towards the seas for both living and non-living resources and the concept of a country's Blue Economy has taken concrete shape, which will take both expertise and capacity to exploit in a sustainable manner. Finally, climate change due to global warming and oceanic pollution has its greatest impact on the seas and its surrounding coastlines, combating which is today a national and global maritime interest. All these factors are important parameters to be taken into account for deciding the force level of the Indian Navy by the middle of the 21st century.

The Indian Navy's task of ensuring maritime security has been vastly complicated by the unprecedented expansion of the People's Liberation Army Navy (PLAN) and its growing presence in the IOR. Recent estimates indicate that the PLAN is already the largest maritime force in the world and will reach strength of 425 blue water combatants by 2030.[7] The PLAN has a three-ship anti-piracy task force permanently deployed in the Gulf of Aden since 2008, and has operationalized its first overseas military base in Djibouti in 2017. China also deploys its oceanographic research and satellite monitoring ships regularly in the IOR. Around 200-250 Chinese fishing trawlers, supported by logistics re-supply ships and factory ships (to process the fish caught by the trawlers) also operate round the year in the IOR. Some of these trawlers are suspected to double-up as maritime militia tasked to gather intelligence in the region.

China is expected to deploy its first carrier task force (CTF) in the Indian Ocean by 2030 and by 2047 would be capable of deploying up to two CTFs in the Indian Ocean in times of conflict or tension. China has already started deploying both its conventional and nuclear submarines in the IOR, and by 2047 could have at least one SSN on permanent patrol in the IOR, with a few conventional submarines based in at least two Chinese naval bases in the region, including the current one at Djibouti and a future base in Pakistan (Gwadar, where China is the port builder and operator) or East Africa. China's Djibouti naval base is now capable of basing an aircraft carrier and already houses a marine brigade. A future war with China could therefore see the deployment of a substantial maritime force—both regular and irregular—in the maritime theatre of operations. China could also bring to bear its land-based anti-ship DF-26 ballistic missiles in the IOR, besides deploying maritime patrol aircraft and unmanned aerial vehicles (UAV) in its bases in the region.

As far as Pakistan is concerned, while the country is financially close to bankruptcy, re-arming and modernisation efforts continue to be bank-rolled by China. Major capability enhancements include eight air independent propulsion (AIP)-capable *Yuan* class submarines and land attack capability from Chinese-built *Azmat* class missile boats, which eventually could be armed with tactical nuclear warheads. Pakistan is also acquiring a modest surface warfare capability in the form of four additional 054-A/P Chinese-built guided missile frigates. It is replacing its US-built P3C Orion maritime patrol aircraft with Brazilian-built Embraer aircraft modified for an anti-submarine warfare role. It can, therefore, be seen that in times of conflict, Pakistan will continue to pose a credible sea-denial capability to the Indian Navy in the Arabian Sea.

Capability Requirements of the Indian Navy

Indian Naval planners, in their first plan paper prepared in 1948, envisaged a 150-ship sea control capable Indian Navy, centred around three aircraft carriers. However, focus and funding on land-based threats emerging from conflicts against Pakistan and China shortly after, ensured that the plan (and its subsequent revisions) did not come to fruition. Even the Indian Navy's finest hour in the maritime theatre of the 1971 Indo-Pakistan war could not substantially shift this focus towards enhancing our maritime capability. From the year 2004 onwards, the Indian Navy has moved towards the formulation of a 15-year maritime capability perspective plan (MCPP), which guides its force-development process and feeds into the LTIPP. The MCPP is supposed to be revised every five years, based on a review of the emerging strategic scenario.

In the face of the offensive maritime capability being acquired by both China and Pakistan, the Indian Navy needs to acquire capabilities to defend its maritime interests, both for a single-front and two-front contingency. It also needs to have adequate capability for ensuring coastal defence of the Indian mainland and its island territories against low-intensity maritime threats, including the capability of transporting and landing a brigade at any time and conducting amphibious operations. Besides, the Indian Navy requires to possess dedicated capability to handle humanitarian and disaster relief (HADR) operations from natural and man-made disasters, not just for India, but also for smaller maritime neighbours who look up to India for assistance in times of need. India also needs a strong hydrographic capability to serve the needs of both India and the wider IOR.

In view of the above, the minimum capability requirement of the Indian Navy by 2047 needs to include the *consistent operational availability* of the following platforms:[8]

- Three aircraft carriers, with two CTFs available operationally at any given time, comprising a carrier, 6-7 escorting destroyers and frigates, logistics support ships and a nuclear-powered attack submarine (SSN). Currently, we have two aircraft carriers, one of which would be due to be replaced by 2045. Discussions on constructing a third aircraft carrier for the Navy have been in progress for almost a decade.
- Forty destroyers and frigates to provide escort forces to two aircraft carriers and also operate independently for offensive roles against enemy warships and merchantmen, and for convoying Indian merchant shipping.
- A force of six SSNs and 18 conventional submarines.
- A nuclear-powered ballistic submarine (SSBN) force to ensure that one submarine remains continuously on deterrence patrol.
- Four landing platform dock (LPD) ships and 15 smaller amphibious ships such as landing ship tank (LST)-(L)s, LST-(M)s and landing craft utility (LCU)s, capable of transporting a brigade-plus for an amphibious operation within the IOR and for re-supplying or supporting our island territories in times of need.

- To sanitise approaches to harbours and specific ocean areas against enemy submarines 12-16 anti-submarine warfare (ASW) ships are needed.
- We need 6-8 logistics support ships to logistically support two CTFs and other blue water forces at sea.
- Coastal patrol forces comprising a mix of 12 offshore patrol vessels (OPVs), 24 patrol boats and around 150 patrol craft.
- Mine-sweeping/mine-hunting forces (manned or unmanned) to ensure our harbours and their approaches are clear from threats of enemy mining.
- A force of at least 8-10 ocean-going survey ships for hydrographic operations in the IOR.
- A force of about 300 manned and unmanned naval aircraft comprising carrier-borne fighters, shore-based maritime reconnaissance and anti-submarine warfare aircraft/remotely piloted aircrafts (RPA), multi-role ship-borne helicopters, airborne early warning helicopters/ aircraft, and utility helicopters.
- Two dedicated marine brigades for conducting amphibious operations. Currently two Indian Army brigades are dual-tasked for maritime operations.
- Adequate satellite communications and surveillance capability to have a fully networked force and complete maritime domain awareness.

Building such a navy will not come cheap. The Indian Navy has always been the 'Cinderella service' in terms of funding due to continental pre-occupations of India's defence. It received only 4 per cent of the defence budget in the decades before the 1971 war. The funding has risen gradually to 19 per cent of the defence budget in 2022-23, in which the Indian Navy's share of the defence capital budget comprised 31.23 per cent. While for the Indian Navy, this year's capital allocation has touched a historic high, it still falls substantially short of the projected capital outlay under the budget estimates (as per the 28th report of the standing committee on defence and defence procurement) by Rs. 20,031.97 crore (30 per cent). To achieve the force levels required to comfortably confront a two-front conflict, it would require a sustained annual increase of at least 25 per cent over the Indian Navy's current level of capital funding over the next 25 years. The additional capital expenditure will be less than 0.1 per cent of India's GDP, and will keep reducing as India's economy grows, which is a very small price to pay for a navy needed to meet our maritime security, and absolutely essential if India aspires to be the leading power in the

Indo-Pacific Region. It also needs to be borne in mind that due to the long gestation period of domestic ship-building, translation of plans into platforms needs to commence today itself, if the projected force levels are to be available a quarter of a century hence, i.e., by 2047.

Conclusion

Theodore Roosevelt had correctly stated that '*A good navy is not a provocation for war. It is the surest guarantee of peace*'. A strong navy is vital not only for India's maritime security, but also to support its diplomacy and enhance its influence in the wider Indo-Pacific Region. It is noteworthy that historically, no country has ever become a great power without commensurate maritime power. With India projected to become a US$ 26 trillion economy by 2047, the third largest in the world, it needs a maritime force commensurate with its economic heft to supplement its comprehensive national power.[9] With China's aggressive ingress in the IOR, and its stated aim of becoming the pre-eminent global power by 2049, the centenary of its independence, India can no longer afford to neglect its maritime sector. It, therefore, needs to focus on developing its comprehensive maritime power, commencing with a strong Indian Navy.

ENDNOTES

1. "Joint Publication JP1-02, Department of Defence, Dictionary of Military and Associated Terms, 08 November 2010 (as amended through 15 November 2012)", https://digital.library.unt.edu/ark:/67531/metadc949822/m1/467/
2. "FY 2021 By the Numbers", 27 December 2021, https://www.dcaa.mol/Careers/Career-Blog/Article-View/Article/2883930/fy2021-by-the-numbers
3. "National Family Health Survey 5", December 2020, https://prsindia.org/policy/vital-stats/national-family-health-survey-5#
4. "Technology Perspective and Capability Roadmap 2018", https://mod.gov.in/technology-perspective-and-capability-roadmap
5. "India's Energy Outlook 2021", February 2021, https://www.iea.org/reports/india-energy-outlook-2021
6. Dick Weisinger, "Internet: 99% of Data is in the Sea, not the Cloud: Underwater Cabling", https://formtek.com/blog/internet-99-of-data-is-in-the-sea-not-the-cloud-underwater-cabling
7. "China's Naval Modernisation: Implications for the US Navy", 1 December 2022, *Congressional Research Service*, https://sgp.fas.org/crs/row/RL33153.pdf
8. It needs to be borne in mind that up to one-third of all naval ships are under various types of maintenance at any given time, some of which can be made ready at short notice for an urgent operational contingency.
9. "EY projects India to become US$26 trillion economy by 2047 with six-fold increase in per capita income to US$15,000", 18 January 2023, EY India, https://www.ey.com/en_in/news/2023/01/ey-projects-india-to-become-a-us-dollar-26-trillion-economy-by-2047-with-a-six-fold-increase-in-per-capita-income-to-us-dollar-15000

8

Indian Aerospace Power: The Way Ahead

Anil Chopra

> "*If we lose the war in the air, we lose the war and lose it quickly.*"
>
> **—Field Marshal Bernard Montgomery**

The Inheritance

The Indian Air Force (IAF) inherited what was left of the British air assets from World War II that was used against the Japanese forces. Independent India was the first Asian country to induct a jet aircraft, the de Havilland Vampire.[1] India initially kept looking towards the British for aircraft like the Hunter, Folland Gnat and the Canberra bomber, but later inducted the French (Toofani and Mystere) fighters and Russian MiG variants. India's threat assessment was regional and land-centric, and therefore the IAF was mostly a tactical air force. The 1965 and 1971 wars saw the classical use of air power in counter-air, strike, and air defence roles. The Bangladesh liberation war saw a major para-drop operation for the first time after the Second World War at Tangail.[2] Also, the Megna River crossing was a classic case of vertical envelopment.[3] For the first time, maritime air power was also seen in action. Subsequently, the induction of the Jaguar, Mirage 2000, and MiG-29 in the early 1980s resulted in significant punch. The induction of the An-12 and later, An-32 and IL-76, made a transformational change to the transport fleet. The Mi-8 and heavy-lift Mi-26 gave huge capability in vertical lift.

The next round of transformation took place after the Kargil war. This saw the induction of force multipliers like airborne early warning and control (AEW&C) and flight refuelling aircraft (FRA). India also acquired a significant fleet of multirole air superiority Su-30 MKI aircraft. Unmanned aerial vehicles

(UAV) were inducted for the first time. The IAF added a host of precision munitions including the Harpy and Harop loiter munitions. The following round of hi-tech purchases were the induction of American P-8I maritime aircraft, the C-130 J-transporters for special operations, C-17 transporters for heavy-lift global reach, and the Chinook and Apache attack helicopters. The latest was the induction of two squadrons of 4.5 generation Rafale fighters.[4]

Meanwhile, India's indigenous light combat aircraft (LCA) evolved into a potent combat asset and is being inducted, albeit a little slower than desired. India also made leaps into space. It has today mastered the positioning of all types of satellites, has a space-based navigation constellation, and is among the few who have demonstrated anti-satellite capability.

Air Power Attributes and Missions

There is a saying that the one who controls the aerospace controls the planet. Armies and navies are investing more and more of their budgets on element air, vis-à-vis their organic tanks, guns and ships and submarines. Aerospace power is technology and cost-driven. Obsolescence sets in early. Most nations spend the bulk of their defence capital budgets on aerospace assets.

Air and space provide the ultimate vantage point. They are thus most suited for intelligence, surveillance, and reconnaissance (ISR). It is thus possible to generate a 'consolidated air picture' that supports situational awareness (SA) for all air, surface and sub-surface operations. Space also supports communications, navigation, and targeting. Mastering aerospace is crucial for successful surface operations. Air superiority is thus a highly desirable requirement. It will prevent an adversary striking our national assets and will prevent its interference in our surface operations.

Speed, range, lethality, accuracy, and flexibility are important traits of air power. It provides a global reach and long-range effects. It is important to understand and exploit the flexibility offered by air power to political, executive, and military commanders. With the evolution of very long range sensors and weapons, the combat engagements are much farther. Neutralising an adversary's air assets through a dedicated counter-air campaign remains an important mission. Interdicting adversary supplies and troop movements can best be done by interdiction missions from the air. The dividends from surface battle are multi-fold. Counter-surface force missions against an adversary in battle-contact with our forces needs very close coordination between the elements, and precision weapons. All missions in the tactical battle area (TBA) require airspace management in a manner that allows maximum freedom to use available weapons and yet avoid fratricide. All missions have to be purposeful, and flown under an effects-based operations (EBO) umbrella.[5] High mission success would have to be ensured by all elements.

Fixed and rotary-wing mobility is a very important capability. They will be the lifeline for intra and inter theatre movements. Vertical lift will be crucial in the mountains for inter-valley transfers or for leapfrogging ahead. They will be required for many other missions including casualty evacuation. Air has a great role of Humanitarian Aid and Disaster Relief (HADR), both in peace and war. Air will always be the first responder, and a great asset for the political authority.

Combat Enhancement Abilities

Advances in secure communications, connectivity and data processing and handling have resulted in all operations becoming network-centric. The entire command and control and decision matrix is supported through networks. Networks have thus become important targets. A successful cyber-attack could cause devastating consequences in milliseconds. Offensive and defensive cyber warfare ability is thus crucial. Networks will have to be rugged and secure. They will need back-ups.

Powerful airborne radars and other electro-optical sensors are major combat enablers. Neutralising them is important and requires sophisticated electronic warfare (EW) ability. Powerful airborne jammers and the latest electronic techniques would have to be in a major air force's inventory.

Artificial Intelligence (AI) greatly supports decision-making and in autonomous operations. Autonomous aerial vehicles are now able to undertake most of the tasks that once required human intervention. Unmanned systems are being teamed up with manned systems to harness the potential of both. In a highly contested battle environment, autonomous aerial platforms could sanitise the air space ahead and saturate adversary defences. The more lethal, heavily armed force of manned platforms could follow. Such manned unmanned teaming (MUMT) could also include drone swarms that can also be used for saturation attack.[6]

Directed energy weapons (DEW) are evolving quickly. They would be an un-expendable asset. They will take on adversary projectiles at distant ranges.

A major hindrance till now was on-board electric power generation to support lasers and DEWs. These capabilities are fast evolving.

Hypersonic platforms and weapons are the other disruptive technologies. Their very high speeds make it difficult to be defended against. Such weapons have already been used in combat in Ukraine. They will be able to take-on very high-value targets like aircraft carriers and large ships on the sea and AEW&C and FRAs in the air. Hypersonic aircraft will being in new dynamics, and disrupt the status quo.

Air Power and Cyber Warfare

War is both timeless and ever changing.[7] While the basic nature of war is constant, the means and methods we use evolve continuously. Actions by a nation-state to penetrate another nation's computers or networks for the purpose of causing damage or disruption can be termed as cyber warfare. Strategic cyber-attacks could be on a nation's critical primary infrastructure and utilities, whilst operational cyber-attacks are against an adversary's military. Since practically all air operations are through data links between platforms and with ground elements of automated integrated air command and control system (IACCS), cyber threats will be real and protection crucial. Similarly, the Air Force Net (AFNET) which is the backbone would have to be secured.

India would also have to build cyber-attack capability to take on adversary networks to neutralise their capability advantage. This would have to be coordinated with other actions such as electronic warfare. Satellite and air-based assets will be crucial. Air will also be used for supporting psychological warfare and the Air Force will have to sanitise its personnel against an enemy's psychological warfare. Social media would have to be extensively used to control and shape the narrative during information warfare and influence operations (IWIO). Extra care would have to be taken while acquiring communications and network equipment, many of which are nowadays originating from China. An interface with the newly-formed tri-service defence cyber agency (DCA) would be important.

Air Power against Terror

Ever since the September 2011 coordinated air attacks in the USA, the Americans have been extensively using air power against terrorists. They have been carrying out precision attacks on their hideouts, and selectively killing key leaders through attacks using combat UAVs. Air can be most effectively used against terrorists without exposing own personnel to landmines or improvised explosive devices (IED). Aerial sensors today allow day-and-night attacks. Terrorist training areas and launch pads make good targets from the air. It is also possible to double-check locations before releasing munitions. Attacks can be fighters, UAVs, or helicopter gunships. Stand-off precision guided munitions (PGM) can be used from long distances, as was the case in the Bamako strike. Helicopters could also be used to extricate terrorists dead or alive.

Multi-Domain Operations[8]

Modern militaries comprise five inter-related domains: land, maritime, air, space, and cyber-space. Future conflicts will face 'multi-domain' challenges. The way a military builds its force, integrates its planning, and synchronizes its operations must change quickly. The cyberspace domain is wholly man-made and is ever-changing. In the emerging 'multi-domain reality', an attack will often come from multiple domains simultaneously—jamming of radios and data-links, persistent surveillance, and precise, long-range fires. The military needs to instil in its commanders the ability to deal with ambiguity and incomplete information—the fog of war in the digital age— and yet continue to operate in a manner consistent with the intent. Force posture, power projection, and presence in all domains will require greater integration of all services and agencies. The services are unfortunately still reluctant to trade proficiency in their core competencies but for futuristic-sounding potentially empty promises of multi-domain prowess. This will have to change.

Joint Operations

Air is the most important element of joint operations. Ground forces and maritime forces require protection from enemy air. Such protection can be provided by the Air Force by creating local air superiority. They also require offensive air support to neutralise the enemy at long ranges so that it cannot subdue on impede own forces' plans. They also need support for air logistics. For any joint plan to succeed, the services need to plan, train, and execute operations in a coordinated manner. Each service has a core task of its own. For joint operations, organisational structures need to be put in place. Each must understand the other's strengths and weaknesses. Also, there is a need for communications and connectivity. It has to be based on equality and trust and not one-upmanship. Joint operations of the future will mean common situational awareness. Joint operations must ensure the freedom of operation to each other.

Current State of Aerial Technology in India

India has already mastered most of the basic aircraft building technologies. It is essentially at 4.5 generation stage in most areas and is gradually catching up in some others. Light combat aircraft (LCA) Mk 1 is a fourth-generation aircraft, the Mk 2 will be a 4.5 generation aircraft. We have mastered the basic aircraft design, the composite materials, and production technologies. For some time, the active electronically scanned array (AESA) radar will continue to be produced through a joint-venture with Israel. The electronic warfare suite will initially be foreign and later move to a joint venture route. India will be dependent on foreign aero-engines for some more years till a joint-venture are evolved and a 'made-in-India' engine is produced. Most other avionics are being built in India, some with foreign help. The LCA Mk 1A and Mk2 will have greater indigenisation and more operational capabilities. Aircraft production rates are still very low and they must go up considerably. Significant private sector participation has begun. Private companies are making the LCA front, central, and rear fuselage.

The design of India's fifth-generation aircraft, the advanced medium combat aircraft (AMCA), has reportedly been frozen. Metal cutting has begun. It will continue to fly with foreign aero-engines. The specifications drawn are among the best globally. India will need foreign help for stealth and some other technologies if reasonable timeframes have to be maintained. As of date, the first flight is officially planned in 2025. A more realistic timeline would be 2026.[9]

With advanced light helicopter (ALH) variants flying in large numbers, we have mastered most parts of helicopter building. The engine is still being built with foreign help. The next logical step would be the larger helicopters. Transport aircraft would normally have been easier to build. However, India floundered with the 'Saras' for long including the loss of precious lives of test crew. Meanwhile, we have been making helicopter and transport aircraft aero-structures for many foreign customers. Finally, the C 295 will be built in India by the private sector in the coming years. We must push the Saras 2 variant development. It would be a good idea to start Indian regional jet development in parallel. It is an infliction point for the aircraft industry, and a time to get our act right.

New Approach for Indigenous Production

Both Hindustan Aeronautics Ltd. (HAL) and the Defence Research and Development Organisation (DRDO) have been re-galvanised. The 220-year-old Ordnance Factory Board has been dissolved and its units are corporatized under seven public sector undertakings (PSU). All are now showing stand-alone profits. The ministry of defence's (MoD) new defence acquisition procedure (DAP) 2020 brings military procurement rules in line with the government's long-running targets to boost indigenous defence capability.[10] The procedure is being continuously revised. Three lists of positive indigenous lists have been released. Nearly 210 items covered in these will have to procured only from Indian manufacturers.

HAL and Israel Aerospace Industries (IAI) recently signed a memorandum of understanding (MoU) to convert a civil airliner to a multi mission tanker transport (MMTT) aircraft in India.[11] Earlier, in September 2021, the DRDO was cleared to convert Air India's six A-319s and A-321 variants into airborne early warning and control (AEW&C) aircraft.[12]

India's Aviation Technology Growth Strategy

Air war in Ukraine has clearly brought out the importance of the use of *ISR platforms*, precision attacks by *UAVs*, smart use of *air defence and anti-tank missiles, air-launched cruise missiles* and even *hypersonic weapons*. The rapid growth of aviation technology has to be factored and imbibed. *Fifth-generation stealth aircraft* are already taking part in operations or flying deterrence missions. India's fifth-generation aircraft may still be a decade away. It is time that India had mostly 4.5 generation fighters to take on adversaries like China. The technology roadmap for the country must be evolved with the participation of stakeholders and with due realism. To be a global power, India must be able to produce an aero-engine for both its military and civil aircraft fleets. Advanced engines with adaptive versatile engine technology will give longer ranges and higher performance.[13] There are some Bengaluru-based companies working on small engines and these could be co-opted. Such engines will be required for UAVs and cruise missiles. Electric and hybrid engines are where the future lies. India must invest in such research also.

India should build latest generation *AESA radars* for airborne and ground systems. 'Uttam' AESA radar also must succeed. It must master the stealth and 'low-observable' design and material technologies. Advanced digital avionics, newer aerospace materials, signature reduction, and highly integrated systems and weapons technologies are a starting point. *Infrared search and track (IRST) systems* are a must. All sensor inputs must be fused for SA and to constantly track all targets of interest around an aircraft's 360 degree bubble. India has a successful missile program, including the BrahMos. Akash Prime and Akash-NG medium-range mobile surface-to-air missile (SAM) systems need newer variants and greater production. The DRDO's *quick reaction surface-to-air missile (QR-SAM)* and *vertical launch short range SAM (VL-SRSAM)* program needs a push. Astra Mk 3 and BrahMos II need to be driven. In many cases, we have partnered with Russia and Israel; the joint venture (JV) route is working well.

There is a major thrust by the government on drones. Development of the DRDO's 'Rustam' and 'Tapas' variants must be completed quickly. The DRDO must find private partners for these. The Adanis are making the Israeli Hermes UAVs in India through a JV with Elbit.[14] As per the Drone Federation of India, the manufacturing of drones and related systems is happening in India, but key components are largely sourced from other countries. These include batteries, motors, sensors, semiconductors, GPS, cameras, etc. Select countries have developed mass production capabilities against aggregated demand of such components. India needs to get into such mass production. Initiatives like the Mehar Baba competition helped identify private sector start-ups. Meanwhile, MUMT technologies need to be mastered.

State-of-the art *electronic warfare systems* would be required. The DRDO has started studies to develop an *airborne electronic attack (AEA) aircraft* on the Su-30MKI platform. Manoeuvre performance gets enhanced by thrust-vectoring engines. AI has great applications in aviation. *DEW* and *hypersonic weapons* would need to be developed and so would be other precision weapons. Significant efforts would have to go to unmanned and autonomous systems and drones, including swarms. The world is moving to *sixth generation technologies*. Things will be built faster, better and more affordably using 3D printing yet ensuring quality and safety standards. Technologies for future aircraft and systems must cater for operations in the anti-access/anti-denial (A2/AD) environment of 2030–50 timeframe.

For India to be part of the big league, the *AMCA* must succeed. The AMCA will be a futuristic fifth-generation aircraft that would also incorporate some features of planned sixth-generation aircraft all over the globe. The development of AMCA will take place in two phases, AMCA Mk-1 and AMCA Mk-2, which would majorly differ in indigenous content and futuristic features. Mk-2 will focus more on stealth, EW, and futuristic pilot-AI interface.

The AMCA Mk-2 will have DEWs and thrust-vectored engines with serrated nose pattern. The aircraft needs to be developed concurrently with *LCA Mk2* and must have a dedicated separate team. Many of these technologies are expensive and no one shares easily. These have to be developed. Dedicated teams would have to be made to drive technology. The private sector would have to be involved. The programs would have to be funded and projects monitored.

A continental sized country like India requires at least 10 large *AEW&C* and 10 smaller 'Netra' class variants, vis-à-vis the 3+3 today. Similarly, India needs at least 15 *FRA* vis-à-vis the six today. These are force-multiplier strategic assets. The urgency has to be understood and action evolved. India must work to build own regional jets and airliners. It must also look at developing *V/STOL aircraft.*

Communications and internet technologies backed by AI and 5 & 6G telecommunications networks will be crucial for aviation design and on-board data handling. They will also be crucial for satellite and ground-based communications. 'Internet of Things' (IoT) and machine-to-machine communications will require these. It will also involve the beaming of millimetre-length microwaves at the Earth from thousands of new communication satellites. These speeds will also be required for cyber-security. Imported electronic hardware of aircraft could be high-risk with embedded chips. Indigenisation is very important.

Breakthrough disruptive technologies keep changing the status quo. High-bandwidth high-speed networks, AI, quantum computing, robotics, hypersonic and DEW are going to change the way air war is fought. Keeping abreast with new technologies is important. Aerial platforms must be built around modularity that will ease regular upgrades.

Core Technology Mission Approach

For long, India has followed a *laissez-faire* approach and left it to scientists in the DRDO to evolve defence technologies. What they could deliver, the armed forces bought. The rest they imported. Scientists are not necessarily good project managers. Therefore, the country could just get low-end products from domestic produce. Things have begun to change. The country has global power aspirations and therefore there is a need for self-sufficiency in defence production. Based on the requirements of the users, core products and technologies need to be identified. Core teams led by qualified well paid program managers, selected scientists, and groups of manufacturing industries should be put together. They should be given seed money to get going. Some tax concessions would be required. There should be incentives for success. Assurance of orders should be put in place. Outsourcing of tasks by each team to MSMEs should be encouraged.

Joint-Venture Approach

With China becoming independent through indigenisation, India is one of the largest importers of defence products. India must leverage this aspect and join up with friendly foreign countries. It is impossible for any country to acquire all technologies and produce all weapons and platforms. The JVs are often a win-win approach for both. The JV should include design, raw material, manufacture, and marketing. Japan is working on a sixth-generation aircraft, and is likely to join up with the United Kingdom (UK). It has both technology and funds. India could join up with them.[15] Small countries like Israel have technology but need markets. Israel has strengths in electronics, radars, missiles, and UAVs. Even the USA collaborates with Israel on them. French could be great partners for aero-engines. We can have more JVs with Russia for specific weapons and armaments.

Indian Private Sector in Aircraft Production

A few big private industrial houses are now well established in aircraft defence manufacturing. Tata Aerospace and Defence (Tata A&D) have been making the AH-64 Apache combat helicopter fuselage. They are also making aero-structures for Boeing's CH-47 Chinook helicopters. All C-130Js delivered to customers around the world have major aero-structure components from India producing 24 C-130 empennages annually. Sikorsky, a Lockheed Martin company, also relies on Hyderabad-based Tata Advanced System Limited (TASL) as the manufacturing base for its global supply of cabins for the S-92 helicopter. The Tata group is working with GE to manufacture CFM International LEAP engine components in India.[16] Lockheed Martin selected TASL to produce F-16 wings in India. There are many private companies making defence electronics, large aero-components, advanced technology components, and sub-systems. Dynamatic Technologies makes assemblies of vertical fins for Sukhoi 30 MKI fighters. They are also supplying aero-structures to Airbus for its A320 family of aircraft and the wide-body 330 aircraft. Hyderabad's VEM technologies manufactures centre fuselage for LCA Tejas.[17] Idea Forge is a product-focused UAV systems company. India's Adani and Israel's Elbit JV have UAV manufacturing complexes in Hyderabad and Bengaluru. Many Indian MSMEs and start-ups are entering defence production. Many private players including start-ups have also entered drone and counter drone manufacturing for the armed forces.

National Level Commonality of Platforms

For any aircraft or system to be built indigenously, there are minimum numbers for it to be economical. Generally, at least 300 aircraft would be considered the break-even point. A single service or organisation may not be able to place such a large order. Helicopters are required by all the three services, Coast Guard, BSF, Police, state governments, and many private operators. Likewise, small commuter/communications aircraft are required by similar agencies. Dornier and ALH could have been bought by many state governments. The 19 seat Saras Mk 2 should evince interest from many players. There is a commonality in air defence weapons, in small arms requirements, speed boats, high altitude equipment, cyber, and electronic equipment, among many others. The service qualification requirements must be adjusted accordingly where possible. Larger orders will improve the economy of scale and support building indigenous industry. The armed forces and defence production must get out of non-core areas like uniforms, boots, and even housing, etc.

Cut Down Red Tape

Cutting of red tape means reducing bureaucratic obstacles for action. Excessive, rigid, or redundant rules and regulations hinder or prevent action and decision-making. They also hamper organizational performance. It is a barrier to businesses, especially the smaller ones. Defence purchases are often linked to bribes to cut red tape and seek favours. Delays of important weapon platforms impacts defence preparedness. A strong political leadership can make sure that red tape is reduced.

The Way Ahead

Nearly 2,500 years ago, Chanakya had envisaged what he called open war, covert war and silent war. He mentioned how the king must exercise the choice and method of pursuing war or peace. He mentions the need to fortify the nation, prepare the armed forces, and give them resources to defend. Capability would mean deterrence and ensure peace without engagement in war, he wrote. He also gave high importance to leadership qualities, intelligence gathering, and information warfare as weapons of war to achieve military objectives. All are relevant today as well as in the foreseeable future. In that, air power is the combined employment of all air and space assets to exercise control over aerospace environments to achieve national security objectives. Air power exploits its unique operational characteristics in the multi-dimensional environment to offer a very broad range of strategic and tactical military options. The inherent characteristics of speed, range, precision, lethality, responsiveness, versatility, and flexibility make it the first choice for strategic effects and options.

The escalating cost of modern fighters, coupled with national priorities, budgetary constraints, a human-resource crunch and newer battlefield challenges leads one to conclude that a new way of war-fighting would need to be employed, especially in the aerospace domain. A national security strategy must be finalised quickly. From this will flow the operational capability building for the armed forces. That, in turn, will lay the road for technology development.

The armed forces need to prepare for asymmetric warfare. Air forces will have to engage in system-of-systems approach to take on multi-dimension, multi-domain operations. Future aerial platforms will have to penetrate dense integrated AD environments that are backed by electronic and cyber-attacks. Since aerial platforms will be used across various military and paramilitary users, a 'whole of nation' vision must evolve.

Undoubtedly, the '*Atmanirbharta*' campaign will drive indigenisation. According to the Defence Ministry, in 2016, the indigenous content of LCA-

Tejas was 75.5 per cent in number and 59.7 per cent in the value of the aircraft.[18] The plan was to reach 70 per cent indigenisation in value in LCA Mk2, and go up to 80 per cent by 2030.[19] Maintaining such developmental schedules is important both for the IAF's operational capability and also to prevent obsolescence setting in. It will have to be an all-of-government approach. Spelling out clear end-states, timelines and regular path-line reviews would be important. Lastly, there is the need for greater R&D funding.

The time to act is now, lest it is too late.

ENDNOTES

1. Aashique Iqbal, From Wapitis to Vampires: Indian Air Force aircraft and the politics of decolonisation 1933-1950, On History, 12 February 2017, https://blog.history.ac.uk/2017/02/from-wapitis-to-vampires-indian-air-force-aircraft-and-the-politics-of-decolonisation-1933-1950/ Accessed on 9 August 2022.
2. Avinash Chikte, How Paradrop Became A Game Changer At Tangail During The Bangladesh Liberation War 1971, *India Times*, 10 December 2021, https://www.indiatimes.com/explainers/news/bangladesh-liberation-war-1971-556392.html Accessed on 9 August 2022.
3. Ratnakar Sadasyula, Meghna Heli Bridge, Tangail Air Drop, *History Under Your Feet*,12 December 2019, https://historyunderyourfeet.wordpress.com/2019/12/12/meghna-heli-bridge-tangail-air-drop/ Accessed on 9 August 2022.
4. Jay Desai, Understanding the Rafale's Induction into the IAF, *South Asian Voices*, 24 September 2020, https://southasianvoices.org/understanding-the-rafales-induction-into-the-iaf/ Accessed on 9 August 2022.
5. Paul K. Davis, Effects-Based Operations (EBO), Rand Corporation, MR-1477-USJFCOM/AF, 2001, https://www.rand.org/pubs/monograph_reports/MR1477.html#:~:text=Effects%2Dbased%20 operati ons%20(EBO)%20are%20defined%20for%20this%20 monograph; the %20application%20of%20military%2C%20diplomatic%2C Accessed on 9 August 2022.
6. Lieutenant-Colonel Livio Rossetti, Manned-Unmanned Teaming, Joint Air Power Competence Centre, Published: January 2020 in Journal Edition 29, https://www.japcc.org/articles/manned-unmanned-teaming/ Accessed on 9 August 2022.
7. C.C. Kruluk, *War Fighting, US Marine Corps*, Chapter 1, Page 17, https://www.studocu.com/row/document/national-defence-university/the-concept-of-modern-marketing/mcdp-1-warfighting-gn-concept-for-modern-warfare/16785772 Accessed on 9 August 2022.
8. Anil Chopra, Cyber Warfare a Key Element of Multi Domain Wars – Time to Push India, Air Power Asia, 3 June 2020, https://airpowerasia.com/2020/06/03/cyber-warfare-a-key-element-of-multi-domain-wars-time-to-push-india/ Accessed on 10 August 2022.
9. Vishal Thapar, Big Landmark For India's Stealth Fighter Programme As Manufacture Of 1st Prototype Begins, *Business World*, 11 March 2022, https://www.businessworld.in/article/Big-Landmark-For-India-s-Stealth-Fighter-Programme-As-Manufacture-Of-1st-Prototype-Begins/11-03-2022-422590/
10. Manjeet Negi, Govt amends Defence Acquisition Procedure 2020 to promote 'Make In India' in military procurement, *India Today*, 26 April 2022, https://www.indiatoday.in/defence/story/govt-amends-defence-acquisition-procedure-2020-to-promote-make-in-india-1941838-2022-04-26 Accessed on 10 August 2022.

11. Ajai Shukla, HAL, Israel Aerospace tie up to turn civil aircraft into mid-air refuellers, *Business World*, 7 April 2022, https://www.business-standard.com/article/companies/hal-israel-aerospace-tie-up-to-turn-civil-aircraft-into-mid-air-refuellers-122040700032_1. html#:~:text=Hindustan%20 Aeronautics%20 (HAL)%20announced%20on,(MMTT)%20aircraft%20 in%20India. Accessed on 10 August 2022.
12. Snehesh Alex Philip, Modi govt okays 6 more 'eyes in the sky' for IAF, DRDO project to cost Rs 11,000 crore, *The Print*, 9 September 2021 https://theprint.in/defence/modi-govt-okays-6-more-eyes-in-the-sky-for-iaf-drdo-project-to-cost-rs-11000-crore/730697/ Accessed on 10 August 2022.
13. Anil Chopra, Contours of a Sixth-Generation Fighter Aircraft, *Indian Defence Review*, 9 February 2021, http://www.indiandefencereview.com/news/contours-of-a-sixth-generation-fighter-aircraft/ Accessed on 10 August 2022.
14. BW Online Bureau, Adani-Elbit JV Expanding To Export Mini UAV Systems, *Business World*, 6 February 2020, https://www.businessworld.in/article/Adani-Elbit-JV-Expanding-To-Export-Mini-UAV-Systems/06-02-2020-183598/ Accessed on 11 August 2020.
15. Kyle Mizokami, Japan, U.K. to Work Together on Sixth Generation Fighter Development, *Popular Mechanics*, 22 July 2022, https://www.popularmechanics.com/military/aviation/a40669920/japan-uk-to-develop-new-fighter/ Accessed on 11 August 2022.
16. Special Correspondent, GE, Tata Group join hands to make LEAP engine parts, *The Hindu*, 15 December 2017, https://www.thehindu.com/news/cities/Hyderabad/ge-tata-group-join-hands-to-make-leap-engine-parts/article21669242.ece Accessed on 12 August 2022.
17. Hyderabad's VEM Technologies manufactures Centre Fuselage for Tejas, *Telangana Today*, 26 July 2021 https://telanganatoday.com/hyderabads-vem-technologies-manufactures-centre-fuselage-for-tejas Accessed on 12 August 2022.
18. PTI, Indigenous content of Tejas 59.7% by value & 75.5% by numbers, *The Indian Express*, 18 November 2016, https://indianexpress.com/article/india/india-news-india/indigenous-content-of-tejas-59-7-by-value-75-5-by-numbers-4383036/ Accessed on 12 August 2022.
19. Ashish Dangwal, IAF Approves Tejas Mark 2 Design; Will Have More Powerful Engines, Larger Payload Capabilities – Experts, *The EurAsian Times*, 31 December 2021, https://eurasiantimes.com/iaf-approves-tejas-mark-2-design-will-have-more-powerful-engines-larger-payload-capabilities-experts/ Accessed on 12 August 2022.

9

STRENGTHENING DEFENCE INTELLIGENCE FOR FUTURE CHALLENGES

Kamal Davar

"... *the reason the enlightened Prince and the wise General conquer the enemy... is foreknowledge.*"

—**Sun Tzu in *The Art of War***

The Science of Intelligence

Historically, the art and science of *Intelligence* has been an integral and significant constituent of statecraft. 'To be forewarned is to be forearmed' is a well acknowledged truism, but equally, it is only when a major security lapse or a catastrophic event occurs that intelligence is accorded some priority in decision-making. It is also a frequently occurring fact that most security failures are conveniently ascribed to intelligence shortcomings even when there might be systemic inadequacies, or lack of planning and anticipation, or sheer laziness in prosecuting laid down checks and balances. Conversely, intelligence successes cannot be publicly flaunted for "there is no place for drum-beating in the business of intelligence!"[1] The Chinese intelligence services (CIS), despite their global footprint and spectacular success in many realms of intelligence, have managed to keep away from the public gaze including that of its enemy intelligence agencies.

It will be worth recalling that since 1947, India has had more than its share of intelligence lapses. In 1962 and earlier, the Intelligence Bureau (IB) failed to forewarn the nation of Chinese intentions, which led to India's debacle when the Chinese gobbled away 38,000 sq km of our territory in the Aksai Chin region. In 1965, the Indian establishment was unaware of Pakistan's 'Operation Gibraltar' which led to the 1965 India-Pakistan war. Consequently, in 1968, the then prime minister Indira Gandhi had ordered the establishment of the Research and Analysis Wing (R&AW) as the exclusive agency for external intelligence. Other serious intelligence shortcomings observed in India were the failure to assess the Pakistani army's atrocities in the then East Pakistan province during the period 1969-71. India did not fully know about the degree of resentment among the East Pakistan populace against their own West Pakistan-dominated government, which ultimately led to the exodus of millions of refugees into India and thence to the 1971 war between India and Pakistan. Pakistan's massive incursions in the Kargil sector in 1999, Pakistani terrorists' attack on the Indian Parliament in 2002, the Mumbai terrorist attack in November 2008, and the Pulwama terrorist strike in 2016 also stand out, among many others, as major intelligence failures.

Chinese incursions into our Eastern Ladakh sector in mid-2020 once again reminded the nation of the failure of our intelligence agencies, including our imagery intelligence (IMINT) set-ups of not being able to detect the massive Chinese build-up in the Aksai Chin region. That led to the Galwan incident in which 20 Indian soldiers were killed in clashes with troops of the People's Liberation Army (PLA). It must be mentioned here that the Chinese build-up for their annual exercises west of the Xinjiang-Tibet highway was known but somehow China's intentions were misread. Anyway, the nation can ill afford to have a re-occurrence of such glaring intelligence lapses.

Challenges for the Armed Forces and Defence Intelligence

India, located in one of the world's politically unstable and violent regions, confronts ever-growing diverse and formidable challenges to its security and economic resurgence. Surrounded by two belligerent neighbours threatening India independently and collusively, security threats, both external and internal, conventional and non-conventional, emerging across the diverse spectrums of warfare make the tasks of intelligence agencies of the nation extremely exacting and mind-boggling.

That the craft of *Intelligence* is not only a force multiplier in the pursuit of a nation's stated and unstated goals, but is also its first line of defence, is a truism which merits no elaboration. The armed forces, being the ultimate bastion of the state and the most critical instrument for ensuring its security and safety, thus has to have in place an adequately structured and a fully responsive intelligence edifice of its own, in order to accord to itself timely and actionable intelligence inputs necessary to thwart emerging threats against the nation. Successful prosecution of a nation's goals, both in peace and war, depends much on the availability of accurate intelligence.

To meet the critical requirements of the armed forces as mentioned above, the vital aspect of *Defence Intelligence* requires re-energising by deliberate, in-depth analyses of the various institutions which constitute the defence or military intelligence structures. Time-bound reviews of the charters and roles, changes and upgrades as warranted, and frank assessments of the capabilities of all the constituents of defence intelligence to fulfil assigned responsibilities in all the realms and nuances of intelligence thus has to be scrupulously gone into on an institutionalized, time-bound basis. Intelligence reforms cannot be merely reactive and incremental.

India's strategic domain extends from the Straits of Malacca in the east to the Gulf of Aden in the west, running southwards along the East African coastline and down to the southern expanse of the Indian Ocean. In addition, the entire Asia-Pacific Region reflects upon our security calculus. India's land borders exceed 15,000 sq km which is shared with seven nations, including a small segment with Afghanistan (presently it falls in the Gilgit-Baltistan region adjoining the Pakistan-Occupied Jammu, Kashmir and Ladakh—POJK&L). Also, India has a 7,683-km coastline and an exclusive economic zone (EEZ) of over 2 million sq km. With an adversarial 'string of pearls' having been established by a militarily powerful China, a congenitally anti-India centric Pakistan constantly exporting terror to India, a few sieges within from Pakistan-sponsored terrorists, and a palpable Naxal/Maoist threat (formally referred to as left wing extremism or LWE), the challenges for India's intelligence agencies, especially defence intelligence, are indeed awesome. China's escalating cyber capabilities, which have the potential to inflict 'electronic paralysis' on India's utilization of cyber space, command and control structures, communications networks, power and nuclear grids, diverse electrical-electronic systems, et al, pose colossal challenges of a diverse and escalating nature for India's defence.

The Indian defence intelligence has to factor-in the rapid and phenomenal growth of China's military and economic might. This growth translates to its aggressive assertiveness against both the unresolved land borders issue and the maritime commons of the Indian Ocean or even the entire Asia-Pacific Region. China's collusive efforts along with its strategic prodigy, Pakistan, in containing India and embarking on the ambitious $ 62-billion China-Pakistan Economic

Corridor (CPEC) project through disputed Gilgit-Baltistan (GB) right up to the Gwadar port are the challenges for our intelligence agencies to monitor. China's successful efforts to lure a hapless Sri Lanka into its debt-trap diplomacy resulting in the latter's current turmoil, political instability and economic distress also need to be carefully monitored by our intelligence outfits. For many years, China has been penetrating various aspects of Sri Lanka's economic and security-related issues which, naturally, will be a cause of concern for Indian security.

A major thrust area for our intelligence agencies, both civil and military, is also to monitor the Pakistan-conceived and implemented terror mischief in Jammu, Kashmir & Ladakh (JK&L), the North-East, Punjab, and in the Indian hinterland. That since the last two years in particular Pakistan's Inter-Services Intelligence (ISI) has stepped up its activities in Punjab is well acknowledged and needs to be carefully observed. Indian armed forces and the Border Security Force (BSF) units located close to the International Border (IB) with Pakistan have to remain extra watchful of increasing hostile drone activities along the IB.

Background: Defence Intelligence

For the Indian Army, its military intelligence (MI) directorate has existed as the primary intelligence set-up since1941 (though it traces its roots well back to 1887). We also have naval intelligence and air intelligence directorates to attend to the intelligence requirements of their respective services, to the extent possible. Though the need for a set-up to provide integrated intelligence inputs and analyses for the three services was felt off and on and expressed by some security analysts since long, it was the rude shock of being surprised by the Pakistani incursions into the Kargil heights in 1999 that prompted the government of the day to review the nation's higher defence organisation (HDO).

In 1999, Vajpayee government set up the Kargil review committee (KRC) under the well-known strategy expert, K. Subhramanyam, to go into the entire gamut of the HDO including the efficacy of the intelligence structure, both civil and military, as prevailing then. The KRC, in its very comprehensive review, put up its findings and submitted to the government a report on various issues concerning the nation's security preparedness. Subsequently, the government instituted a high-powered group of ministers (GOM) under the then Deputy Prime Minister and Home Minister, L.K. Advani to study these recommendations. The GOM, in turn, constituted a task force under a former R&AW chief, Gary Saxena, to have an in-depth look at the nation's intelligence challenges and structures in their totality in relation to the recommendations of the KRC.

In its candid exposition, the KRC had opined that "the resources made available to the defence services are not commensurate with the responsibility assigned to them. There are distinct advantages in having two lines of intelligence collection and reporting with a rational division of functions, responsibilities and areas of specialization. Indian threat assessment is a single process dominated by the R&AW..."[2] It went on to state that for its own threat assessment, the army had to depend upon inputs from the R&AW. The KRC observed that "the Indian intelligence structure is flawed since there is little back up or redundancy that goes to build the external threat perception by one agency, namely the R&AW, which has a virtual monopoly in this regard. It is neither healthy nor prudent to endow one agency with multifarious capabilities for human, communications, imagery and electronic intelligence."[3]

The KRC and the GOM reports and the task force on intelligence strongly advocated the setting up of a *Defence Intelligence Agency* (DIA). Besides, many other recommendations were made to energize the civil intelligence set-up, including raising of the National Technical Facilities Organisation (NTFO, rechristened later as the National Technical Research Organisation or NTRO) for technical intelligence (TECHINT). Importantly, the KRC and GOM had both recommended the appointment of a five-star Chief of the Defence Staff (CDS) to render single-point military advice to the Government of India.

The Defence Intelligence Agency (DIA)

Based on the recommendations of the GOM which were duly accepted by the Vajpayee government, the DIA was established on 5 March 2002. The DIA was established primarily for "coordinating the functioning of the different service intelligence directorates". It was created to ensure better integration of intelligence collected by the three service intelligence directorates (SIDs) and serve as the principal military intelligence agency. It was also chartered to produce integrated intelligence assessments as regards defence matters for national security planners.

Strategic intelligence assets of the services, namely, the defence image processing and analysis centre (DIPAC) and the signals intelligence directorate were placed under the command of the DIA. Defence attaches (DAs), posted abroad, were also put under command of the DIA, albeit partially. The Director-General DIA (DG DIA) is also the deputy chief of the integrated defence staff (DCIDS Int) and is the principal military intelligence adviser to the Raksha Mantri, the CDS, the Chairman of the Chiefs of Staff Committee (COSC), and the Defence Secretary. The DG DIA is member of various intelligence committees at the apex level like the intelligence coordination group (ICG), technical coordination group (TCG), the national information board (NIB), etc.

Aspects of Defence Intelligence Meriting Analysis

The major issue as regards defence or military intelligence (the terms are synonyms) is to, first and foremost, arrive at or define the capabilities which we want the DIA to acquire in its pursuit of serving the nation and the armed forces. The inter se responsibilities for overall military intelligence acquisition between the DIA and the SIDs also require further clarity and definition.

Areas of Concern/Major Intelligence Acquisitions Sought

The armed forces have to be prepared for successful prosecution of conflicts in the entire spectrum of war fighting for which accurate, actionable and timely intelligence is required. For successful prosecution of its various tasks in the next 25 years, the armed forces require hard intelligence on China, its military and nuclear capabilities, infrastructure, modernization, cyber capabilities, build up in space in the years ahead and its activities along our borders as well as the Indo-Pacific maritime regions. Intelligence is also needed on China's collaboration with Pakistan, its growing footprints in Gilgit-Baltistan, Pakistan Occupied Kashmir (POK) and Gwadar deep sea port activities, its 'string of pearls' initiatives, etc.

Similarly, regular intelligence on Pakistan in virtually every area of military significance is needed. That rogue nation has to be kept under constant surveillance over its nuclear activities and the state of its nuclear readiness; the USA may be doing so but we have to be sure ourselves. Pakistan's devious activities against Indian interests in Afghanistan and Bangladesh have also to be in deeper focus of India's military intelligence. Importantly, Pakistan's activities with the Afghan Taliban in power, the Haqqani network and the

Islamic State in Khurasan (ISIK) in an instability-prone Afghanistan require careful, long-term monitoring. As earlier, the growth of the Pakistani deep state and its terror infrastructure, its continuing proxy wars, terrorism in JK&L and the Machiavellian measures it adopts to keep the pot boiling in that sensitive state need to be monitored.

Specialized military intelligence requirements over the coming decades from our vast areas of military interest and influence from the Straits of Malacca to the Gulf of Aden will be huge and endless. At present, the R&AW is chartered to provide for military requirements. However, it will be worthwhile to look at the entire gamut of tasks and responsibilities in concert with the R&AW to assess as to where all military professionals have to step in and where does the R&AW have to continue and enlarge its intelligence coverage. The division of tasks and responsibilities for external intelligence between the R&AW and DIA. and internally between the IB and DIA have to be further formalized.

External Intelligence

The mandate for acquisition of all forms of external intelligence, including military intelligence, currently rests with the R&AW. Have we got the desired quality and depth of military-oriented inputs from this arrangement so far? The R&AW comprises officers and operators primarily from police organisations and various other civil streams, and thus their expertise in military-specific intelligence is, naturally, not of the required levels. The R&AW primarily focuses on political, economic and diplomatic intelligence and therefore military-specific intelligence requirements take a back seat. As is the practice in many other nations, the DIA should be accorded the capability for acquisition, analyses and dissemination of military intelligence, external as well as internal. This will require upgrading its means like human intelligence (HUMINT), electronic intelligence (ELINT), IMINT—in fact, all forms of TECHINT—and selective augmentation of staff and equipment with the missions abroad. It is important that both the R&AW and DIA be more strictly mandated to share inputs as required.

As military diplomats, our DAs and military attaches (MA) do not have the legal or moral sanction to undertake covert activities. This aspect may require careful re-examination. It is opined that India's military attaches, who are specifically selected officers from the three services, are, apart from enhancing our understanding of the host country's language and systems, left somewhat under-utilized. To optimally utilize the DA or MA appointees, formalized intelligence training to sniff out and filter important information and to discreetly handle HUMINT resources will be required. The desired intelligence picture and an actionable mosaic, would, however, have to be carefully acquired with adequate safeguards.

HUMINT

As regards HUMINT tasking is concerned, there is also an aspect of covert operations. Currently the R&AW bears exclusive responsibility of external operations. For internal security (IS) operations, the IB is mainly tasked. However, in actual practice, every organization having stake in internal security indulges in it independently with hardly any worthwhile cooperation, and that can often turn out to be counter-productive. We need to streamline the roles and responsibilities for HUMINT operations in the counter-insurgency grid. For counter-LWEHUMINT operations at the grass root levels, the local police have vital roles to play.

A plethora of security organisations have their intelligence set-ups and are simultaneously engaged in IS and counter-insurgency (CI) operations. Howsoever efficient or otherwise they , effective coordination in reality would be a localized or state-level affair and a game changer. Seamless intelligence sharing by all agencies operating in the IS domain in different regions will be most essential. Within the military organisation, SIDs should control such operations while keeping the DIA in the loop. The responsibility should rest with the SIDs who anyway must share the collected information for the DIA to build larger and clearer pictures.

Along our coastlines, where the Coast Guard shares intelligence with the Navy and vice versa, inputs must also come to the DIA which, with its excellent TECHINT assets, will be prepare the overall mosaic for the Navy, Coast Guard, the Joint Intelligence Committee (JIC) and the National Security Council (NSC). Maritime domain awareness (MDA) is an area which is becoming critical for India and thus all efforts must be made to ensure enhancement of our capabilities in this field.

Globally, the Indo-Pacific expanse is now unquestionably the most strategically-contested region, with highly significant implications for Indian interests. Along with the intelligence agencies of friendly foreign nations and the groupings of the QUAD and AUKUS, India's defence intelligence too will have to carefully monitor growing Chinese ambitions and assertiveness in the Indo-Pacific. The Indian Navy's information management and analysis centre (IMAC), the nodal agency for maritime data fusion, and the 'information fusion centre for the Indian Ocean Region' (IFC-IOR) keep track of both military and non-military shipping. These need to be further strengthened. The IFC-IOR, though earmarked only for non-military shipping, coordinates with a large number of nations and intelligence agencies.

Building Domain Expertise

The frequent transfer of officers from the DIA and SID to units and formations for mandatory command, staff, and instructional appointments need to be controlled for it reduces the build-up of the requisite experience and capability to achieve domain expertise of the desired level.

Cross-Postings between Intelligence Agencies. Within the armed forces, officers from the three services are adequately represented in the DIA. However, the main problem lies in the cross-postings of military officers to other civil intelligence agencies, basically because of eschewed seniority versus the rank structure. This hierarchical aspect needs to be worked out. Officers from the armed forces in civil intelligence organisations also must be posted abroad and be utilized in an equitable manner.

Developing Linguistic Skills. The armed forces are woefully short of officers and personnel who are adept in key languages like Mandarin, Dari, Pashtu, Uzbeki, Sinhalese, and even Kashmiri, Persian, Burmese, Arabic, Turkish, etc. Language skills do not get sharpened overnight and so the DIA made a modest beginning with the National Defence Academy (NDA) and the Director-General Military Training (DGMT) to get the neighbourhood languages their due slot during training. At the Army Education Corps Centre and other regimental centres, specific language training responsibilities should be allocated and trainees encouraged and taught accordingly. We have some bright young soldiers who are exceptionally computer savvy; some of them could also become linguistic experts. To augment own linguistic expertise, the DIA should also not hesitate to employ youngsters directly from the civilian world.

Boosting TECHINT and Cyber Intelligence. China, having acquired breath-taking capability in hacking and disrupting cyber networks of even advanced Western nations, India and its military need to take speedy action to build-necessary offensive and defensive capabilities in all aspects of cyber warfare. China, as mentioned earlier, is assessed to be very well equipped to inflict 'electronic paralysis' upon target countries, and India and its armed forces need to be well prepared to counter this cyber challenge. The armed forces should accord adequate importance to the recently established defence cyber agency to meet cyberspace challenges in the coming years. In the years ahead, as cyberspace assumes a higher significance in the domain of warfare, this agency will surely require to upgrade to a cyber command. Importantly, the armed forces must be adept in all nuances of information warfare (IW) in the foreseeable future. The NTRO, the premier TECHINT agency, has been given a massive mandate to plan, design, set up and operate new TECHINT facilities, including establishing secure digital networks and monitoring missile launches by countries of interest. Some experts feel that the NTRO has been grossly overloaded with TECHINT and is facing problems in fulfilling its assigned role—the USA has three agencies looking into various aspects of TECHINT. As regards TECHINT for military operations, the DIA, DIPAC and Signals Intelligence need to better coordinate and cooperate with the NTRO. With maturity and clarity in thinking, we can arrive at suitable answers by better division of necessary tasks. The Corps of Signals can be more optimally utilized based on its reservoir of expertise and talent.

Countering China's Information Warfare (IW). For the last three decades in particular, China's war-fighting doctrines have included IW as a central pillar. It has been developing a force to fight and win 'limited wars under modern informationised conditions'. Indian intelligence has its task cut out to monitor China's phenomenal growth in IW and will require a wide variety of military satellites for intelligence, surveillance and reconnaissance (ISR), signal intelligence (SIGINT), ELINT, communications intelligence (COMINT) and navigation capabilities. As India develops its own IW capabilities, there will be no harm in coordinating with friendly foreign nations to safeguard own information domains and keep a check on Chinese ambitions. China's clandestine activities directed against the Dalai Lama and its covert operations in concert with Pakistan need to be constantly monitored. Chinese business set-ups in India also need to be kept under strict watch.

Countering the Dragon in Space. Unquestionably, China today is a space-faring nation, next only to the USA in its overall space capability in both military and civil applications. The continuing exploitation of space-based

ISR by China will enable it to monitor preparations of its adversaries' battle deployments. China's counter-space capabilities are a threat to India's limited ISR, communication and navigational satellite capabilities. China has hard and soft kill capabilities to deny India the requisite battle space awareness. India's defence intelligence will have to be speedily geared up to monitor China's designs in space, including the use of Pakistan as its space warfare proxy. The recently established defence space agency may be upgraded to a defence space command and has to work in very close coordination with the DIA.

Other Shortcomings in Defence Intelligence

(a) The services themselves, traditionally speaking, do not accord due importance to intelligence. With all sorts of unimagined challenges appearing and the massive destructive powers and reach of modern weaponry, response times are becoming virtually zero. Due importance to intelligence has to be accorded by the three services and, most importantly, by the Ministry of Defence (MoD).

(b) With the much awaited institution of the CDS being established it is hoped that long term intelligence planning and a synergetic approach from the three services on intelligence will be implemented.

(c) Most officers posted to the DIA and SIDs have minimal intelligence backgrounds; short tenures too inhibit talent building and retention of organizational wisdom.

(d) Our digital databases are hardly of the desired quality. They have a life span that is generally co-terminus with an officer's tenure. Most of them are not-so-well collated and tagged, making data mining difficult.

(e) Information-sharing networks between the DIA and SIDs, and the DIA and its sister civilian intelligence agencies need far better coordination. We all talk about the *Need to Know* principle while sharing information with each other but conveniently forget the gospel of the *Need to Share*.

(f) Turf battles and one-upmanship, where existing, need to be eliminated in larger national interests.

(g) It must be appreciated that no organization or service can ever have year-round, foolproof intelligence, and thus their systemic preparedness must be adequately maintained to prevent catastrophic incidents.

(h) Overall, intelligence gathering, collation and analysis must optimally utilize the acquisition and penetrative capabilities of technology which is growing at a phenomenal pace. India has vast yet untapped talent in technological prowess which should also be utilized for intelligence operations encompassing all domains of warfare. Intelligence expertise in space with the newly created defence space agency in concert with the Indian Space Research Organisation (ISRO) must be commenced without any further delay; notably, the Chinese may soon surpass the USA in this capability.

(i) The Military Intelligence School, Pune, should be upgraded to a 'defence intelligence school'. Necessary resources and expertise, including that from the three services, the civil intelligence fraternity, and the niche areas from friendly foreign nations should be utilized.

(j) In today's internet-driven world where transparency in governmental actions or the build-up of forces cannot be hidden, intelligence agencies must become far more adept in gathering and collating open sources intelligence (OSINT). By conservative estimates, information data even with the world's top intelligence agencies constitute 80 per cent from OSINT! China's intelligence strategy is based on the 'thousand grains concept' which includes synergising, directly and indirectly, inputs from the media, academics, Chinese businesses and civilians to gather information.

Summation

Firstly, the DIA has to be substantially strengthened both in terms of manpower and TECHINT. Secondly, the DIA must be given sufficient and official oversight over the SIDs—it cannot work on mere goodwill or personal equations. There is no alternative but to make the SIDs answerable to the DIA's strategic intelligence tasking; for tactical intelligence activities they can report to their respective service headquarters. Thirdly, the armed forces must raise a 'defence intelligence corps' which includes the current intelligence corps set-up and intelligence elements drawn from the three services. Its expertise in snooping, various intelligence techniques, acquisition of information and analysis, knowledge of languages, neighbourhood areas and the region needs to be substantially built up.

Despite much hype over India being a great information technology (IT) power, we have not channelized our resources and energies towards software and secure databases tuned to military requirements. A common architecture and secure information networks for information-sharing between the SIDs and DIA and the DIA with other intelligence agencies can be developed. The DIA and other national-level intelligence agencies need to cooperate far more with each other than hitherto. Information dominance and a decision advantage for own military commanders and national security planners have to be earnestly strived for by synergizing our resources and genius. Accordingly, establishing a 'future technologies unit' and a 'digital academy' in the emerging technical intelligence domains to train intelligence officers from the armed forces and from the civil intelligence agencies should be strived for. The DRDO must be tasked along with chosen Indian institutes of technology (IIT) to look into future technical threats and put into place suitable architectures to confront them. There is no alternative but for India to develop a credible indigenous capability in this field.

The Indian armed forces can strive for intelligence-sharing with friendly foreign countries—currently we are rather conservative on such matters. The DIA and SIDs need to vastly augment their HUMINT and covert operations capabilities. The DIA must attain expertise for operations with the special forces as also in coordination with the R&AW. With technology on a rapid march and acquiring vast advancements in its reach and capabilities, the strategic assets of the DIA will need to be sharpened further. The government must allocate adequate resources towards the same. Research and development (R&D) needs to be promoted and the highly talented private sector incorporated into the schemes. The DIPAC's imagery intelligence and signals intelligence organizations with the DIA must be accorded all the support for future development. The security of our military satellites in space will have to be carefully ensured.

Most security analysts are of the opinion that currently the national security adviser (NSA) has too much on his plate to be able to devote to rising intelligence requirements. A major suggestion is that all the 14 intelligence agencies in the nation should report to a 'national intelligence authority' (NIA). As in the USA, we need a 'director national intelligence' (DNI) to whom all these agencies report. Some intelligence experts also opine that creation of the DNI may result in the rise of an 'intelligence czar'. However, the government can institute checks and balances to control that possibility. The NIA can issue a classified doctrinal document to lay down the responsibilities of each of the intelligence agencies. The NIA should also issue 'a annual tasking plans' for each of the intelligence agencies.

Notwithstanding certain political and partisan motivations, the much discussed issue about governmental and parliamentary oversight over the intelligence agencies, which is essential in a democracy, remains an important legislative shortcoming. Surprisingly, barring the NIA, no intelligence agency in India has any formally sanctioned legal status and are currently functioning through executive orders issued by successive governments from time to time. Operating outside the purview of legislation makes them immune from financial, operational and administrative accountability which is not a healthy practice in a democracy. The Indian Parliament must therefore frame suitable legislative enactments for the functioning of these intelligence agencies.

Practitioners of military intelligence (DIA and SIDs) should note that while governments may use civil intelligence agencies for political purposes, the armed forces intelligence fraternity have to remain totally apolitical. Even the Raksha Mantri had opined in Parliament in March 2016 that "military intelligence has been sacrificed at the altar of political goals."[4] It is imperative that military intelligence agencies keep clear of politics and political parties.

Finally, institutionalized reviews on a time-bound basis—say every 10 years—must be undertaken and remedial measures sought and implemented. We do not need crisis situations to occur and must improve and streamline our structures. As regards the overall military intelligence structure, we need an in-house inter-services, MoD-driven commission to look into the complete system.

Conclusion

As India strives to take its rightful seat on the global high table, it will have to strengthen its overall intelligence edifice in which *defence intelligence* will have a significant role to play in contributing to the nation's security as its first line of defence. Accordingly, our leadership must provide the necessary primacy, direction and support for the defence intelligence organisation to fulfil national objectives. The significance of intelligence in enhancing the nation's comprehensive national power will always remain a national imperative.

ENDNOTES

1. Interview of Lt-Gen Kamal Davar by Josy Joseph, rediff.com, 15 April 2003.
2. *From Surprise to Reckoning: The Kargil Review Committee Report*, Sage Publications, New Delhi 2000.
3. Ibid.
4. ORF Paper: India's Enduring Challenges of Intelligence Reforms, ORF Issue Brief No. 428 by Vinayak Dalmia, Vindra Kapoor and Saikat Datta, December 2020, ORF, Delhi.

10

India's Military Vision: Mismatch with Reality?

Rajesh Isser

Introduction

An emerging India's comprehensive national power and threat analysis for the next quarter of a century will decide its place in the world. Military capabilities to mitigate threats and project capabilities to protect its interests would be the key. This requires hard assessments of lessons from recent history, present status, and trends and scenarios of the future. Technology will continue to drive military transformation, as, for a resource-constrained nation, it is imperative that individual agencies and services' visions and capability wish lists be converted into an optimised clear path with clear timelines on progress. This paper examines this issue albeit with selective cases.

Uncertainty and Complexity

If there was any doubt on an emerging India's rising clout and sovereign dispensation that has been completely dispelled during the Ukraine crisis. Juggling our best interests with competing super powers, yet earning the praise of lesser ones, India has been able to generate confidence and goodwill; her performance and magnanimity in handling the COVID-19 pandemic is one specific example. A robust foundation of national security is mandatory for India to sustain that rise.

On the issue of national security, Kanwal Sibal puts it very succinctly, "*Today, there is much greater focus on national security in policy making. Defence sector reforms, emphasis on creating indigenous manufacturing capacity in defence manufacturing, involving the private sector to achieve that objective, boosting defence exports to solidify partnerships with key countries, rapid improvement in military infrastructure in border areas are all part of this new outlook.*"[1]

'All plans go awry on the first shot' is an old military adage and probably the only one that has withstood pressures to change like everything else has. This is just acknowledging that the only thing certain in a conflict is 'uncertainty'. While newer terms are being framed around it, the sheer power to adapt quickly is the most important quality in leaders to mitigate uncertainty and complexity. That is also applicable to the importance and usefulness of doctrines and principles of war in a real battle. These can never be rigidly stuck to, and only provide a framework when deliberating on a next course of action. In fact, with the rapid change in the character of combat, many of these principles could contradict each other, 'massing of forces' for example. Blind adherence to any principle is foolhardy. However, the framework they provide, especially in relativity with each other, can provide for deeper intellectual investigation and better understanding of the conduct of war.

Problem Statement

Will India's military vision and thrust on self-reliance be able to close the gap between development of capabilities and emergence of requirements in the next decade? This paper attempts to explore the issue by first examining some factors that are changing the character of joint war-fighting, followed by a case-study to deliberate on of some aspects of the Indian Air Force's (IAF) vision, and finally, highlighting some challenges in an attempt to initiate discussion on the problem statement. Overall, there is focus on aerospace, but similar issues need to be examined in all other domains.

Changing Character and Trends of War

Technology at Play

Civilian technologies in cyber, information, and space fields present strategic options to a nation competing against an adversary. Mining data and advanced analytics is one such field where the defence sector can learn by establishing ecosystems wherein the military, academia, and industry can develop innovative options. While emerging and breakthrough technologies are truly revolutionary in their effects on the military, more important are the slower experimenting and trial-by-error efforts that take time and suffer failures. The useful convergence of technology and tactics is normally guided firmly by the military without curbing the creativity of scientists.

It is commonly understood that "each age has its own wars and its own forms of warfare."[2] Some analysts even predict that "significant ongoing changes in the security environment will alter the character of warfare beyond recognition."[3] Most breakthroughs in war-fighting have come about due to convergence of varied fields that have transformed tactics and operational approaches to conflict. Some have even predicted a change in the nature of nature which had been heretofore considered a heresy. "The era of disruptive technologies, with potential to change both the nature and character of war, is swiftly approaching."[4] It is highly probable that the emerging technologies of the Fourth Industrial Revolution such as artificial intelligence and robotics, quantum computing, additive manufacturing, neuro- and bio-technologies, new materials, and energy technologies, among others, would reshape the ways of conflict.[5] More significantly, a convergence of areas such as drones, the dark web, malware, synthetic biology, and 3D printing, which are more and more accessible, could allow non-state or proxy belligerents to create havoc.[6]

Fighting and Surviving in the Networked Age

An entirely new generation of network-enabled weapons, possessing both precision and potency, and aided by real-time intelligence by pervasive sensors and high-speed analytics, is fast changing the nature of warfare. Most of the damage, both material and psychological, will happen before contact by troops. Importantly, all such weapons will have sensors and networking to enable real-time battle damage assessment, a vital issue in combat. The entire gamut of sensing, planning, deciding, and acting will necessarily need coordination across all five domains. However, the sixth domain—the people-will need to be indoctrinated in this newer way of networked war fighting to achieve results on the ground.

Information dominance will entail a myriad of issues such as the ability to protect your data and networks, high-speed processing, and dissemination capability in an uninterrupted manner, and denying them to the adversary. Multi-domain synergised operations would demand shared battle space awareness among men, autonomous machines, and commanders of different sub-units. In such a networked high-pace battle, decision-making and allocation of targets/tasks will have to be quick, keeping a battle space whole-picture framework. Only artificial intelligence (AI)-enabled decision-making can do this for sustained long-term operations.

On the other hand, the above also point to the vulnerability and susceptibility of networked weapons, in particular to cyber or electro-magnetic attacks, which could be in the form of jamming or a lethal attack, data corruption from a cyber-attack, or slowing down of network which affects guidance, navigation, and control of weapons in flight. It will also need a secure network incorporating encryption, redundant paths and nodes, and high reliability. Since accurate and secure navigation data will be the foundation of autonomous platforms and loitering or network-enabled weapons, security in the space domain including satellites and data flow, is critical. So are the issues of bandwidth usage that need solutions for data prioritisation and sharing protocols, all being done at high speeds. Everything points to the imperative for a newer model of joint-targeting, and points of decision-making at different levels that caters to optimisation, timing and desired effects.

Lessons from Recent Conflicts

If anything, the Russo-Ukraine war has only reiterated the complexity and uncertainty of modern conflict. Assumptions such as short-swift conflicts, non-vulnerability of supply lines and optimal stockpiling armaments, and just-in-time maintenance concepts are being severely questioned. Campaign coherence and sustainability are two major concerns affecting all actors irrespective of the colour of their uniforms. The Indian Air Chief recently remarked on the "need to reassess the IAF's strategic priorities" and realign actions to ensure that the service does not get left behind. Quite pointedly, he asserted that while a well-crafted strategy may not guarantee success, absence of a coherent and sustainable strategy will surely lead to failure.[7]

Hybrid and whole-of-nation nature of conflict that allows weaponising of all leverages available, including economic, cyber-infrastructure and technology, is changing the very foundations of norms and rules underpinning the international order and competition. One thing standing out is the criticality of dependencies which can severely affect sovereign decision-making; and therein is the importance of self-reliance and having national force structures and capabilities based on inherent strengths.

Take for example the realm of space, so intrinsic to networked warfare. To deter an adversary offensively taking on own space assets, a nation must have a variety of capabilities and actions in hand. It must understand the motivation and risk-taking propensity of the adversary to promise severe consequences along with a built-in resilience to make an attack not worth the effort. Therefore, capacity to retaliate lethally against enemy space elements and redundancy in own satellite surveillance assets will form a core of the deterrence.

Some view emerging technologies in the fields of network, artificial intelligence, and space as shifting the balance back to defence.[8] However, there is always a danger of 'techno-romanticism', i.e., relying on technology to provide all solutions and breakthrough innovations. The see-saw of defence-offence dominance has been part of military history, and there is no reason for it not to continue.

Joint War Fighting

The US Air Force's operational-level doctrine on 'agile combat employment' is a way to mitigate China's technological advancements in intelligence, surveillance and reconnaissance, and all-domain long-range fire-enabled anti-access and area-denial or A2AD. The counter demands a reduced, dispersed, and fast changing airpower deployment with full protection by all available jointly-owned assets. Ideally, it aims to complicate the Chinese targeting process, pose political and operational dilemmas, and creates flexibility for friendly forces. This demands very effective integration of all legacy and modern weapon sensors and shooters available, and sensible employment to avoid wastage and shortages. With a preponderance of ground-based deep strike weapons in the future, this 'coordination of fires' would become more complex. There are lessons for the Indian military here.

Space is not only a 'final frontier' but an imperative to defend India and protect its interests abroad. The Government of India is already in an expedited process of energising and revamping this domain—expanding and building on the Indian Space Research Organisation's (ISRO) success so far. The Indian military would look at a comprehensive model such as the US global information grid (GIG) which along with the transformational satellite communications system (TSAT) allows for protected satellite communications and links satellites in geo-stationary orbit (GEO) with smaller satellites in low earth orbit (LEO), all connected to terrestrial nodes. This allows a hybrid mix of switching technologies (radio frequency (RF) circuit, optical circuit and packet switching), and supports far more interfaces and a wider range of military missions than the previous templates.

Multi-domain operations essentially orchestrate and synchronise military with non-military activities across all domains to deliver unexpected converging effects. NATO now talks of joint all-domain operations (JADO), growing out of its current multi-domain operations. It shifts the focus from 'multi-domain', in which individual services tend to operate, to back on joint operations. Another concept by the USA's defence advanced research projects agency or DARPA is of 'mosaic warfare' which takes advantage of secure high-bandwidth networking to obtain an interconnected and interoperable force package, using the best of different platforms.[9]

Transparency on the battlefield is adding to the headaches of attacking forces. With deep-strike precision available, massed forces or strung-out supply lines are easy targets with disproportionate damaging effects on the battle scheme. A good example was in the 2020 Nagorno-Karabakh conflict. Though Armenian-backed Artsakh forces occupied the high ground and were well dug-in and camouflaged, arrays of Azerbaijani sensors detected those forces and allowed them to be quickly destroyed with loitering munitions, drones, and precision fire.

Military Adaptation to Emerging Technologies

Unmanned and Autonomous Warfare

"One hundred years ago, Douhet and Mitchell predicted that aerial warfare would erase the distinction between civilians and combatants entirely. They continue to be right as drone warfare expands in the twenty-first century."[10] According to the Chief of the Royal Air Force, UK, "Air forces of the future will no longer be able to rely on traditional platforms alone". The British define a sixth-generation platform as an 'optionally manned' one, aiming to blend the best of human-flyable technology with whatever the next decade offers. In one example, the Boeing Company has invested heavily in its Loyal Wingman and MQ-25 Stingray drones. The former is an unmanned vehicle, demonstrating how future fighter pilots could use technology to command one or more robot wingmen. The MQ-25 is intended to be a refuelling tanker, enhancing ranges and radii of action of all platforms. In another example, the Russian S-70 Okhotnik drone, powered by an AL-31 turbojet engine, will fly at 1,000 km per hour with a range of 6,000 km. Equipped with electro-optical targeting, radio, and other types of reconnaissance equipment, its two internal bays will carry up to 2.8 tons of weapons including air-to-air missiles and unguided bombs. Trials are on to operate in collaboration with the Su-57 aircraft, which will extend the latter's radar field and strike capabilities.

Emerging capabilities of loitering munitions have lapped up the Ukraine war as a proving ground. Suddenly, the tank, a symbol of mobility and lethality in manoeuvre warfare, finds itself in a supporting, secondary role. No-contact engagements through missiles are playing a dominant role. However, these are initial days and successes; further advances and counters from better equipped and discerning air defence systems in the future are expected.

The 'IAF Vision 2020' (presented in 2000) recommended 55 fighter squadrons, including 16 multi-role, 18 strike, 16 air defence and a few reconnaissance and electronic warfare squadrons. However, the government of the day approved 42-45 squadrons, to be raised by the end of the 13th Plan period ending 2027. The important question is whether 45 squadrons will meet the requirements of a worst-case scenario, i.e., a two-front war. More importantly for a developing nation like India, are there other less expensive and optimal ways to mitigate this kind of threat? The answer may lie in honestly examining the assumptions and frameworks of our earlier assessments as well as taking into account factors such as the emergence of technological development and the changing character of warfare, among others.

A tussle between manned fighter aircraft on one side and AI-enabled capabilities such as unmanned combat platforms and surface-to-surface long-range precision missiles on the other is at hand. Keeping in mind longer times of actualisation after decisions over force acquisitions are taken, the deliberations had to be done yesterday! And this is talking of only a sub-part of one domain. In an age of multi-domain warfare, decision-making at the government level gets even more confounded. To add to all this is the vulnerability conundrum of the space and cyber domains that enable the conduct of networked warfare. The first shots fired, as well as hostile acts even before the formal commencement of conflict, will be in such domains that are mostly non-attributable or will at least take time to identify and prove the perpetrator(s).

Unmanned combat autonomous vehicles or UCAVs score over manned options in high-risk missions that have suddenly become very do-able. It is not only cheaper in human and monetary terms but also a game-changing menu of strategic and tactical options. When employed as intelligent swarms they are able to beat most current air defence systems either by overload or hard kill. Combining manned UCAVs and loitering weapons pose even greater dilemmas for an adversary. Undoubtedly, in the coming decade, force structures will veer less towards manned options.

Aerospace Plans

The IAF's 'centre of excellence for artificial intelligence' under the aegis of the 'unit for digitisation, automation, artificial intelligence and application networking' or UDAAN was set up in July 2022. A big-data analytics and AI platform, it aims to handle all aspects of analytics, machine learning, natural language processes, neural networks, and deep learning algorithms. The high-end computing relies on the latest servers powered with graphical processing units.

The next generation combat jets will be highly software-centric, and combat engagements would involve processing of data for target detection, tracking, and combat operations. For example, fifth-generation F-22s and F-35s of the USAF have target engagement activities that are heavily software generated (up to 95 per cent). Algorithms fly the planes, and provide optimum solutions after processing high-speed data from multi-sensors and sub-systems. Importantly, the 'multi-platform multi-sensor data fusion' (MPMSDF) system creates real-time awareness to integrate the entire battle space. This is the essence of AI-based decision support systems (DSS) that is an imperative in such complex environments. Notably, the Defence Research and Development Organization (DRDO) has initiated the development of such frameworks that are conversant with the algorithms like 'multi-criteria decision-making' (MCDM), swarm-and-search algorithms, game theoretic approaches, etc., to improve and optimise resource allocation.

AI will be crucial for the advanced medium combat aircraft (AMCA) program, which is being designed and developed as a fifth-generation medium-weight fighter aircraft. The level of autonomous functionality is planned on sixth-generation technologies, e.g., the 'smart wingman' concept and optionally manned/unmanned combat platforms. India's ambitious unmanned projects—Rustom–II unmanned aerial vehicle (UAV) and Ghatak—are in the development phase. Such intelligent unmanned systems are based on computer vision processing and artificial intelligence. 'Ghatak' is a stealth unmanned combat aerial vehicle (UCAV) initiated under the autonomous unmanned research aircraft program, AURA. AI-enabled systems will be critical in the development of target detection and use of lethal autonomous weapon systems.

Case-Study: The IAF Vision

IAF Vision 2040: Wish-list or Imperative? Some issues are now highlighted that seem to be part of the IAF's stated vision. These have been gleaned mainly from Air Chiefs' speeches over the last few years, as well as stated policy pointers in the open source domain. Accordingly, the challenges that the IAF may face are discussed in the following part of this paper.

Force Structure. According to a leading international strategic expert, "Despite being a world-class combat arm, the IAF's falling end-strength and problematic force structure, combined with its troubled acquisition and development programs, threaten India's air superiority over its rapidly modernizing rivals, China and Pakistan. India's air dominance is vital for deterrence stability in southern Asia and for preserving the strategic balance in the wider Indo-Pacific region. Resolving India's airpower crisis, therefore, should be a priority for New Delhi."[11] As the resources of the IAF depleted, a former Chief of Air Staff (CAS) had warned that "our numbers are not adequate to fully execute an air campaign in a two-front scenario. The probability of a two-front scenario is an appreciation which you need to do. However, are the numbers adequate? No! The squadrons are winding down."[12] Indeed, to ensure 'punitive response' capability against the western threat and 'credible deterrence' against the northern threat, IAF force structures require major transformation and a focused effort to that purpose.

Fighters. While highlighting the challenges faced by the IAF in fulfilling its mandates, Shushant Singh states, "The IAF would be challenged to fulfil its mandate, as it currently holds no numerical advantage over Pakistan. It has only 30 squadrons of fighter aircraft while it requires at least 50 combat squadrons—if not 60—for a possible two-front war."[13] Hence, the IAF needs to quickly achieve authorised strength, and thereafter re-assess capability requirements in terms of strength and type—bomber, fighter, fighter-bomber, stealth, and unmanned—to effectively counter the possibility of collusion. It should seek to accelerate design, development, and flight testing of the AMCA and its integration with indigenous weapons. Realization of the multi-role fighter aircraft (MRFA) project and upgrading the fleet of Su 30 MKI and first versions of the light combat aircraft (LCA) becomes an additional necessity. Some foreign strategic experts have opined that the IAF should be prudent about investment in Tejas and consider expansion of the MMRCA component, while also stating that "India should also reassess the decision to develop the AMCA indigenously and avoid weakening the collaboration with Russia on the PAK-FA/SU 57 program."[14]

Weapons. A credible and indigenous kinetic and non-kinetic weapon capability is a must to address various types of hostile target systems as well as ensure proportionate response to any security situation. Twin focus on achieving first-shot capability in air-to-air and long-range stand-off precision capability would ensure a firepower edge over adversaries. To achieve this in the requisite timeframe, Indian policy makers need to be realistic about their domestic capacity to produce sophisticated combat capability and diversify investments in advanced munitions to provide for the best of capabilities.[15] The proliferation of drones, i.e., small unmanned and remotely or autonomously operated aircraft, has thrown up a new challenge. This challenge exists on the cusp of air and ground defence and needs a focused response with customized capability and equipment. The IAF needs to be in the vanguard of development of national counter-drone capability, driving the policy, ensuring standards, and possibly even networking.

Battlefield Transparency. Effective command and control or C2 and decision making depends on seamless coverage of all domains of the battlefield and situational awareness represented in actionable form. Secure and redundant communication, fully integrated data link, versatile and fused intelligence, surveillance, and reconnaissance (ISR) capability including that from satellites are necessary ingredients of battlefield transparency that must be developed. Better battlefield transparency would decide the outcome of future wars that would have no clear delineation of domains. Discussing the future of warfare, Lt-Gen Panag has stated that "Future warfare will be all about airpower, missile power, cyber warfare, and electronic warfare. The application of force in the future will be for a short duration, with a very specific aim and with high-end military technology."[16]

Combat Enablers. Airborne sensors in adequate quantity and quality are essential to enable seamless battlefield transparency and C2, especially in sub-continental conditions and amidst topographical challenges. Across the military academia, the IAF's AWACS and its aerial refuelling aircraft are considered extremely inadequate to conduct air operations effectively on a sustained basis around the Indian subcontinent.[17] Airborne warning and control systems (AWACS) in good numbers—we are already much behind both the adversaries—and flight refueller aircraft (FRA) must be purchased till such time indigenous projects fructify. Also, acquiring credible, swift, and adequate strategic and tactical lift capability would be necessary to enable successful performance of combat tasks in all domains.

Electronic Warfare and Next-Gen Technology. While emphasizing the importance of niche technology in airpower, an IAF chief has stated "Looking at the northern neighbour, we have to have niche technologies which must be built in-house by our own industry for reasons of security."[18] He added that "There are areas of indigenous industry where very good progress has taken place. The most critical is our effort towards research and development and how much we will devote there. The major advantage of doing indigenous development is very important. This is an area that needs focus straight away."[19] Towards that, we need to focus on dedicated airborne and ground-based electronic warfare (EW) and communications jamming (COMJAM) capability. All combat and combat-enabling aircraft must have indigenous EW suits. In unmanned systems, the IAF operates extremely small number of UAVs and armed drones and that too in limited roles."[20] This capability must be expanded with indigenous production of all class of UAS, e.g., medium altitude long endurance (MALE), high altitude long endurance (HALE), unmanned combat aerial vehicles (UCAV), armed UAVs, Stealth UAV/UCAV, swarm drones, with their integration into the operational philosophy. The quick realization of AI in all combat and non-combat roles like the manned unmanned teaming (MUM-T) concept is an important milestone of future vision. The IAF must also make the transition to seamless net-centric operations through the incorporation of hardened networks and adequate redundancy, both on the ground and in the air through operational data links. This also implies a high level of expertise in, and requisite infrastructure for, dealing with the ever evolving threats in the cyber domain.

Aerospace Defence. On reports about the use of hypersonic weapons in the Ukraine war, the IAF has stated that it was also planning to have them in its arsenal.[21] It was further amplified that "Due to very high speeds, hypersonic missiles are difficult to intercept, making existing air defence systems redundant.

The Air Force is actively involved in research and development for such weapons as well as counter-measures."[22] Accordingly, the IAF must adopt measures to achieve active defence against hypersonic and ballistic missiles, UCAVs, long-range rockets and drones through indigenous means. It should indigenise and integrate all types of surface-to-air missile (SAM) systems as well as the sensors in its integrated air defence setup. With the growing military use of space, there is a requirement for the IAF to enhance its in-house expertise and knowledge levels in this domain. There is a need to acquire the requisite capability to counter threats 'from' and 'in' space. Furthermore, as new generation threats emerge that transit seamlessly from space to air and vice versa, there is a need to develop and operationalise a comprehensive concept of aerospace defence.

Conceptual Development. We must establish robust joint structures to enable rightsizing joint training and operations while maintaining service-specific core competencies.[23] While highlighting the need for a concerted joint approach to war-fighting, the IAF has emphasized on in-depth reference to service-specific doctrines and well-trained manpower to evolve employment philosophy and concepts.[24] While elaborating on this aspect further, it is stated that this task will require joint planning and joint execution of plans. "No single service can win a war on its own and this holds true for the future. The primacy of as to who will do what cannot be determined by pro-rata systems based on who has a larger mass of forces and equipment.[25] This thought process must change, and it will be important to appreciate the capability of each service to make 2+2=5, and that there is a need for us to develop joint command and control structures for integrated and synergized application of combat power."[26] Thus, the conceptual development should follow a measured approach from 'jointness' to 'integration', while incorporating future technology and force structure in the military decision making process (MDMP) and operational philosophy.

Force Development

Atmanirbharta. As per the IAF chief, "A focused action plan needs to be developed for indigenization of all critical components in order to achieve the nation's mandate of *Atmanirbharata* (self-reliance)".[27] Towards a holistic Atmanirbhar approach, we must prevent strategic vulnerabilities by building self-reliance and reduce dependence on foreign support by creating an end-to-end seamless development, production, and maintenance support. The focus has to be on material specifications and indigenization of all rotables and spares. The national level self-reliance in state-of-the-art military technology is possible by progressively expanding from mere co-production of advanced foreign weapons in India to development, manufacturing, and integration of entirely indigenous systems in the service.[28] The long-term vision should be to develop the concept of a 'military industrial complex' with a concerted shift from 'threat based and demanded' to 'capability demanded' force requirements.[29] This will also reduce the gap between the 'capability demanded' and the 'capability supplied'.[30]

Operational Infrastructure and Logistics. The IAF must follow a theme of 'credible force preservation.' The focus should be on development of protected bases in adequate numbers, up-grade of existing infrastructure and equipment by expeditious construction of newer-type hardened shelters, underground storages and functional complexes, while ensuring protection measures against electro-magnetic pulse (EMP) attacks. There is an utmost requirement of expanding the scope, capability, and capacity of operational logistics. Towards that end, we also have to review our procurement strategies to reduce lead time for supplies and pre-empt problems of supply chain obsolescence. During contingencies, roads and railheads would be choked due to simultaneous movement of the Army along the same axes. Towards this, we need to formalise an integrated road-and-rail management plan and explore the feasibility of increased containerisation and the use of civilian wide-bodied aircraft.[31] Towards faster realization of this goal, a leading effort can be made to integrate into unified logistics interface (ULIP) as a part of Project GATI SHAKTI. Also, logistics doctrines should be evolved and complete digitization of logistics processes be achieved while ensuring last-mile connectivity, both virtual and physical. Moreover, a flexible stocking policy with modern forecasting techniques would be essential to shorten the demand-supply chain.[32]

Realistic Training. The entire training structure should be based on emerging security trends and the evolving role of aerospace power to be effective as an instrument of military response. This aspect is brought out by the IAF stating that "There has been a paradigm shift in security threats, and newer ways of pursuing strategic objectives are coming to life. These are also creating newer and unknown vulnerabilities. These challenging security dynamics will continue to pose tough choices and would require novel and innovative solutions."[33]

Post identification of the nature and type of operations envisaged by each platform, infrastructure (airspace, targets, full-scale electro-magnetic spectrum, and emerging non-kinetic trends in warfare) should be established. A right mix of "synthetic" and actual training models should be determined and functionalized, with the networking achieved to the best possible level. Accordingly, the unmanned systems and AI-based models in training should be quickly adopted.

Administration. Adequate and appropriate operations and administration infrastructure is the key to force protection against air and ground, conventional and sub-conventional threats. Thus, underground weapon storage areas, hardened shelters, underground hangars and C2 centres, rapid runway rehabilitation capability, and an integrated multi-layered security system are needed. Bases also need to be future ready and in synchronisation with the highest standards of productivity and sustainability. Internal processes need to be revamped to be more operations oriented. The IAF's legal, accounting and medical services need to be developed as responsive, technology-ready, and efficient. They need to be able to provide desired services, and develop expertise to handle complex challenges on a global scale as can be expected when IAF operations expand in line with national aspirations, apart from improving every air warrior's quality of life.

Human Resource Development

Evolving Strategic Thought. There is a necessity of directed professional military education (PME) towards enhancing strategic thought in medium-level leadership and establishment of in-house think tanks for doctrinal evolution, strategy formulation, and strategic communication. Resonating with these aspects, the IAF, while commenting on the necessity of revitalising military education states that "Technology, training and education are vital dimensions of preparing a military officer for future war. In such a scenario, there is an evolving need to upgrade and fine-tune our education and training pattern. We need to make a roadmap for strengthening training programs and research, stimulating innovation, and supporting incubation of emerging technologies, which calls for bringing military, academia, and industry—the three critical pillars of national security—on a common platform."[34]

Talent Management. Resource rightsizing and re-structuring of existing resources is necessary to improve teeth–to-tail ratio and economy of effort. The theme should be, "Right Person, right equipment, and right weapon for the job".[35] With technology in focus, the IAF must maximise skill, follow an approach of "Being an Expert and Master", and diversify the skill development program in accordance with the needs of the future—in other words, an adaptive skill development program that is open to newer demands and ideas. Along with this is a need for a 'retention of talent' program. Airpower being technology sensitive, retention of qualified manpower that is fully conversant and adaptive to the modern trends of warfare is an inescapable necessity. In view of the growing and lucrative avenues outside, there is a requirement to examine career progression profiles and methodology to accommodate individual aspirations and foster motivation to continue in the service.

Challenges and Mismatches

Indian Self-Reliance in Defence in the Decades Ahead: A Visionary Move or a Trap?

The Government of India through its Ministry of Defence (MoD) is laying considerable stress on defence indigenisation, domestic procurement, and defence exports. The Government's Aatmanirbhar Bharat Abhiyan (ABA) aims to unlock the potential of domestic industry and manufacturers to meet the country's growing requirements in the future. Some indicators bode well, e.g., the 2021–22 defence budget earmarks Rs. 1,000 crore for procurement from start-ups; budgetary support of Rs. 500 crore has been kept for iDEX (Defence Innovation Organisation) till 2025–26 for start-ups, micro, small and medium enterprises (MSME) and individual investors. More than 80 start-ups are currently developing 30 cutting-edge products. The MoD has reserved 25 per cent of its research and development (R&D) budget for industry and start-ups indicating a preference for a industry-led design and develop model.

The strategic partnership model with global original equipment manufacturers (OEMs) is an effort to energise the domestic defence industrial ecosystem. The Government had introduced a separate domestic capital expenditure of Rs. 51,930 crore in 2020–21, which increased in 2021–22 to Rs. 71,438 crore (63.6%). A 'positive' list of indigenisation has grown to 209 items. The contract for 83 light combat aircraft (LCA), worth over Rs. 48,000 crore is the biggest domestic procurement contract ever with 500 MSMEs involved in executing it.

In a resource-constrained nation, careful thought, balancing and juggling of competing demands, hedging on bets, among others are common headaches of highest leadership of national security. However, clear directions of timelines and capabilities are needed to be laid out by the political leadership. This will help temper down the wish-lists, and also clear and enable vision among all players in order to fight jointly in multi-domain engagements. The Government has already shown this inclination in moves such as increasing spending on R&D, motivating the private sector to take up flagship technology development projects, building a competitive R&D ecosystem and focusing on emerging technologies.[36]

While India is establishing a strong aviation ecosystem by bringing together all stakeholders, private industry will be the real crusaders in defence production, particularly in the UAV vertical. This will have a major link with the economy. In future, the perspective of private industries will influence and add value to government policies. However, like the proverbial 'slip' there could be serious gaps and mismatches in considering the kind of threats or opportunities India may have to face in the next decade and the corresponding grand plan. It is important to examine if this could be a critical issue for India. The main hypothesis to be tested would be that *'the self-reliance thrust may not be able to close the gap between developing capabilities and emergent requirements in the next decade.'*

The first would be an assessment of threats, vulnerabilities, and worst-case scenarios in the decade ahead. This should consider among other issues, the multi-polar trends, increased protectionism in trade and multi-engagements among major players as well as the regions. Future scenarios such as of that a two-front threat alongside a laggard progress on indigenisation could be noted.

Second, after a brief examination of historical factors that have plagued our indigenisation, the focus should move to the impetus given since 2014—the *Atmanirbhar* campaign. This vision should be examined for flexibility and adaptability in an environment where economic prioritisation would be a difficult balancing act. The background is an imperative for self-reliance in defence not only that dictated by economic pressures but also by unpredictable geopolitical trends and events such as the current Ukraine crisis.

Finally, an honest and realistic examination of progress in the *Atmanirbhar* campaign would allow the main hypothesis to be examined with focus on the aerospace sector and defence corridors. This sector is critical to developing asymmetries against China which currently has an edge over India in budgets and technology.

Hybrid: Anything New?

Hybrid warfare is the current buzzword in conflict-analysis circles. However, it has practically always existed from the time humans started quarrelling. Chanakya used it famously in his works as a strategy of '*saam, daam, dand, bhed.*' Qiao Liang and Wang Xiangsui in their acclaimed work, *Unrestricted Warfare,* defined future conflict as an 'extended domain', not necessarily where lethality took precedence, but where paralysis of the decision makers and the will of the people were the primary targets.[37] Well before the purported Russian doctrine by Gen. Gerasimov, the USA and the Western powers had been using every means available to undermine challenges to their hegemony worldwide. It begs the question, '*Do you plan to fight with the capabilities you have or do you plan capabilities to fit the fights ahead?*'

In India's case, the threats, currently and for the next two decades, are geographically clear to be coming from China and Pakistan, and even more so, with their collusion. At the same time, there would be requirements to project limited capabilities out-of-country, especially around the Indian Ocean Region (IOR). In terms of aviation capabilities, the acquisition of C-130J Super Hercules, C-17 Globemasters, Apache, and Chinooks helicopters—both air transportable—provide ample quick-reaction ability across the IOR. Long-range and potent fighters such as the Rafale aircraft, along with force multipliers like air-to-air refuellers and airborne early warning systems, give a sting capability across the IOR. With air-launched, long-range precision weapons like the Brahmos missiles, the Indian peninsula becomes a virtual unsinkable aircraft carrier in the IOR.

Threat Assessment and Theatre Commands

Threat Manifestation. As brought out in a recent article on the formation of the first 'Theatre Command' by Dwight D. Eisenhower's Allied Force Headquarters (AFHQ) in 1942, the step was driven by dovetailing integrated support to a large campaign. However, it was largely a meshing of existing plans, command structures, and allocation of responsibilities among other assets that allowed it to succeed in the Atlantic theatre.[38] In the Indian scene, manifestations of threat from the two prime adversaries will range across all domains, especially in the gray-zone below the red-line thresholds. In such a continuum of threats of hybrid warfare, would the simple military theatre commands suffice? Can they plug into a whole-of-nation effort to counter to such persistent threats? Would we need to reconceptualise the all-encompassing domains and actors without limiting them to those 'under command'? Is it possible to have fluid models of task-allocation, responsibilities and accountability as we have sometimes seen in mammoth humanitarian and disaster responses by our armed forces in the form of task-forces?

Formal Promulgation of Strategy. Another issue is the demand for a national security strategy (NSS) document. It is almost assumed by its proponents that this would be a panacea to overcome uncertainty and give direction to capabilities to focus on. However, in the current calculus of gray-zone competition and tool-kits such as covert cyber-attacks on infrastructure and proxy-enabled strife, it is a moot point whether such a definitive document can serve any real purpose. Except for long-term strategic signalling on geo-political or economic issues, which are debatable under such uncertainties, it may be wiser to be ambiguous and keep the adversaries guessing. Even in a war-like campaign, any strategy and plans would need adequate adaptability, as has been witnessed by Russia in Ukraine.

Air Defence. The incumbent CAS's recent articulation in a seminar on issues related to an air defence command, which caused quite a flutter, was incisive and persuasive. Airspace or aerospace is an indivisible entity, without demarcated borders or theatres for all sides in a conflict. This all-pervasive character presents opportunities to calibrate and control coherent battle execution over land and sea. Importantly, ownership or control of this is dynamic in time and space unlike over land or the sea. Also, dominance over this airspace is fleeting and nearly impossible to be achieved sustainably, even by powers with the latest and largest air arsenals. Therefore, there are limits to exploitation of airspace in a sustained manner. Technological means at the disposal on both sides and its innovative employment adds unpredictable dimensions to the air battle which can swing either way, either in offensive or defensive engagements. These two engagements are inseparable and often cannot be differentiated in the fog of war. Synergy between the offensive and defensive assets, strategies, tactics and orchestrating them for the best possible outcome is key to airspace battles, and that will substantially influence any surface battles. There can be no stand-alone air defence operations either on land and/or sea and/or in the air. An integrated air defence across the battle space or the theatre is the only answer. Any deviation could undermine the unique and intrinsic strengths of airpower such as flexibility, reach, surprise, and firepower, besides precision and the shock effect.

Surface-Based Deep Strike. Many Indian analysts and think-tanks have been advocating for a long time for an independent rocket force. In the light of recent conflicts and China's capabilities, it is an imperative to have a highly mobile, protected, and fully Integrated rocket force (IRF). This will allow quicker responses and strategic strike opportunities against enemy centres of gravity such as command and control posts, air defence sensors and sites, force concentrations, staging areas and logistics nodes which are relatively hard to intercept with ground-launched vectors.

Conclusion

This paper has attempted to initiate a discussion on whether India's military vision is realistic while highlighting certain challenges facing this proposition. That is a vast canvas to cover; however, the attempt has been to deliberate over the major trends in warfare; technological imperatives; lessons from recent conflicts indicating rapid changes in the character of war; the IAF's vision on selective issues; and some mismatches and glitches that prosecution of joint-fighting may have to contend with.

As a case-study and looked at in isolation, the IAF's discerned vision is quite logical, forward-looking and holistic. However, in the all-domain no-holds-barred threat environment, there are similar wish-lists among not only the other two services but also every other agency involved in the nation's defence. As professed by each service headquarters, a synergised version that multiplies rather than just adds capabilities needs to be agreed upon.

In an environment of complexity and uncertainty of the gray-zone and non-contact vectors, a vision for all agencies in a multi-domain integrated battle is imperative. Such visions have to be tempered at the highest levels to fit a whole-of-nation approach to conflicts and competitions. Additionally, with clearly defined geographical adversaries and our capacity building for long-term security, it is a must to evaluate both the defined threats and the capabilities. More importantly, our political leadership must be decisive and clear in intent so that all the stakeholders are fully on board with due compromises made over their wish-lists. At the same time, in the planning and conduct of modern wars, adaptability to fast-learning curves in war and peace must be seen as a real strength.

ENDNOTES

1. Kanwal Sibal. India@75: Focus on China, G20, I2U2, How Our Foreign Policy Has Evolved Post Independence. www.firstpost.com accessed on 20 August 2022.
2. Hans-Georg, Ehrhart, "Postmodern Warfare and the Blurred Boundaries between War and Peace", *Defence & Security Analysis* 33, no. 3 (2017): 263. Accessed at www.oclc.org on 20August 2022.
3. Jeffrey J. Becker and John E. DeFoor, "Exploring the Future Operating Environment", *Joint Force Quarterly: JFQ* no. 89 (Second, 2018): 121.
4. F.G. Hoffman, "Will War's Nature Change in the Seventh Military Revolution?" *Parameters* 47, no. 4 (2017): 20.
5. Klaus Schwab and Nicholas Davis, *Shaping the Future of the Fourth Industrial Revolution* (New York: Currency, 2018), 6-11.
6. Gregory D. Koblentz, "Emerging Technologies and the Future of CBRN Terrorism", *The Washington Quarterly* 43, no. 2 (2020), 178-183.
7. Suchet Vir Singh. *The Print*, 24 June 2022. https://theprint.in/defence/coercion-is-new-strategy-iaf-chief-chaudhuri-flags-cyber-space-domains-as-new-battlefields/1010586/
8. David Johnson. Ending the Ideology of the Offense, Part-I. 15 August 2022. warontherocks.com
9. https://othjournal.com/2018/09/17/defining-the-domain-in-multi-domain/
10. Remote Warfare: New Cultures of Violence. (ed.) Rebecca A. Adelman and David Kieran. Minneapolis, MN: University of Minnesota Press, 2020.
11. https://carnegieendowment.org/2016/03/28/troubles-they-come-in-battalions-manifold-travails-of-indian-air-force-pub-63123 published 28 March 2016, accessed on 14 August 2022.
12. Express News Service, "IAF: Don't Have the Numbers to Fully Fight a Two-Front War," *The Indian Express*, 11 March 2016; cited in "The Challenge of a Two-Front War - India's China-Pakistan Dilemma" by Sushant Singh, Stimson Centre, Asia Issue Brief, April 2021, pg. 2.
13. Ibid, pg. 9.
14. https://carnegieendowment.org/2016/03/28/troubles-they-come-in-battalions-manifold-travails-of-indian-air-force-pub-63123 published 28 March 2016, accessed on 14 August 2022.
15. https://carnegieendowment.org/2016/03/28/troubles-they-come-in-battalions-manifold-travails-of-indian-air-force-pub-63123 published 28 March 2016, accessed on 14 August 2022.
16. Political leaders are too involved in politics and not in their actual jobs: Lt–Gen. H. S. Panag-Edexlive, published 31 December 2021, accessed on 14 August 2022.
17. Ashley J. Tellis, *Troubles, They Come in Battalions: The Manifold Travails of the Indian Air Force*, 2016 Carnegie Endowment for International Peace, pg. 7.
18. Ibid, pg. 7.
19. IAF to procure 350 aircraft as part of 'Atmanirbhar Bharat' over next 2 decades | *India News* (republicworld.com), 8 September 2021, accessed on 14 August 2022.
20. Ashley J. Tellis, *Troubles, They Come in Battalions: The Manifold Travails Of The Indian Air Force*, 2016, Carnegie Endowment for International Peace, pg. 7.

21. *IAF chief says air force needs to prepare for intense, short duration ops | Latest News India - Hindustan Times*, 28 April 2022, accessed on 14 August 2022.
22. Ibid.
23. IAF Basic Doctrine, 2022.
24. 'No single service can win a war on its own': IAF chief seeks jointness, but with a caveat (theprint.in), 24 February 2022, *The Print*, accessed on 14 August 2022.
25. Ibid.
26. Ibid.
27. Need to prepare for intense, small duration operations: IAF Chief, The *Economic Times* (indiatimes.com), 28 April 2022, accessed on 14 August 2022.
28. Ashley J. Tellis, *Troubles, They Come in Battalions: The Manifold Travails of the Indian Air Force*, 2016, Carnegie Endowment for International Peace, pp. 60-61.
29. IAF Basic Doctrine, 2022.
30. Ibid.
31. https://www.thehindu.com/news/national/need-to-prepare-for-short-swift-wars-says-iaf-chief/article65362561.ece 28 April 2022, *The Hindu* Bureau, accessed on 14 August 2022.
32. Ibid.
33. Need to upgrade education patterns in military: IAF chief - *The Hitavada*, 11 August 2022, accessed on 14 August 2022.
34. Ibid.
35. IAF Basic Doctrine, 2022.
36. Sameer Patil & Neeraj Singh Manhas. Accelerating the pace of India's defence research. www.orfindia.com accessed on 22 August 2022.
37. Liang, Q. & Xiangsui, W. *Unrestricted Warfare*. Beijing, CN: PLA Literature and Arts Publishing House Arts, 1999.
38. J. Bryan Mullins. Insights on Theatre Command and Control from the Creation of Allied Force Headquarters. JFQ 106, 3rd Quarter, 2022.

11

Towards a Comprehensive Security Architecture

Dhruv C. Katoch

Introduction

Every nation needs a capable military to protect both its sovereignty as well as its economic and other vital interests. A strong military is a deterrent to conflict, and only through the overall ambit of such protection can a nation peacefully pursue its development agenda. History bears testimony to the fact that great civilisations flourished when they had the protection of a strong army. When military power waned, the state withered away. The invasion of Sindh in 711 CE by Muhammad bin Qasim, an Arab military commander of the Umayyad Caliphate, is an apt example. After defeating Raja Dahir, the ruler of Sindh, Qasim established, for the first time, Muslim rule in a part of India. Other invasions followed over the course of the next thousand years, till the arrival of the British and other Western powers. We can never allow that to happen again.

From ancient times, military capability has been a sum total of well-trained and equipped soldiers with a sound organisational structure, good fighting doctrines, and possession of superior technological capability. The same holds true today. As an example, in ancient times, elephants were used to fulfil a variety of military functions. Generally, elephants were used for their routing ability, being able to get rid of enemy soldiers with one sweep, and also in scaring the enemy horse cavalry and for trampling chariots. The shock-and-awe effect was psychological, a function performed today by tanks and armoured personnel carriers, artillery, missiles and fighter aircraft. The advent of the cavalry provided mobility in the battlefield, which became a lethal weapon system when the riders were equipped with swords or mounted as archers. Battlefield communications was done by visual signalling, flags and runners, who carried messages during the battle. Fundamentally, the principles of war which were true for those days remain true today. It is the means of warfare which have changed, providing advantage to the side that is mobile, and has better battlefield transparency, precision long-range weapon systems, good and secure communications and well equipped and trained soldiers.

Technology and its adaptation have shaped the outcomes of wars since ancient times. However, it was only in the nineteenth century that gigantic leaps in technological developments started taking place. The machine gun invented by Hiram Maxim was used in the Boer and Spanish American wars. It became notorious for the deadly manner in which it was used by European powers in their pursuit of colonialism.[1] Used extensively in both the world wars, the machine gun is now a standard weapon in the armies of all nations. Likewise, the British invented the tank during World War I to provide troops with mobility, protection, and firepower. These were used for the first time in the Battle of Flers-Courcelette on 15 September 1916.[2] Since then, the tank has become a sophisticated and powerful tool of war. The first successful flying machine was invented in 1903 by the Wright Brothers. Today, its widespread use of both fixed and rotary wing aircraft to control airspace is vital for observation, reconnaissance, air-to-air combat and engaging ground and maritime targets. In recent times, the Gulf wars and the US war in Afghanistan has brought home to the world the power which long-range precision weapon systems bring to the battlefield. This, combined with advances made in communication technology, has given rise to what came to be known as the 'Revolution in Military Affairs'.

However, technology, though a major war-winning factor, cannot by itself win wars. The USA, despite its superiority, could not subdue the Taliban in Afghanistan. The Gulf wars too, have still not come to any final conclusion. When fighting battles far from one's shores, different geo-political and geo-strategic factors come into play. There is also a need for boots on the ground for successful mission accomplishment. A strong and capable armed force is hence a sum of multiple factors, including political will, speed of decision making, training, and morale of troops, organisational structures, war fighting doctrines, and exploitation of technology. All this must be supported by a strong domestic military industrial complex.

Securing National Interest

Broadly, the term 'national interest' (NI) refers to protecting and defending a nation's physical, political and cultural identity.[3] In specific terms, it means preserving one, territorial integrity of the state; two, the politico-economic structure; and three, the nation-states' cultural ethos and traditions. Post-World War I, US President Woodrow Wilson, while formulating US foreign policy, drew upon the work of scholars and philosophers like Sir Alfred Zimmer and Nicholas Murray Butler. The effort was essentially Utopian in concept and was dedicated to promoting a more peaceful world. American foreign policy took on a more realistic hue, post-World War II,

Post the Second World War, American foreign policy was driven by a sense of realism promoted by the work of authors such as Hans J. Morgenthau, Reinhold Niebuhr and others. Morgenthau was a German-American jurist and political scientist, considered one of the founding fathers of the realist school in the 20th century, who propagated the role of the nation state in international relations, viewing the same as primarily concerned with the study of power. Niebuhr was a theologian, whose work looked at "Christian Realism", laying stress on egoism and the pride and hypocrisy of nations and classes. In India, however, the political leadership formulated foreign policies sans an institutionalised doctrinal approach. Consequently, India's national security policy-making process was neither institutionalised, nor was the role of stakeholders incorporated and defined. India's foreign policy formulations remained personality-driven and highly individualistic.[4]

In 1995, Shri Jaswant Singh referred to the 'operational directive' as the document which brought out the threat assessment against India. This was formulated by the three services, the Ministry of External Affairs, the Home Ministry and the Prime Minister's Office, and finally approved by the Defence Minister.[5] Jaswant Singh stated that the document required considerable changes because of the enormous changes that had taken place in India since.[6] This statement by Shri Jaswant Singh, who has served as India's defence as well as external affairs minister, was telling and indicative. No surprise then that George Tanham came to the conclusion that India's political elites lacked the due strategic vision.[7] Tanham, however, had little understanding of India's civilisational ethos and history. It was ancient India's Sanskrit treatise on statecraft, Kautilya's *Arthashastra*, which spoke of political science, economic policy and military strategy—a veritable treatise on the science of governance.

Similar references are found in our ancient scriptures like the *Mahabharata* and the *Ramayana*, *Hitopadesa*, *Manu Smriti*, *Bhagavatam Purana* and others. Statecraft finds prominent mention in all of them. India had a strategic culture, which enabled it to be a leading nation in the world for millennia.[8] We need to get back to our roots and reclaim our heritage.

Much however has changed since 2014, when the National Democratic Alliance (NDA) government was swept to power with an overwhelming majority. The objectives of India's National Security were clearly defined to include one, national stability and integrity; two, social, political and economic progress; and three, global peace and stability. India's national security, as an essential component to securitise its national interests, must be seen in terms of these larger goals.[9] The government, as it assumed power in 2014, started the process to achieve all that. India's foreign policy is consequently seen to be more bold, proactive, innovative and ambitious; it is a policy that will not compromise on the nation's integrity and honour. The era of reticence is over. The era of proactive engagement has begun. We now see a greater engagement with India's Diaspora, renewed emphasis on building relations in the neighbourhood, cooperation in the field of counter-terrorism, renewed economic vigour and emphasis on physical and cultural connectivity.[10]

Countering Chinese Belligerence

The India-China relationship remains strained, the unresolved border issue being the major irritant. China refuses to recognise the legal status of the McMahon Line and, consequently, besides being in illegal occupation of the Aksai Chin plateau in Ladakh, lays claim over the Indian state of Arunachal Pradesh. Within Tibet, China has concentrated on upgrading infrastructure having a distinct military bias, thus enhancing its military capability, in the process posing an exponential military threat to India.

Chinese transgressions across the un-demarcated line of actual control (LAC) have been a constant feature for many decades. Presently, however, such transgressions are being responded to with an element of firmness which was absent earlier. For example, in 2017, when China's People's Liberation Army (PLA) transgressed into Doklam, a tri-junction between Bhutan, India and China, India responded with a matching response. The stand-off continued for 70 days, during which time the Chinese state-controlled media as well as the spokespersons of the Chinese Communist Party (CCP) resorted to issuing statements threatening India. India however refused to budge and the PLA personnel finally had to halt.[11] The clash in Galwan in June 2020 was the first incident which led to loss of lives on both sides. The face-off continues till date, with both India and China building-up their force levels in the area. Once again, China tried to intimidate India, but received a firm response, displaying the strength of India's political and military leadership.[12] For the first time, India also took over, her security considerations, certain economic measures against China, banning over 320 Chinese apps as well as adopting firm measures on diplomatic and other fronts.[13]

As a part of its overall effort to counter China across the Himalayas, a massive push has been given to infrastructure development both in Arunachal Pradesh and in Ladakh. Key infrastructure development projects include construction of roads, tunnels, bridges, and airfields. One of these projects is the strategically important 300-km long Nimmu-Padum-Darcha road between Himachal Pradesh and Ladakh. This is an all-weather road nearing completion and will provide all-year connectivity to Ladakh as also an alternate axis to the Leh-Manali highway.[14] On the Manali-Leh axis, the Rohtang Pass, lying on the eastern end of the Pir Panjal range, connects the Kulu Valley with the Lahaul and Spiti valleys. This remains closed for about four months in a year due to heavy snowfall in winter. Now, a nine-km long tunnel has been constructed under the Rohtang Pass, to provide year-long connectivity to the region. This tunnel, named the 'Atal Tunnel' was inaugurated on 3 October 2020.[15] Many such projects are coming up all across the border to provide strategic mobility to the military throughout the year. The Border Roads Organisation (BRO) which is responsible for these projects was allotted Rs. 3,500 crore for FY 2022-23—a record increase of 40 per cent over the Rs. 2,500 crore allowed in FY 2021-22. This is a reaffirmation of the government's resolve to focus on border development to enable speedy mobilisation of the armed forces to strategically important sectors, further bolstering own security environment.[16]

India's space capability will also play a major role in countering Chinese actions. In the event of hostilities breaking out with China, the key to victory for either side will lie in information dominance, battlefield transparency and air superiority. *Inter alia*, both sides will leverage space to get that edge. Space is thus the final frontier. Criticality for India will lie in monitoring, in real time, Chinese troop movements, build-up of artillery and logistic nodes, command and control centres, missile bases and aerial assets. That would require continuous satellite coverage over the Tibetan Plateau, for which India would need adequate satellites of her own or leverage information from satellites of friendly partner-countries. Towards that end, India's space capabilities are also being enhanced to take on any threat.

The Pakistan Factor

Pakistan has been hostile to India since Independence. Ideological and other differences have led to four India-Pakistan wars. Pakistan continues to support terrorist activity within India, using terrorism as an in instrument of its foreign policy. The interests of both Beijing and Islamabad converge when it comes to dealing with New Delhi, and for long, Beijing has been using Pakistan to contain India. Besides cross-border terrorism, it is the nuclear, missile and military hardware nexus between China and Pakistan that is of concern to India. India is thus geographically placed between two hostile neighbours, both of whom are nuclear armed, which imposes its own security dynamics upon India.

At the economic level, the China-Pakistan Economic Corridor (CPEC), which is a part of China's Belt and Road Initiative (BRI), connects China's Xinjiang province to Gwadar in Balochistan, Pakistan. The CPEC consists of two major projects. One, the development of Gwadar Port, and the other, construction of roads, and a rail, pipeline and optical fibre corridor between Gwadar and Xinjiang province.[17] China has invested more than USD 55 billion in infrastructure development and the energy sector but the CPEC continues to face many hurdles in terms of financial constraints and security concerns due to a host of internal security problems within Pakistan. Since 1948, the Baloch people have been engaged in their freedom struggle which the Pakistani establishment has not been able to suppress. While Baloch freedom fighters target Pakistan's security forces, they also consider Chinese workers in Pakistan as legitimate targets. The TTP (Tehrik-e-Taliban Pakistan), an umbrella group of a number of militant organisations based at the Pakistan-Afghanistan border, also pose a serious security threat to Pakistan. The TTP seeks the imposition of Islamic law in the country and poses a threat to the Pakistan military as well as to the CPEC. As the CPEC runs along militant-infested areas, there are huge costs involved in protecting it. In the prevailing circumstances, it is unlikely to be reasonably operational in the near to mid-term. India opposes the CPEC because it passes through Gilgit-Baltistan, which is illegally occupied by Pakistan.[18]

India's response to Pakistan-backed terror activity in India was reactive for many years. This changed with India calling out Pakistan's nuclear bluff and carrying out surgical strikes on terrorist bases across the Line of Control.[19] The messaging in both these attacks was important. It conveyed the will of the Indian state to protect its security interests by hitting out at targets far beyond its borders. The abrogation of the special status given to Jammu & Kashmir (J&K) under Articles 370 and 35A of Indian Constitution on 5 August 2019 has further reduced Pakistan's ability to support terrorist operations in India, though such support continues still, albeit on a far lower scale than hither-to-fore.

India's firm policies in taking on the threat from Pakistan-supported cross-border terrorism have led to a reduction in levels of violence in J&K, though much work still remains to be done for total normalcy to return. Pressure at the political, diplomatic and military levels being applied against Pakistan are yielding results, but that would require to be vigorously continued till such time as Pakistan abandons its policy of using terrorism as an instrument of state policy and hands back to India the territory that it has illegally acquired.

India's focus, therefore, over the next decades, must be on recovering lost territories through political, diplomatic and if necessary, military means.

The Indian Ocean Region

India's location in the Indian Ocean gives it great importance as a maritime power. While India's focus since Independence has been based on her land borders, due to the necessity of dealing with two hostile neighbours, the focus now is increasingly on harnessing India's maritime resources. India's 'Neighbourhood First' policy has seen a distinct push towards improving relations with West Asia in securing energy supplies and supporting the Indian Diaspora working in these regions. Similarly, India's 'Act East' policy helps expand trade with South-East Asia. This marks a shift from a more militarised continental approach towards an economically focused strategy for the region.[20]

India enunciated her vision for the Indian Ocean Region (IOR) through the idea of 'SAGAR' or 'Security and Growth for All in the Region'. Further, India's area of interest is defined as that stretching from the East African Coast to the West Pacific, marking the Indo-Pacific as a new domain in India's foreign policy engagements. This enunciation marks a shift in New Delhi's strategic environment. Now, besides her focus on continental borders, India is increasingly looking at her maritime space.[21]

India's emphasis in the IOR is focused on trade and freedom of navigation. As trade is an important component of India's economic growth, India's interests lie in keeping the sea lanes of communications safe and secure. This would be a challenge for India in the coming years. Chinese belligerence in the South China Sea and the increasing presence of the PLA Navy (PLAN) in the IOR poses challenges for India that would require further strengthening of India's naval capability. India would need to look into the indigenous manufacture of another aircraft carrier, as well as strengthening its submarine fleet. The 'QUAD' (Quadrilateral Security Dialogue) grouping of India, Australia, Japan and the USA has seen a fillip over the last few years with annual summit-level meetings and periodic meetings between the defence and foreign ministers of the member-countries. The QUAD, as of present, is an informal strategic grouping which works for a free, open, prosperous and inclusive Indo-Pacific Region.[22] The coming years are likely to see the QUAD expanding to what can be termed as a 'QUAD-plus' to counter possible Chinese aggressive moves. It would also see a deepening of economic, diplomatic and military ties amongst the member-countries.

Enhancing Military Power

A major initiative to enhance India's military power is to focus on indigenisation, through the *'Atmanirbhar Bharat'* push in defence production capability. India has been one of the world's largest importers of weapons and this is now set to change with emphasis being laid on restricting imports and on 'Make in India' schemes. Two defence corridors have come up—one in Tamil Nadu and the other in Uttar Pradesh. Investments of Rs. 20,000 crore by public as well private sector companies have been envisaged in these corridors by the year 2024. When fully functional, these will facilitate production of indigenous military hardware, making India a major defence manufacturing hub in the world.[23]

The role of the public sector in defence production has also been streamlined. The erstwhile Ordnance Factory Board has been dissolved and in its place seven new defence public sector undertakings have been carved out.[24] This would provide the much-needed accountability in the system, enhance speedy decision making and lead to greater user satisfaction in terms of timely delivery of weapons and equipment with appropriate quality control.

Another important initiative has been in providing a greater role to the private sector in defence production. This is significant as earlier defence production was reserved for the public sector. A slew of measures taken over the last few years are by the revision of defence procurement procedure (DPP)-2016. The DPP has been revised to defence acquisition procedure (DAP)-2020, which is driven by the tenets of the defence reforms announced as part of '*Aatmanirbhar Bharat Abhiyan*'. In the capital acquisition budget, the major share now goes for domestic capital procurement. In addition, in order to promote indigenous design and development of defence equipment a 'Buy Indian' (indigenously designed, developed and manufactured, or IDDM) category has been accorded the topmost priority for procurement of capital equipment. We now also have a positive indigenisation list which will impose an embargo on imports according to the timelines indicated against them. This would offer greater opportunities to the Indian defence industry to manufacture using their own design and development capabilities so as to meet the requirements of the armed forces in the coming years.[25]

The 'Make' procedure for capital procurement has also been simplified. Under the 'Make-I' category, there is provision for government funding to Indian industry up to 70 per cent of development costs. In addition, there are specific reservations for micro, small and medium enterprises (MSME) under the 'Make' procedure. The procedure for the 'Make-II' category (industry funded), introduced in DPP-2016 to encourage indigenous development and manufacture of defence equipment, has a number of industry-friendly provisions such as relaxation of eligibility criterion, minimal documentation, provision for considering proposals suggested by industry and individuals, etc. Foreign direct investment (FDI) in the defence sector has been enhanced to 74 per cent through the 'automatic route' for companies seeking new defence industrial licences, and up to 100 per cent by the 'government route' whenever it is likely to result in access to modern technology or for other recorded reasons.[26]

Another major initiative is the opening up of the defence sector for exports. This is a marked shift from earlier policies which were reticent on this front. The government has set up a target of achieving USD 5 billion in defence exports by 2025. India has started exporting Brahmos missiles to the

Philippines. The chairman of BrahMos Aerospace has stated that there are expectations of more such orders and that the company will by itself be able to achieve the target set by the government. With India manufacturing its own aircraft carrier, fighter jets, helicopters, artillery pieces and a host of other advanced weapon systems, the field of exports appears bright. More importantly, such developments would make India's defence industrial base more robust, decrease our dependence on imports, provide jobs for the Indian work force, give a fillip to the economy and lead India to be Aatmanirbhar in defence capability.

In terms of organisational structures, the creation of the post of the Chief of Defence Staff (CDS) was a much-needed reform. The CDS acts as the principal military adviser to the defence minister on tri-service matters. He is a member of the defence acquisition council and defence planning committee, and also heads all specialised tri-service, special operations, cyber and space divisions, and formations.

One important scheme announced by the Ministry of Defence has been in the recruitment of soldiers. The '*Agnipath*' scheme envisages the enrolment of selected candidates in the armed forces for a period of four years, after which they soldiers will go back to civil society as a disciplined, dynamic, motivated and skilled work force, with 25 per cent being retained in the service. The aim is to reduce the pension bill, maintain a youthful profile in the armed forces and attract young talent from society to effectively exploit, adopt and use modern technologies. The scheme is yet to be proved, and is still a work-in-being; it is expected to be modified and improved as more experience is gained during its implementation.[27]

Conclusion

Presently, there is a greater focus on addressing India's security concerns. That is being accomplished through multiple initiatives being taken both in the realm of foreign policy as well as through defence sector reforms. The focus over the next decade will be on holistic management of India's security for which the driving force will be political and military leadership, supported by a strong defence industrial base.

ENDNOTES

1. https://guides.loc.gov/machine-gun-its-history-development-and-use
2. https://www.iwm.org.uk/history/how-britain-invented-the-tank-in-the-first-world-war
3. Hans J. Morgenthau, *Dilemmas of Politics,* University of Chicago Press, 1958, p. 65.
4. Gautam, S, *Institutionalising National Security Policy-Making in India*, Issue Brief No. 81, Centre for Land Warfare Studies, July 2016.
5. Jaswant Singh, *What Constitutes National Security in a Changing World Order: India's Strategic Thought,* Issue 6, CASI Occasional Paper, 6 June 1998.
6. Ibid.
7. Tanham, G. (1992). Indian Strategic Culture, *The Washington Quarterly,* pp. 129-142.
8. Shakti Sinha, *Indian Strategic Thought*, Dhruv Katoch (ed.), India's Foreign Policy: Towards Resurgence, Pentagon, 2019.
9. Sen, G, *India's National Security Policy-Making Prism, CLAWS Journal,* Winter 2016.
10. Madhav, Ram, Panch Amrit: The Five Pillars of Indian Foreign Policy, Dhruv Katoch (ed.), India's Foreign Policy: Towards Resurgence, Pentagon, 2019.
11. Sajjanhar, Ashok, *The Diplomatic Crisis ends: A Diplomatic Victory for India*, available at https://www.orfonline.org/expert-speak/the-doklam-crisis-ends-a-diplomatic-victory-for-india/
12. https://www.hindustantimes.com/india-news/what-does-the-2020-galwan-clash-say-about-india-101655355460675.html
13. https://www.thehindu.com/sci-tech/technology/india-bans-54-more-chinese-apps-over-security-concerns/article65052287.ece
14. https://timesofindia.indiatimes.com/city/shimla/padum-darcha-road-opens-for-heavy-vehicles/articleshow/92609973.cms
15. https://www.indiatoday.in/information/story/pm-modi-inaugurates-manali-leh-tunnel-12-interesting-facts-to-know-about-atal-tunnel-1727798-2020-10-02
16. https://pib.gov.in/PressReleaseIframePage.aspx?PRID=1794833
17. https://www.scirp.org/journal/paperinformation.aspx?paperid=110152
18. https://economictimes.indiatimes.com/news/defence/india-expresses-strong-opposition-to-china-pakistan-economic-corridor-says-challenges-indian-sovereignty/articleshow/57664537.cms?from=mdr
19. Pakistan vows retaliation if India attacks, *Financial Times*, 19 January 2019.
20. Hannah, Harri, I, The Great Game Moves to Sea: Tripolar Competition in the Indian Ocean Region, available at https://warontherocks.com/2019/04/the-great-game-moves-to-sea-tripolar-competition-in-the-indian-ocean-region/
21. https://carnegieendowment.org/2020/06/30/india-in-indo-pacific-new-delhi-s-theater-of-opportunity-pub-82205
22. https://www.business-standard.com/about/what-is-quad#collapse
23. https://www.makeinindia.com/defence-industrial-corridors-india
24. https://www.hindustantimes.com/india-news/ordnance-factory-board-dissolved-here-are-7-new-defence-companies-launched-by-pm-modi-on-dussehra-101634284729696.html
25. https://pib.gov.in/PressReleasePage.aspx?PRID=1739049
26. Ibid.
27. https://indianarmy.nic.in/writereaddata/documents/FAQsAgnipath170622.pdf?MnId=wZKaTvhq6pc+/CjfB48LQ&NewsID=ILHkTiCMdQs3r0e7wOgDIg==

12

TECHNOLOGIES TO BE DEVELOPED FOR THE INDIAN ARMED FORCES

P. K. Chakravorty

Introduction

The process of military modernisation primarily results in infusion of *Technology* into *Doctrine*. Technology and modern weapons are force multipliers for enhancing combat potential. The improvement of capabilities by technological methods would also enhance *Deterrence* which is a mind game to avoid conflicts.

The future battle field is likely to have the following features:

- Practically no warning, with periods of high tempo and density.
- Transparency of the battlefield will be enhanced.
- Non-linearity of operations. Multi-domain operations linked to artificial intelligence (AI) could commence with destruction of satellites in outer space, cyber warfare, operations by special forces, and covert actions in depth areas, followed by multiple intrusions and offensive across weaker spots of the enemy.
- Combat zones for land warfare would be deeper and wider. The entire combat zone would be net-centric and would be, to a large extent, fed by autonomous systems.
- Future warfare would be asymmetric in nature and to a large extent depend on flexibility of mind as well as equipment to deal with the conditions.
- Current operations in Ukraine have vindicated the need for joint operations and a combination of firepower and manoeuvre.
- Operations in the Indian subcontinent would be against a nuclear backdrop.

It would be interesting to take note of the critical technologies that would be important for the Indian military, development of which would lead to enhanced combat capabilities.

Critical Technologies for the Military

Critical technologies for the futuristic requirements of the Indian military are as under:

- Nano-technology.
- Big Data.
- Quantum Technology.
- Bio-Technology.
- Artificial Intelligence (AI) and Robotics.
- Micro-Optronics.
- Information Security.
- Radar and Microwave.
- Satellites.
- Rockets and Missiles including Hypersonics.
- Material Science.
- Nuclear Technology.

There is a need to realistically look at these technologies to understand their applicability to military purposes and the process of indigenisation.

1. NANO-TECHNOLOGY

General Aspects

Nano-technology is science, engineering, and technology conducted at nano-scale of approximately 1 to 100 nano-metres (nm).[1] Nano-technology has opened new frontiers to mankind. Precision in science and engineering with smaller particles is the core area of this unique technology. Though science has spoken of atoms and molecules for many years, much remains to be analysed about their behaviour at the nano-level.

There are 25,400,000 nano-metres in an inch. Nano-structures can be nano-scale in one dimension as in the case of thin film and sheets. In a two-dimension mode it would be carbon nano-tubes. It is also possible to have items in three dimensions which are nano-scale as in the case of nano-particles. These are nano-porous structures where the cavities are nano-sized, while the bulk material remains macro sized. Illustrations are nano-sponges and nano-porous membranes.

Indian Military and Nano-technology

Nano-technology has the potential to influence warfare in a number of ways. Lighter, stronger, heat resistant nano-material could be used in manufacturing all types of war like equipment, weapon platforms, and missiles, and enabling mobility over all types of terrain on land including mountains, water, and air. With regard to troops deployed, military use of nano-technology will ensure better protection, more lethality, enhanced endurance, and better repair capabilities in the battle space.[2]

Aspect that nano-technology would directly impact on the military would be as under:

- Focus on the combat soldier.
- Information dominance.
- Weapons.
- Vehicles and weapon platforms.
- Logistics.

The **combat soldier** is keen that the weight of his equipment is reduced. The sensors he carries would need lesser electrical output for the same functional capability. The soldier of the future should carry a battlefield management system in the form of a wrist watch which would provide him all details including the common operating picture. His weapon would be lighter and he would be camouflaged against infra-red (IR) devices. The future soldier will have an all-impact suit enabled by nano-materials combined with macro fibres offering protection against bullets, grenade fragments and biological and chemical agents. His back pack, weapons, and ammunition would be light and precise. His smart helmet is light weight and he will have a light system for preservation of food and water.

In the field of **Information Dominance**, nano-electronics will lead to improved equipment and quality for sensors and other communications equipment. Microchips will consume lower power, less noise and have higher processing speeds. Equipment with nano-electronics will take on cognitive functions, leading to higher human applications. These will lead to better command functions. The Indian Armed Forces, which have a wide surveillance network, will be deeply impacted by these changes.

In **weaponry**, nano-materials will assist in creating a smoother control of energy release and can create shorter diffusion paths for high explosive ammunition blasts. Nano-particles can also permit greater penetration of kinetic shells. With nano-particles, the construction flexibility can be improved, as can be the stealth capabilities of the materials because light falling on these particles get scattered. In the next decade, the impact of nano-technology would result in light weight guns, rifles, and automatic firing systems. Other militaries are using nano-weapons to correct body-shaking while firing bullets.

Future **vehicles and weapons platforms**, be it land, sea or air assets, have to be lighter, faster and more lethal. Armoured and other vehicles should fit in greater numbers into heavy-lift aircraft like the IL-76, C-130, or Globe Master. The aim would also be to develop light-weight nano-composite plates to cover critical parts of tanks, infantry combat vehicles, and other vehicles and platforms like combat aircraft. Nano-materials will enable electronic systems and other components of military platforms to be light-weight. Besides, nano-particles would scatter the incident light and infrared, thus making the Indian military hardware stealth-capable. Unmanned vehicles made of nano-materials would be able to produce better capabilities in the battle space.

An essential element of future warfare is **logistics**. In the Indian Armed Forces, supply chain management forms an important component of logistics. This should support operations in the field to ensure that food, water, ammunition and fuel, are at the right place on time and in the desired quantities. In order to undertake such tasks, there is the need for modular containers which can be of various sizes for moving to desired military destinations. Nano-technology would make these containers light and enable their easy movement by transport aircraft and utility helicopters. All these aspects combined with AI would make the delivery of items in the battle space easy.[3]

The Way Ahead

The military's design bureaus need to have comprehensive discussions with the Defence Research & Development Organisation (DRDO) on application of nano-technology to military hardware. In a one-day workshop held in 2012, the DRDO informed that there were more than 30 laboratories working on nano-technology.[4] To expedite the matter, it would be best to involve the military and the DRDO with the Indian Institute of Science, Bangalore (IISc) which is a premier institution dealing with the subject. Discussions must lead to some pilot projects undertaken on combat battle gear, sensors, platforms, and containers. Active participation of these agencies would lead to optimal development of nano-products.

2. BIG DATA

Defining Big Data

A database is the beginning of any military operation. 'Big Data' is that enormous amount of data which is huge in size, so large and complex that none of the traditional data management tools are able to store or process it efficiently. The military has a use for Big Data in the following fields:

- Surveillance.
- Processing of intelligence.
- Prioritising of targets.
- Engagement of targets.
- Post-strike damage assessment.
- Entire field of military logistics.
- Human resource management.

Applicability to the Indian Armed Forces

The Indian military has stressed the need to focus on incorporating artificial intelligence (AI) and big-data computing in our armed forces systems, adding that our northern adversary (China) was investing large amounts on such projects. Apart from inducting equipment, there is also a need to invest in these technologies to have a grip on non-contact warfare.[5]

Intelligence is the heart of all defence planning and implementation. With joint command, control, communications, computers, intelligence and information (C4I2) systems in place, there is no dearth of data. The need of the hour is a Big Data strategy as well as recognition of its crucial importance from the top echelons to the front-line soldier. Accordingly, our decision-makers have focused on the need for collaboration with industry. It is pertinent to note that the European defence agency has made numerous recommendations how data is to be analysed and thereafter fed to each combatant. The Europeans have included modelling and simulation (M&S) applications over the 'Cloud', and utilisation of predictive analysis data in the development of M&S models.[6]

Big Data will also play an important part in the field of human resources and logistics. Handling of manpower within the Indian Armed Forces needs a higher degree of optimization which would immensely benefit the military. Handling of logistics data is a nightmare for any military. The need to form a 'distributed logistics agency' in a combat zone would need automation to ensure free flow of items to troops without the need for indents, and replenishments taking place on an on-line system.

3. QUANTUM TECHNOLOGY

From the military point of view, quantum technology can send information down the fibre optics network using an entangled pair of photons. If someone tries to intercept the message and view the contents, they will not be able to put it back in the same state. The message will arrive scrambled and the recipient will know that someone tried to eavesdrop on the communications en route. For quantum technology to be useful to the Indian military, quantum computers must be available in the field. This would take some time.[7]

Experiences in Application

The integration of quantum technologies is extremely important for the Indian military. Quantum technology is expected eventually to have far-reaching effects for the forces in the field, intelligence elements, and other strategic and analytical establishments. However, the precise impact is difficult to gauge.

The field of quantum information science is giving rise in multiple new defence-related applications that are often grouped under the head 'quantum'. Quantum key distribution (QKD), quantum cryptoanalysis and quantum sensing, all promise to significantly affect strategic security by varying methods. There is no doubt that quantum technology is expected to have far-reaching effects for military forces, intelligence services and law enforcement agencies, but like all domains of warfare, it would be difficult to quantify the amount of impact this will have in terms of success in operations. The most common form of quantum encryption is the transmission of cryptographic keys. QKD technology is applicable to existing systems for encrypted communications and offers a valuable means of knowing if communications have been intercepted and examined. The process is under trial and is currently a challenge over long distances; it would take some time to fine-tune this issue.

Quantum cryptoanalysis refers to the specific application of quantum computing for decrypting encoded messages. Current encryption standards primarily rely upon mathematical algorithms for encoding data, which are effectively unbreakable in any reasonable period of time. Quantum computers will eventually be able to replace the trial-and-error methods of processing such mathematical problems with alternative means, thus permitting a number of possibilities simultaneously. This is an extremely attractive proposition. A few countries are already beginning to collect encrypted foreign communications with the expectation that once quantum cryptoanalysis stabilizes, these would be able to extract valuable secrets from that data. Once cryptoanalysis data is available, it will impact international relations by making intercepted communications open to decryption.[8]

It is imperative we understand which other countries are contemplating such a development, so that the Indian Armed Forces assimilate the nuances of quantum technology and accordingly decide on a road map. The US "National strategic overview for quantum information science' defines quantum sensing as leveraging quantum mechanics to enhance the fundamental accuracy of measurements and enabling new regimes or modalities for sensors and measurement. These capabilities would offer military advantages.[9] The United Kingdom's Defence science expert committee has highlighted the potential importance of improved gravity sensors which could detect moving objects on the land border as well as under water such as submarines and unmanned water boats. Further, quantum radars could be used for locating low-flying aircraft, particularly unmanned aerial vehicles (UAVs) and unmanned combat aerial vehicles (UCAVs). These are also being used in atomic clocks which are being used in navigation systems. It is also important to note that quantum computers will not be a replacement for the current computers but be alternative and complementary to the current networks to deal with problems the others cannot solve.

Several nations are heavily investing in quantum research to gain economic and military advantage. The private sector and academia will play an important role in inventing and adapting these new technologies. The USA, China, Russia and the United Kingdom and many other countries are also into advanced research on quantum computing. As a matter of course, a new security dilemma would be created when data is available to technically advanced countries whereas the others, with no access to quantum technology would stand exposed to political and military concern. The Indian military, with the DRDO, private industry, and academia, must work to have the demonstrated capabilities within a respectable time frame to ensure that we are not left high and dry in the field of quantum computing.

4. BIO-TECHNOLOGY

Importance

There are speculations about misuse of bio-technology and genetically engineered materials particularly those meant to strengthen military programmes.[10] It is reported that the technology could lead to disasters which could be more dangerous than nuclear accidents, the reason being that genes can replicate, spread, and recombine indefinitely. The cloning of 'Dolly the sheep' was visualised as a step which would lead to human cloning. Initially, the USA imposed a five-year ban on human cloning while the British at that time wanted cloning to be made illegal.[11] Currently in the USA, cloning is permitted for bio-medical research; however, many states have passed laws on human cloning and some of them forbid cloning of children. The United Kingdom permits cloning for producing stem cells but it is very tightly controlled by the government.

As genetic engineering can boost horizontal gene transfer, which is to transfer genes to unrelated species, it may be used to create new pathogenic bacteria and antibiotic resistance among pathogens. It is reported that such horizontal gene transfers are already occurring due to improper handling, storage, and disposal of genetically-engineered material. It has been alleged that previously unknown bacterial strains responsible for the outbreak of Streptococcus epidemic and E-coli in Scotland were the result of genetic recombination subsequent to horizontal gene transfer.[12] According to WHO reports, at least 30 new diseases including AIDS, Ebola and Hepatitis-C have emerged over the last 30 years. Genes for antibiotic resistance are also believed to have spread horizontally. Such microbes are a cause for concern because infections with these and other similar strains will not respond to known treatments and therefore accidental or intentional release of such genetically engineered organisms into the environment may be disastrous.

Applications in the Indian Armed Forces

The present pandemic of corona virus has impacted the armed forces of all countries of the world. Currently, the immediate focus is on defensive measures with an aim of keeping personnel fit. Overall, the Indian Armed Forces have to deal with surveillance, diagnosis, offensive and defensive measures. First of all, we must see as to what is the position of India with regard to this subject. The armed forces have to be prepared for all kinds of threats.[13]

On 27 March 2020, on the occasion of the 45th anniversary of the Biological and Toxin Weapons Convention (BTWC) coming into force, India underlined the need for international cooperation, including institutional strengthening of the World Health Organisation. The COVID-19 issue was discussed in detail, and ahead of the ninth review conference of the convention in 2021, India reiterated its call for putting in place a comprehensive and legally-binding protocol having a non-discriminatory verification mechanism to strengthen the norms to deal with biological weapons.[14]

A few issues which need consideration as far as the Indian Armed Forces are concerned, are as under:

- The bio-technology industry surpasses the aerospace industry.
- India is at a nascent stage in the field of bio-technology.
- Bio-technology should not be seen in isolation. A biological weapon can be used easily.
- BTWC does not provide enough space to control existing developments in the field of bio-technology.
- Issues need to be discussed by India at the regional level.
- Bio-technology is likely to be a lead technology in the current century.
- India has to be cautious on agro-terrorism and pharmaceutical companies spreading a biological agent for earning high profits.
- The bio-technological threat is increasing exponentially and there is a need to analyse the threat to get methods to solve the problem.[15]

Prior to getting on to the tasks for the Indian Armed Forces, it is important to note the process of bio-engineering development systems.[16] The Armed Forces must take a fresh look at bio-technology and undertake the following measures:

- The Department of Military Affairs should form a special project comprising of the three services, DRDO, and representatives from the ministries of Health, Finance, and Defence.
- The project could function as a biological warfare commission. It must have the capability of knowing the latest viruses and also details of Case X genetically engineered viruses and keep ahead of impending biological weapons and genetically engineered products. It should also

look at the possibility of India's crops and livestock being harmed and provide a response mechanism for the same.

- The project could suggest innovative ideas on the subject like ducks eating locusts. It must be given due importance like the Atomic Energy Commission and the Indian Space Research Organisation (ISRO) so that results are produced early. These together should create a 'biological warfare doctrine' and measures to develop offensive and defensive biological warfare. The Institute of Nuclear Medicine and Allied Sciences (INMAS) should actively cooperate with the project.

Once the project takes off, it will enable us to be proactive in dealing with biological warfare. It is pertinent to note that the intelligence community in the USA had been warning about corona virus for the last five years. They predicted with uncanny accuracy many of the medical supply shortages which are troubling the US Government today.[17] Adoption of the suggested model would provide us rich dividends.

5. ARTIFICIAL INTELLIGENCE (AI) AND ROBOTICS

Introduction

AI traditionally refers to an artificial creation of human-like intelligence that can learn, reason, plan, perceive or process natural language. It is further defined as 'Narrow AI' and 'General AI'. 'Narrow AI' is designed to perform specific tasks within a domain like language translation and 'General AI' is hypothetical and not domain-specific.[18]

Impact of AI on the Indian Army

Needless to say, the Armed Forces need AI. The DRDO has a laboratory specifically dedicated to AI, known as the centre for artificial intelligence and robotics (CAIR). The laboratory focuses on the following areas:

- AI, Robotics and Control Systems.
- Command, Control, Communication and Intelligence Systems.
- Communications and Networking.
- Communication Secrecy.

The CAIR has already developed robots for non-destructive testing of composite parts of light combat aircraft (Teas). Apart from these, the following projects are under development:

- AI techniques for net-centric operations (AINCO). This is a suite of technologies for creation of a knowledge base, semantic information reception and handling, interference reasoning and event correlation.
- Development of a family of robots for surveillance and reconnaissance applications. These comprise Ribose, a mobile robot system for patrolling, reconnaissance and surveillance. It is capable of autonomous navigation in semi-structured environments with obstacle avoidance capability and continuous video feedback.
- The next is a miniaturised man-portable unmanned ground vehicle (UGV) for low-intensity conflicts and surveillance in urban scenarios. A wall climbing, a flapping wing and a walking robot with four and six legs for logistics support tasks are being developed.
- CAIR has also developed the network traffic analysis (NETRA) which can monitor internet traffic. It can analyse voice traffic passing through software such as Skype, Google Talk and intercept messages with key words 'attack, bomb, blast, kill' and other words in real time.[19]

AI could have numerous applications. Robots can perform numerous functions from a sentry to a surgeon in the battle field. Gradually, these would depend on the level of technology which we can have to make computers and machines analyse and think like soldiers. At the level of planning, it can provide multiple options at the strategic, operational and tactical levels. In terms of equipment, UAVs already exist and soon UGVs and unmanned water vehicles would be developed. Operations like mining, demining, launching of assault bridges, flying across water obstacles and Para-dropped robots for tasks with Special Forces and field logistics tasks would be undertaken with AI.

Swarms have attracted a lot of attention and a comprehensive view on its usage is imperative. The process would result in corresponding modernisation of various functions thereby enhancing operational efficiency. Currently, the Indian military is closely working with CAIR on its project of a multi-agent robotics framework (MARF). The types of robots include the Snake, Legged Robot, the Wall Climber and the UGV. Apart from these there is a need to jointly focus on the following:

- Image interpretation for target identification and classification. AI techniques could automate the extraction of low-level map features from imagery.
- AI for managing platforms, cyber security, logistics, and transportation.

- Systems for diagnosis and maintenance of sophisticated weapon systems.
- Target range and trajectory analysis for evaluation of kill zones, launch times and simulation to assist in qualifying missile performance.
- Enhanced use of robots for anti-improvised explosive devices, extraction of personnel, firing of guns and other applications.
- Swarming of UAVs and use of them for destruction tasks.
- UCAVs have been used in operations during the current war in Ukraine and also in the recent killing of Al Qaeda leader, Adman Al Zawahiri, in Kabul.

Robotics

Military robots are autonomous or remote-controlled mobile equipment designed for military applications. These could be used for transport, search and rescue and attack related tasks. Use of robotics has been extended from autonomous UCAVs firing Hellfire missiles, UGVs, unmanned ships and submarines, production of Dragon Fire II autonomous guns to automation of loading and ballistics calculations. Autonomous fighter jets have also been developed which are at the trial stage. It is stated that currently robotics are being used with drones like the DRDO's Daksh, Israel's D9T Panda, Shomer Gvoluth (Border Keeper) and Elbit Hermes 450, the Goalkeeper Close-in Weapon System (CIWS), Pack Bot, TALON and Samsung SGR-A1, MQ-9 Reaper, MQ-1 Predator, Iran's Shahed 129, etc.

A few projects which are under development are listed below:

- US Mechatronics has produced an automated sentry gun which has to be refined for military use.
- MIDARS, a four-wheeled robot outfitted with several cameras, radars and possibly a firearm that automatically performs patrols at random or pre-programs around a military base or any other fortification. On detecting an intruder, it alerts the human observer and helps in taking suitable decisions. It would also scan radio frequency identification tags (RFID) of the inventories and report any missing items.
- Tactical autonomous combatant (TAC) units as specified in 'Project Alpha Study on Unmanned Effects'. This project focuses on development of robots that would be capable of replacing humans to perform many, if not most combat functions in the battle field. The study suggested that as early as in 2025, the presence of networked

and integrated autonomous robots on the battlefield might not be an exception but a norm.

- The autonomous rotorcraft sniper system is an experimental robotic weapon system being developed by the US Army. It consists of a remotely-operated sniper rifle attached to an unmanned autonomous helicopter. This system has been tried on the unmanned Vigilante 502 helicopter. [20]

The Way Ahead

We have to bear in mind that the Chinese are developing all aspects of AI to enable them to use robotics and autonomous technologies in undertaking UAV swarm attacks.[21] They are also contemplating the use of robots to capture objectives and to hold ground and guard installations. Further, they intend having their guns, rockets and missiles fully autonomous with a high degree of intelligence interpretation to shoot down enemy aircraft and missiles. The Chinese may share the same with Pakistan and it is a matter of time that our Western adversaries too develop capabilities in this field.

It is of interest to note that in January 2018, the Russian Ministry of Defence reported that its forces at the Khomeini air base of the Tartus naval base in Syria were attacked by a swarm of homemade drones in a coordinated attack. The attack was launched during dusk and the Russian air defence had observed that these were approaching the airbase and the naval facilities. Six of the drones were intercepted by electronic warfare units, three exploded on contact with the ground and three were made to land outside the base. The remaining seven were eliminated by the Pantsir-S anti-aircraft missiles. It is not known who launched them as it has been denied by all. That was followed by the Saudi Arabian Aramco oilfields attack by UCAVs flown by Houthis on 14 September 2019 that paralysed the entire set up. On 31 July 2022, Al Qaeda leader, Ayman al-Zawahiri, was killed by US forces with a Hellfire missile fired from an UCAV, the Reaper. Indeed, the age of drones and swarms has arrived; it is to be noted by all countries.[22]

The Indian military must address the issue with alacrity and speed. This can be achieved if the in-house design bureaus, the DRDO and the private sector look at AI with a sense of urgency. CAIR by itself would find it difficult and needs the assistance of the private sector to ensure that development in this field is expedited. For AI to produce decisive results, there is a need to have a state-of-the-art sensor based on quantum communications. This would ensure that the robots and the autonomous vehicles are controlled with precision and speed. The issue is urgent and demands the highest priority.

6. MICRO-OPTRONICS

Opto-electronics or Optronics is the study and application of electronic devices and systems that source, detect and control light waves. Optronic devices are electrical to optical or optical to electrical transducers to convert night into day, thus enabling precision attacks by night.[23] Some of these devices are Infra-red binoculars and sights, Charge coupled imaging devices, Image intensifiers, Thermal imagers, Telescopic sights, N cross, Long-range reconnaissance and observation systems (LORROS), Optical contrast seekers, Laser range finders, etc. Israel is a reliable manufacturer of these equipment. It has also developed a hand-held battle field management system computer to be carried by every soldier to receive the common operating picture. Payloads of the UAVs also have a variety of cameras and electronic devices.

The Indian military currently depends on optronics equipment from Bharat Electronics, DRDO laboratories and private sector companies like Alfa Technologies, Bengaluru. These have improved our capability to fight by night. The future lies in laser weapons capability.

Direct energy weapons (DEW) are capable of destroying targets by emitting and transferring extreme levels of energy at them. DEWs can be used against unmanned and light aircraft and many other targets like tanks, guns and fortifications. The energy emitted by DEWs can be in the form of electro-magnetic radiation, microwaves, lasers and masers, and particles with mass. Laser weapons lead the DEW pack. These are precise and capable of destroying targets like weapons and hardware.

India is currently working on a series of DEWs. According to the laser science and technology centre (LASTEC) of the DRDO, the effort is to fire a laser beam with a potency of 25 kilowatts to intercept and destroy incoming ballistic missiles in its terminal phase within a range of 7 km. LASTEC projects include the following:

- Hand-held laser dazzler to disorient enemies at 50 metre range, without collateral damage.
- Lasers to neutralise improved explosive devices from a safe distance.
- Air defence dazzlers to take on enemy aircraft and helicopters at a range of 10 km.

- 25-kilowatt laser systems to destroy missiles during their terminal phase at a range of 5 to 7 km.
- At least 100-kilowatt solid state laser systems, mounted on helicopters/ UAVs and aircraft, to destroy missiles in their boost phase.[24]

7. INFORMATION SECURITY

Information Technology (IT) has transformed the nature of warfare and given a boost to electronic, rocket and cyber warfare. Strategists have analysed the way in which IT has transformed warfare resulting in wars which will be fought on 'digital borders'. Aspects that would need attention are as under:

- IT vulnerabilities include the ease of infecting computers with virus, denying connectivity to adversaries, disrupting daily life through denial of financial transactions, defacing electronic data and spreading disinformation.
- IT could be used to disrupt, disable, delay and corrupt rather than physically destruct an adversary's capabilities.
- IT has enabled non-state actors, terrorists and criminal organisations to undertake information warfare.
- The primary issue is to prevent cyber-attacks on own data. The aim would be to gain electro-magnetic superiority to neutralise the enemy's command, control, communications, computer, surveillance, intelligence and information acquisition systems. This would result in a psychological paralysis of an adversary rather than capture of territory or destruction of forces.
- *Information warfare* primarily consists of *electronic warfare* (EW), *cyber warfare*, *psychological warfare* and *deception operations* (MILDEC).

To provide continuous capability advantage, EW systems of the future must be able to operate in a complex, multi and cross organisation domain to couple EW with cyber effects.[25] The Indian military must have an active EW policy with all communications and non-communication equipment duly upgraded with modern electronic devices. Cyber warfare is a form of information warfare utilised to destroy, degrade, exploit or compromise the adversary's computer-based systems while ensuring protection of own assessments. It involves the use of technology to gain intelligence, speedier processing and dissemination of intelligence, identification of friend or foe, and jamming and overloading an adversary's networks. Offensive cyber warfare includes physical destruction of communications infrastructure as also to gain access to enemy's information systems or networks. Psychological warfare gets linked with cyber warfare when messages, pamphlets, leaflets, and scam mails are used to impact the mind of the enemy. Further, there are extremely effective defensive cyber actions to focus on denying access and protecting own systems. Integrity of own data is also maintained in the defensive mode. During peace, cyber operations would comprise espionage activities, civil communications, interference with rail, air and financial operations to paralyse the operating systems. Cyber-attacks on the web sites of Estonia (2007) and Georgia (2008) are some examples.[26]

While technologies in the information domain have a profound impact on the battle field, there is also the use of 'nerds' as 'information warriors'. The US army has created new intelligence, information, cyber, electronic and space warfare battalions. It is also reorganizing a new cyber warfare support battalion and is edging towards reorganizing its army cyber warfare command into an information warfare command.[27] The British have unveiled a new cyber division which would operate above and below the threshold of conventional conflict to counter Russia's malignant activity and threats from technologically sophisticated terror groups such as the Islamic State. A new specialised information warfare formation named 6 division comprising 77 information warfare brigade and about two signal brigades will seek to influence the adversary's public behaviour.[28]

China has also paid great attention to the subject; its policy is in consonance with its military strategy. China describes the primary objectives of cyber space capabilities to include cyber situation awareness, cyber defence, support for the country's endeavour in cyber space and participation in international cooperation.[29] In the People's Liberation Army's (PLA) strategic support force (SSF) is the coordinator of information operations. Its network spreads from the central military commission to the theatre commands and is directed at gaining information superiority in joint operations. Its network systems department has integrated cyber and electronic warfare to optimize its information operations. The SSF's role in psychological warfare could enable the PLA to exploit the nexus of cyber and psychological warfare capabilities.[30]

Considering these aspects, it would be prudent for the Indian armed forces to focus on information warfare forces in cyber, electronic and psychological domains and optimise its capabilities.

8. RADAR AND MICROWAVE

Radar

Radar systems have been used in military applications for ground surveillance, missile control, fire control, air traffic control, moving target indication weapons location and search of vehicles. It has grown into everyday military use for surveillance and fire control, to engage stealth, short range and quick reaction and other missiles, etc.[31]

Some important developments to focus on are:

- *Phase Array Technology.* Active electronically switched array (AESA) radar can produce multiple beams for multiple target tracking. India has produced an indigenous AESA radar with the Akash missile system.
- *Varied Band Spectrum.* Radars which operate in very high frequency (VHF) bands are difficult to jam and can detect targets with low cross sections.
- *Over the Horizon (OTH) Radar* uses the bounce effect of high frequency (HF) waves with a detection capability of thousands of kilometres. It is primarily used for surveillance and anti-stealth tasks.
- *Multi Band Spectrum* functions simultaneously in multiple frequency bands with the help of AESA. It has very effective ECM capability.
- *Fire Control Systems* like forward looking infra-red, infra-red search and tracking, thermal imagers, charged couple devices and cameras are important.
- *Stealth* is detected by multi-band passive systems. Research has indicated that passive radar systems can detect reflections from three different bands—the frequency modulation (FM), digital audio broadcasting and digital video broadcasting terrestrial bands. Laser technology is also being explored to detect stealth.[32]
- *Weapon Locating Radar* (WLR) is an electronically scanned phased array system to locate hostile guns, mortars, rocket launchers and also to track own artillery fire and give corrections to hit targets. It detects small cross-section projectiles and has the capability to handle simultaneous fire from weapons deployed at multiple locations. Algorithms for trajectory computations consider environmental parameters while estimating both launch and impact points of accuracy. The radar is mobile and facilitates quick deployment.

The Indian armed forces have to continuously work with the DRDO and Bharat Electronics Limited to ensure that its radars acquire all the latest capabilities.

Microwave

Microwaves are a form of electro-magnetic radiation with wavelengths ranging from about one metre to one millimetre. Its broad definition includes both ultra high frequency (UHF) and extremely high frequency (EHF). Microwaves travel by line of sight and are not reflected by the ionosphere. Accordingly, microwave links are restricted to 64-km post World War II, microwave radar became the central technology to be used in air traffic control, maritime navigation, anti-aircraft defence, ballistic missile detection and radar and satellite communications. High power microwaves were used by the USA to disrupt and destroy Iraqi electronic systems.

An active denial system (ADS), a non-lethal, directed energy weapon system has been developed by the USA for area denial, perimeter security and crowd control at 700 metres. The weapon is often called the 'heat ray', as it heats up the surface of targets such as human beings. The system was introduced in Afghanistan but was withdrawn without witnessing combat. This is a non-lethal weapon which is also reported to be developed by China and Russia.[33] It can have multifarious defensive uses.

Kilo-Ampere Linear Injector (KALI)

India is developing a weapon 'KALI' to be used against missiles and aircraft for soft kill. It is being developed by the DRDO and the Bhabha Research Atomic Research Centre (BARC). The project was initially started for industrial purposes but its capabilities help in making it a powerful weapon. Important issues regarding the project are as under:

- The KALI series (KALI 80, KALI 200, KALI 1000, KALI 5000 and KALI 10,000) are described as 'Single shot pulsed gigawatt electron accelerators'. The single shot devices use water-filled capacitors to build the charge energy.
- Beams from the weapon can shatter any satellite, UAV or UCAV.[34]
- It emits powerful pulses of electrons which can be converted into electro magnetic radiation. That has fuelled a hope that the KALI could be used in a high-powered microwave gun. Successful trials and induction would make it a game changer

9. SATELLITES

Military Satellites

Satellites, especially in lower earth orbits (LEO), are extremely important for providing information regarding military operations. Military satellites have imaging resolutions of 12 to 15 cm or larger and can pick up men, vehicles, defensive positions and other equipment. Key hole class (KH) reconnaissance satellites use charge coupled devices (CCD) to gather digital images to be transmitted back to Earth from an altitude of about 320 km. Since the satellites are in orbit, they cannot hover over a given area or provide real time video of a single location. Accordingly, to provide a constant surveillance over a specified area one would need numerous satellites with different visit timings.

Indian Perspective

India currently has about 47 operational satellites. Out of these, about fourteen are used for remote sensing. Recently the Prime Minister launched the Indian Space Association to make India a global leader in the space arena. This incorporates the private sector in space applications. On 10 June 2008, the former defence minister had announced the formation of an 'integrated space cell' under the Headquarters Integrated Defence Staff which would integrate space requirements of the armed forces with the Department of Space and the ISRO. While India has not formed a dedicated space force like the USA, it does make extensive use of space technology for its military needs. Currently, the satellites are in a dual role for these tasks.[35]

India's experiments with reconnaissance satellites started with the technology experimental satellite (TES) in October 2001. With images of 1 metre resolution, it can be possibly termed as India's first satellite used for military purposes. The next variety of satellites with a synthetic aperture radar (SAR) purchased from Israel were the series of radar imaging satellites (RISAT). RISAT-2B, being on an inclined orbit, is better for revisiting areas of interest. The satellite can operate day and night with all-weather monitoring capability in different modes including very high-resolution radar imaging models of 1m × 0.5m and 0.5m × 0.3m resolution. It can be utilised for high resolution spot imaging of locations of interest with evident military applications.

The CARTOSAT variety of satellites is probably India's most capable variety of satellites for use by the military. The first satellite was launched in

2005. CARTOSAT 2F was launched in January 2018; it has four MX detectors which can deliver imagery at a two-metre ground resolution along a 10-km swathe. While its primary tasks are for disaster management, cartography and environmental monitoring, its military applications are evident. On 27 November 2019 CARTOSAT 3 was launched with an image resolution of 25 cm. The swathe is 16 km with four bands and it is at an altitude of about 500 km. It has also a midwives infra red (MWIR) camera with 5.7 m resolution.[36] It is at an orbit of 509 km at an inclination of 97.5 degrees to the Equator. Its images allow an observer to distinguish a truck from a car and take our country to higher resolution capabilities.[37] The mission duration is planned up to November 2024. The satellite would be dual purpose and will be used for a variety of Earth observation applications such as cartography, weather mapping, forest surveys, urban planning, coastal studies, mineral prospecting, disaster relief operations and, most important of all, military purposes.[38]

Way Ahead for the Armed Forces

The 'integrated space cell' was formed on June 2010 to counter the growing threat to India's space assets. Notably, offensive counter-space systems like anti-satellite weaponry, anti-satellite weaponry, new classes of heavy lift and small boosters and an improved array of military space systems have emerged in India's neighbourhood which need to be countered.[39] Then followed 'Mission Shakti' to launch the anti-satellite weapon test (ASAT) on 27 March 2019. The interceptor was able to strike a test satellite at a 300-km altitude in low earth orbit (LEO).

India's capabilities for using space for military purposes are extremely limited. While its lone ASAT test gives a limited capability, we have a long way to go in the domain of military use of space and in the area of counter-space technologies. Currently, there are just a little over a dozen satellites having limited military purposes whereas China has possibly ten times the number. Imagery satellites like CARTOSAT and RISAT may provide useful imagery, but there is a long way to go before the Indian military can have near real-time imagery or electronic intelligence that is essential in maintaining the tempo of modern warfare.[40]

The moot question is, how many satellites do the Indian armed forces need for keeping a close eye on India's adversaries? The answer is difficult. However, to keep a closer eye on the activities of the Chinese military, both near Indian territory as well as in its depth areas all along the 4,000-km line of actual control (LAC), the agencies feel there is a requirement of four to six dedicated satellites, which can help them keep a check on Chinese movement.[41] This would be an *ad hoc* requirement to enable near real-time data to be available to the Indian military. Currently, it would be important for the Chief of Defence Staff and the Department of Military Affairs to jointly work out the priorities and arrive at the number of satellites that are required for joint application in the threatened sectors.

The issue that gradually dawns on the DRDO is that it would not be possible to rely entirely on the ISRO and it must look at other alternatives. The armed forces must harness the changes due to the *Aatmanirbhar Bharat* special economic stimulus package. As a matter of fact, the Government must permit extensive and deep outreach by the services to see how some of the innovations accruing from the start-up segment can generate benefits to military intelligence. Small satellite technology by space start-ups is one core area which the services must exploit. These space unicorns will fulfil the need for numerous satellites by the defence forces.[42]

At this stage, it can be assessed that the requirement of satellites by the armed forces would be large and could be met by start-ups manufacturing small satellites. Currently, India has two military communication satellites, GSAT-7 with the Indian Navy and GSAT-7A with the Indian Air Force. The Indian Army will soon receive the GSAT-7B satellite. This will gradually pave the way for more acquisitions.

10. ROCKETS AND MISSILES

Existing Capability

This is an area where India has been upbeat with its own technology. Truly, India has the ability to indigenously develop and manufacture all types of missiles. Currently our focus has been on the following:

- Enhancing the range of rockets.
- Developing a state-of-the-art indigenous anti-tank guided missile.
- Develop missiles with air defence capability through a process of co-development.
- Develop hypersonic capability for supersonic cruise missiles.

Enhancing the Range of Rockets

A multi-barrel rocket launcher Grad BM 21 is currently ranging 40 km with extended range ammunition. The Smerch rocket launcher is ranging 90 km with an extended variety of ammunition. There is little scope in upgrading these two multi-barrel rocket launchers. Pinaka is an indigenous multi-barrel rocket launcher which currently ranges 60 km. This is a rocket which could be first extended to 90 km and thereafter to 120 km. This is an area on which the Indian Army must focus at the earliest. Further, the system is required to cater for incendiary ammunition which needs to be developed by the Armament Research Development Establishment (ARDE), Pune.

Developing a state-of-the-art Third-Generation Anti-Tank Guided Missile (ATGM)

In terms of *Aatmanirbharta* or attaining self-reliance, a need arises for a third generation ATGM that can effectively engage anti-tank and anti-structure targets. The DRDO is making a man-pack ATGM; this would cater primarily for the special forces and infantry battalions.[43] It would be an industry-funded indigenously designed, developed and manufactured project. The indigenous content will be a minimum of 60 per cent. The maximum range of the ATGM would be 2.5 km by day and night with a minimum range of 200 metres. Considering that the missile is similar to the DRDO's Nag, the incorporation of lock-on-after-launch parameter should be feasible.

Indian Navy

The Indian Navy has missiles which are surface-to-surface, surface-to-air, air-to-air missiles and torpedoes. There are also missiles launched from submarines which are primarily ballistic missiles and torpedoes. Missiles under development are:

- BrahMos hypersonic cruise missile.
- Takshak torpedoes.
- Advance version of Barak surface-to-air missiles.
- Naval anti-ship missile short range (NASM-SR) being developed by the DRDO.
- K-5 and K-6 submarine launched ballistic missiles.

Developmental progress is steady and the missiles should be in service after due process of user trial evaluation. Modernisation needs to be a regular process.

Indian Air Force

The Indian Air Force has numerous missiles. State-of-the-art missiles inducted and to be inducted are Spice and its variants (Israeli origin); Brahmos hypersonic under the DRDO's development; Astra (DRDO); Python (Israeli); HeliNag (variant of the DRDO's Nag missile); Novator KS 172 (Russian, AWAWCs killer); Hammer AASM (French air-to-ground); Advanced short range air-to-air missile (ASRAAM, UK origin); Anti-radiation missile NGARM or Rudra-1 (under development by the DRDO).

The Indian Air Force needs to have state-of-the-art missiles to effectively deal with our adversaries. Modernisation needs to be a sustained commitment.

11. MATERIAL SCIENCE

Material science deals with the properties of solid materials and how they are determined by a material's composition and structure. Knowledge of properties enables materials to be designed for numerous applications ranging from structural steels to computer microchips. Material science is essential for important engineering activities such as electronics, aerospace, telecommunications, information processing, nuclear power, and energy conversion.[44]

There are numerous applications for material science in the defence services. The Department of Defence outlines the critical needs for materials needed for research and development to meet 21st century defence needs, as enumerated below:

- Structural and multi-functional materials.
- Energy and power materials.
- Electronics and photonic materials.
- Functional organic and hybrid materials.
- Bio-derived and bio-inspired materials.

Research investments must be made in the design of materials, devices and systems, duly assisted by computation and phenomenological models of materials and their behaviour. Today's breathtaking improvements in computational power enable material scientists to move beyond trial and error and predict structures from first principles. Further convergence with other sciences would help in producing the desired metals needed for weaponry, modern radio sets, etc., for the armed forces. Future defence systems would employ advanced materials that are self-healing, can interact independently with local environments and can monitor the health of a structure or component during operation. Advanced materials could also be used for state-of-the-art technologies like embedded sensors and integrated antennas. Advanced materials must also deliver traditional high performance in structures. That would lead to protection against corrosion, fouling, erosion, and fires.[45] All the three services of the Indian military must collaborate with the DRDO to invest in these areas.

12. NUCLEAR TECHNOLOGY

Nuclear weapons have important roles to play in India's military calculations. Ideas, concepts and doctrines of nuclear weaponization change with time. Most of the contemporary military conflicts are regional conflicts, and often countries like the USA and France have to participate in operations far from their country. With regard to India, most of the conflicts would be of a hybrid nature. Considering these aspects, the Indian military must have a vision to anticipate possible nuclear postures in the future.

Two more areas where nuclear energy could be used by the military would be to use portable nuclear reactors to produce potable water from the sea, and use it as nuclear fuel. Demand for desalination of sea water is likely to grow as inadequate fresh water supplies become an urgent global concern. Using waste heat from nuclear reactors and mobile desalination plants can be used to convert water from brackish lakes in high-altitude regions. Similarly, the idea of using nuclear power to produce synthetic fuels, originally proposed 57 years ago, is even more relevant today.[46] That could replace carbon-based fuels and eliminate the grip of the oil sector on the armed forces.

Research is continuing on the design of miniature reactors that would enable a variety of military applications. The Indian military, in conjunction with the Atomic Energy Commission, must analyse the various futuristic uses of nuclear power for military operations.

Conclusion

The Indian armed forces would need to develop frontier technologies to modernise and be prepared to undertake military operations across India's areas of interest on land, sea and air. With sworn adversaries as well as other advanced militaries regularly inducting high-technology weapons, there is no option but to develop the above stated technologies so as to be able to undertake precise and effective military operations in the defence of the nation.

ENDNOTES

1. "What is Nano-Technology?" www.nano.gov.
2. Frank Simonis & Steven Schilthuizen, "Nano Technology : Innovation, Opportunities for Tomorrow's Defence", *TNO SCIENCE and Industry*, 2006, at http://www.futuretechnologycenter.eu/downloads/nanobook.pdf accessed on 9 June 2019.
3. Frank Simmons & Steven Schilthuizen, "Nanotechnology, Innovation Opportunities for Tomorrow's Defence", at www.futuretechnologycenter.eu
4. "*DRDO Newsletter*", Volume 32, No. 11, November 2012 available at www.drdo.gov.in
5. Press trust of India, "Army Chief tapping AI, Big Data for Defence Forces", *Economic Times* at www.economic times.indiatimes.com, 21 January 2019.
6. Air Cmdre I Chand, "Big Data Analytics and Its likely application in Defence and Security Organisations", www.cenjowsgov.in
7. Aaron Dalton, "Quantum Technology Comes off Age", www.sciencemag.org 15 November 2019.
8. International institute for Strategic Studies, "Quantum Computing and Defence", *The Military Balance* 2019, at www.iiss.org February 2019.
9. Subcommittee on Quantum Information Science "National Strategic Overview for Quantum Information Science", National Science and Technology Council.
10. I. H. Miller, "UN based biotechnology regulation: Scientific and Economic havoc for 21st century", *Trends in Biotechnology*, 1999, pp. 17, 185-190.
11. J. R. Ferguson, "Biological weapons and US law", *JAMA*, 1997, pp, 278, 357-360.
12. J. A. Poupart & Miller, "Biological Warfare" in *Encyclopedia of Microbiology*, J Lederberg (ed.), London Academic Press, 1992, pp. 297-308, www.publications.drdo.gov.in
13. Press Trust of India," India must be prepared for biological warfare: Manohar Parrikar", *The Economic Times*, 11 July 2018, www.economictimes.indiatimes.com
14. Press trust of India, "Ensure strict compliance of treaty on banning biological weapons: India", *The Economic Times*, 27 March 2020, www.economictimes.indiatimes.com
15. Gunjan Singh, "Role of Biotechnology in Defence", Fellows Seminar, IDSA, 5 September 2008, www.idsa.in
16. The National Academies Press, "Chapter-2, *Biotechnology band The Army", Opportunities in Biotechnology for Future Army Applications*, 2001, www.nap.edu
17. Ken Klippenstien, "Exclusive: The Military knew years ago that Coronavirus was Coming", www.thenation.com
18. "Artificial Intelligence and Machine Learning" Policy Paper, 18 April 2017, www.internetsociety.org/ai/how-ai-works
19. "Products CAIR", www.drdo.gov.in0
20. David Hambling, "UAV Helicopter brings Finesse to Air Strikes", *Popular Mechanics*, May 2009, www.popularmechanics.com/technology/military_law/4313331.html accessed on 23 June 2020.
21. Anthony Blair, "AI Army", www.dailystar.co.uk 27 January 2018.
22. Peter Dockrill, "First Ever Drone Swarm Attack has struck Russian Military Bases, sources claim", www.sciencealert.com 11 January 2018,
23. Norbert Koch," Supramolecular Materials for Opto Electronics", Royal Society of Chemistry, Cambridge 2015, www. pubs.rsc.org/en/content/ebook/978-1-78262-694-7
24. Defence Update, "Directed Energy Weapons: India's Strategic Game Changer?", *Indian Defence News*, www.defenceupdate.in

25. Global Defence Technology, "The Future of Electronic Warfare in Europe", www.defence.nridigital.com and www.army-technology.com
26. Lt-Gen Rakesh Chadha, "Emerging Role of Information Warfare in Indian Subcontinent", *Future of Land Warfare beyond the Horizon*, CLAWS, Pentagon Press LLP, New Delhi, 2020.
27. Carmine Cicalese, "How to give the military's tactical information warriors a chance", 9 August 2019,www.fifthdomain.com
28. Dominic Nicholls, "British Army to engage in social media warfare as new cyber division unveiled", *The Telegraph*, 1 August 2019, www.telegraph.co.uk
29. Lyu Jinghua, "What are Chinese Cyber capabilities and intentions?", Carnegie Endowment for International Peace, www.carnegieendowment.org
30. Elsa. B. Kania, "The Strategic Support Force and the Future of Chinese Information Operations", 2017, www.cyberdefensereview.army.mil
31. Jack Browne, "Radar Grows from Military tool to Everyday use", Microwaves & RF www.mwrf.com
32. Lt-Gen Naresh Chand, "Future Trends in Army Air Defence Systems", *SPs Land Forces*, Issue 5/2013, www.spslandforces.com
33. David Hambling, 'Why Russia Will Be the First to use the Pain Ray: Analysis", *Popular Mechanics*, www.popular mechanics.com 18 June 2012.
34. *India Today* Web Desk, "KALI: India's weapon to destroy any uninvited missiles and aircrafts", www.indiatoday.in 21 September 2019.
35. Sanjay Badri Maharaj, "India's Military Satellite Options", *Magzter News Stand*, January 2020, www.magzter.com
36. Gunter's Space Page, "Cartosat 3, 3A,3B", www.space.skkyrocket.de
37. Sandhya Ramesh, "Cartosat-3 images are so clear that you can tell a truck from a car, read road markings, *The Print*, 31 January 2020, www.theprint.in
38. Sandhya Ramesh, "Cartosat-3 images are so clear that you can tell a truck from a car", *The Print*, 31 January 2020. www.theprint.in.
39. Global Security.org, "India to set up space cell to counter threats to space-based assets," www.global security.org 10 June 2008.
40. Manoj Joshi, "India has a Long Way to Go Before it can use Space for Modern Warfare", *Science the Wire*, 16 June 2019, www.science.thewire.in
41. ANI, "Security agencies seek four to six dedicated satellites for keeping close eye on Chinese military activities", *The Times of India*, 6 August 2020, www.timesofindia.indiatimes.com
42. Kartik Bommakanti, "AatmaNirbhar: Indian Space Start-ups and the Armed Services", ORF, New Delhi, 23 May 2020, www.orfonline.org
43. Prashant Pande, "Invitation for Expression of Interest (EoI) for procurement of 3rd generation ATGM system for Indian Army", Ministry of Defence, Govt. of India, www.ddpmod.gov.in
44. Louis A. Girifalco, "Materials Science", *The Britannica Encyclopedia*, www.britannica.com
45. National Research Council of United States, *"Materials Research 21st Century Defence Needs"* Princeton University,, The National Academies Press, Washington, D.C. www.scholar.princeton.edu
46. R.A. Pfeffer and W.A Macon Jr, "Nuclear Power: An Option for the Army's Future",www.alu.army.mil.

13

Restructuring Special Forces for the Future

Prakash Katoch

The Scenario

The threats to India's national security are increasing day-by-day. The China-Pakistan anti-India alliance eyes our territory and is engaged in destabilizing India through terrorism and other asymmetric means. China eyes large tracts in our North-East and Eastern Ladakh. In our neighbourhood, Nepal is drawn into China's strategic sphere through Nepalese communist parties and the Belt and Road Initiative (BRI) for which China has recently pledged a US$ 118 million grant to Nepal. Chinese territorial advances in Bhutan aim to secure the Jhampari Ridge together with Saktang wildlife sanctuary, and bring the Siliguri Corridor within range of China's long-range weaponry. US sanctions on Myanmar are pushing it closer to China. China has secured a major role—positive or otherwise—in the Sri Lankan economy. Having secured the first island chain in the Western Pacific, China is reaching out to the Pacific and Indian Ocean islands.

China views India to be in the American camp. However, even if America would want India (even Taiwan) to become the Ukraine of the Indo-Pacific, it will not fight China directly. The Ukraine conflict has proved that the USA cannot directly engage Russia for avoidance of nuclear escalation. The same applies to the USA vis-a-vis China and vice versa. The US leaders' solidarity visits to Taiwan notwithstanding, for a long time China has conveyed to foreign delegations that Taiwan will be integrated into mainland China by 2025.

India is further afflicted with multiple insurgent and radical organizations which are externally supported. Forty-two terrorist organizations and 13 unlawful associations are banned in India. However, the Kerala-headquartered Popular Front of India (PFI) having an armed wing and whose five cadres were nabbed in Kupwara, Jammu & Kashmir (J&K), while trying to cross into Pakistan Occupied Kashmir (POK) in 2005 is not yet banned. On 30 July 2022, the All India Sufi Sajjadanashin Council (AISSC) adopted a resolution in the presence of our NSA that organizations like the PFI, indulging in anti-national activities and creating discord, must be banned and acted against as per the law. Apparently, the case seems to be some distance away from ripening.

Special Forces

Special Forces provide multiple low-cost high-gain options to governments for achieving military, political, economic, and psychological objectives, including in conditions of grey zone and sub-conventional war. Employment of Special Forces on politico-military missions at the strategic level can provide rich dividends as an extension of foreign policy in shaping the environment in the nation's favour. Special Forces should be central to asymmetric response including against irregular forces though asymmetric warfare does not automatically equate it with physical attack. A physical attack is only the extreme and potentially most dangerous expression of asymmetric warfare. The key lies in achieving strategic objectives through application of minimal resources packaged with essential psychological elements.

The ultimate aim in employing Special Forces must be to secure strategic advantage. Counter-terrorism will remain a task for the special forces along with other hitherto-fore tasks. However, rapid technological advances will also require an expansion of special force employment on additional domains like cyber and space.

The Indian Set-up

The Army. Numerically, India has a large number of Special Forces. The Army has 10 PARA or Parachute (Special Forces) battalions including one being raised. These battalions are distributed among the various army commands with one as reserve at Army Headquarters level. With the setting up joint theatre commands, this distribution may undergo changes and perhaps also their locations in some cases. In addition, there are five parachute battalions in the same Parachute Regiment whose designation on modification has recently been upgraded to PARA (SF) airborne battalions to bring all at par.

Navy. The Navy has the marine commandos (MARCOS). Their strength is in the region of 2,000. The Navy's proposal for raising a marine brigade has been pending with the Ministry of Defence (MoD) for over two decades.

The Air Force. The Garud Commando Force was established in the Indian Air Force (IAF) in September 2004. It has a current strength of over 1,500 personnel.

The Armed Forces Special Operations Division (AFSOD). The AFSOD is a tri-service command established on 29 September 2018. This came about with the Naresh Chandra task force recommending the establishment of a special operations command as one of its recommendations.

Training. The Army maintains a Special Forces Training School (SFTS) and a Parachute Regimental Centre (PRTC) for the Parachute battalions. The IAF conducts its airborne training at the Paratrooper Training School (PTS), Agra. In addition, the headquarters of the integrated defence staff (IDS) has been conducting tri-service exercises for out-of-area contingencies.

The National Security Guard (NSG). 51 and 52 special action groups (SAGs) are manned completely by army personnel on deputation. These groups classified as Special Forces could have been part of the Special Forces orbat. A few decades ago a proposal to place them under the Army was nixed on the ground that anti-hijack tasks were not part of the Army's role. The optimisation of Special Forces capabilities thus remains below par.

The Special Frontier Force (SFF). The SFF was in being much before the three services raised their special forces. Within the SFF, the two special groups (SGs) are fully manned by army personnel on deputation. For cost-efficient operational management, these two SGs need to be integrated with the tri-service Special Forces.

Observations

Some steps are being taken to strengthen India's Special Forces; much more needs to be undertaken with due alacrity. The matter is discussed in the following parts.

Employment

Other than the employment of the then three para commando battalions (whose designation was changed to PARA (SF) later) under the Indian Peace Keeping Force (IPKF) in Sri Lanka, employment of our special forces has largely been within the country. In one instance, a PARA (SF) battalion and later some Special Forces elements were sent on UN missions in recognition of their good work. Besides that, over the past eight years or so, cross-border employment of special forces has been restricted to just one 'surgical strike' in Pakistan Occupied Kashmir (POK) and one raid inside Myanmar in response to the casualties suffered in an army camp at Uri and the ambush of an army convoy in Manipur, respectively. These were retaliatory operations and not strictly classified as pro-active.

In counter-insurgency (CI) operations in Jammu & Kashmir (J&K), Special Forces are invariably being used, for immediate and expedient responses to incidents rather than for cross-border tasks, even when 'Ghatak platoons' of the infantry battalions can undertake the same tasks. The Northern Command also has the 31 Rashtriya Rifles whose manpower is also provided by the PARA (SF) and the Parachute Regiment.[1] There have been instances of the SAG of NSG and SG of SFF having been deployed for CI tasks in the Kashmir Valley. However, due to diffused command and control, these have seldom been employed, have little coordination with the Army in the area, leave alone with the PARA (SF), and invariably have arrived late on the scene of action after the counter-operations have already been launched.

Command and Control

The Army's Special Forces, Navy's MARCOS, Garud Commandos of the Air Force, 51 and 52 SAGs of NSG and SGs of SFF, all have separate channels of command and control. That denies holistic optimization of these assets and their strategic employment in furtherance of India's national interests. The AFSOD is placed under the headquarters IDS, whereas dynamic tasking of the Special Forces on strategic purposes can only be sanctioned by the highest political authority. This aspect that affects the employment of the AFSOD at the strategic level needs to be examined.[2] Similarly, there is a need to reorganise and streamline the functions and systems of the AFSOD in relation to the CDS, the department of military affairs (DMA), the Chiefs of Staff committee (CoSC), and the department of Defence. Four years after the AFSOD had been raised, it remains below strength, split at various locations, and short of essential support elements that such a formation should have.

The command and control of Special Forces units must be exercised by the highest headquarters in the theatre. As mentioned above, PARA (SF) battalions are allotted to various commands but they tend to group these units to corps headquarters. Moreover, at the theatre level, the level of integration among the Special Forces and the other force multipliers—like intelligence field surveillance units (IFSU), electronic warfare (EW) units, long-range artillery, aviation and the like—have to be enhanced to avoid suboptimal employment of the Special Forces.

Training

Since they can be launched without notice, the Special Forces must train continuously to hone multiple skills and remain at the peak of combat efficiency. Because of separate channels of command, training of Special Forces is organized by the individual services. Headquarters IDS has been organizing tri-service exercises for the task forces earmarked for various out-of-area contingencies (OOACs). These exercises involve Special Forces of the three services, but the elements may not come from the same unit/subunit—these keep changing, thus losing out on consolidating on the experience. The SFF and the Army's Special Forces both might have tasks on the Indo-Tibet border and therefore need to be jointly exercised. Similarly, 51 and 52 SAG of NSG and SGs of SFF, all manned by Army personnel on deputation, have to begin exercising with the PARA (SF), for under certain contingencies they may have to be deployed in tandem or jointly.

There are some other impediments to be addressed. As an example, there are limitations of the availability of training ammunition for the Special Forces personnel who fire their primary weapons on a daily basis. For combat free-fall (CFF), the designated personnel of PARA (SF) battalions need to undertake their full schedule of jumps with combat loads without the schedule being delayed or missed out altogether. Capacity at the Para Training School (PTS) at Agra run by the IAF needs to be substantially augmented to meet the essential requirements of all the special and parachute forces.

Equipping

The MARCOS and GARUD units being small in number are well equipped.

This is not the case with the Army's Special Forces where the accent has been on expansion at the expense of consolidation. Rapid expansion of PARA (SF) battalions has also to be speeded up with the rising requirements of equipment scales, a problem which is further compounded when indigenous production remains short while restrictions rule over 'Buy Global'. The requirements being in small numbers, the private sector does not appear interested while the Defence Research & Development Organisation (DRDO) gets afflicted with red tape and quality issues. Also, the NSG and SFF have to follow one procurement procedure to avoid a situation when one faces critical deficiencies of key and urgently needed ammunition and equipment while the other holds adequate stocks.

There is a need for an exclusive procurement procedure for Special Forces which should be fast-track and akin to emergency procurement procedures. Moreover, dedicated funding is a must for equipping Special Forces. For effective employment of Special Forces, these issues need to be further resolved.

Special Forces should be at the vanguard of new weaponry to be introduced in the military. In developed countries, they have their own mini workshop-R&D facility to experiment and modify the latest and futuristic weapons and choose the best among them. The Defence Innovation Organisation (DIO), Army Design Bureau and such in-house development initiatives need to be boosted beyond their present levels to meet that end.

Army's Coriolis Problem

Within the Army, the Special Forces have been affected with the 'Coriolis Effect' as exemplified by raising and later disbanding of a Special Forces regiment and brigade-level headquarters. Besides, there are instances when the Army's various directorates dealing with manpower, training and equipment for Special Forces have pulled in different directions contrary to the requirements of the military operations directorate. The level of synergy therefore needs consolidation through streamlined capability development functions.

Analyses

Call for Doctrinal Upgrade

In the overall context, it would be apparent that there is much to be done in terms of intelligently re-structuring, organizing, training and equipping our special forces for them to be able to counter the 21st-century threats to India's national security. For that, appropriate changes in our somewhat defensive military doctrines need to be upgraded. For example:

- Seventy-five years after Independence, it is time to formalize a national security strategy.
- The Raksha Mantri's directive, a generic document, needs to be revised.
- A long pending strategy to counter asymmetric threats from Pakistan requires to be studied afresh and approved.
- The Special Forces Doctrine needs to be scripted at Headquarters IDS with wider participation of Special Forces specialists.
- The Army's Sub-Conventional Warfare Doctrine has to cover cyber, information operations and even border skirmishes.
- The Special Forces Doctrine needs to look beyond confining the forces just to the *'internal scene of infiltration and exfiltration of terrorist groups'* while *"other elements of national power address the external dimension of the terrorist smuggling in/out of warlike material"*. Past hesitancy over trans-border employment of Special Forces needs to be got over and long-proposed revisions instituted with continued vigour.[3]

Right-Tasking of Special Forces

Exploiting an enemy's fault-lines, deterring him from taking advantage of our fault-lines and provision of platform(s) for strategic force projection are intrinsic to the Special Forces potential. However, our successive Indian governments have limited the tasking of Special Forces only to direct actions. Even as intelligence agencies globally are working in tandem with their special forces, R&AW remains an exclusive agency to undertake trans-border operations. We have to elevate our concept of covert employment of Special Forces beyond using just the R&AW operatives who would be not enough in the future. In an era where space is becoming another front for employing Special Forces, we are not even using them for cyber and information operations. This mindset is unlikely to change without the indulgence of the highest political authority. Future governments may have to grasp the modern nuances of Special Forces employment. Out-of-area deployment alongside friendly foreign Special Forces and conduct of trans-border operations are effective means to gain experience as well as to secure strategic dividends. Rather than being fixated to the past, such options may be carefully considered in the future.[4]

Our Special Forces potential has to be considered to cover surveillance gaps in areas of our strategic interests, in countering the asymmetric and hybrid wars, and in shaping the strategic environment in India's favour. No matter the rhetoric, at sub-conventional level, we continue to remain at strategic disadvantages vis-à-vis China and Pakistan. Besides, chemical, biological, radio-active and nuclear (CBRN) terrorism is round the corner. There is concern that we cannot strike terrorists on foreign soil like Israel does because it enjoys US and Western support. But then Israel also traces out and eliminates terrorists through clandestine operations. In our case, our protests and repeated knocking at the doors of the United Nations to book terrorists and perpetrators of dozens of terrorist attacks in India fail when China vetoes any action against them.

Right Recruitment and Training

According to some reports, the '*Agnipath*' scheme of recruitment will not be applied to the Special Forces. However, if '*Agniveers*' are posted to the PARA (SF) battalions, they must undergo full-fledged probation training. Also, retention of only 25 per cent after four years of service should not be mandatory for PARA (SF) even if the numbers are small in the overall context of the Army. Similarly, *Agniveers* coming from other units to PARA (SF) as volunteers must also undergo the full probation.

Opinions and Suggestions

China is using de facto groupings, termed 'deep coalition', as part of its 'unrestricted warfare'. Its repeated invocation of the political role played by non-state actors ranging from credit rating agencies to narco-mafias, and its emphasis on the 'civilianization of war' thesis, are precisely similar to the manner in which modern technology is changing the weapons and the battlefields. China's deep coalition could consist of some nation-states, civil society organizations, narco-mafias, private corporations having their self-interest at stake, individual speculators, and other unknown components—the last could well consist of intelligence operatives, terrorist organizations and Special Forces. With all these groups operating all the time in a continuous flow—multiplying, fissioning, and fusing into others—the deep coalition is multi-dimensional.

The expanding China-Pakistan nexus will remain a constant impediment to India's growth. To counter the China-Pakistan hybrid war, India could establish multiple 'deep coalitions' with strategically autonomous strategic partnerships. The aim should be to: one, isolate Pakistan as a terror-exporting country; two, deter and weaken the China-Pakistan nexus; three, secure India's land access to Afghanistan-CAR; four, assist in stabilizing Afghanistan and protect Indian interests abroad; five, deter establishment of Chinese naval bases in the Indian Ocean Region (IOR) and protect the Sea Lines of Communications (SLOC); six, contain China's aggressive moves by forcing it to look inwards; seven, weaken China's gravitational pull in the strategic neighbourhood; eight, generate a pronounced global response to nuclear terrorism; and finally, enable progress of the campaign for nuclear disarmament (CND).

The above strategy is achievable, especially with India viewed favourably in the global balance of the power game. It would promote our grand strategy as a regional and global power. It however, needs more finesse in crafting and steady implementation. Special Forces and intelligence agencies themselves have a major role to play in this process. *Employment of Special Forces for full spectrum optimization (CT, cyber, space, information operations included) needs to be evolved at the national level, with full indulgence of the nation's highest political authority.* Similarly, the roles, organisations and command and control of PARA, PARA (SF) and PARA (Airborne) battalions need to be further deliberated, formalised and operationalized. For all this, establishment of a 'special operations forces (SOF) cell' in the Department of Military Affairs (DMO), to oversee the organization, equipping, training, employment and monitoring of Special Forces may be considered.

In order to optimize the special forces assets in the country, 51 and 52 SAG of NSG and the SGs of the SFF should be integrated with the AFSOD which, if needed for semantic reasons, may be renamed as the 'national special operations division' (NSOD). The AFSOD (or NSOD) should be linked to the NSA, CDS, R&AW, NTRO, DIA and IB. The verticals under it should include an intelligence cell, training cell, SOF teams group, insertion and extraction group, support group, logistics group, cyber cell and an R&D group. Here is highlighted the need to train and employ multiple *SOF teams country and region-wise*. We need *to develop and employ 'publicized' overt capabilities and 'deniable' covert capabilities as credible deterrence against the irregular wars thrust upon us*. The number of SOF teams in the SOF teams group could gradually be increased with the initial focus being on our immediate neighbourhood. The training cell should be linked to the SFTS and training centres of the NSG and SFF. The training cell will also be responsible to organise training with foreign Special Forces.

The rest of the Special Forces would remain with their respective services. However, the following upgrades are suggested:

- Within the Army, all Special Forces functions of policy, planning, employment, manpower (postings included), training and equipping must be more effectively centralized under the designated special operations directorate of the Directorate-General of Military Operations.
- The current practice of posting a colonel-level officer at command headquarters would need to be upgraded to the establishment of a 'special operations branch' at the joint theatre command level. This should be a natural corollary to the establishment of integrated theatre commands.
- More focused and regular exposure of our special forces with their counterparts in the USA, Russia, Israel and France would be good. The present scope and frequency of such events will not stand up to the nation's future mandates to the special forces,

Conclusion

We cannot remain a nation in the 'reactive' mode and keep hoping that rational diplomacy backed with moderately empowered conventional forces alone can deter our enemy's irregular forces. The notion that Special Forces are meant for only cross-border strikes up to a particular distance and that strategic tasks are the forte of the R&AW alone must be laid to rest. Competent external intelligence agencies of leading nations (e.g., the USA's CIA and the UK's MI are just some examples) act in sync with their military and their special forces and so is the case even with Pakistan. As suggested, the NSOD/AFSOD will have to be employed for strategic tasks in the future in concert with the R&AW and NTRO.

Finally, blurred foresight, both at the political and military hierarchical levels, has resulted in India mostly using the Special Forces just as storm troopers within our borders. This must change. To reiterate, *we must develop and employ publicized overt capabilities as well as deniable covert capabilities as credible deterrence against the incessant irregular war thrust upon us.* As former ambassador R.S. Kalaha wrote in his book, '*The Dynamics of Preventive Diplomacy*', "*It is often said that idealism has no place in making of foreign policy. But the argument is not that idealism should not be a stand-alone factor, but that the costs of always following an inward looking policy may be that much higher. Therefore, the most effective foreign policy for any country, whatever its weight is one that balances realism and idealism—that in effect makes idealism realistic."*

The NSOD/AFSOD should be reorganized on the above lines in a few years' timeframe. That should not be a problem with the indulgence of the Prime Minister's Office (PMO). Then, depending on India's progress towards her great power destination, this arrangement could become a precursor for the eventual creation of a full-fledged national special operations command in a longer time frame.

ENDNOTES

1. In a recent case, the Nagaland Police filed an FIR against personnel from 21 PARA (SF) employed on bonafide duty under the Armed Forces' Special Powers Act or AFSPA for 'murder and culpable homicide not amounting to murder' for killing 13 civilians. These are purported charges because of involvement of the state police with Naga insurgents, drug mafia and illegal tax collection. Based on a petition filed by family members of the concerned PARA (SF) personnel, the Supreme Court has granted an interim stay on any proceedings. However, such incidents are not conducive for Special Forces employment. (https://news4masses.com/special-forces-under-attack/).
2. There had been some unsubstantiated talk in the media regarding splitting the posts of CDS and Secretary Department of Military Affairs (DMA). Actually, the need is to better integrate all such departments of the MoD.
3. K.P.S. Gill, former DGP Punjab, had stated in 2001, "Unless our Special Forces go for trans-border operations in the mantle of R&AW, the Army will continue to remain at the receiving end".
4. Maloy K Dhar, former Joint Director IB, wrote in his book, '*Open Secrets–India's Intelligence Unveiled*', ... "advocate for an aggressive and proactive counter and forward intelligence thrust against Pakistan ... sabre rattling of 'coercive diplomacy' cannot convince the Islamist Establishment to desist from the roots of the jaundiced Islamist groups ..."

14

Information Warfare: Time for a Relook

P. K. Mallick

> *"I began to understand that I was caught up in two wars: one fought on the ground with tanks and artillery, and an information war fought largely, though not exclusively, through social media. And, perhaps counter-intuitively, it mattered who won the war of words and narratives (rather) than who had the most potent weaponry."*
>
> —**David Patrikarakos, *War in 140 Characters*, 2017**

Preliminaries

We live in the data-rich Information Age. The ability to share information in near real-time, securely and anonymously, is a capability that is an asset as well as a potential vulnerability to our adversaries and us. The ubiquity of information and the pace of technological change are transforming the character of warfare. Old distinctions between peace and war, public and private, foreign and domestic and state and non-state are increasingly getting out of date. Information Warfare (IW) is a medium through which nation-states achieve strategic objectives and advance foreign policy goals. It is virtual, as these strategies do not employ direct kinetic attack or destruction. It is also societal since both targets and contestants in such campaigns stretch across societies and the goal is to weaken their efficient functioning, levels of trust and their very solidity. It is 'warfare' because it is an activity for achieving supremacy over rival nations and gaining a decisive victory.[1]

Further, IW is a well-developed element of national power as well as a strategic, operational, and tactical weapon that operates at as well as below the level of armed conflict. If used in a timely and logical manner, it can generate advantages over the opponent through subversive customisation of messaging, narrations, and persuasions that deliver mass effects of disrupting, confusing, agitating, and radicalising the population. As cyberspace presents a cost-effective and easy method to communicate a message to a large population, most IW today occurs on the internet. This leads to some confusion between cyber warfare and IW.

Confusion of Terminologies

Various terms used in the doctrines of IW and Information Operations (IO) are somehow confusing and lack clarity. Strategic communities use the terms IW, IO, psychological operations, perception management, military information support operations (MISO), strategic communication, influence operations, cognitive warfare, public field diplomacy, cyberspace operations, etc., rather inter-changeably, though they are not synonymous. Other terms used in the literature include hybrid warfare, grey zone warfare, new or next-generation warfare, ambiguous warfare, full-spectrum warfare, non-linear war, etc.[2]

These inconsistencies eventually can create conceptual confusion that results in misallocation and misalignment of resources and capabilities. For instance, such confusion will make it difficult to recruit, hire, and train the right people for cyber and psychological operations positions due to a lack of understanding of what skill sets different missions require.

Defining Information Warfare (IW)

The Rand Corporation defines IW as, "...conflict or struggle between two or more groups in the information environment". Dan Kuehl of the US National Defence University defines IW as "military offensive and defensive actions to control/exploit the environment". IW is a mix of military and government operations to protect and exploit the information environment. Whether attacking government organisations, political leadership, or the news media to compel decision-makers to take specific actions or to influence public opinion, the final target of IW activities remains human cognition. That is why IW is sometimes referred to as *influence operations* or *psychological operations.*

IW is a strategy for using information to pursue a competitive advantage, including defensive and offensive efforts. IW is a mean through which nation-states achieve strategic objectives and advance foreign policy goals. It may be an end in itself and an attempt to achieve them without the use of force. It may be a prelude to an armed conflict and may begin from below the level of armed conflict to set conditions to gain the support of locals through Information Operations (IO).

Most of the IW today occurs on the internet. This leads to some confusion between *cyber warfare* and IW. There is a subtle difference; cyber warfare operates exclusively in its digitised and operationalised form, IW does so in a much broader sense. With IW, information itself is the weapon. For example, the National Cyber Mission Force of the U.S. Cyber Command carries out operations to target and dismantle violent extremist websites that cause operational threats to troops on the ground. However, this cyber force is structurally and conceptually separated from the troops responsible for conducting information operations. The two forces operate under separate doctrines.

IW and Information Operations (IO)

Information warfare occurs at the strategic level, while IO use various information-related capabilities to implement strategy, when campaigns and major operations are planned, conducted, and sustained to achieve strategic objectives within theatres or other operational areas. Information Operations link these strategic objectives with particular tactics, techniques, and procedures to achieve them.[3]

Information Operations. IO is an evolving construct. The late 1970s saw the emergence of IW and command and control warfare (C2W) as war-fighting concepts integrating several diverse capabilities. These further evolved into IO, thus recognising the role of information as an element of power through the spectrum of peace, conflict, and war.

In the 2003 version of U.S. Department of Defence (DoD) Joint Publication 3-13 and the IO Roadmap, IO consists of five pillars:

- *Computer Network Operations* (CNO), which consisted of computer network attack (CNA), computer network defence (CND) and computer network exploitation (CNE).
- Psychological operations (PSYOP).
- Electronic warfare.
- Operations security (OPSEC).
- Military deception (MILDEC).

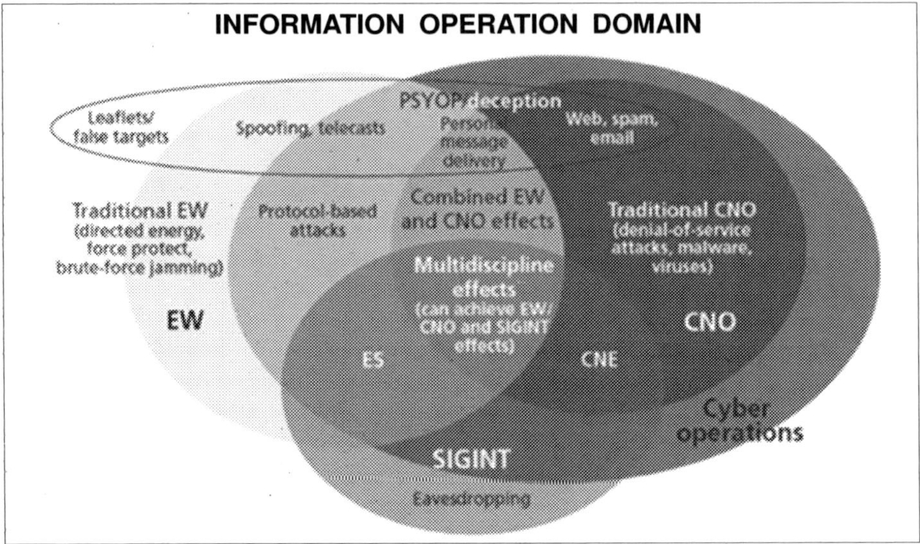

Source: CERDEC I2WD. RAND MG1113-5.2

Cyberspace Operations. Later, computer network operations (CNO) became *cyberspace operations*, offensive and defensive, with its separate doctrine. In the latest U.S. DoD Joint Doctrine JP 3-04, joint operations call for 'information forces' to conduct operations in the information environment (OIE).

Information Forces. Information forces would comprise the following:

- Psychological operations forces to conduct military information support operations (MISO).
- Civil affairs actions planned, coordinated, executed and assessed through civil resources to impose costs through conventional and unconventional activities.
- Public affairs (PA) organisations to concentrate on informing the domestic, international, and international audiences of the operational information environment (OIE).
- Electro-magnetic spectrum operations (EMSO) elements to organise, execute, and oversee the conduct of electro-magnetic warfare and spectrum management operations.
- Cyberspace forces to defend the nation from threats from cyberspace, and project power in support of combatant commanders' objectives.

Space Operations Elements. These would ensure that commanders and staffs have a common understanding of space operations by providing space domain awareness and coordinating space capabilities for the OIE.

Political Warfare. The term 'IW' is often used interchangeably with other terms such as *political warfare*. George Kennan has defined political warfare as the employment of all the means at a nation's command, short of war, to achieve its national objectives. Such operations range from overt actions like political alliances, economic measures, and 'white' propaganda, to such covert operations as clandestine support of 'friendly' foreign elements. Political warfare also covers 'black' psychological warfare and even encouragement of underground resistance in hostile states. By this definition, IW is a form of political warfare where targets are a nation state's government, military, private sector and the general population but there are issues in carrying out IW in democratic countries. The attack surface of a country inevitably includes various elements of civil society, private industry, and civilian government. Most democracies legally differentiate between the role and responsibilities of armed forces vis-a-vis intelligence agencies, law enforcement, and other elements of civilian government. IW operations therefore take the form of hybrid strategies that involve the mixed use of military force alongside other activities.

Cyber Operations and Information Operations

Information Operations can be used in support of conventional military operations, military coercion and those utilising proxies like deniable paramilitary forces, through offensive cyber operations and lawfare. Traditional techniques, such as assassination, deception, economic coercion, espionage, theft of intellectual property and subversion, all gain potency through clever use of cyberspace, digitised information, and social media. Emergence of state-sponsored actors and allied organisations with more advanced cyber warfare capabilities is a fact of life. Many states will have offensive cyber warfare capabilities to interrupt an adversary's cyber-enabled systems. They will use this capability to create social unrest. Attacks will weaken the trust and data integrity in financial, legal, and technical infrastructure which is central to advanced societies.

When 'fake news' appears to originate at home, it gains credibility and reach. It fuels confusion, disagreement, division, and doubt in societies. The 'front' is no longer in some distant theatre of operations but within the country's electro-magnetic spectrum, space and networks. Sub-conventional operations are carried out continuously by adversaries to weaken own military readiness, critical national infrastructure, the economy and the way of life.

Urbanisation and wider access to social media will increase operational complexity. Soldiers and commanders may be deluged with information and face multiple dilemmas across multiple operational domains. The overall operational complexity will require defence personnel to perform their duties with greater skill and understanding of information and cyberspace. Military commanders have to seek information advantage to operate and fight. They have to think beyond the enemy and examine the additional effects relevant to the achievement of the objective, which have to be applied to many other actors, especially the local population, before coordinating an appropriate mix of physical, virtual, and cognitive actions. Information advantage facilitates improved understanding, assessment, decision-making, and execution.[4]

The successes of *psychological* IO carried out by autocratic countries against democracies in recent times have exhibited that truth does not always prevail, in part because lies spread faster than truth. Authoritarian governments exercise control over the information that flows out of their borders. So how to conduct IO against such adversaries or non-state actors needs careful examination.[5]

Information Environment (IE)

Information Environment (IE) is part of the operational environment. All instruments of national power, diplomatic, informational, military, and economic can be projected and employed in the information environment. Activities occurring in and through the IE substantially affect military operations and their outcomes. Cyberspace is a domain within the IE.[6]

IW is conducted in three dimensions of IE:[7]

- **The physical layer**. Command and control systems and associated infrastructure.
- **The informational layer**. Networks and systems where information is stored.
- **The cognitive layer**. The minds of people who transmit and respond to information.

These dimensions continuously interact with individuals, organisations, and systems. A hypothetical example would be a commander using a laptop (physical dimension) to send an encrypted message (informational dimension) to a subordinate who, after reading the message, takes a decision and acts on the information contained in the message (cognitive dimension).

Conduct of IW by the Armed Forces

The conduct of IW by the Armed Forces is governed by the following considerations:

- How can emerging technologies provide ways for faster and reliable development of a common operating picture and understanding to enable effective decision-making?
- What challenges and opportunities does IO provide to swift and effective decision-making? What communications can it have with other domains?
- How does IO impact governments and stakeholders? What would constitute the 'centre of gravity' in IO?
- How should governments and stakeholders combat misinformation as a tool of modern conflict?

Components of IW

Psychological Operations (PSYOPS). PSYOPS involve the prepared use of information (propaganda) to influence the emotions, objective reasoning, motives and, ultimately, the behaviour of foreign governments, organisations,

Source: GAO. I GAO-22-104714

groups, and individuals. PSYOPS employ several mediums such as newspapers, magazines, leaflets, radio, television, email, etc. At the strategic level, PSYOPS are the activities to influence foreign target audiences in support of own nation's goals and objectives. PSYOPS at the operational level are conducted to support the combatant commander's mission accomplishment either independently or as an integral part of other operations. In the US military, the PSYOPS term was changed to military information support operations (MISO)—All-round skill sets needed to perform psychological operations. These skills come from communications technologists, behavioural scientists, cultural anthropologists, educators, historians, religious scholars, economists, linguists, political scientists, business managers, television programmers, and ethnographers and so on.[8]

Electronic Warfare (EW). EW is defined as military action involving electro-magnetic and directed energy to control the electro-magnetic spectrum to attack the enemy. Examples are jamming command and control systems, satellites used for global positioning systems and radio communications.

Operational Security. It is a system of identifying critical information and analysing friendly actions attendant to military operations and other activities.

Military Deception. These are actions to mislead an adversary's military, paramilitary, or extremist organisational decision-makers, thereby causing the adversary to undertake specific actions or inactions that will contribute to accomplishment of own missions.

Public Diplomacy. Public diplomacy is defined as the efforts by a country's government to communicate and interact openly and directly with foreign audiences, including academics, NGOs, businesses, institutions, and even the general public, to deepen mutual understanding and promote its national interests.

Strategic Communication. Strategic communication is defined as synchronization of words, deeds and programs and their perception among select audiences in public affairs, public diplomacy, and information operations professionals.[9]

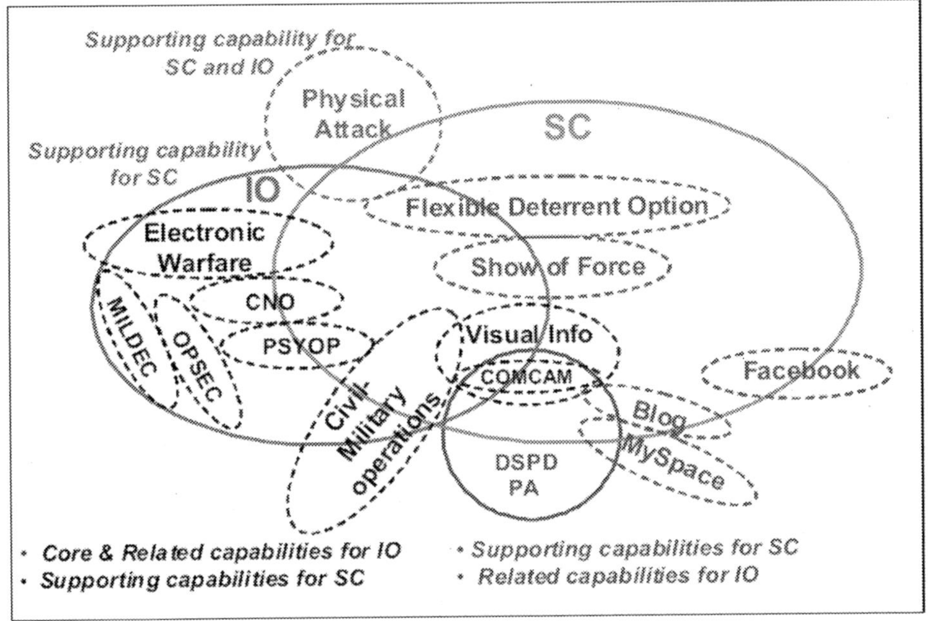

Relationship between Strategic Communication (SC), Information Operation (IO), Public Diplomacy (PD), and Public Affairs (PA)[10]

Cognitive Warfare

The Chinese have started using the term 'Cognitive Warfare'. Fighting in the cognitive environment directly affects the brain, influencing emotions, motives, judgments, and actions and even controlling the enemy's brain. As the engine of cognition, the brain could become the main battlefield of future warfare. The ability to control the brain is the key to combat in the most critical cognitive domains of future warfare.[11] In 2020, the president of the Information Engineering University of the PLA's Strategic Support Forces, Guo Yunfei, argued that of the physical, information, and cognitive domains, it is the cognitive domain that will prevail in any military confrontation between major powers.

Chinese strategists feel that directly interfering with or subconsciously controlling the enemy's brain can induce mental damage, confusion, and hallucinations in the enemy, forcing them to lay down their arms and surrender. According to them:[12]

- The cognitive domain is the key domain for the transformation of military superiority into political victory.

- Military operations have a key role in cognitive shaping.
- Cognitive counter-measures are increasingly being directly used in warfare.

Cognitive Manipulation through Social Media

Social media platforms (SMP) like Facebook, Twitter, YouTube and Instagram are websites, tools, applications and gizmos that provide social media services. The SMP industry has created an addiction. It has a damaging side-effect on democracy. Social media is not just a communication space but a new kind of battle space. The boundaries between foreign and domestic sources of information chaos and dysfunction are blurring. Nation-states and non-state actors alike are leveraging social media to manipulate like-minded populations' cognitive biases to influence conflict dynamics.

The use of propaganda, disinformation, deception, and IW is not new. What is new is the ease, efficiency, low cost, global reach and propagation speed with which people's political sensitivities to national and international opinion can now be manipulated. We cannot control who accesses this capability. The agile player who can shape perceptions will more likely achieve his objectives. Philip N. Howard, referring to deliberate and systematic attempts to steer public opinion using inauthentic accounts and inaccurate information describes them as, "countries with dedicated teams are meddling in the affairs of their neighbours through social media misinformation". The private sector now owns the popular platforms. They shape and influence what we think. Responding to these challenges will not be easy. It will involve making complex and controversial decisions about the private sector's responsibility, restrictions on speech and national security issues.

Freedom of Speech in Social Media versus National Security Concerns

Social Media. The rise of the internet and social media companies, whose profit model is based on an 'attention economy', has been a game changer. Social media platforms are global private players. They have no public accountability. They do not have a mandate to address issues of national security. They have no regulatory oversight. They are not law enforcers. They do not police their platforms. They do all these as per their internal policies. Social media platforms make decisions about content take-downs according to criteria that include corporate risk factors. New tools have emerged for creating and spreading information and disinformation, whether it is beneficial or harmful, true or untrue, on a global scale. Social media companies are reluctant to let intelligence and law enforcement agencies look behind the privacy walls of active accounts. However, making those walls impenetrable prevents those agencies that are responsible for keeping us safe from doing their job. A balance has to be struck as our safety depends on it.

National Security Concerns. Due to the very structure of the internet, there is no solution to stop or deter malicious foreign cyber activity. It is nearly impossible to know quickly and with certainty as to who is behind a disinformation campaign, ransomware implant or data theft. The approach of social media platforms to curb this menace is not encouraging for security professionals. Moreover, the mechanisms put in place by the platforms to identify what is termed fake news are unsuitable for this task. These rely on an obscure fact-checking exercise whereas hostile states use highly sophisticated techniques.

Privacy Rights. There is the sensitive issue of the state demanding to see data without being intrusive to individual rights. However, one must understand that the 'Big Brother' is no longer the state. Technical giants have taken that position, who misuse privacy protections based on their own politically driven algorithms rather than submitting themselves to the government's due process. Recent data shows that requests by the governments to access user data are growing. The challenge for both social media platforms and government agencies is to devise mechanisms and implement regulations that make accounts linked to terrorist groups accessible to law enforcement agencies in real time. Protecting communications between traffickers and terrorists should not be taken as privacy. Platforms know who these people are and can see what they are posting, even if they lie behind privacy settings. Owners of social media must understand that freedom and privacy are not an 'all-or-nothing' game. A balance has to be struck as our safety depends on it.

Cyber-Enabled Information Operations (CIO)

Cyber-enabled information operation (CIO) is defined as the conduct of IW that uses modern information technologies like the Internet, social media, search engines, artificial intelligence and traditional communications media technologies. Military commanders have to seek information advantage because it is central to how militaries operate and fight. Commanders have to think beyond the enemy and examine the additional effects that are to be applied to the many other actors, especially local populations relevant to the achievement of the objective, before coordinating the appropriate mix of physical, virtual, and cognitive actions. Information advantage facilitates improved understanding, assessment, decision-making, and execution.[13]

In the digital age, IW is generally viewed in terms of the attack surface of network-enabled information and communications systems. Whether the target for decision-makers is political or military, reliance is mostly on internet-enabled infrastructure—from data stored in computers and codes that makes them work to sensors employed on the battlefield. However, there is a difference between cyber-enabled psychological operations and offensive cyber operations. Whereas cyber security is centred around technical expertise in computer science, communications, mathematics, etc., for defence against psychological operations, the practitioners need to learn techniques for inoculating against misinformation. It requires a whole-of-the-government approach to bring all of the relevant expertise to address the problem.

Strategic Goals and Tactics of CIO. A CIO campaign aims not to degrade a computer system's functional integrity but to use those computer systems against the target to benefit the attacker's objectives. Many such activities are intended to shape a society's perceptions, choices and behaviours, and in some cases, to make the target dysfunctional as a society. This is not merely propaganda, fake news, or manipulation of perception. It is a battle over what people believe is reality and the decisions each individual makes based on those beliefs. The winners in this battle are the attackers who have convinced a large number of victims to make decisions that directly help them.

In the twenty-first century, digital platforms have become the primary sources of perception-shaping information. Anyone can publish any kind of information, true or false. Digital platforms provide numerous advantages for current information operations, including low cost, no oversight, anonymity, and ease of multiplication.[14] China, Iran, Syria, and the Islamic State have all carried out political warfare regularly via digital platforms, often augmented by cyber means, against Western polities during the past few years with increasing intensity and sophistication.[15] The same technologies can also be used for defensive purposes. Technology can help researchers to search massive amounts of social media data.[16]

IW AND INDIA

Doctrine

The Indian Army's Doctrine of October 2004 gave different forms of IW as:

- Command and Control Warfare (C2W);
- Intelligence-Based Warfare;
- Electronic Warfare;
- Psychological Warfare;
- Cyber Warfare;
- Economic IW;
- Network-Centric Warfare.

The Doctrine was revised in November 2010 to state, "IW battle space deals with physical, information infrastructure, and perceptual realms. From the Indian Army's perspective, IW will comprise cyber warfare, psychological warfare and electronic warfare." The Indian Army's Land Warfare Doctrine published in 2018 points to development of capabilities to prosecute IW operations over the entire spectrum of conflict, as well as in a 'No War No Peace' scenario, to achieve full spectrum information dominance over an adversary. It will have the following components: cyber warfare (CW), electronic warfare (EW) and psychological warfare (Psy W).[17]

India's Joint Doctrine for Perception Management and Psychological Operations was published by the Headquarters Integrated Defence Staff (IDS) in March 2010.[18] In Jammu & Kashmir, the Northern Command has used the term 'Perception Management' to address own people affected by counter-insurgency/counter-terrorism operations (CI/CT Ops), whereas the term 'Psychological Operations' has been used to address the people across the border. There is a clear-cut division of responsibility.

Organisation

The Ministry of External Affairs (MEA) has a 'Public Diplomacy Division', which was established in May 2006 to "educate and influence global and domestic opinion on key policy issues and project a better image of the country commensurate with its rising international standing". The Public Diplomacy Division also partners with major domestic and international universities, think tanks, and research facilities to organise seminars and conferences. The Ministry of Information and Broadcasting supports the public diplomacy initiative with its strategic media use. However, currently, this organisation is dormant. The Ministry of Defence (MoD) has an existing organisation named 'Directorate of Public Relations'. The Armed Forces and other agencies have some organisations for cyber warfare, but no organisation exists specifically for psychological operations.

The respective service headquarters have their own organisations for public information operations. In the Army, the Additional Directorate-General of Public Information (ADGPI), now renamed ADG Strategic Communications (Strat Comn), comes under the Directorate-General of Military Intelligence. It deals with public relations activities, media relations and monitoring, information release, publicity, image projection and perception management. It aims to establish conditions that foster confidence in our Army and its readiness to conduct operations in war and peace.[19] Recently, there has been some reorganisation in this field. A new post of Director-General of IW has been created under the Deputy Chief of Army Staff (Strategy) to function as the 'single-point advice' to the Vice-Chief of Army Staff (VCOAS). From outside, it looks as if an additional layer has been included in the chain of processing but it is too early to judge the efficacy of this reorganisation.

Information warfare capabilities, both offensive and defensive, must be integrated with traditional warfare for success on the modern battlefield. Its ability to drive offensive operations while denying or manipulating enemy perceptions of the battlefield, if applied in isolation, will not get us victories. IW capabilities defined as combat capabilities will only be effective in the context of consequences. Ultimately, a war is won on the land, which involves violence, death, and destruction.

RECOMMENDATIONS

I. Mark Responsibilities

Unlike in the UK (foreign ministry) and the USA (DoD), in the case of India, it is not clear who has overall responsible for IW. For information operations, the various stakeholders are the MoD, the Ministry of Home Affairs (MHA) and intelligence agencies, the MEA, and the ministries of Information and Broadcasting, Electronics and Information Technology, Communications, Education, Law and Justice, among others. Close coordination between these ministries will be needed to carry out IW against an adversary. However, as of now, there is no central agency to coordinate and direct such a task.

For allotment of budget and ability to prevail upon the MHA, the MEA and intelligence agencies, the MoD can definitely not be considered as the lead agency. At the most, it can lead in perception management activities in CI/CT operations within the country. In such an environment, the army, central and state intelligence agencies, paramilitary, central and local police forces, concerned ministries, etc., all come together and carry out perception management, including 'Winning Hearts and Minds' (WHAM) of the population. Invariably they do a good job taking an *ad hoc* approach.

For carrying out psychological operations at the strategic level, the Central Government has to take a whole-of-the-government and whole-of-the-society approach. The strategy has to be chalked out at the highest level. The lead agency, given India's notoriously stove-piped bureaucracy, cannot be the MoD. A specific organisation under the National Security Council could be responsible for IO. The organisation should have experts from psychology, sociology, media, area specialists, language experts, legal, armed forces, political science specialists, foreign affairs, country experts, communications, and social media.

II. Find the Right Term

Currently, India's armed forces and strategic community blindly follow US jargons and also like the USA, the DOD, seems to be confused. To succeed in IW, we have to define terms like *information operations, psychological operations, strategic communications, influence operations, perception management, public information operations, cognitive operations, public field diplomacy* and other similar terms. Presently these terms are being used interchangeably even if they are not synonyms. The Indian armed forces must coin their own common terms and develop indigenous concepts, tactics, techniques, and procedures for IW.

III. Formulate IW Strategy and Doctrine

The Indian government must enunciate a formal integrated strategy for IW and psychological warfare encompassing all international and national facets to empower a doctrinal framework for thinking, communicating, planning, and acting within the information environment. The armed forces should then chalk out their own tactics, techniques, and procedures for IW operations in their respective service domains.

IV. Organise for IW Tasks at the Strategic Level

India should establish a whole-of-the-government organisation responsible to defend India in the information environment. During the Kargil War, an *ad hoc* organisation was created which did a good job. However, this was never institutionalised. There is a feeling that in the Balakot incident, India lost the plot in the IW domain. Currently, the Indian government does not have a lead organization to manage offensive or defensive psychological operations. At the apex level, the establishment of a 'Centre for Cognitive Security' may be considered to bring together experts in all relevant fields to manage full-spectrum security issues of the information environment. It should have close ties with government, industry, academia, think tanks, and public interest groups. It should have the following functions:

- Develop a strategic, multi-lateral cooperation and information sharing arrangement with friendly countries focused on countering IW misinformation efforts.
- Create clear and practical technology objectives in support of adopted policies and strategies to develop practices and technologies to identify, disrupt, fact check, and verify disinformation campaigns.
- Create training and research schedules for strategy and policy formulation, implementation and supporting technologies.
- Maintain a response team that will coordinate with all communities to identify influence campaigns and issue alerts and warnings.

Normally, governments find it difficult to work effectively across traditional departmental boundaries. This bureaucratic vulnerability can lead to poor information flow, competition for resources and influence or exclusion of key stakeholders. These shortcomings underline the need to work more effectively across government agencies to integrate own IW activities. The concerned ministries must break out of their silos of national security thinking, coordinate more effectively, and provide space for cross-sector cooperation.

V. Factors to be Considered at Strategic Level

The following factors may be considered at the strategic level:

- What are the current objectives and how likely can they be achieved?
- What strategies (e.g., force or negotiation) are most likely to influence the targeted groups and yield the desired outcomes?

- What message sources, contents, and formats are most likely to be accepted and lead to fostering the desired changes?

The misuse of social media by our adversaries, both external and internal, has to be checked. The government should promote international coordination to stop the adversarial disinformation campaigns and bring cross-border cybercriminals to justice. It may consider setting up a *national counter-disinformation centre* as successfully done with the National Counter-Terrorism Centre. India should have its own mitigation strategy to thwart hostile psychological operations campaign and to launch own campaign with due subtlety. The government may even consider joining externally controlled social media platforms like Weibo and WeChat to reach the target population and put forward India's viewpoints.

VI. Considerations at the MoD Level

Presently, the MoD or the HQ IDS do not have any established definition for IW, nor are there any comprehensive concepts of operations. Though with the raising of the *Defence Cyber Agency*, initial steps are being taken with regard to cyber warfare, no control organisation exists for IW which actually is a superset of cyber warfare. To begin with, the MoD may think of expanding the role of the Defence Cyber Agency and rename it as *Defence IW Agency*; at least the pros and cons may be discussed and analysed.

IW related imperatives for the MoD are:

- Define IW, develop IW operational concept and designate IW leadership hierarchy.
- Coordinate with MEA, MHA, intelligence agencies, and concerned ministries to improve whole-of-government synergy. Seek to incorporate their insights into military responses to political-military threats. Identify critical information requirements for emerging threats across the entire spectrum of warfare.
- Train the armed forces to recognise and resist foreign disinformation campaigns. Build a database of adversarial disinformation operations to identify patterns and vectors of delivery.
- Establish a presence on opponents' social media platforms so as not to cede valuable communications territories to the adversary. Engage with concerned friendly foreign countries to share information and

best practices for identifying and countering adversarial disinformation on social media.

VII. Oversight of IW Preparedness at MoD Level

The state of our preparedness in IW may be regulated by the following considerations and by activating suitable enabling mechanisms:

- How can the MoD develop consistent policies, plans, doctrines and a common lexicon for the department as a whole?
- To what extent has the MoD established priorities for use and protection of the information environment, and outlined the priorities for training and exercises concerning that environ-ment?
- What steps have been taken towards protection and accountability against mal-information generated or spread by service members, civilian employees, and the public at large?
- What controls have been put in place to enhance the cyber-security of the systems and networks owned by defence establishments, the defence industrial base, contractors and civilian companies that MoD relies on for its purposes?
- To what extent has the MoD established a comprehensive plan to identify and fill the requirement of personnel related to the information environment?

There is the possibility that our armed forces could be the target of adversarial psychological operations to influence their emotions, motives, objective reasoning, and behaviour. If the MoD is not in a position to lead a society-wide defence against the IW threat, it should at the least take action to defend its service members and their families. The MoD should augment its basic training and professional military education requirements to identify foreign and domestic enemies.

Conclusion

In the information age, it's not just whose army wins, but whose story wins.

—Joseph Nye

IW will be a critical core competency in future armed conflicts. The battlefield is expanding from kinetic effects towards networked and information-driven outcomes. We must define its terms, develop operational concepts, doctrines, leadership, and resources to empower our forces to fight and win in the information age. A healthy democracy requires the ability to produce, share and access quality information supported by trusted institutions of government, media, academe, non-profit organisations and others. When the integrity of that information is compromised, attacks against the fabric of democracy would be telling.

In recent years, cyber operations have boosted deft manipulation of the algorithmic underpinnings of modern media platforms to reinforce and project attempts to sell prejudice, skew opinions and coerce and distract democratic populations. Through social media and other internet technologies, attackers can incentivise and manipulate exchanges directly with citizens of another country, bypassing government efforts to insulate their citizens from a deluge of disinformation. These attacks exploit human vulnerabilities more than technological ones and capitalise on psychological and emotional dimensions like fear, uncertainty, cognitive biases, and others.[20]

There was a report in early September 2022 by *Graphika* titled '*Unheard Voice: Evaluating Five Years of pro-Western Covert Influence Operations*'. Concerns have been raised that Pentagon agencies had engaged in "attempted manipulation of audiences overseas".[21] The *Washington Post* has published, in a story, "Our joint investigation found an interconnected web of accounts on Twitter, Facebook, Instagram, and five other social media platforms that used deceptive tactics to promote pro-Western narratives in the Middle East and Central Asia". The report cited data from a group of accounts removed from those social media sites in July and August 2022. Behind the 'bamboo curtain', China is not far behind in this activity. There is a certainty that the USA, China, UK, Russia, even Pakistan, are carrying out extensive IW with India being one of their main targets. We have no choice but to prepare for both defensive and offensive aspects of IW.

ENDNOTES

1. Mazarr et al., The Emerging Risk of Virtual Societal Warfare, Rand Corporation, p. 154.
2. Caroline Jack, Lexicon of Lies: Terms for Problematic Information (New York: Data & Society Research Institute, 2017), p. 6.
3. Catherine A. Theohary, Information Warfare: Issues for Congress, Congressional Research Service, 5 March 2018.
4. The Integrated Operating Concept 2025 (accessible version), UK Ministry of Defence, 30 September 2020 available at: https://www.gov.uk/government/publications/the-integrated-operating-concept-2025/the-integrated-operating-concept-2025-accessible-version

5. Matt Field, Congressional testimony: How the Pentagon can fight information warfare, *The Bulletin*, 4 May 2021 available at: https://thebulletin.org/2021/05/congressional-testimony-how-the-pentagon-can-fight-information-warfare/
6. Isaac R. Porche III et al, Redefining Information Warfare Boundaries for an Army in a Wireless World, RAND Corporation, 2013 available at: https://www.rand.org/pubs/monographs/MG1113.html
7. The Conduct of Information Operations, ATP 3-13.1, October 2018, available at: https://irp.fas.org/doddir/army/atp3-13-1.pdf
8. Ibid.
9. Maj-Gen P. K. Mallick, VSM (retd.), Strategic Communications Opportunities and Challenges, 18 March 2018 available at: https://www.vifindia.org/sites/default/files/SC%20PPT%2018%20mar.pdf
10. Lysychkina, Iryna. (2017). The Image of Security Sector Agencies as a Strategic Communication Tool. *Connections: The Quarterly Journal.* 16. 5-22. 10.11610/Connections.16.3.01.
11. Koichiro Takagi, What Is Cognitive Warfare? The Future of China's Cognitive Warfare: Lessons from the War in Ukraine, *The Hudson,* available at: https://www.hudson.org/research/17991-the-future-of-china-s-cognitive-warfare-lessons-from-the-war-in-ukraine 2/6
12. Megha Pardhi, Security Assessment Measures, *5th Digital China Summit*, Issue 40, 22 August 2022 available at: https://chinatechdispatch.substack.com/p/battle-in-the-quasi-cognitive-domain
13. The Integrated Operating Concept 2025 (accessible version), UK Ministry of Defence, 30 September 2020 available at: https://www.gov.uk/government/publications/the-integrated-operating-concept-2025/the-integrated-operating-concept-2025-accessible-version
14. Rid, *Active Measures*; Clint Watts, *Messing with the Enemy*, New York: Harper Collins, 2018.
15. Dr. Christopher Whyte, Protectors without Prerogative: The Challenge of Military Defence against Information Warfare, Christopher Whyte, PhD, https://doi.org/10.21140/mcuj.2020110108
16. Christopher Paul and Miriam Matthews, The Russian "Firehose of Falsehood',' Propaganda Model, Santa Monica, Calif: RAND Corporation, PE–198–OSD, 2016.
17. Indian Army, 'Land Warfare Doctrine 2018', available at: https://www.ssri-j.com/MediaReport/Document/IndianArmyLandWarfareDoctrine2018.pdf
18. Joint Doctrine for Perception Management And Psychological Operations, JP-9, Headquarters Integrated Defence Staff, March 2010.
19. Manvendra Singh, Army has a new head of information warfare. *The Print*, 7 December2020 available at: https://theprint.in/opinion/army-has-new-head-of-information-warfare-but-stop-hiding-facts-from-indians/561524/
20. James J. F. Forest, *Political Warfare and Propaganda An Introduction*, Marine Corps University Press, MCU Journal, JAMS-vol-12-no-1 available at: https://www.usmcu.edu/Outreach/Marine-Corps-University-Press/MCU-Journal/JAMS-vol-12-no-1/Political-Warfare-and-Propaganda/ https://doi.org/10.21140/mcuj.20211201001
21. Stephen Silver, Defence Department to Investigate Military-run Fake Social Media Accounts, *National Interest*, 20 September 2022 available at: https://nationalinterest.org/blog/techland-when-great-power-competition-meets-digital-world/defense-department-investigate

15

Indian Air Power—2047

Diptendu Choudhury

> "*It was the best of times, it was the worst of times, it was the age of wisdom, it was the age of foolishness, it was the epoch of belief, it was the epoch of incredulity, it was the season of light, it was the season of darkness, it was the spring of hope, it was the winter of darkness, we had everything before us, we had nothing before us...*"
>
> —**Charles Dickens**[1]

Preamble

The opening lines by Dickens in his seminal novel set in the times of the French Revolution are a fitting description of the times of India's independence. As we are a quarter away from the completion of a century as a free nation, our winter of darkness is definitely past, and it is possibly our age of wisdom and certainly the season of light. By 2047, manned powered flight will be 144 years old from the benchmark set by the Wright brothers, and the Indian Air Force (IAF) will have completed 115 years in the service of the nation. So, where do we see Indian air power twenty-five years later?

The question draws us to take an overview of the nation's complex relationship with this versatile instrument of national power up to the present, before we delve deeper into its foreseeable contours in the distant future. Winston Churchill's observation, "*Air power is the most difficult military force to measure or even express in precise terms*", rings true even today and will possibly continue till 2047 and beyond.[2] Though the world over there is a much greater understanding of the invisible domain of air power and leveraging the third dimension, in India it still remains a little understood force, both in the military and civil domains. This two-part piece looks at air power from the strategic perspective of India's security construct and hopes to contribute towards greater awareness and understanding in the larger national interests, so that all its present and future capabilities and capacities are made the most of.

The first part—The 'Adrishta' or the 'Unseen'—after a very brief contextual overview of the past till the present, seeks to clarify some popular conceptual misunderstandings about air power and its invisible dimension. It also highlights the growing unseen threat due to the increasingly sophisticated exploitation of the aerospace domain by our adversaries. The second part—The 'Akasha Drishti' or 'Sky-Space Vision'—focuses on the multi-domain salience of air power in India's future security construct and endeavours to bravely envision the future vectors of aerospace power in the last quarter of the centennial of our independence.

PART ONE: THE *ADRISHTA*

A Forgotten Past and a Turbulent Present

The tryst with the destiny of India's air power began against tremendous odds of the deep-seated feelings harboured by the British, articulated by Air Marshal Sir John Steele, the Air Officer Commanding in Chief, India, between 1931 and 1935, *"Indians will not be able to fly and maintain military aeroplanes. It's a man's job."*[3] While born of an imperial heritage, the IAF became an independent service way back in 1932.[4] It was the sheer grit of the intrepid Indian airmen that not only proved Steele wrong, but earned the enduring professional respect and admiration of the sceptics as well, *"Never before have so many castes, creeds, and races been united in one single endeavour as they are in the Indian Air Force"*, and, *"her sons fought with matchless brilliance and courage."*[5] Post-Independence, *"In almost every war that we had to fight, air power tilted the balance of success between victory and loss in our favour in all, except one. Our land forces (and naval forces in 1971) have performed admirably in wars, often against severe odds. But we need to recognise that air power played a key role in each and every one of them, mostly providing the critical factor that created opportunities for the land forces to defeat the aims of the enemy."*[6]

With the sole exception of unfettered offensive employment of air power during the 1971 Bangladesh War, its use in all other wars was politically constrained. Even in the Kargil conflict of 1999, the IAF was prohibited from crossing the line of control in its operations. The constrained employment has unfortunately led to the faded memory of the larger role air power plays in carrying the war deep into the enemy's heartland and attacking counter-value and strategic targets, thereby impacting his ability and will to fight. It has even more disconcertingly led to atrophy not only in the understanding of the role of air power in India's military strategy, but also to its inadequate strategic leveraging in the larger interests of national security.

Over the last two decades or so, due to the prevalent narrative of 'short-swift-limited-border' wars, the role of air power has unfortunately come to be perceived as a support element in the border-oriented security construct and thinking amongst the military practitioners and strategists. The possibility of a full-scale conventional war appeared to have receded from India's military strategy as economic progress took the centre stage in our national priorities. This is a mind-space the nation cannot afford since we share long disputed borders with two adversarial neighbours.

On the west, despite Pakistan's internal and economic challenges, it is not likely to implode as vested nations will continue to keep it on life support. Thus, given the military-driven political construct, its India-centric threat obsession is unlikely to change anytime soon. To our north and east, China's aggressive foreign policy actions in the South China Sea and closer home in North Ladakh, combined with the deepening and reaffirmation of its strategic partnership with Pakistan, serve as a reality check that the days of 'peace and tranquillity' on the borders are over.[7,8] Its threat perception from India, due to the disputed borders and a challenge to a unipolar Asia, has moved up in the priority list of its strategic imperatives. To Beijing, its ports being the wellsprings of its economy and the 'One-China' policy continuing to fuel the Taiwan dilemma, its eastern seaboard remains its greatest security challenge. To cater to the possibility of the consequent two-front overstretch for its military, the recent adoption of the land border law to secure its borders amidst the heightened tensions underscores the intent to '*resolutely defend territorial sovereignty and land border security*.'[9] Connecting the dots, Beijing's recent actions of creating and populating villages in the disputed border areas is a strategy of creating 'new normals' as a follow on to its salami slicing game plan, and an indication that the unresolved border issue will continue to underpin all future Indo-China dynamics.[10,11]

While it bides time for the 'China Dream' to become a reality by 2050 when its economic might will be reinforced with a world-class military, China will continue with its doctrine of 'unrestricted warfare' in the realm of international policy, geo-economics, attacks on digital infrastructure and networks, and terrorism, where political and economic systems of an adversary are targeted without resorting to military confrontation.[12, 13] This effectively ensures that India's national security threat of the future encompasses the entire spectrum of the non-conventional, conventional, sub-conventional, and hybrid zone to the no-war-no-peace (NWNP) conditions. It would therefore be a *grave strategic mistake on India's part to under-prioritise conventional war as an unlikely possibility that can be allayed by diplomacy alone.*

Greater Understanding of the Invisible

Given India's justifiable great power aspiration and its contemporary stature and credibility as a rising power today, the nation is well poised to transform the aspiration into an achievable ambition. However, it is a path strewn with security challenges of living in a tough neighbourhood. What should the vectors of air power for securing India in the present, as well as enabling and ensuring its security in the future be? For an answer, while we need to shed some shibboleths of the past, we also need to take into account the important enduring structural aspects of air power, and most importantly, consider doctrinal and paradigm changes relevant for the future. Unless we do so, understanding the future of air power and what it can do for the nation will remain a challenge.

The invisible vertical dimension of a nation's sovereign air space was internationally affirmed in the Paris Convention on the Regulation of Aerial Navigation (1919) and subsequently by various other multilateral treaties.[14] The security of India's sovereign air space is an unequivocal responsibility of the IAF and this stretches over both land and sea, occupying a volume that has presently no international law or agreement on its vertical boundary or limit. And so it is that the terms 'aerospace power' and 'air power' are often used interchangeably, with the understanding that air power capabilities and exploitation today extends up to 'near space.' Despite the contrarian views of some on this issue, three points are irrefutable: In the absence of an internationally agreed dividing line between air and space it is indeed a continuum of the third dimension above the Earth's surface; India's growing economic power, trade expansion, and commercial interests will necessitate the continued pursuance of the aerospace continuum in our national interest;

military operations of the future will increasingly use this continuum for the furtherance of national security. In an Indian security context, Pakistan has a near peer and well trained air force. The People's Liberation Army (PLA) Air Force on the other hand is a stronger air force overall, but presently its operational capability and training is constrained compared to the IAF. That means that in any future war, conflict or any security contingency, the air space and indeed all of India's battle spaces would be intensely contested.

Control of the Air

This leads to the core-concept of 'control of the air' whose centrality comes from the defining military advantage of 'owning the skies,' that is possibly the most misunderstood aspect of air power even today. According to Kapil Kak, "*Command of the air or air superiority, the raison d'être of the counter air campaign has often not only generated inter-service controversy but as a key doctrinal component remained little appreciated. The overall strategy is to seize the initiative, carry the war into enemy territory, neutralise air power, and establish control of the air to provide freedom of action for our surface forces. Such an air offensive is aimed not only to further land, maritime and other operations, but also for the very successful pursuit of overall war aims and defence strategy.*"[15] But the skies are inherently difficult to own, especially if the adversary has a strong air force. The quantum of enemy air opposition, whether weaker, peer or stronger, decides the degree or spectrum of control. Therefore, in reality, the control of the air has several '*degrees of ownership*' or a '*spectrum of control*' and are termed accordingly. These terms are often used synonymously and are also mistakenly confused with each other.

Air superiority and air supremacy are the two original conditions that are widely accepted. It allows for friendly air operations '*without prohibitive interference from the opposing force*,' while the enemy is actively denied the use of the air. Air supremacy is a step higher, where the opposing air force has been rendered 'incapable' of air interference. Gaining air superiority is not an end in itself but a means to an end. It has a two-fold objective of creating the necessary conditions for the full exploitation of the third dimension offensively, and ensure the full freedom of own air and surface operations from enemy air interference.[16] However, in contested airspaces, situations such as it will be for India, such a condition in its true sense is an unrealistic expectation.

Control of the air required for joint operations involve time and space which will vary greatly depending on the scenario, mission objectives, and phase of conflict. According to Kainikara, control of the air is a comparative state, ranging between command of air, control of air, air superiority, favourable air situation, and tolerable air situation to air parity at the other end.[17] As per the US Air Force Doctrine, '*Control of the air provides the joint force with freedom of action while reducing vulnerability to enemy air and missile attacks. Control of the air is normally one of the first priorities of the joint force. This is especially important whenever the enemy is capable of threatening friendly forces from the air or inhibiting a joint force commander's (JFC's) ability to conduct operations.*'[18] In 2016, the US Air Force initiated an 'Air Superiority 2030 Enterprise Capability Collaboration Team' to develop capability options to enable joint force air superiority in the highly contested environment of 2030 and beyond, indicating the continued relevance of control of the air in the future and its high priority in the US military strategy.[19]

Post the Gulf War saw the increasing usage of the term 'air dominance', which, while not defined, is a condition mentioned in most Western air power doctrines and modern war-fighting discourses. The word 'dominance' is a 'condition' of what can be considered as the highest state of the skies being 'owned' and implies that the adversary is dominated totally in the third dimension. If supremacy is difficult to achieve, then domination is even more difficult, and can only be achieved if the enemy air is not there, or defeated or grounded. In the Gulf War, the enemy air was effectively missing in action, and hence the coalition air forces could dominate the operational airspace. While the popular concept did find temporary traction in its initial days in the IAF, it was quickly pushed aside with the thought that while air dominance was possible in a certain time space construct, it was not possible to achieve it for extended periods in the present and the future, given the highly contested Indian battle-spaces.

Doctrinal Construct

The least understood is the *doctrinal construct of air power for creating vertical air spaces or corridors deep inside enemy territory, well beyond the spatial limits of surface forces, and dominate them temporarily for the conduct of depth-offensive missions* by the IAF. Jasjit explains, "*Air Dominance in both dimensions of the concept also implies that India would have the ability to achieve coercive capabilities that could be calibrated in time and space to exploit the strategic space below the nuclear level and above the level of sub-conventional war.*"[20] Even past practitioners, with dated assessments of the IAF's doctrinal precepts, must realise that with every change in technology in platforms, weapons, and systems, the service not only adapts to the changes in technology, it also adopts new tactics, operational concepts, strategies and doctrines.[21] Its latest doctrine released in June 2022, is remarkably future-centric and elaborates on the full spectrum of capabilities, hard and soft, kinetic and non-kinetic, that can and must be leveraged in India's future national security and interests. As the current war in Ukraine underscores, the war-fighting salience of the invisible dimension, control of the air has re-emerged as a vital military strategy imperative, a truism that is widely accepted by all modern powers and militaries. It is time that its salience is understood, accepted, and included in India's military strategy.

Matter of Indivisibility

Indivisibility of air power is another concept difficult even for aviators from other services to come to terms with. The fact is that all military arms need air power in their individual domain-specific service strategies, and therefore are unable to reconcile to the concept of its indivisibility. It was Field Marshal Bernard Montgomery who perceptively said, "*Air power is indivisible. If you split it up into compartments, you merely pull it to pieces and destroy its greatest asset—its flexibility.*"[22] The indivisibility rests on the fundamental premise of '*unity of application*' of air power as a whole, and not in parts thereof based on individual domain or service-specific requirements. Neither can it be divided based on the terms of strategic and tactical, which broadly classify as to how the instrument is used. Indivisibility is a conceptual framework of how air power is to be used as a comprehensive force, and not as specific roles, missions, and tasks; definitely not as a mere firepower provider or weapon, based on its size, speed, range, payload, employment domains of air, land and sea, or service or command affiliation.

Very few nations have the luxury of each military arm owning its own air assets, but for most, this remains an aspiration given the extremely cost-intensive overheads to own and maintain service-specific aviation capabilities. In most nations, each service concentrates on developing individual areas of core competencies, and relies on joint strategies to meet their service-specific needs of air power. Considering the individual inventory and capability shortcomings of India's military and the 'never enough' defence budget, it is time each service found the balance between understanding the limits of owning and the necessity of sharing their individual requirements of air power. In our vast and populous nation, and our growing power stature, security requirements will continue to compete for its share of the national budget in the foreseeable future. Understanding the larger responsibilities of air power at the national level and its inclusion in the larger military strategy will therefore serve the interests of jointness better wherein each service must grow to strengthen their individual core capabilities towards the joint application in a larger national interest or end.

Some have chosen to interpret the IAF's certainty about the 'indivisibility of air power' from the narrow perspective of 'ownership issue,' and that the IAF is against the belief that for other services, aviation must be an integral resource, available at their disposal. Nothing could be farther from such understanding of ownership vis-a-vis the very basic premise of joint warfare that 'you do not need to own' your partner's assets to have assured access to their capabilities. The essence lies in the clarity of understanding that the necessity of air power requirements of any individual service is but one amongst the many in the IAF's overall role and responsibility to the nation. The application of force in air power is different from the other services who inherently need to 'own' or at the least have a military capability 'under command' in order to employ it. The multi-dimensional and multi-domain capabilities of air power are its greatest strengths and the nation needs to come to terms with the reality that it is best employed as a service and as a single entity in the larger joint military construct, rather than in piecemeal packets for the limited role-specific requirements of individual services.

Employment of Air Power

Other services need to come to terms with the fact that the IAF is not only the nation's air power, it is also an instrument with both independent and joint capabilities. More importantly, each service needs to introspect its future institutional role as a military instrument, how it will fight future wars and conflicts, and the role air power will play in its operational strategies. They need to lay on the table their core competencies and resources for providing the nation multi-domain bespoke solutions based on the specific threat context. Only then can the services hope to train, plan, and execute joint strategies in the employment of force aimed at the larger national outcomes.

The employment of air power today is no longer considered escalatory as its offensive kinetic employment can be escalation-controlled with a widespread spectrum of applications across all levels of conflict and war. While it continues to remain the air delivery vector in non-conventional roles, it is the enormous offensive capabilities of air power which provides and will continue to provide in the future valuable asymmetry in India's 'defence oriented' security approach and deterrence capability. Its offensive capabilities are seamlessly employed across the strategic-operational-tactical levels, with parallel simultaneity. Against the persistent challenge of diminishing combat squadrons, it is this offensive capability that needs to be strengthened and leveraged as an asymmetric advantage in India's deterrence strategy. The IAF's is already a strategic force with the strategic reach and effects which has grown beyond the air defence of India to the defence of the nation. Building this asymmetry into a coercive deterrent capability will go a long way in bolstering India's national security and interests in a China-dominant regional security context in the region.

Air defence, which is the Siamese twin of offensive air power, is no longer a defensive construct, and has become an offensive capability. Expanded areas of surveillance coverage, advanced fighters armed with extended range beyond visual range (BVR) missiles, and surface-to-air guided weapon systems whose lethal envelopes extend well beyond the tactical battle spaces, are all fused together into extended integrated air defence systems. The Jabba Top (Balakot) strike was the crossing of the Rubicon in India's application of kinetic air power in peace time as a political strategic communication to our adversary that sponsored acts of terror will attract consequences. Today, the significant capabilities of air power have extensive applications in the sub-conventional hybrid zone of conflict as well. A separate chapter on No-War-No-Peace has been included in the recently released IAF's Doctrine-2022 to provide for air power applications in the grey zone; however, the decision and the extent of employment of kinetic air power in internal security situations remains a political one.

The Unseen Threat

As the Russia-Ukraine war drags on and many lessons emerge, four key aspects stand out for India. The *first* is that it has brought back the possibility and salience of a full-fledged conventional war, and the harsh reality that limiting the war in scale and duration in the Indian context is unlikely to be orchestrated, let alone dictated, by one side alone. The *second* is the fundamental necessity of synergising political goals and military strategy when taking a nation into war, particularly since India's future wars will have to be fought alone. The *third* is that a surface-centric single-service dominant military strategy has the very high possibility of running into a quagmire of attrition warfare, especially in our context, since the erstwhile strategies of the capture of large swathes of territory have become untenable. And *finally*, unless the larger capabilities of offensive air power are included in a nation's military strategy, the possibility of successful strategic outcomes reduces significantly.[23]

Since conventional wars with both our adversarial nuclear-armed neighbours with strong air forces remain the persistent danger, the threat dynamics are no longer the same. Threats can no longer be seen from the isolated continental or maritime threat perceptions alone, primarily because adversarial air power will play a significant role in any conflict with any or both our neighbours. Let us see why is this so?

Pakistan's Air Force

The Pakistan Air Force (PAF), remains the blue-eyed boy of its nation. It has played an active role in all its wars except Kargil, where it had deployed its fighters in Skardu airfield north of Srinagar, but did not participate.[24] It has remained active in kinetic operations in the Federally Administered Tribal Area (FATA) and Afghanistan region from the days of the Soviet invasion till the present and is an important player in Pakistan's military capability.[25] The Pakistan Air Force (PAF) has benefitted immensely from its close relations with the US Air Force over the decades in terms of technology, training, and tactics. Even today, PAF remains a high priority for the USA in terms of engagement and leverage despite the matured Indo-US relations.[26] True to form, the USA has swung back yet again, possibly to revive its strategic engagement with Pakistan, with its very recent 450 million dollar package to upgrade its mainstay fleet of 75 F-16s.[27] The Pentagon stated that this proposed sale was to support the foreign policy and national security objectives of the USA by allowing Pakistan to *"retain interoperability with the USA and partner forces"* in ongoing counter-terrorism efforts and in preparing for future contingency operations.[28]

Meanwhile, the Pakistan aviation industry and the PAF have been actively engaged with Beijing for years. It has stepped up the pace of the modernisation of its platforms, airborne radars, and BVR missiles to counter the Rafale advantage and to achieve and maintain air dominance.[29] It is also actively seeking to enhance its strike capability against India.[30] It has deftly managed to upgrade and modernize its force structure and due to a combination of its steady expansion and the IAF's steadily dwindling numbers, has today become a 'near peer adversary'. However, while Pakistan remains a threat, in recent years the Chinese threat has emerged as our long-term concern.

PLA Air Force

The PLA Air Force (PLAAF) has long been recognised by the party leadership as a strategic force.[31] With the rise of Xi Jinping to the presidency of the People's Republic of China (PRC) in 2013, the then PLAAF Chief, Ma Xiaotian, used the PLAAF's anniversary to rephrase its goals to reflect Xi's priorities as '*...powerful people's Air Force for integrated air and space operations that is capable of attack and defence and of providing a strong support for the realization of the China Dream and the dream of making the armed forces strong*'.[32] China has been systematically strengthening its air power over the last two decades as is evident from its three consecutive China Defence White Papers of 2013, 2015, and 2019.[33, 34, 35] Today, in effect, the PLAAF inventory is adapting to its anticipated future employment which includes its Taiwan mission, maritime interests in the East and South China Seas (ECS&SCS), and the larger Indo-Pacific construct, and, more recently, the Tibet Autonomous Region (TAR).[36] General Ding Laihang, the previous PLAAF chief had stated on China National Radio, *"In the past, our strategies and guidelines focused on territorial air defence. Now we have been shifting our attention to honing our ability in terms of long-range strategic projection and long-range strike."*[37]

PLAAF Strategy

The Chinese have been far-sighted in expanding and modernising the PLAAF capabilities. For some time now, the PLAAF has emerged as an instrument of choice with the implementation of its 'Anti-Access-Area-Denial' (A2AD) concept and along with the extensive conduct of regional air exercises, as an integral part of its coercive foreign policy strategy. The concept essentially comprises two concurrent strategies, which are both offensive and defensive in nature. *Anti-access* is the ability to keep the adversary out of its theatre or area of interest and therefore involves larger strategic spaces. *Area Denial* is somewhat more tactical, where it seeks to prevent the use of air and sea spaces like preventing over-flights or the use of a defined maritime space. The strategy employable across the East and South China Seas is primarily aimed at denying the effective employability of the US carrier strike groups in the region, with the intention of securing strategic control over maritime and air spaces up to the 'Second Island Chain' in the future. China's artificial island air bases bolster the A2AD bubble in the SCS by allowing forward deployment of fighters, sensors and weapons, thereby increasing the range and the volume of air cover.

Consider Mao's view, "*Every quality manifests itself in a certain quantity, and without quantity, there can be no quality*", which resonates in China's current and future approach to its air power.[38] To the Chinese leadership, the definitive role of air power and its performance in the Gulf War of 1991 was a turning point that led to the transformation of the PLAAF. With its rapid advancements and growth, the future role of the PLAAF is of serious concern even to the USA, because controlling the 'airspace above the maritime spaces' of its national interests effectively enables China to control, if not own, the contested waters. This would also enable it to control the fishing, oil, and gas explorations in the region, and use it as a coercive leverage on the region. Build-up of PLAAF capabilities will enable the PRC to extend its airspace control and force projection across the sea and land frontiers. An increase in PLAAF's power projection missions is the new normal, and is an effort to establish its regular presence in the region. This will result in the increased Chinese control of the regional air space in the long term, which would inevitably make the Indo-Pacific realm more contested.[39]

Threat appreciation among India's strategic community on the other hand has been somewhat obsessed by the PLA Rocket Force (PLARF) and PLA Strategic Support Forces (PLASSF), thereby continuing to overlook the consequences of PLAAF's growing capabilities and future goals. India's diminishing combat squadrons below the critical mass is a way more serious national security issue than merely an IAF problem of the future. Continuation of this situation would be a serious strategic mistake in our security assessments. Jasjit Singh had summed it succinctly, "*But no one can say that Beijing has not put its neighbours, if not the world, on notice regarding how it plans to use aerospace power and to what purpose*".[40]

PART TWO: THE AKASHA DRISHTI

Old ways of thinking, old formulas, dogmas, and ideologies, no matter how cherished or how useful in the past no longer fit the facts. The world that is fast emerging from the clash of new values and technologies, new geopolitical relationships, new life-styles and modes of communication, demands wholly new ideas and analogies, classifications and concepts.

—**Alvin Toffler**[41]

Multi-Domain Salience of Air Power

From a continental threat perspective, the parameters of the PLA's military actions in Ladakh and Sikkim have deeper strategic underpinnings. While there is no doubt on the resolute, robust actions by the Indian military against China's territorial transgressions during the Doklam stand-off and more recently in the Galwan crisis; however, one factor tends to be overlooked in the eyeball-to-eyeball headline-grabbing border confrontations. The IAF's swift and extensive offensive deployment in both cases indicated India's intent to bring offensive air power into the equation that was prepared to execute the entire range of air operations that are envisaged in case of any high-altitude conflict with China.

For the first time after the Cho La and Nathu La skirmishes in Sikkim in 1967,[42] India reacted robustly to signal that till the border issues are resolved, any attempts to alter the *status quo* would not be acceptable and would be countered. Unnoticed by most was that every element of the IAF's offensive operational experience at high altitudes and lessons of the Kargil War as well as the threat-specific pan-India air power exercises in a joint military construct, were put into action here.[43] This brought in a strategic coercive asymmetry into the Ladakh crisis, similar to Sikkim, where according to a post-Doklam report, the *'PLA's strategic options were constrained by the IAF's asymmetric advantage over the PLAAF.*'[44]

Regional Salience of Air Power

China evidently recognises the asymmetric air power advantage India currently enjoys in the Tibet Autonomous Region (TAR). To close the gap, it is rapidly expanding infrastructure and assets, and increased its air activity and combat training.[45] The IAF has been taking deterrent air defence actions by swiftly responding to all such attempts, leading to complaints of increased Indian air activity by the Chinese who '*were taken aback by the Indian response to their activities*'.[46] Consequently, for the first time, the IAF has been included in the Army's border talks with China, with the possibility of a hotline between the two air forces.[47]

The PLAAF has till date conducted nine iterations of its bi-lateral series of air exercises called 'Shaheen' with Pakistan, deploying its latest aviation hardware in its bases in the region. The flagship exercise simulates near-realistic war-fighting scenarios, which include land attack strikes, air-to-air combat, electronic counter-measures (ECM) and electronic counter-counter-measures (ECCM), naval target strikes, and surface-to–air strikes, among others.'[48] Interoperability being the fundamental premise of this exercise series, it highlights two key aspects: one, the salience given to air power in their military strategies; and two, the high probability of collusive air operations in future conflicts.

In August 2020, Gen Xu Qiliang, the senior vice-chairman of the central military commission (CMC) and therefore the senior-most military officer of the PLA in active service, visited Pakistan. He is said to have succeeded in impressing upon Pakistan the significance of making the PAF the lead service in the war, and that the PLA was ready to share select virtual war domain capabilities with the PAF for war in the North Kashmir and Ladakh regions. So, how important is air power in the Ladakh or Arunachal regions? Let us assume that the IAF is not a factor in Ladakh or Arunachal. Will it give the PLA the option to use more coercive tactics? Will it enable the PLA to now take use of the PLAAF's asymmetric edge to strengthen its coercive advantage? Will this compel the IA to a wholly defensive holding posture against China's coercive actions? If the answers are in the affirmative, then it is imperative that in the future, joint strategies are adopted and air power included in all our continental response options. Even the slightest consideration of any continental contingency in the region without offensive air power will be a 1962-redux—a disastrous strategic error for India rather than merely a local tactical one.[49]

The Indian Ocean Region (IOR) is the vital lifeline for energy, trade, and commerce, and therefore is a security imperative for India's growth and future. While the wider multi-lateral Indo-Pacific construct of the 'QUAD' by Japan, the USA, Australia and India, renewed their '*steadfast commitment to a free and open Indo-Pacific that is inclusive and resilient*', clearly with reference to China, the IOR will remain India's core interest.[50] Prime Minister Modi in his Shangri La Dialogue articulated, "*...promote a democratic and rule-based international order, in which all nations, small and large, thrive as equal and sovereign. We will work with others to keep our seas, space and airways free and open.*" Regarding the Indo-Pacific region he said, "*We should all have equal access as a right under international law to the use of common spaces on sea and in the air*". It was the first time any PM had referenced air and space in a regional geopolitical context. The huge region is mostly left in the hands of an overworked Indian Navy; therefore, a stronger and collaborative strategy is required to protect our interests.

Due to its pre-occupation with carrier-based airpower, maritime strategic thinking tends to neglect the enormous capabilities that land-based air power brings to the table. Without doubt, a carrier battle group has significant strategic capabilities, but it has a definite 'response-reach' lag as it takes time to sail to the desired region of presence or the location of force application. Till it reaches its destination, in the interim, the lag can be made up by using the swifter response and long reach of land-based air power. Inclusion of additional resources of land based air power in India's expansive maritime domain not only reinforces the nation's strategic capability, both qualitatively and quantitatively, it also enhances our strategic options.

Today, the IAF brings a formidable capability to the table of strategic hard and soft power options. The technology-enabled transformation of the core characteristics of air power—reach, mobility, flexibility, responsiveness and offensive lethality—gives it a unique 'strategic agility'. It is this strategic agility which enables the service to spin up swiftly, deliver a wide spectrum of bespoke kinetic and non-kinetic solutions with speed, create calibrated effects and outcomes, plug in with other elements of the CNP and military instruments, and operate across multiple domains simultaneously.

Future Vectors of Aerospace Power

What would or should be the contours of the development of air power in India's future? By 2047, India will certainly be a major power in a possibly multi-polar world, and while, as a 'modestly ambitious' nation, we may not aspire to be 'the' leading power, we definitely are geo-politically and strategically poised to become a great one. Given the developments in the power equations of the world, with China emerging as an antipodal alternative to the USA, and the rise of middle powers, India may quite as well become the balancing power and the 'third alternative.'

Wherever time takes us, the need for a strong, credible and powerful military will be a precursor for any future major power standing or geopolitical equation. According to Chatterjee, active rising powers are on the path to great powers due to economic power, military power and the narrative or '*idea advocacy*' of becoming a great power.[51]

With capture of territory no longer a normative state behaviour, the expanded threat domains of the present and future necessitate a multi-domain security approach. Therefore, the fusion of the hitherto geographically independent domains of land, sea, air, cyber and space into a multi-domain security approach will be a defining change in India's strategic thinking, growth, power, and security calculus. Aerospace power will play a vital role in the multi-domain security environment simply because of its continued future ability to transcend geographical limitations with its strategic agility. Thinkers on the future of air power as an effective military instrument in the Indian context need only to examine the growing evidence of its strategic leveraging by China, the USA, Japan and Taiwan. This is not to say that *air power* is likely to become the leading instrument of military prowess, but the importance given by China to its development along with the PLARF and the PLASSF are certainly a clear indicator of the imperative assigned to the vertical dimension of its future power projection and application strategies as these two services were essentially developed to offset the disadvantage of the dominance of the military power of the USA.

Future Contours of *Air Power*

The above-mentioned considerations help provide insights into what must India's *air power,* as a component of *aerospace power,* be expected to provide to the nation over the next transformational two-and–a-half decades, and how the IAF must evolve and adapt to ensure this. These are not easy questions to answer, and while the onus on the formulating the future contours of *air power* lie with the IAF, some signposts are suggested. All these actions would have to be spread over a period of the next two-and a-half decades to coincide with the completion of India's hundred years since independence.

I. Reverse the Inventory Downturn

In February 2009, the then defence minister had written in a reply to the Rajya Sabha on the IAF that during the period from 2007 to 2022, the numbers would increase to 42 squadrons.[52] Unfortunately, the medium multi-role combat aircraft proposal sucked all the oxygen pushing all other IAF requirements to the margin, and in the end, from the global tender floated in 2007 till its cancellation in 2015, eight valuable years were lost.[53,54] Reducing the strength of the IAF has led to the Parliament Standing Committee on Defence express its concern and called for time-bound procurements to replenish it.[55] The reduced strength may still be just adequate to hold our own in the current stage while we can still rely on the asymmetric deterrence advantage, it is certainly not enough to address a future scenario of an increasingly coercive PLAAF. Further, the question is will the authorised strength of combat squadrons based on threat assessments of the past be adequate for a future of a changed world order, geo-political context and India's great power trajectory? The Air Chief has recently pointed out that while "*numbers do matter, and our inventory needs expansion*", due to the blend of the hybrid and conventional wars, the future lay in developing multi-domain capabilities.[56]

The future plans of the IAF is tied up in a Gordian Knot, severely constrained by budget realities and the harsh fact that the 'fill rate' of induction of new squadrons will be slower than the 'obsolescence rate' of the older fleets. The greatest challenge with force structuring air force inventories the world over is that the rapid pace of technological advancements in the aerospace domain runs contrary to the fundamentals of long-term planning, and is not unique only to India or the IAF. Without undermining its importance, possibly a shift of focus away from the 'authorised numbers' is needed in favour of a capability-capacity-balancing approach.

The near to mid-term priority in the decade ahead should be to prevent any further slide in the IAF's strength and balance it with global procurements till the *Aatmanirbharta* driven production of the Tejas MK 2 and the Advanced medium combat aircraft (AMCA) stabilise, and also ensure upgradation of the mainstay fleets of Sukhois and Rafales. For this, as an interim measure in the near term over the next five years, bold steps are needed to fast track the procurement process through the government-to-government route. By the mid-term of ten years, we should have been able to reverse the slide by increasing our fill rate to a point where accretions overtake the obsolescence. Over the mid to long term, the focus should be towards accelerating our accretion to build a force structure to ensure a *counter-coercive air power* with an expanded *depth strategic targeting capability and capacity.*

The future combat squadron strength should be reviewed based on India's position in the world, dynamics of USA-China relations and future contours of the PLAAF. A decrease or increase needed from the benchmarked number would emerge from close strategic analysis of these three variables which must be monitored continuously. A 'mid-course inventory review' in a decade's time would provide greater visibility of the future security environment. It will also allow a reality check of the capability and production rate of the indigenous aircraft and weapons industry. To achieve this, as the IAF Chief stated, "*The need of the hour is to re-imagine, re-invent, re-train, and re-dedicate.*"[57]

II. Develop a Full Spectrum Force

Sub-conventional and No-War-No-Peace (NWNP) tasks in the Indian context, which are likely to be in a permissive or semi-permissive environment, will primarily entail utilisation of lower-cost and lower-capability assets whereas conflicts against our adversaries who have advanced capabilities will necessitate utilisation of the full spectrum of air power capabilities as well as a joint approach to bring to bear the entire military might of the nation. Since air power already contributes across the entire spectrum of warfare from non-conventional to the hybrid, it must continue to be sensitive to future threat transformations and remain agile to innovate and adapt its kinetic and non-kinetic applications. With the air vector continuing to remain an important element of the nuclear triad due its swift response and flexibility, extended long range air delivered stand-off missiles with adaptable warheads will be essential for our continental deterrence.

Bolstering conventional deterrence, where force numbers and capability volume are vital against militarily stronger adversaries, will necessitate a balance of manned and unmanned platforms. Uninhabited combat aircraft can change that giving the Air Force affordable power projection. Unmanned aircraft will operate in tandem with manned aircraft, either as 'loyal wingmen' in close proximity or potentially as detached wingmen, moving forward to reconnoitre, jam, or strike targets. These aircraft will not be fully autonomous. Instead, they will employ operationally relevant autonomy—enough autonomy to reduce the bandwidth requirements such that they are manageable with stealthy, jam-resistant A2/AD communications. Human aviators will remain in command, 'quarterbacking' the fight and making key decisions, such as target selection and engagement.'[58]

While the IAF is already working on the concept, what is of relevance is that future force structure will have advanced kinetic and non-kinetic air power platforms, weapons and systems which are today on the design boards. The vector of the IAF's full spectrum capability should be to develop a family of agile capabilities that operate in and across the air, space and cyberspace domains, which are a 'system of systems' and not isolated next-generation capabilities. Agile communications, data, and information networks, real-time persistent-stare intelligence, surveillance and reconnaissance (ISR), advanced high speed analysis and decision tools, futuristic aerospace battle management and command and control (C2) systems, enhanced aerial and ground asset survivability and threat mitigation, etc., must be the focus areas of capability enhancement.

The sheer seductiveness of advanced technologies makes it very easy to get 'swept away' with their future prospects. Future needs have to be carefully calibrated given the wide range of advanced and emerging disruptive technologies in artificial intelligence, robotics, quantum technology, space and cyber capabilities, nano-technology, directed energy weapons, hypersonic weapons, and the various platforms. These are expensive, research-intensive works in progress, have niche applications, and not an end in themselves. Importantly, they have limited shelf lives, till a 'counter' is produced or the 'next one' comes along. The IAF will do well to remember that given the costs, these should be cherry-picked to enhance future roles, applications and strengthening of core competencies amidst competing budgetary demands, so as to produce joint outcomes in the larger national interest. The asset profile of future force structuring will have to factor the balance of cost versus utilisation. Sub-conventional and NWNP tasks which are likely to be in a permissive or semi-permissive environment, will primarily entail utilisation of lower-cost-lower-capability assets whereas conflicts against our adversaries who have advanced capabilities will necessitate utilisation of the full spectrum of air power capabilities jointly with all the stakeholders of CNP.

III. Enhance Strategic Capability and Capacity

The IAF's strategic capabilities have been regularly demonstrated by its regular participation in international air and maritime exercises. However, from India's security perspective, its strategic capacity is seriously constrained due to inadequate flight refuelling aircraft, airborne early warning and control aircraft, dedicated electronic warfare platforms, etc. These are no longer desirable force multipliers but have become mandatory critical mission enablers. Capacity increase of critical mission enablers must not only meet the IAF's requirements of swift reach, response, spatial coverage and operational persistence; ideally, it must also meet inter-operability and inter-usability requirements of the Indian Navy and our strategic partners. Building a robust and bespoke critical enabler force must be a national priority in the near future as it not only enhances joint war-fighting capabilities, but also significantly expands India's future regional security, stability, and influence.

Development of extended continental and maritime strategic reach, capability, and capacity is no longer an option but an imperative, which must be invested in the mid-long term. Strategic penetration and target engagement capability and capacity building for conflicts in contested to highly contested environments is another critical requirement. Our indigenous defence industry needs to accelerate its programs to be able to produce long-range aerial platforms and kinetic vectors, air-surface stand-off precision weapons, long-range surface-to-air guided weapons and air defence systems, extended beyond visual range air-to-air, air-to-surface missiles, etc.; weapons that have strategic capabilities and are able to target and apply pressure on our adversaries deep inside their territories and areas of interest.

There are contrarian views amongst Indian practitioners and the strategic community over *bombers* in the future, primarily on the need and the cost, given our depleting combat bench strength. Interestingly, the USA, Russia and China are continuing to invest in their long-range stealth bomber programs. The future US B 21 (which the US Air Force expects to order 200), and the Russian PAK DA are extremely low observable long range hypersonic cruise missile shooters which are designated to penetrate advanced integrated air defence systems to swarm, saturate and destroy multiple target systems.[59,60,61,62] There is no denying the fact that from an international perspective, bombers lend enormous strategic power projection capability and gravitas to a nation's military and will continue to do so well into 2050. Given India's growth and power trajectory, the IAF will do well to consider that option in the long term strategic interests. Until we upgrade our air power capacity to its stated squadron strength, leasing a squadron of long-range bombers, as an interim measure and despite contrarian views, will complement our surface and sub-surface inventories to provide a potent strategic power projection capability. It will also send out a strong strategic communication to signal India's seriousness of intent in the maritime and air space realms, to ensure its security and national interests in the larger IOR and Indo-Pacific region.

Development of futuristic 'Extended Integrated Aerospace Defence Systems' (EIADS), which have the capability to dominate the vertical dimension well into the adversaries' heartland are a vital future requirement as they create vertical splits in the battle space for penetration and targeting. Future EIADS, capable of engaging multiple cruise and ballistic missiles, are also a vital imperative for aerospace defence of our sovereign territories and India's future areas of strategic interest.

IV. Expand Regional Strategic Presence

An inescapable strategic necessity is the development of fighter-capable air fields in our island territories, the Andaman and Nicobar chain on the east and the Lakshadweep chain on the west. Air bases on these islands serve as India's strategic bulwarks, both as forward defensive arcs to the mainland and regional aerospace defence. These are equally vital for deterrent power projection and regional influencing. With increased roles of air power, the missions and tasks in supporting India's 'Security and Growth for All in the Region' (SAGAR) mission and in contributing to net security in the IOR become important. Thus, enhanced interoperability and military cooperation engagements are the future air power imperatives towards fostering regional stability, and most importantly, deterring China's attempts at imposing maritime hegemony.

Alongside building Air Force-to-Air Force relationships as 'air bridges of friendship and cooperation' by exercising and operating with the countries on our east and west will give the IAF the additional reach and access to support the nation's long term strategic interests.[63] Unlike the strategies of the USA and China, India does not need to create 'bases' but just needs access to these countries to enable a wider swathe of sustainable air power coverage in the region.[64,65] Apart from enhancing regional power projection and influence, these could be equally vital pivots of counter-pressure against vulnerability of China's multi-front threat. For that kind of access, Tajikistan, Oman, Kenya, Mauritius, the Maldives, Indonesia, Myanmar, Indonesia and Vietnam are the countries which must be engaged from a strategic perspective.

In the near to mid-term, the IAF must step up development of its air power capability and capacity by exploiting its Air Force-to-Air Force connects amongst these nations. Ranging from conducting training and exercises, capacity building with assistance from our aeronautical and defence industrial base, sale and supply of air defence radars, surface-to-air guided weapons and strategic weaponry, to potential joint tasks and missions in the future, the scope is immense. That would also provide the much-needed asymmetric advantage to our maritime power and enable the creation of a game-altering collective airpower deterrence capability in the security matrix of the nations affected by China's military coercion.

Amongst the South-East Asian countries, Taiwan, Indonesia, Malaysia, the Philippines and Vietnam, all have small air forces. Most of them have a mix of combat aircraft of varying vintage and very limited modern air defence capability which they are struggling to upgrade. Simply put, none of the air forces of these nations can individually match up to the PLAAF. Yet, all of them are running programs to modernise their air forces since they realise that a credible conventional deterrence against China is only possible with a strong air force with a modern inventory. This is an area that can be easily developed given that India has already engaged and exercised with most of the air forces in the region. Access to air bases in these countries will provide India a security counter-leverage in future border conflicts, and also enable us to become a serious player in the Indo-Pacific construct. An increase in our air power capability and displayed intents towards stability in the South-East Asian region will not only increase the confidence of these countries in India but will also serve to reinforce India's position regionally and internationally as a mature and responsible future global power.

V. Enable Fusion of Aerospace Domain

The merger of the vertical dimension of the air and space domains into a fused aerospace volume will impact all surface operations and activities increasingly in the years to come. Air power has long since transformed into aerospace power not only due to applications like navigation, imagery, surveillance, targeting, meteorology, communications, cyber, command and control, etc., but also because of the vast array of ever-increasing space dependant kinetic capabilities and aerospace defence. Without seeking ownership, space must be dealt with as a 'national common' and integrated into a '*fused aerospace domain*' for India's future civil and military national security calculus which all the services will do well to integrate and plug into.

This is a mid-long term goal, for which our strategies and policies will have to be formalised in the near term.

Given the range of threats, aerospace defence needs an integrated approach to include both air and near-space defence and offence capabilities. Outer space will need extensive civil-military handshaking and handholding to balance budgets and capabilities into a synergized credible national power instrument. Advanced layered missile defence, and kinetic and non-kinetic defensive and offensive systems will have to be invested in to develop joint coercive lethal capabilities. These must be able to penetrate enemy air and missile defence systems deep into adversarial airspaces in the continental and maritime domains, so as to target diverse weapon systems, static and mobile theatres and ballistic missile networks, as well as strategic centres of gravity. This will again need a timeline of prioritised multi-layered embrace across public, private and military domains, and to begin with, a policy for military use of space.

Knowledge of what 'lies across the hill' is now available to all, but what matters is the ability to have the information on call in real time. Intelligence and 'constant-stare' visibility across our borders over disputed areas and future conflict zones are India's Achilles' heel in our defence and deterrence. The urgent need for real-time, perpetual surveillance and analysis capability of our adversarial airspace, air defence identification zones, in-depth look across our borders, and over the sovereign maritime spaces must be fused to provide information dominance. Multi-domain space-based command, control, communications, computers, intelligence, surveillance and reconnaissance (C4ISR) capability will become the very bedrock of India's future military instruments of power. A multi-fold enhancement of this capability is a national security imperative of possibly the highest priority in the near term. Creation of a *national multi-service-multi-domain-multi-sensor fusion centre*, where inputs from all types of sensors, imagery and intelligence systems are employed to provide a 24×7×365 visibility of the entire volume of our domains of interest—i.e., airspace, continental, and maritime spaces—and duly analysed in real-time for all our national security requirements must be a near-term priority.

VI. Invest in Aerospace Technology and Production (ATP)

The rapidly changing operational environment entails that the IAF can no longer afford to develop aerospace systems on the traditional linear acquisition and development timelines. Increasing the capability development pace is critical to narrow and close the gap against an adversary whose pace and capacity in the aerospace field is way ahead of us. There is no option but for the Indian aerospace industry to evolve swiftly so that capability development remains future-relevant. The ATP has to become adaptable, affordable and agile to stay ahead of the curve of future aerospace power needs. In the immediate-near term, the idea is to maximise collaborative research and development in science and technology between the academia, industry and the military. Simultaneously, the need is to bring-in agile acquisition processes and time-sensitive acquisition policies which shrinks the lag between the development-production-operationalisation cycle. Continuing with the traditional approaches will result in a fatal technology gap in our critical war-fighting capabilities vis-à-vis our technologically superior adversary.

Digital engineering must be leveraged to ensure smart commonality and inter-operability across all fleets and systems across all the services wherever possible—common support equipment, system configurations, interfaces, and architecture, even common components that simplify logistics and maintenance in the field.[66] The pace of technological advancements can only increase if the IAF and industry synergistically short circuit the synapses between the development of future operational concepts, identifying operational requirements, industrial research, development and production, and finally operational testing and evaluation. These matters should be addressed on the highest priority given the long distance and lead times between the drawing board and the field.

Civil aviation along with the IAF and aviation elements of the other services, constitute the nation's comprehensive air power (CAP), and the nation must realise the immense potential of the defence and civil aviation industry. There are vast areas of overlapping between civil and military aviation in national security due to inter-operability of capabilities and capacity redundancies. It also has enormous untapped potential in contributing to economic growth, foreign policy support, diplomacy, political support and signalling, humanitarian support, etc., and will certainly have more to offer in the future. A new approach is needed that embraces public-private-partnership and invests heavily to flip it into a profit-making economic venture. India's aviation industry expects Rs. 35,000 crore (US$ 4.99 billion) investment in the next four years, as the Government plans to invest US$ 1.83 billion for the development of airport infrastructure, aviation navigation services, and build 220 new airports by 2025.[67] India is already known for cost competitive space research, development and production. Expanding this model to the integrated military-civil aviation industry will be truly a strategic investment for the future, given the immense regional necessity for affordable combat platforms, critical enablers, air defence radars and weapon systems, aerial weapons, fixed and rotary wing civilian passenger and transport aircraft, unmanned platforms, etc.—the list of possibilities is endless. It will not only fill our inventory gaps, but by generating extensive low-cost competitive exports and creating technology dependencies will serve to expand our regional influence. There is a strategic window of opportunity for India to create an ecosystem of cooperative development and production with regional partners to our strategic advantage.

VII. A Force of Future-Ready Scholar Warriors

The IAF today has a very clear understanding of its future responsibilities in securing the nation and fostering growth, and has initiated future relevant doctrinal changes. The onus of sharing the knowledge of what air power has to offer rests with an operationally obsessed IAF which has been historically reticent in projecting itself as a military instrument in its own right. This has been due to three organisational mindsets—'We don't believe in blowing our trumpet'; 'our efforts and achievements are there for all to see and don't have to prove ourselves'; and most commonly, 'we don't have time for all this'.[68] This needs to change to communicate as to what the IAF can and cannot do to policy makers, security establishment, industry, academia, media, and the citizens.

Today there is greater awareness of the need to encourage discourse over proliferation of air power in both military and civil domains. As an aerospace force which will continue to face rapid technological changes and will consequently keep adapting and adopting to future war-fighting paradigms, the biggest area of investment by the IAF must be its human resource. Though the root concepts of air power are enduring, its technology-intensive character and the molecular level of technology dependency in peace and war mandates its practitioners to be techno-agile to absorb, imbibe, innovate, and offer to the other services and the nation, the best possible range of offerings of the third dimension. This awareness is evident in the future need expressed by the IAF brass for 'scholar warriors' rather than 'air warriors'.[69] The pre-existing technology intensive basic training of the IAF is being made more robust with further infusion of technology and simulation that allows for stringent preparation of the entire spectrum of skilled sets for the future.[70] It has also introduced critical thinking and aerospace strategy development amongst its leadership.[71] However, while significant, these are foundational steps for the transformation of India into a leading aerospace power of the world in the years ahead.

More needs to be done in the immediate future, and for the nation to appreciate the immense potential of the aerospace domain, an important first step would be to invest in an aerospace advisor. The National Security Council Secretariat has advisors from all the services except the Air Force, despite it having fought in all the wars the country has faced, being the fourth-largest in size in the world and ranked third among global air powers, ahead of the PLAAF, in 2022.[72] In the continued absence of one, the nation will be bereft of professional inputs on an important instrument of a multi-domain full-spectrum military power, but will also be constrained in leveraging the immense future potential and capabilities of India's CAP. The articulation of India's air strategy should be the next step. This should provide a wider eagle's eye view of how CAP will secure and support the nation in its great power journey, and how this versatile force must be developed in the intervening years, en route to the destination.

Concluding Thoughts

Internationally acknowledged economic progress and recognition of India's emergence as a rising power has drawn the nation into the complex arena of global realignments and realpolitik. With every rise comes greater expectations of international responsibility. As a rising power, the world is closely watching India and what it brings to the high table in terms of international responsibility. To secure the nation's future, and to counterbalance and stabilise the regional China-dominated dynamics of Asia, India will have to mitigate the myriad challenges and create its own strategic space. Its firm belief in '*multi-polarity, rebalancing, fair globalization and reformed multilateralism*', and the willingness to shoulder greater responsibility toward its goal of becoming a developed nation in the next 25 years is its vision statement.[73] To achieve this goal, the strategic agility of aerospace power has much to offer in the future, and will therefore become increasingly indispensable for securing and supporting national interests, both independently, and jointly with the other services.

India's past experience with air power is extensive, but its leveraging has been less than desirable, primarily due to its complex nature and its relative youth compared to other instruments of military power. Also, the rapid technology-enabled changes in its capabilities and the accompanying changes in doctrines, strategies and tactics, makes it difficult to keep pace with a wide spectrum of kinetic and non-kinetic choices and options it has to offer to the nation. It is necessary today to update our legacy ideas on *air power* with a wider understanding of the future relevance of *aerospace power* to leverage the invisible medium better. The unseen threat from the third dimension posed by the adversarial near-peer and stronger air forces against our future national security needs to be *recognised.* The responsibility is best described in the prescient words written over a decade ago, "*The purpose of the Indian Air Force in the 21st century is to provide the nation with an unparalleled range of options and capabilities through the exploitation of the aerospace continuum. And that it is best done by the Indian Air Force as long as it maintains an integrated vision that seeks to match ends and means, and provides it a strategic direction.*"[74]

ENDNOTES

1. Charles Dickens, *A Tale of Two Cities*, Penguin Classics, UK, 2003.
2. Air Vice-Marshal Tony Mason, *Air Power A Centennial Appraisal*, Brassey's, London,1994, p. 2.
3. Mike Edwards, *Spitfire Singh,* Bloomsbury Publishing India Pvt. Ltd., New Delhi, 2016, p. ix.
4. H. C. Deb. Army and Air Force (Annual) Bill, 29 March 1946, Vol. 421, cc. 701, https://api.parliament.uk/historic-hansard/commons/1946/mar/29/army-and-air-force-annual-bill
5. Squadron Leader Rana T. S. Chhina, *The Eagle Strikes*, Appendix E, *Tribute to Indian Airmen* by Air Marshal Sir Patrick Playfair, Centre For Armed Forces Historical Research, United Services Institute, Ambi Knowledge Resources, New Delhi, 2006, p. 317.
6. Air Commodore Jasjit Singh AVSM, VrC, VSM (retd.), *Defence from the Skies*, Second Edition, KW Publishers Pvt. Ltd., New Delhi, 2013.
7. Rajeshwari Pillai Rajagopalan, 'The China-Pakistan Partnership Continues to Deepen', *The Diplomat,* 9 July 2021, https://thediplomat.com/2021/07/the-china-pakistan-partnership-continues-to-deepen/
8. PTI, 'Pak, China Reaffirm Their 'Strategic Partnership in the Challenging Times', *Business Standard*, 13 June 2022, https://www.business-standard.com/article/pti-stories/pak-china-reaffirm-their-strategic-partnership-in-the-challenging-times-122061200756_1.html
9. Shuxian Luo, *China's Border Law: A Preliminary Assessment*, Order From Chaos, Brookings, 4 November 2021,https://www.brookings.edu/blog/order-from-chaos/2021/11/04/chinas-land-border-law-a-preliminary-assessment/
10. 'Second Chinese village along Arunachal border: Satellite images', *TNN* 19 November 2021, https://timesofindia.indiatimes.com/india/second-chinese-village-along-arunachal-border-sat-images/articleshow/87788526.cms

11. The author's interpretation of a Chinese strategy of carrying out such activities that seek to alter the status quo repeatedly so that it becomes an accepted norm. The example of China's maritime claims, presence and actions in the South China Sea, embellished by the creation of militarised artificial Islands, which it expects will become an accepted 'new normal' over time. In India's case, a similar strategy is evident with China setting up villages in the disputed areas on the borders of Arunachal Pradesh, which it expects will alter the territorial status quo in its favour over time, once they are allowed to remain.
12. https://www.economist.com/china/2019/06/27/xi-jinping-wants-chinas-armed-forces-to-be-world-class-by-2050
13. Qiao Liang and Wang Xiangsui, *Unrestricted Warfare*, Beijing: PLA Literature and Arts Publishing House, February 1999 at https://www.c4i.org/unrestricted.pdf
14. https://www.britannica.com/topic/air-law
15. Kapil Kak 'A Century of Air Power: Lessons and Pointers', *Strategic Analysis*: A monthly journal of the IDSA, March 2001 (Vol. XXIV, No. 12).
16. *Air Superiority 2030* (AS *2030*) *Enterprise. Capability Collaboration Team* (ECCT) https://www.af.mil/Portals/1/documents/airpower/Air%20Superiority%202030%20Flight%20Plan.pdf
17. Sanu Kainikara, 'A Fresh Look at Air Power Doctrine', Air Power Development Centre, Canberra, Australia, 2008, p. 53.
18. https://www.doctrine.af.mil/Portals/61/documents/AFDP_3-01/3-01-AFDP-COUNTERAIR.pdf, p. 2.
19. Air Superiority 2030 Flight Plan Enterprise Capability Collaboration Team, United States Air Force, https://www.af.mil/Portals/1/documents/airpower/Air%20Superiority%202030%20Flight%20Plan.pdf
20. Jasjit Singh, Chapter *Indian Air Power*, Global Air Power, John Andreas Olsen, (ed.) Potomac Books Inc., p. 257.
21. Arun Prakash, 'Why India's Military Leaders Must Have a Free and Frank Discussion on Demarcation of Air Power Roles and Missions', *Indian Express*, 12 August 2021, https://indianexpress.com/article/opinion/columns/why-indias-military-leaders-must-have-a-free-and-frank-discussion-on-demarcation-of-air-power-roles-and-missions-7447880/
22. Editorial, Journal Edition 6, Joint Air Power Competence Centre, NATO, https://www.japcc.org/journals/journal-edition-6/
23. Air Marshal Diptendu Choudhury, 'Russia's Military Understanding of Air Power', VIF Article, 23 May 2022, https://www.vifindia.org/article/2022/may/23/russia-s-military-understanding-of-air-power
24. Nasim Zehra, *From Kargil to the Coup: Events That Shook Pakistan,* Sang-e-Meel Publishers, Lahore, 2018, p. 508.
25. Shahzad Chaudhry, 'PAF and the Afghan War—II', *The Express Tribune* , 17 September 2021, https://tribune.com.pk/story/2320524/paf-and-the-afghan-war-ii
26. Jonah Blank, Richard S. Girven, Arzan Tarapore, Julia A. Thompson, and Arthur Chan, *Vector Check, Prospects for U.S. and Pakistan Air Power Engagement,* 2018, https://www.rand.org/pubs/research_reports/RR2107.html
27. World Directory of Modern Military Aircraft 2022, Pakistan Air Force Current Fighter Inventory, https://www.wdmma.org/pakistan-air-force.php#:~:text=Current%20Active%20Inventory %3A% 20818%20 Aircraft&text=The%20following%20represents%20an%20overview,in%20its%20active%20aircraft%20inory
28. Snehesh Alex Phillip, 'Biden Administration Approves Upgrade of Pakistan's F-16 Fighter

Aircraft in $450-Million Deal', *The Print*, 8 September 2022, https://theprint.in/defence/biden-administration-approves-upgrade-of-pakistans-f-16-fighter-aircraft-in-450-million-deal/1120715/

29. Sana Jamal, 'Pakistan Air Force Speeds up Fighter Force Modernisation with JF-17 Block III', *World Asia*, 16 January 2022, ttps://gulfnews.com/world/asia/pakistan/pakistan-air-force-speeds-up-fighter-force-modernisation-with-jf-17-block-iii-1.84992034
30. Adnan Aamir, *Pakistan to Boost Air Strike Power with 50 Enhanced Fighter Jets*, 6 February 2022, https://asia.nikkei.com/Politics/Pakistan-to-boost-air-strike-power-with-50-enhanced-fighter-jets
31. Diptendu Choudhury (2020), 44:6, 521-541, https://www.tandfonline.com/doi/full/10.1080/09700161.2020.1841100
32. Ma Xiaotian and Tian Xiusi 'Speed Up the Building of a Powerful People's Air Force for Integrated Air and Space Operations That is Capable of Attack and Defence—Studying Chairman Xi Jinping's Important Expositions on the Building and Development of the Air Force', , *Seeking Truth*, 30 October 2014.
33. Andrew S. Erikson, *China Defence White Papers—1995-2019*, 23 July 2019, https://www.andrewerickson.com/2019/07/china-defense-white-papers-1995-2019-download-complete-set-read-highlights-here/
34. Ibid.
35. Ibid.
36. Diptendu Choudhury, 'Expanding Role of PLAAF in China's National Security Strategy', *Strategic Analysis*, Taylor and Francis, 44:6, 2020, pp. 521-522.
37. http://usa.chinadaily.com.cn/china/2017 09/05/content 31577141.htm (Accessed on 30 August 2020).
38. Quotations from Chairman Mao Tse Tung, *The Little Red Book,* Chapter 10, Leadership of Party Committees, Peking Foreign Languages Press, eBook format 2019, pp. 379-80, https://www.marxists.org/reference/archive/mao/works/red-book/ch10.htm
39. Diptendu Choudhury, 'Expanding Role of PLAAF in China's National Security Strategy', *Strategic Analysis*, 44:6, 2020, p. 536.
40. Jasjit Singh, 'Indian Air Power, Global Air Power', John Andreas Olsen (ed.), Potomac Books Inc. 2011, p.249.
41. Alvin Toffler, *The Third Wave*, Bantam Books, New York, 1980, p. 2.
42. Probal Dasgupta, *Watershed 1967, India's Forgotten Victory Over China*, Juggernaut Books, New Delhi, 2020, pp.139-178.
43. Dr. Arvind Gupta, 'Significance of Exercise 'Gagan Shakti-2018', 7 May 2018, https://www.vifindia.org/article/2018/may/07/significance-of-exercise-gagan-shakti-2018
44. Frank O'Donnell and Alex Bollfrass, *The Strategic Postures of China and India,* Report, Belfer Centre, Harvard Kennedy School for Science and International Affairs, March 2020, https://www.belfercenter.org/sites/default/files/2020-03/india-china-postures/China%20 India%20 Postures.pdf
45. Huma Siddiqui, *Financial Express*, 12 August 2022, https://www.financialexpress.com/defence/china-continues-to-expand-infrastructure-and-upgrades-air-bases-in-tibet/2627807/
46. ANI, 'India, China likely to have Air Force-to-Air Force hotline to Prevent Flare ups at the LAC', *Times of India*, 9 August 2022, https://timesofindia.indiatimes.com/india/india-china-likely-to-have-air-force-to-air-force-hotline-to-prevent-possible-flare-ups-on-lac/articleshow/93460533.cms
47. Ibid.

48. Samran Ali, 'Importance of Shaheen Exercises for Pakistan Air Force and Indian Concerns', Centre for Strategic and Contemporary Research, Islamabad,https://cscr.pk/explore/themes/defense-security/importance-of-shaheen-exercises-for-pakistan-air-force-and-indian-concerns/
49. Author, https://www.vifindia.org/article/2021/june/16/the-absence-of-air-power-in-india-s-security-narratives
50. QUAD Leaders Joint Statement, The White House Briefing Room, Statements and Releases, 24 May 2022, https://www.whitehouse.gov/briefing-room/statements-releases/2022/05/24/quad-joint-leaders-statement/
51. Manjari Chatterjee Miller, *Why Nations Rise*, Oxford University Press, 2021, p. 145.
52. PTI, 19 February 2009, 'IAF fighter squadrons to rise to 42 by 2022: Antony', *The Times of India*, https://timesofindia.indiatimes.com/india/iaf-fighter-squadrons-to-rise-to-42-by-2022-antony/articleshow/4151093.cms
53. MRCA RFP: 'India Floats its Biggest-ever Global Tender for Jet Fighters', *Aviation and Aerospace*, 28 August 2007, https://www.domain-b.com/aero/20070828_mrca_rfp.htm
54. Atul Chandra, 'India Ends MMRCA Fighter Acquisition,' *Flight Global*' 5 August 2015, https://www.flightglobal.com/india-ends-mmrca-fighter-acquisition/117851.article
55. Krishn Kaushik, 'Parliament panel says IAF strength down, calls for time-bound purchase', *The Indian Express*, 17 March 2022, https://indianexpress.com/article/india/iaf-strength-down-go-for-time-bound-purchase-7823340/
56. Prakash Nanda, '114 Multi-Role Fighters, LCA Tejas, AMCA Jets, S-400 Missiles – IAF Chief Outlines His Game Plan For Possible Conflict With China', *Eurasian Times*, 30 August 2022, https://eurasiantimes.com/114-multi-role-fighters-lca-tejas-amca-jets-s-400-missiles-iaf/?amp
57. Ibid.
58. Paul Scharre, 'Yes Unmanned Aircraft Combat Aircraft are the Future', 11 August 2015, https://warontherocks.com/2015/08/yes-unmanned-combat-aircraft-are-the-future/
59. Dr. Mel Deaile, 'The Future of the Bomber in an Air Superiority Role: Fighting an Adaptive, Complex Enemy in the Pacific', *Journal of Indo-Pacific Affairs*, Air University Press, 1 August 2022,https://www.airuniversity.af.edu/JIPA/Display/Article/3111116/the-future-of-the-bomber-in-an-air-superiority-role-fighting-an-adaptive-comple/
60. Secretary of the Air Force Public Affairs, 'B-21 bomber to be unveiled first week in December', 20 September 2022, https://www.af.mil/News/Article-Display/Article/3164776/b-21-bomber-to-be-unveiled-first-week-in-december/
61. Kyle Mizokami, 'Russia Will Fly a New Heavy Bomber in 2024 ... If Sanctions Don't Kill It First', *Popular Mechanics*, 8 August 2022, https://www.popularmechanics.com/military/aviation/a40813053/russia-new-heavy-bomber-2024/
62. Sakshi Tiwari, 'Two Distinctive Models Of China's H-20 Stealth Bomber Surface Online; Experts Decode The Mysterious Images, *The Eurasian Times*, 24 August2022, https://eurasiantimes.com/two-distinctive-model-of-chinas-h-20-stealth-bomber-surfaces/
63. Air Marshal Diptendu Choudhury, 'Salience of Air Power in Asian Waters', *Naval War College Journal*, Volume 32, Annual Issue, 2020.
64. Michael W. Pietrucha, 'Making Places, Not Bases a Reality', US Naval Institute vol. 141/10/1,352, 28 March 2016.
65. Daniel J. Kosteca, 'Places and Bases, The Chinese Navy's Emerging Support Network in the Indian Ocean', *China Brief*, vol. 10, no. 15, The Jamestown Foundation, 22 July 2010.
66. Dr. Will Roper, '*Take the Red Pill: The New Digital Acquisition Reality*'. Cited by Valerie Insinna, *Defence News*, 15 September 2020 https://www.defensenews.com/breaking-news/

2020/09/15/the-us-air-force-has-built-and-flown-a-mysterious-full-scale-prototype-of-its-future-fighter-jet/

67. Aviation Industry Report, June 2022, https://www.ibef.org/industry/indian-aviation#:~:text=Market%20Size,airplanes%20operating%20in%20the%20sector
68. D. Choudhury, 'Aerospace Doctrine and Strategy: A Time for review', *Asian Defence Review,* 2021, KW Publishers, p. 34.
69. Prakash Nanda, '114 Multi-Role Fighters, LCA Tejas, AMCA Jets, S-400 Missiles – IAF Chief Outlines His Game Plan For Possible Conflict With China', *Eurasian Times*, 30 August 2022, https://eurasiantimes.com/114-multi-role-fighters-lca-tejas-amca-jets-s-400-missiles-iaf/?amp
70. Diptendu Choudhury, 'The Fire Walking Braves', *ORF Expertspeak*, 20 June 2022, https://www.orfonline.org/expert-speak/the-firewalking-braves/
71. Manjeet Negi, 'IAF Conducts Capstone Seminar for 1st Warfare and Aerospace Strategy program', *India Today*, 25 June 2022https://www.indiatoday.in/india/story/iaf-conducts-capstone-seminar-warfare-aerospace-strategy-program-1966529-2022-06-25
72. Global Air Power Ranking 2022, https://www.wdmma.org/ranking.php
73. India's Statement delivered by the External Affairs Minister, Dr. S. Jaishankar at the General Debate of the 77th session of the UN General Assembly, MEA Media Centre, 25 September 2022, https://www.mea.gov.in/Speeches-Statements.htm?dtl/35757/Indias+Statement+delivered+ by+ the+ External+Affairs+Minister+Dr+S+Jaishankar+at+the+General+Debate+of+the+ 77th+ session+of+the+UN+General+Assembly
74. Jasjit Singh, *Defence from the Skies*, KW Publishers, New Delhi, 2013, p. 286.

16

Future Organisation for Joint-Services Air Defence

V.K. Saxena

Setting the Perspective

In order to get to the main issue of a desired future organisation for the country's air defence, a few essentials need to be put on record. These are briefly stated as follows:

- Air defences the world over exist to counter the network of cumulative air threat from our potential adversaries.
- Since the said air threat can manifest on land, sea, sub-surface, or air (including space) either singly or simultaneously, air defence weapons exist in each of these domains to take on the challenge.
- Weapons in each specific domain are tailored to be core-competent in their medium of operation. Crews (implying the services—Army, Navy, Air Force, Coast Guard, etc.) operating these have perfected the techniques and experiences over the years and decades to use their arsenal most optimally.
- Notwithstanding the rationale and logic of service-wise holding of domain-specific weapons, optimal conduct of the air defence battle demands that irrespective of the weapons, crews or their medium of operation, the most lethal of the weapons must be brought to bear on the threat continuously and seamlessly till the threat is destroyed or negated.

Some examples to indicate the magnitude of challenges in the context of air defence are illustrated below:

- Imagine a deadly air threat package closing in to destroy a critical asset of the country. The challenge is to detect this threat as far ahead as possible. Within a matter of minutes and seconds, the threat has to be identified to be either a friend or a foe (IFF). Among multiple threats of such kind in the battle space, the one most deadly is to be prioritized based on its 'immediacy' and 'lethality'. In near-real time thereafter, the threat has to be designated to the most optimal weapon, be it aircraft or missile or ship/sub-surface-based weapon. Once battle is joined, air defence fire has to be shifted weapon-to-weapon across the entire spread of firearms across multiple domains till the threat is killed/negated. All this must be completed in a matter of a few fleeting minutes! This is the challenge.
- The entire edifice of air defence rests on three verticals, namely, sensors, shooters and battle management command and control (BMC2) system. Basically, the sensors (implying multiple types of radars and a host of electronic and electro-optical (EO) devices), are meant for detecting air threats. The shooters, comprising fire-arms represented by air defence aircraft, surface-to-air-missiles (SAMs), towed and self-propelled air defence guns, and sea and sub-surface launched air defence weapons are for interception and destruction of the threat while the BMC2, typically called the 'air defence control and reporting system' (ADCRS) is for the management and control of the air defence battle. It controls the battle functions of detection, identification, prioritization, target designation, and continuous punishment of the target while seamlessly shifting from weapon-to-weapon as stated earlier.
- Another important point to make here is the eternal cause-effect duel between the prosecutors of the air threat and the defenders. Based on the dictum 'to every sword a shield', air threats drive air defences. In that, as the air threat revamps in quality and quantum, so does the means to destroy them.
- In the above light, it is important to highlight that the air defences of today and tomorrow must recognise the emerging threats like small drones, drone swarms, hypersonic weapons and soft-kill threats, to name a few, and shape up to counter them.

Integration: A Basis for Future Organisation

Future organisations will be driven in a big way by the unambiguous understating of what are the integration needs of the organisation. As regards air defence, integration will be required at two levels; one, at the level of the conduct of the air defence battle, and two, on the pedestal of policy and procedural framework. This is explained further.

Integration Requirement for Conduct of Air Defence Battle

While it will be logical to state that the air defences of the three services must be integrated to ensure that a cumulative punch of the nation's capability is delivered optimally on the aggressor, it does not imply that the air defences of the three services need to be beaten into one lump of minced meat. In fact, the requirement is that some portion of the air defences needs to be seamlessly integrated while the other must remain distinct and vibrant in its respective domains of core-competence.

Taking a cue from what has been stated in building the perspective, while the air defence weapons tailor-made for each domain and operated by crews with expertise gained over decades must remain distinct and vibrant and continue to operate in their respective mediums, what must be integrated is the entity that threads them all together into one whole. That involves the following:

- The countrywide integrated capability of sensors on land, sea, and air that can detect the enemy's air threat at the longest possible ranges.
- Capability to auto-fuse inputs from multiple sensors to cut out duplication of the same target being painted by different sensors.
- Near real-time capability to identify threats as hostile and prioritize them on the basis of the sequence of their likely impact and the comparative lethality of the threat they pose.
- Auto-designation of the threats to the most suitable weapons based on their geographical positioning and the effectiveness in achieving a kill.
- Coordinating air combat in real-time by guiding own interceptors on to the threat in case the air defence battle has opened up with ingress-mode interception.
- Controlling the ground air defence battle all across the firearms so as to ensure a seamless punishment of the threat.
- Carrying out auto-de-confliction of the finite air space so that multiple users can exploit the air space with minimum restriction and maximum freedom of operation.

All this is a huge task. As stated, the organ of the air defence that makes the above happen is called the ADCRS. It must be fully integrated across the entire vertical of air defence

Integration Requirements in Other Areas

Besides the above, the future air defence organisation must be integrated along several other verticals. These are briefly captured as follows:

- That air threat drives air defence has been stated earlier. The organ of air defence that collects, collates and interprets the entire body of intelligence from multiple sources (NSCS, IDS, SHQ, IB, RAW, NTRO, etc.) so as to generate one assessed perception of the air threat to the nation must be fully integrated across land, sea and air.
- Another important aspect for integration is capability development. Air defence is a close-knit battle fought with multiple weapons spread across the services. The organ of air defence which will decide what type of weapons, what type of sensors, what type of command and control systems must be procured and fielded across the nation for the prosecution of national air defence capability as one cumulative punch has to be one central agency. This will not only ensure that best war waging assets are purchased overriding the service turfs, but also drive economy of scale in progressing joint cases in a tri-service mode. Such an approach will also ensure a holistic view of emerging threats and will field optimal counters well in time.
- Another area of centralisation and optimization is in the field of budget allocation. It is imperative to ensure that the allotted funds are utilised most optimally by ruthlessly cutting out non-essentials, skewed procurements, and duplications. Funds for fielding the air defence of the nation must be received centrally and utilized by one central authority responsible for national air defence.
- Air defence weapons are cost-prohibitive. No nation can afford a frequent changeover of inventory. What is resorted to is the extension of operational effectiveness of weapons and support systems through phased overhauls and qualitative enhancements through repeated product upgrades to absorb emerging technologies. Huge logistic and infrastructure support goes into this. In order to cut out service-wise duplication of efforts, drive economies of scale, and ensure a most effective utilization of men and machines, it is reiterated that the entire

gamut of sustenance of the air defence war-waging potential of the country must be controlled and executed by one central agency.

Another important aspect which needs to be integrated is training. The nation faces one air threat and all air defence warriors must be trained to counter it following the same ethos and achieving the same training threshold. Persons trained in different service environments will achieve different standards. Integrating them in one common thread of national air defence will indeed be a herculean task.

- Also, anything not tested, inspected, evaluated, and scored is actually not fit for war. This is particularly true in training. All training must be evaluated and all war-waging potential must be inspected regularly. It is obvious to state that this important responsibility must be executed by one single agency against one common benchmark.

A Word About the Current Organisation

Having presented an analysis of the requirements of a future air defence organisation, here is a word about our current air defence organisation. Before that, a word about the naval air defence will be in order. Naval air defence as connected to the other two services basically relates to the air defence of naval shore-based assets and vulnerabilities (dockyards, ammunition installations, naval bases, etc.). Air defence of the fleet at sea by multiple air defence weapons (aircraft, helicopters, ship-borne guns and missiles as also sub-surface air defence weapons) is an exclusive naval domain executed by the Navy end-to-end.

The salient points about the rest of the air defence set-up are briefly stated as follows:

- The responsibility for the air defence of the national air space is that of the Indian Air Force (IAF).
- In the execution of this responsibility, the IAF exercises overall control of the air defence battle across the three services by permitting or restricting the fire of air defence weapons held by all the three services.
- This control is exercised by the IAF through a system called the integrated air command and control system (IACCS). This is a system responsible for nation-wide ADCRS in the manner explained above.
- IACCS is configured on the SATCOM network referred to as Air Force Net (AF Net). It features a series of ADCRS nodes starting from the national level down to formation headquarters.

- IACCS provides one common thread of air defence command and control, handshaking with networks of air defence sensors and shooters of other two services in a seamless manner and extending from the highest level right down to the tactical battle area.
- There is a whole body of standing instructions, fire control orders and emergency control orders as tools of control. Suffice it to say, no air defence opens fire unless cleared by the IACCS.

  It will amount to treading on the CLASSIFIED domain, if the current status and deficiencies of IACCS are cited in an open source. The need of this paper will however be served if the desired attributes of IACCS are briefly stated. These are as under:
- The IACCS must have its full complement of ground and aerial sensors to generate a comprehensive and a dynamic air situation picture (ASP).
- It must feature state-of-the-art technologies for executing functions like the multi-sensor tracking and fusion, identification of friend or Foe, 3D dynamic displays of ASP, near-real time data transfer, encrypted data and voice connectivity, capability of auto de-confliction of airspace, and more.
- Most importantly, the inter-service network connectivity on the AF Net has to be perfect and seamless with due redundancies.

A Perception of the Future Organisation

Having enumerated all the desired features of a possible future air defence organisation, it is now possible to define its contours to some level of clarity. Here is an attempt:

- The future organisation could be called integrated air defence command (IADC).
- Keeping in mind the primacy of the IAF in all matters of air defence and their position of responsibility as stated earlier, it will be in order to have the IADC headed by an IAF three-star ranking officer.
- It must be stated here that the IADC is not an air force command; it is a national entity that is responsible for the execution of the country's might of air defence in a cumulative manner.
- That said, the next level of hierarchy right under the C-in-C must be tenanted by two-star officers of the Army Air Defence and Navy as Deputy C-in-Cs.
- For administrative convenience, it would be ideal to co-locate the IADC with an existing Air Force Command.

- In the upward command and control channel, it will be logical to place the IADC under the CDS or under the permanent chairman of chiefs of staff committee.
- The entire IACCS network must remain under the unified control of the Air Force. For this, a two–star officer under the IADC must be put in charge of all IACCS networks.
- The above stated IACCS network must become the backbone of IADC. It must get seamlessly integrated with the networks of the other two services as explained earlier.
- Based on the other needs of integration explained earlier, the IADC must have an intelligence wing, a capability development wing, a sustenance wing and a finance department.
- Each of these wings must have a proportional representation by the three services in the ratio of 3:2:1 for the IAF, Army and Navy, respectively. The broad rationale of each of these wings has been explained earlier. Detailed tasking could be worked out in due course.
- Weapon verticals should remain with the original services on an as-is-where-is basis to start with. Further enhancement of capability should be the responsibility of the capability development (CD) wing.
- That said, while there may be a case for the CD wing to examine a re-ordered holding of ground-based air defence weapons (GBADWS) among the three services, the same is not recommended, being non-executable in practice.
- IADC should interface with the theatre commands as and when established by having an IADC cell in each of them. These cells will be responsible to provide all air defence support to the command. Detailed modalities and operating procedures could be worked out accordingly.
- This author is not in favour of rigid or prioritised distribution of air assets to theatre commands. Such a division is against the very DNA of air power and its application for offence or defence. Air power must remain integrated and undivided as one cumulative whole. This can be best utilised by IADC in providing air defence support to each theatre command and exploiting the inherent signatures of air power, namely, flexibility and dynamic deployment.

That such an organisation will see the light of the day in the near future is the hope of the author.

17

Building India's Counter-Terror Capability

Bipin Bakshi

Preamble

Images of a mystery boat carrying arms and explosives flashed across media channels and TV sets on 23 August 2022, bringing back memories of the Mumbai terrorist attacks in 2008.[1] While the boat's arrival on Indian shores did not lead to any hostile action, it brings to the fore the difference between just raising a few counter-terrorist units and building a robust counter-terrorist capability. Building such a capability entails a comprehensive understanding of how India has been facing the threat of terrorism and how our security forces have evolved to meet the challenge. Taking into context India's hostile neighbourhood, external forces have been fomenting trouble and trying to destroy our nation's unity for decades. As Gen V.K. Nayar articulated, external forces in conjunction with internal dissent would endeavour to exacerbate India's security problems.[2] Terrorism is the most lethal derivative of this dangerous nexus and India has been confronting it for the longest period of time in comparison to any other nation.

Building the necessary capabilities to counter the threats of terrorism and insurgency will be the key to securing India in the years to come. This would fundamentally require a comprehensive analysis of the evolving dynamics of modern terrorism.

Elements of Terror Attacks

Renowned counter-terrorism expert David Otto illustrated through *The Terror Triangle* Model, the necessary elements of a successful terrorist attack and the

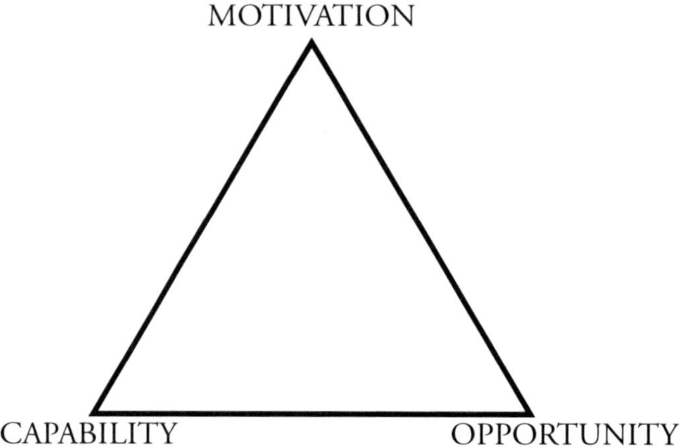

Figure 1: David Otto's Terror Triangle Model

methodology by which modern terrorism is propagated (Figure 1).[3] According to the above model, terror outfits or states supporting terrorism first seek to motivate vulnerable and at-risk individuals to commit acts of terrorism through indoctrination of ideology and narrative. This is followed by building the capabilities of the recruited individuals to carry out terror attacks through training in weapons and logistical support. At this stage, terrorists are trained and equipped according to the intended target. According to Dr. Otto, training varies from carrying out terror attacks against hard targets (military personnel and installations) and soft targets (civilians and civil establishments). Finally, the terror outfits seek opportunities to execute their attack by capitalizing on security lapses and voids in the security architecture.[4]

In a recent incident along the Line of Control (LoC) in Jammu Sector, on 21 August 2022, a captured Pakistani national revealed on media that he had been promised Pakistani Rs. 30,000 (US$ 125) by Pakistani "Col Yunus" for carrying out an attack on Indian forces.[5] Another recent example is the Islamic State (IS or ISIS)-motivated terror suspect apprehended in Russia with stated aims of carrying out a blast in India against a VIP.[6] Such attacks can take place anywhere in the vast expanse of the country and we have to deal with such threats employing various state and central resources. A successful counter-terrorism strategy encompasses, firstly, a robust intelligence mechanism that can detect and disrupt attempts by terror outfits to motivate and recruit from the vulnerable population; secondly, we need to build the capacity to degrade and prevent the capability of terrorists and opportunity to execute attacks;

and finally, we need specialized forces with the required strike capabilities and tactics to bolster the nation's effort to combat terrorism and defeat such terrorist attacks.

One of the examples of a successful counter-terrorism strategy is that of the United Kingdom. Despite its rapid evolution over the years, however, experts have noted that it still needs better synchronisation among various government departments involved in the effort as well as the communities served by the strategy.[7] As per the Global Terrorism Index, India figures in the top 15 countries in the world affected by terrorism, with a score of 7.432 out of 10, calculated as an average of four indicators: terrorist incidents, fatalities, injuries, and property damage. To measure the impact of terrorism, a five-year weighted average is applied by the Institute for Economics and Peace (IEP) based at Sydney, using data from the *Terrorism Tracker* and other sources.[8]

Taking all these factors into consideration, this paper will explore the various nuances of building a robust counter-terrorism capability through an analysis of the history and evolution of counter-terrorist (CT) operations in India while deriving lessons from international experiences.

Historical Timeline of Counter-Terrorist Operations

The first instance of the involvement of the Indian armed forces in carrying out operations inside the country happened within13 months of our Independence. Major K.C. Praval notes that some infantry units of the Indian Army were employed for military operations during the Hyderabad police action in 1948.[9] Prolonged counter-terrorism campaigns by the Indian Army started with the upheaval in Nagaland from the 1950s onwards. Secessionist groups in Nagaland began the revolt as early as 1952 over the demand for an independent state. Initially, the Assam Rifles and State Armed Police were tasked to counter the insurgents, but by 1956 the Indian Army was mobilized to carry out anti-insurgency operations in the region. The insurgency in Nagaland was a prelude to the series of insurgencies throughout the North-Eastern region that demanded specialized and complex combat tactics. Subsequently, terrorist activities began to emerge in other border regions of our nation and also in the hinterland. The history of military involvement in CT operations has been illustrated in Table 1.

Table 1: History of Military Involvement in CT Operations[10, 11, 12]

Nagaland 1950s	Assam Rifles and State Armed Police mobilised in March 1952. Indian Army mobilised in February 1956.
Mizoram 1960s	Indian Armed Forces along with Air Assets were mobilised on 5 March 1967.
Manipur 1960s/70s	Insurgency started with the formation of the United National Liberation Front (UNLF) on 24 November 1964. In 1981 the Indian Army was mobilized for counter-insurgency operations.
Punjab 1984	The Army was mobilized on 3 June 1984 to neutralise the terrorist stronghold in the Golden Temple in Operation Blue Star and subsequently to assist the police in fighting terrorism.
Assam 1990	The State of Assam was declared disturbed on 27 November 1990 and Operation BAJRANG launched. Due to the pressure of the Security Forces, the United Liberation Front of Asom (ULFA) agreed to a truce in March 1991. Renewed violence led to launching of Operation RHINO in September 1991.
Jammu & Kashmir 1990	The Army was deployed in the Valley with the enactment of the Armed Forces Special Powers Act (AFSPA) on 10 September 1990.
Mumbai Attack 26/11/2008	Ten armed terrorists began the attack at 2130 hrs on 26 November 2008. The National security Guard (NSG) arrived in Mumbai from Manesar at 0630 hrs on 27 November 2008 and began the operations. Military/Police elements including Navy MARCOS were also involved.
Myanmar 2015	Surgical strikes were carried out by Army Special Forces on militant strongholds inside Myanmar in June 2015, in response to a major strike by militants in Chandel District.
Pathankot Attack 2016	Commandos from the NSG, Indian Air Force (IAF)Garud and Indian Army Special Forces neutralised the terrorists who attacked the Pathankot Air Force Base on 2 January 2016.
Uri Attacks & Surgical Strike	On 18 September 2016, terrorists from Pakistan attacked the Indian Army brigade headquarters in Uri. On 29 September 2016, the Indian Army retaliated by carrying out a surgical strikes across the Line of Control (LoC) targeting the terrorist launchpads.

These incidents in India's long history of CT operations have underscored the importance of military, paramilitary as well as armed police forces in India's counter-terrorism architecture. Consequently, the Armed Forces, Central Armed Police Forces (CAPF) and State Armed Police Forces have raised various specialized units for conventional and sub-conventional operations which have evolved with the changing threat environment and operating conditions. While standard Army units and airborne battalions handled the initial force requirements in the first two decades after independence, certain specialized forces were later felt necessary for CT tasks with varying capabilities for different envisaged employment.

India's Response to Terrorist Threats and Challenges

The Army raised para commando units post-1965, commencing with only two units, and a special group. These units had different domains of specialized training and capabilities, varying from mountain and high-altitude warfare, operating in deserts, plains and riverine sectors and various other specialized capabilities like counter-hijack, counter-terrorism and amphibious operations. These units were primarily designed for deep penetration into hostile territory by land, sea, and air in keeping with the capabilities of the best special forces of the world. The National Security Guard (NSG) was later raised as a Federal Contingency Deployment Force post-Operation Blue Star in 1984 to undertake precise, small team CT operations, while obviating collateral damage.[13] Counter-hijack (CH), Bomb disposal (BD), and personal security of protected persons were added to the role of the NSG, with certain roles overlapping the existing special units. The Special Protection Group (SPG) was also raised for the sole purpose of providing proximate security to the Prime Minister of India.[14]

In subsequent years, the Indian Navy raised marine commandos (MARCOS) and the Indian Air Force raised its Garud commandos.[15] After the Mumbai attacks of 2008, it was felt that one single CT-CH node in the National Capital Region would not be able to respond in time to urgent response situations in the entire country. Therefore, the states and some of the Union territories started raising CT, counter-IED/BD, counter-left wing extremism and K9 (dog) units of varying sizes, capability and strength. The NSG units have also increased in number with the establishment of five regional hubs post the Mumbai attacks of 2008, which have been set up at Mumbai, Hyderabad, Chennai, Kolkata, and Gandhinagar.[16] Meanwhile, the Indian Army para commando units have been renamed as special forces units and their numbers have been increased from initially two to 10 today.

We thus see a multitude of units designed for various roles to augment the nation's capabilities in the conventional and sub-conventional space. There are some overlaps and some voids that exist in their mandates, jurisdiction, powers to investigate, arrest and their capabilities under various operational situations. Coordination between various agencies that would be required to facilitate operations, especially in an urban environment, thus becomes a critical requirement. None of the special forces that need air effort for airborne and heliborne operations have been provided with a dedicated air wing, thereby increasing the complexities of coordination in vertical envelopment and air insertion operations. This void in air effort will need to be filled up as swift insertion in an urban scenario using helicopters is an inescapable requirement for which close affiliation of pilots with the force and regular training is essential.

The concept of having a specialist force for urban counter-terrorism was immediately validated when the Black Cat commandos proved successful in the stand-off siege of the Golden Temple, i.e., Operation Black Thunder I & II. In April 1986, the NSG was tasked to flush out terrorists in the Golden Temple complex and the operation was codenamed *Operation Black Thunder I.* The second part of the operation, code named *Operation Black Thunder II* was carried out by the NSG between 10 and 11 May 1988. This time by using their snipers from surrounding vantage points, the NSG successfully neutralized terrorists without entering the Golden Temple complex.[17] In these operations, superior weapons and urban warfare tactics employed by the NSG could achieve the desired results with minimal collateral damage. In contrast with Operation Blue Star of June 1984, this operation was relatively bloodless with 30 terrorists neutralised and no casualties among the security forces. The operation inflicted a major tactical and psychological blow to terrorism in Punjab.[18] There have been over 60 operations by the NSG since then, though only a few are in public memory, like *Akshardham 2002, Mumbai 2008,* and *Pathankot 2016.*

Response to Counter-Terror Operations

The NSG model for counter-terrorist, counter-hijack and bomb disposal (CT/CH/BD) operations within national borders is well proven and should be continued. There are, however, command-and-control issues and the role of the NSG in conventional operations that need review.

The first responders in any situation in the hinterland are the local police, with the exception of certain areas, wherein it would be the Army, the Rashtriya Rifles (RR), Assam Rifles, or CAPF units. The present response matrix within the country may be summarized as illustrated in Table 2.

Table 2: CT Response Matrix

Nature of Threat	*Location*	*Force*	*Response*
Limited terrorist incidents	Hinterland less J&K/Northeast	State police	First contact and information
		State special forces/ CAPF	Graduating to second responders
Intense terrorist strike/hijack/ hostage situation	Federal contingency	NSG	Second responders - response time - 2.5 hrs
Left Wing Extremism (LWE) incidents	LWE areas	State Police/ CAPF	CAPF with support of state police
Proxy war/ terrorist activities	J&K/Northeast	Indian Army & CAPF	Supported by state police

State CT forces would be the second responders unless the situation warrants deployment of the NSG as the second responder. It is only if the intensity of the terrorist action is higher than the capability of the state CT forces to manage, that the federal contingency force should be called. For example, when three terrorists attacked the Dina Nagar police station in Gurdaspur district of Punjab, only the state forces were employed to neutralise them in an operation that lasted for almost 12 hours. Despite the Ministry of Home Affairs offering the services of the NSG and even the Army rushing its special forces, the Punjab Police insisted that the SWAT unit of Punjab Police would handle the operations.[19] A seamless response matrix therefore needs to be worked out depending on the location of various units and their capabilities. The list of state CT units/forces is given in Table 3.

Table 3: List of State CT Forces

Andhra Pradesh	Organisation for Counter Terrorist Operations (OCTOPUS [AP])
Arunachal Pradesh	Special Task Force (STF)
Assam	Assault Groups of Black Panthers, Assam Commando Battalion
Bihar	Anti-Terrorist Squad (ATS)
Chandigarh	Chandigarh Special Force
Chhattisgarh	Special Operations Group (SOG)
Delhi	Special Weapons and Tactics (SWAT)

Goa	Altinho
Gujarat	Chetak Commando Force & Special Operations Group (SOG)
Haryana	Haryana Police Commandos Wing
Himachal Pradesh	Special Service Unit (SSU) & Quick Reaction Teams
Jammu & Kashmir	SOG in Kashmir and ATS & ERT in Jammu Division
Jharkhand	Jaguar Force & ATS
Karnataka	Garuda & SWAT
Kerala	Thunderbolts & Special Operations Group
Madhya Pradesh	Hawk Commandos
Maharashtra	Force One & C 60
Manipur	State Police Commando Wing
Meghalaya	Special Operations Team
Mizoram	State Police Commando Platoons
Nagaland	Police Commandos
Odisha	Special Tactical Unit & Special Operations Group
Punjab	Special Operations Group, SWAT
Rajasthan	Anti-Terror Squad and Emergency Response Team
Sikkim	Special Task Force
Tamil Nadu	Tamil Nadu Commando Force and Quick Reaction Teams
Telangana	OCTOPUS (Telangana) & Greyhounds
Tripura	Special Weapons and Tactics Units
Uttar Pradesh	Special Police Operations Team
Uttarakhand	Anti-Terror Squad
West Bengal	Special Commando Unit, Special Striking Force Battalion and Counter Insurgency Force

Refining CT Operations Capabilities for the Future

During the period 2009to 2012, when an increasing number of CAPF units were being inducted into LWE areas for operations, a need was felt to re-orient them for CT operations in jungles and rural areas, and this training was conducted by Indian Army units. Training teams of army units located in the vicinity of CAPF units, which were being moved to Chhattisgarh, were tasked to carry out intensive training for the CAPF.[20] Simultaneously, the Counter-Insurgency and Jungle Warfare School was being established at Kanker, in Jagdalpur District of South Chhattisgarh, and manned by instructors drawn from the Indian Army. Subsequently, the states also set up special training cells with military officers on deputation.[21] Garuda-Karnataka is one such example of an urban CT Force of the state armed police where Army instructors form the training team that is on deputation to the state government. Besides, a senior-rank officer is appointed as the Director of the Centre for Counter-Terrorism (CCT), Karnataka Police.[22] This team assists the state in honing the skills of the police commandos and is also available to the state government for advice on CT matters.

A considerable amount of regular training is also being carried out by the NSG for the State and Central Armed Police Forces, and their CT and BD teams since 2014. Besides a monthly module, there are annual exercises conducted by the NSG and most of the states have benefitted from the training.[23] This concerted effort has resulted in a steady improvement of state armed police CT equipment, training, and capabilities.

A central study was carried out with the participation of the state police and CAPF to recommend a standardized structure for organizing, equipping, and training CT forces in all the states and Union territories, recommendations of which were promulgated to all the states.

A suggested unit structure that may be suitable for all state CT units is illustrated at the Appendix. This is a modular structure of the smallest unit that would be able to carry out effective operations independently, and it can be scaled up depending on the requirements of each state. It has been drawn up in a manner suitable for the police forces while drawing on the experience of NSG units working with the states, during several joint exercises with state police forces.

Many of the states are now raising their commando training schools which will be used to further enhance the capabilities of the state armed police forces for CT operations. However, the following training centres of the Army, CAPF and State Police can be utilized as zonal and sub-zonal CT training centres rather than committing more resources towards creating new training infrastructure:

1. Army Counter Insurgency and Jungle Warfare School, Vairengte, Mizoram.
2. Army Commando Wing, Infantry School, Belgaum, Karnataka.
3. Counter-Insurgency and Anti-Terrorism (CIAT) School (CRPF), Silchar, Assam.

4. Training Centre & School (TC&S) BSF, Hazaribagh, Jharkhand.
5. Premavatipet Training Centre, Telangana.
6. Commando Training School, Jodhpur, Rajasthan.
7. Counter-Terrorism and Jungle Warfare School (CTJWS), Kanker, Chhattisgarh.
8. CoBRA School of Jungle Warfare and Tactics (CSJWT), CRPF, Belgaum, Karnataka.

An audit of all state CT forces carried out in 2018 revealed certain voids in some of the states, while other states have developed fairly robust counter-terrorist capabilities.[24] It is essential to carry forward this upgrade exercise so that all state police forces become self-sufficient to handle most terrorist-related situations while Army, RR/AR can be relieved for other tasks. We are already seeing the redeployment of RR and Assam Rifles units away from population centres and their increasing role in border management. This trend must continue and be accelerated so that the military components may focus on external threats and trans-border roles which are likely to increase in the future. The raising of the armed forces special operations division is significant in this regard and presents opportunities for greater specialization with a sharper focus on strategic roles and on the development of niche capabilities with various units.

Lessons from International Experiences

The USA has been conducting an anti-terrorism assistance (ATA)[25] programme for our armed police forces for about 20 years.[26] The training content varies from room intervention to post-blast investigation. Joint exercises have also been carried out between the NSG and the Green Berets of the US Army.[27] Therefore, we can see that the special forces of the USA, like the Green Berets, and the Special Air Service of UK, drawn from the military, continue to conduct CT operations under the defence ministries of these countries. However, these are practically island nations with no hostile land borders, unlike Israel and India, who cannot afford to have a large component of the armed forces looking inwards. It is significant to note that Israel no longer employs military units for CT operations within its borders.

The joint working groups set up for Indo-Israel cooperation included a sub-group on CT training, of which the author was a member in 2018.[28] The training cooperation was envisaged between the elite *Yammam* units of Israel

Police and the NSG. The famed Sayeret Matkal of the Israeli defence forces (IDF), which is believed to have been a part of significant CT operations in the past, is now organised and trained for conventional operations while the *Yammam*, from the police, has been prepared as the prime CT force.[29] It may be recalled that Operation Entebbe is among the most daring CT-hostage rescue operations which are studied by special forces the world over as an example of a successful rescue action.[30]

Looking at the Future

The counter-terrorism response matrix as depicted in Table 2 will largely continue to apply in so far as terrorist incidents within our national borders is concerned. Simultaneously, military involvement in the form of the 'first responder' in Jammu, Kashmir and the North-east should be progressively reduced. Signs of this are already visible with the withdrawal of the Army from parts of Assam where the Armed Forces Special Powers Act (AFSPA) has been repealed recently. The Indian Army's Eastern Command has clarified that as the situation improves and violence parameters reduce, the Army is being de-inducted from specific areas where the CAPF and state police have taken on the responsibility of ensuring peace and stability.[31]

Presently, except for one brigade, all Indian Army troops have been pulled off CT duties and redeployed along the Line of Actual Control (LAC) in tune with the overall re-orientation towards the LAC carried out by the Army since the May 2020 stand-off with China. This re-orientation will gradually progress further, thereby enabling military special forces to focus on strategic and operational level tasks, while tactical level CT operations would slowly shift to the armed police forces.

As India rises in the global order and emerges on the world stage as a preferred security partner in the region, the need for special forces to operate beyond our borders is likely to emerge in the future. We have already seen trans-border employment of special forces during the *surgical strikes* in recent years, besides the international intervention operations in The Maldives in 1988. Accordingly, overseas employment of our military special forces could be expected in CT or hostage rescue situations, besides the various other operational and strategic tasks in the conventional and sub- conventional space.

An operational role for the counter-terrorist/counter-hijack units in the NSG, manned by elite Army commandos, for employment under the aegis of the 'Armed Forces Special Operations Division', needs to be considered. The specialized training, equipment and capabilities that these NSG units have developed for room, aircraft, metro rail intervention and response to a hostage situations in confined spaces while limiting collateral damage, cannot be mirrored by the military special forces. Employing the NSG when the need arises to undertake such tasks outside the nation's borders could also be considered in the future. One such situation was the IC 814 hijack situation in December 1999, when it was finally decided not to use the NSG.[32] However, situations in the future may require specialized NSG capability to handle an international terrorist incident involving Indian or friendly citizens. It will therefore be prudent to hone specialised intervention skills under the aegis of the NSG and mandate it to be available under the Armed Forces Special Operations Division for overseas employment.

Conclusion

The overall structure of our military and armed police forces needs to factor-in various operational contingencies, of which, CT operations would be a part. In this overall context, the entire spectrum of employment of the various kinds of units and forces at the central and state levels will need to be considered while evolving their future structures. The future structure of military special forces would need to be harmonised within this overall spectrum of CT-CH operations to achieve synchronization and coordination while ensuring a robust capability to respond in various situations that may arise in the future.

ENDNOTES

1. D. Sivanandhan, "How a 16 Foot Yacht Points to Nation's Vulnerability to a Terror Attack", *The Indian Express*, 25 August 2022, retrieved from https://indianexpress.com/article/opinion/columns/how-a-16-foot-yacht-points-to-nation-vulnerability-to-terror-attack-8109628/
2. V. K. Nayar, *India's Internal Security Compulsions*, New Delhi: Centre for Policy Research, July 2003, p. 3.
3. David Otto, "Top Counter Terrorism Expert Says UK Counter Terrorism Strategy was Based on Luck All the Time", *Biomedical Journal of Scientific & Technical Research*, 15 June 2013, retrieved from https://biomedres.us/pdfs/BJSTR.MS.ID.000134.pdf
4. Ibid.
5. PTI, "Captured Pakistani Terrorist was Sent to Attack Indian Post: Army", *The Economic Times*, 25 August 2022, retrieved fromhttps://economictimes.indiatimes.com/news/defence/captured-pakistani-terrorist-was-sent-to-attack-indian-post-army/articleshow/93760793.cms
6. "IS Terrorist Arrested in Russia for Plotting Attack in India over Prophet Remark", *Hindustan Times*, 23 August 2022, retrieved from https://www.hindustantimes.com/india-news/is-

terrorist-arrested-in-russia-for-plotting-to-carry-out-attack-in-india-over-prophet-remark-101661190182981.html

7. Nodin Muzee, "The 'Terror Triangle' and British Counterterrorism", European Eye on Radicalization, 19 October 2020, retrieved from https://eeradicalization.com/the-terror-triangle-and-british-counterterrorism/
8. "Global Terrorism Index 2022: Measuring the Impact of Terrorism", Institute for Economic and Peace, March 2022, retrieved from https://www.visionofhumanity.org/wp-content/uploads/2022/03/GTI-2022-web-09062022.pdf
9. K.. C. Praval, *Indian Army After Independence*, New Delhi: Lancer Publications, 1987, p. 549.
10. Annual Reports, Ministry of Home Affairs, Government of India, retrieved on 17 September 2022 from https://www.mha.gov.in/documents/annual-reports
11. "Datasheet-India", South Asia Terrorism Portal (SATP), retrieved on 17 September 2022 from https://www.satp.org/datasheet-terrorist-attack/fatalities/india
12. Vivek Chadha, *Low Intensity Conflicts in India: An Analysis*, New Delhi: Sage, 2005.
13. P. C. Katoch and Saikat Datta, *India's Special Forces: History and Future of Indian Special Forces*, New Delhi: United Service Institution, 2013, p. 93.
14. The Gazette of India, *SPG ACT*, 7 June 1988, New Delhi: Ministry of Law and Justice.
15. P. C. Katoch and Saikat Datta, *India's Special Forces: History and Future of Indian Special Forces*, New Delhi: United Service Institution, 2013, p. 93.
16. *Annual Report 2020–21*, Ministry of Home Affairs, Government of India, p. 102.
17. Ibid.
18. Shekhar Gupta, "Success of Operation Black Thunder in Amritsar Clears Golden Temple Complex of Terrorist", *India Today*, 15 June 1988, retrieved from https://www.indiatoday.in/magazine/cover-story/story/19880615-success-of-operation-black-thunder-in-amritsar-clears-golden-temple-complex-of-terrorists-797338-1988-06-15
19. Aman Sharma, "Gurdaspur Attack: Punjab Police Handle Operations; NSG, Army Wait", *The Economic Times*, 18 July 2015, retrieved from https://economictimes.indiatimes.com/news/defence/gurdaspur-attack-punjab-police-handle-operation-nsg-army-wait/articleshow/48244994.cms?from=mdr
20. Rahul Tripathi, "Army to Train State Forces, More IAF Ops: New Plan to Take On Naxalites", *The Indian Express*, 7 May 2017, retrieved from https://indianexpress.com/article/india/army-to-train-state-forces-more-iaf-ops-new-plan-to-take-on-naxalites-4644252/
21. Smruti D, "Befriend the Forest", *Force*, retrieved on 31 August 2022 from https://forceindia.net/cover-story/befriend-the-forest/
22. Akhil Kadidal, "Most Terror Attacks in 2019 were on Hotels: Brigadier S. Bubesh Kumar, Director of the Centre for Counter-Terrorism", *Deccan Herald*, 29 January 2021, retrieved from https://www.deccanherald.com/state/most-terror-attacks-in-2019-were-on-hotels-brigadier-s-bubesh-kumar-director-of-the-centre-for-counter-terrorism-945041.html
23. "Working Conditions in Non-Border Guarding Central Armed Police Forces (Central Industrial Security Force, Central Reserve Police Force and National Security Guard)", Report No. 215, Department Related Parliamentary Standing Committee on Home Affairs, Rajya Sabha Secretariat, 12 December 2018, retrieved from https://rajyasabha.nic.in/rsnew/Committee_site/Committee_File/ReportFile/15/107/215_2018_12_15.pdf
24. "10 Years after 26/11, NSG Audit Shows Chinks in 20 States Armour", *The Hindustan Times*, 28 October 2018, retrieved from https://www.hindustantimes.com/india-news/10-years-after-26-11-nsg-audit-shows-chinks-in-20-states-armour/story-uei1fwyl7Khne5C4l UK9aP.html

25. "Anti-Terrorism Assistance (ATA) Program", U.S. Department of State, 26 July 2016, retrieved from https://www.state.gov/anti-terrorism-assistance-ata-program-summary/
26. "India and US Enhance Partnership in Joint Anti-terrorism", *Indian Defence Review*, 17 May 2011, retrieved from http://www.indiandefencereview.com/news/india-and-us-enhance-partnership-in-joint-anti-terrorism/.
27. Jayanta Gupta, "US Special Forces, NSG Carry Out Joint Drills in Kolkata", *The Times of India*, 1 March 2018, retrieved from https://timesofindia.indiatimes.com/city/kolkata/us-special-forces-nsg-carry-out-joint-drill-in-kolkata/articleshow/63119460.cms
28. "India, Israel Steering Committee Meeting on Homeland and Public Security Held", Press Information Bureau, Ministry of Home Affairs, Government of India, 28 February 2018, retrieved from https://pib.gov.in/newsite/PrintRelease.aspx?relid=176848
29. Judah Ari Gross, "Bennett Declares 'Yamam' Israel's National Counterterrorism Force", *The Times of Israel*, 1 December 2021, retrieved from https://www.timesofisrael.com/bennett-declares-yamam-israels-national-counterterrorism-force/
30. "Operation Entebbe", Israeli Defence Forces, 1 February 2018, retrieved from https://www.idf.il/en/mini-sites/wars-and-operations/operation-entebbe/
31. "Insurgency Down in Northeast, Army Shifts to LAC", *The Hindu*, 19 September 2022, retrieved from https://www.thehindu.com/news/national/northeast-insurgency-losing-public-support-recruitment-down/article65906559.ece
32. "NSG Came Close to Raid IC-814 in Dubai", *The Times of India*, 7 July 2015, retrieved from https://timesofindia.indiatimes.com/india/nsg-came-close-to-raid-ic-814-in-dubai/articleshow/47967046.cms

APPENDIX

COMPOSITION OF A STATE CT UNIT

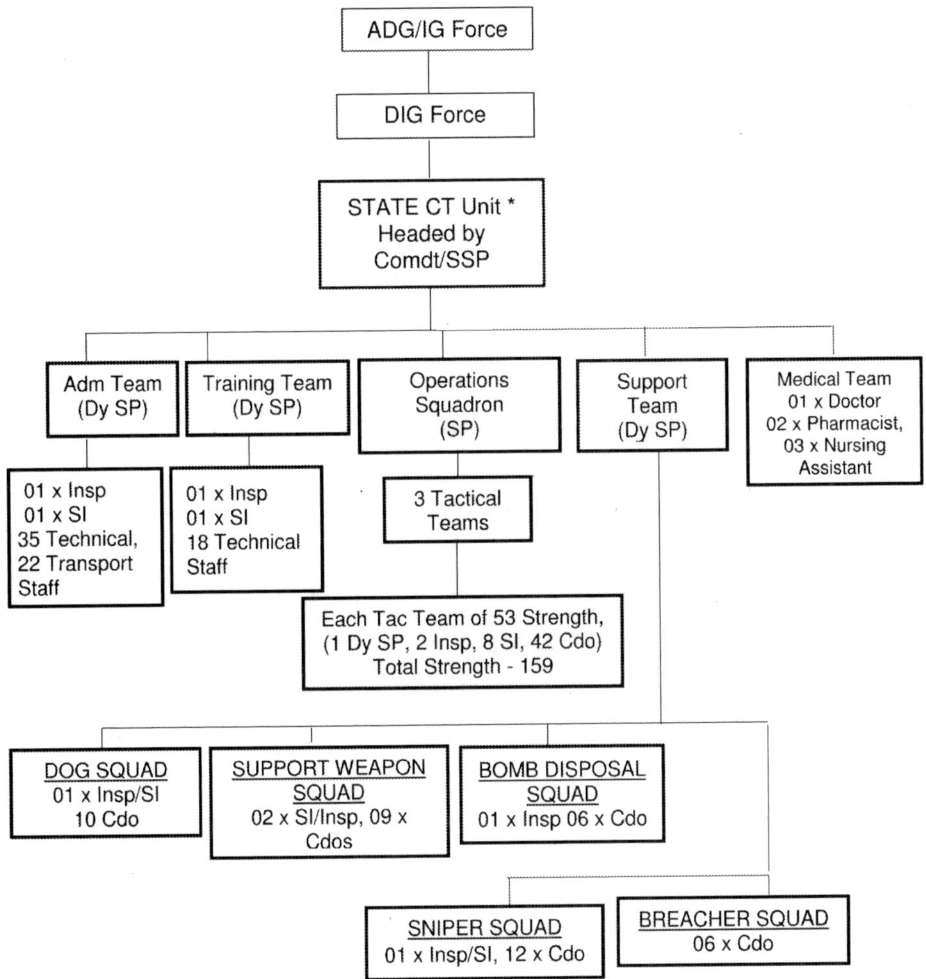

Total Strength - 298

*Number of Units/teams/squads in each state may vary as per specific requirements.

18

Future Technology and Security Landscapes: Trailblazing Pathways towards Self Reliance

N.B. Singh

Technology Security

The war in Ukraine has brought into focus the importance of staying power of a field force and the immense destructive power of long-range precision weapons in striking bases, industrial infrastructure, field formations, and logistics chains. The halting of the Russian offensive was essentially a technological surprise delivered by autonomous platforms. As Ukraine lost most of its artillery and ammunition to precision fires, the war also highlighted the importance of regeneration of combat forces after suffering an initial surprise, lost engagements, and grounding of operations. To prevent loss of territory, boots on ground, supported by sustainable technology-driven capability that is spread across many domains is essential. That calls for not only increased resources but a high-technological orientation of human resources.

The current strategic environment is complex, featuring a rising power in the neighbourhood that is executing its military modernization strategy aimed at countering the USA. It could well achieve technological dominance in that direction. In addition, globalization is also making it easier for both state and non-state actors to acquire the latest military technology. The probability of employment of these capabilities against the Indian state is high. It is therefore essential that some forward-looking decisions are taken today to shape the future course of defence technology strategy, acquisitions, and engineering sustainment of our military capability. The limited budget likely to be available for research and development (R&D) has to be maximized for its impact on India's march towards self-reliance.

The aim of this analysis is to identify areas as to where the government and private sector investments in R&D need to be channelized so as to maximise its impact on self-reliance, and to evolve a road map for development of indigenous capabilities, which would help us achieve *technology security* and *strategic assurance* by 2050. 'Technology Security' implies local availability of underpinning technologies that India needs for reasons of security and sovereignty. It mitigates the risk of being surprised by an adversary's weapons and launching capabilities by employing technology.

Innovations have been the driver of comprehensive national power of a nation. These do not take place in isolation; one needs to find pathways for these to enter the development pipeline. Defence R&D enhances operational effectiveness, improves export performance, and also finds civilian end use. For this to happen, the entire eco-system comprising the Ministry of Defence (MoD), the military, the Defence Research & Development Organisation (DRDO), academia, industry majors and micro, small & medium enterprises (MSME) have to play key roles in shaping and balancing the demand-supply mechanism.

The industry has not found the much-needed handholding by the military in fine tuning their innovations. Consequently, most efforts are getting abandoned after some initial forays. Barring a few industry majors, for the rest it is increasingly difficult to plug into our complex defence acquisition-procurement process due to lack of understanding as well as inadequacy of resources for the long haul ahead.

Improving the Internal Workings of Military Industrial Ecosystem

As a consequence of barriers that retard the tempo of capability development, there are several capability gaps and vulnerabilities in our equipment capabilities. Even today, a large number of components and aggregates continue to be imported by the defence public sector undertakings (DPSU). This could create major vulnerabilities during war as the conflict in Ukraine has demonstrated. Many critical sub-systems like propulsion, navigation, target acquisition, surveillance, and armaments have been imported and integrated on indigenous platforms. Some have referred to them as an assemblage of imported technologies. Even if the threat of sanctions can be addressed through politics and diplomacy, the risk of manifold cost escalation of components looms large. It is critical to reduce this vulnerability through timely indigenization to drive the state of readiness. The high cost of these components has already derailed base refit of the platforms. The cost of supporting a platform post acquisition is well illustrated by the Iceberg effect:

- Life cycle support costs far outweigh acquisition costs over the life cycle.
- Complex platforms require 2-4 times acquisition costs for engineering support over a life cycle of 40-50 years.
- Arjun, Tejas, and other indigenous platforms would need substantial outlays for retaining mission capabilities over their service lives.
- Total life cycle cost can best be explained by the 'Iceberg Effect':

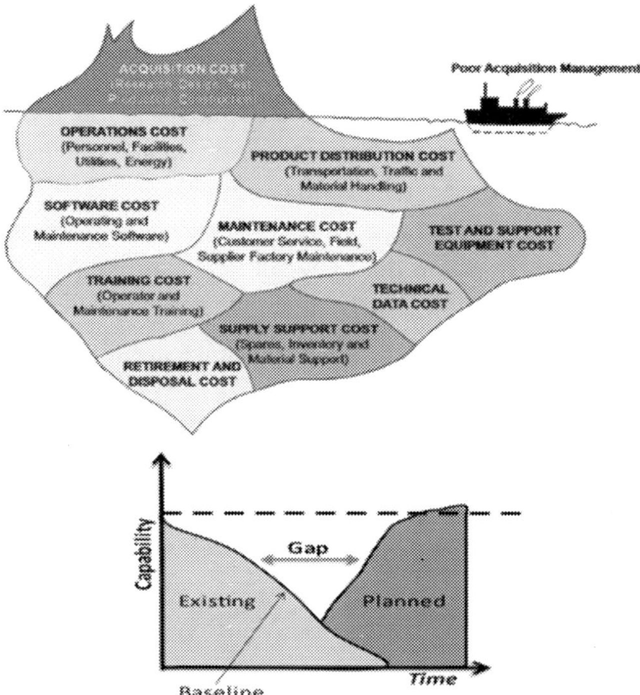

The "do nothing" syndrome creates capability gaps

In addition, the 'do nothing syndrome' aggravates hollowness. Acquisition of new platforms is further delayed due to complex procedures, and due to high costs the legacy systems do not get upgraded. Moreover, many times new features get added to the qualitative requirements of the procurement items. Due to quality and time limitations of indigenous products, the military wants to acquire high quality foreign made platforms despite their many unwanted conditions. It also prefers to retain manpower and old organizational structures alongside acquisition of modern technologies whereas inadequate attention to readiness and support activities creates new vulnerabilities. Addressing these vulnerabilities requires financial resources. Thus arises the need to optimize manpower, operation and support costs. The war in Ukraine has driven home an important lesson: It is not enough to have several thousand platforms in the inventory; these have to be kept mission-capable through periodic reset by maintainers. Through life capability readiness (TLCR), this vulnerability could be addressed and therefore needs consideration at the acquisition stages. The MoD has to usher in a strategic culture of indigenous capability development and continued investments in next-generation and game-changing technologies.

In order to leverage commercial technology, the government could adopt management and commercial ways of working. A shift from 'L1' (lowest cost) to 'T1' (technology competency) regime and life cycle costing would greatly facilitate defence MSMEs and start-ups. Sustained performance in our terrain, especially in high altitudes and extreme weather conditions, should be the core criteria for acquisition of platforms, not just the claimed attributes. The country's efforts for self-reliance in weapon platforms cannot be brought to fruition without the military taking ownership and demonstrating its inclination to operate systems, as an interim, with scaled down attributes. System maturity can be achieved in the continued development stride. The three specific areas to be addressed are: The people's competencies; industrial capability gaps; and, consistent funding.

It is time to review the internal workings of the industrial and commercial ecosystem in this era of knowledge sharing and cooperation between various stake holders. Interaction will help capture, share and codify new knowledge and consolidate the existing cache of knowledge. The culture of doing things differently which the present government has been stressing will be feasible only if all the stakeholders agree to attempt a change.

Game-Changing Technologies

Though improved ground combat vehicles, faster ships and stealth aircraft would continue to sustain military operations, in our context of human-centric operations, large scale technological developments in China could change the essential contours of military operations in the future. We cannot allow China to achieve technological dominance over us in the way the USA has enjoyed over its adversaries. High-powered microwaves and directed energy weapons, if operationalised by the People's Liberation Army (PLA) by solving engineering complexity and power requirements, could dramatically alter the Indian Army's offense-defence balance on ground. Unmanned and increasingly autonomous robotic systems, artificial intelligence (AI), data mining technologies and electronic warfare can usher in a local revolution in military affairs. The next few decades are likely to be the most disruptive as the Chinese military continues its quest for killer technologies. What makes a technology 'disruptive', 'game changing' or 'killer' is that it offers unique capabilities to launch a technological surprise. We need to work towards achieving pragmatic technology security to safeguard against capability surprises that could make our forces vulnerable.

Wars in Ukraine and Afghanistan have demonstrated the potential of unmanned systems and precision-guided munitions. Unmanned systems have proven to be a killer technology. The 'Predator Drone' technology was actually operationalised in the 1990s Balkan War but became a wunderwaffe with GPS enablement after 9/11. The Turkish 'Bayrakter' drone has emerged as a game changer responsible for widespread attrition. Nano swarms, also called 'civilian air power', have enhanced surveillance, target acquisition, and remote targeting of combat platforms. Ironically for India, serious capability gaps exist even in foundational areas like engines, propulsion systems, armaments, energetics, and early warning. The tie up to manufacture AK 103 assault rifles, designed as far back as 1994, reflects such gaps.

It is important that in the next two decades, R&D efforts are directed at achieving significant home-grown capabilities in game changing technologies. The task ahead is fairly daunting but not impossible, provided a capability-centric approach to technology development is strategized.

Key Pathways to Technology Development

Making Legacy Systems Future Ready. The import ban list taken out by the MoD some time back has indicated a firm resolve of the government to go the

'Make in India' way. The military needs to evaluate equipment capabilities of the legacy systems along with their vulnerabilities against enemy counter-measures and work towards plugging them. It would be wise to cover current operational shortcomings by subjecting the combat platforms to technology insertion. Modern-day complex systems like tanks and aircraft are expensive with a service life of four to five decades. Sabre jet aircraft had a life of 17 years as compared to four decades for the more contemporary F15/16s which are being modernized through upgrades. The M1Abrams and T 72 tanks are already 40 years old and are still in the inventory of many countries after incorporating technology upgrades.

Consolidation of Defence Industrial Capability. A unique advantage with us is that the local industrial base matches global standards with adequate availability of local talent. The same cannot be said for the supply chain though. In defence manufacturing, the fact that the country has demonstrated capabilities to design its own fighter jets, helicopters, tanks, howitzers, frigates, submarines and aircraft carriers indicates the versatile capabilities created. However, platform performance has been achieved mostly by incorporating foreign-made sub-systems like propulsion, navigation, sensors, weapons, etc. This vital capability gap has to be plugged using the enormous intellectual fire power of our youth and overseas talent of the Indian Diaspora. The MoD and the military needs to encourage an adaptive, interactive approach to sponsor new projects. The Technology Development Fund and Innovation for Defence Excellence (IDEX) should provide mission-oriented funding for defence innovations that seek to address vital operational and strategic capability gaps based on due scrutiny of technology trees of complex platforms.

Localising the Supply Chain. Large-scale indigenization of spare parts can address hollowness, reduce expenditure, and provide economy of scale to MSMEs. Approximately 30,000 x T72s are in service all over the world. Supply of affordable spare parts could boost exports significantly.

Incubation of Disruptive Technologies. Current technologies are getting deeply impacted by digitization, automation, and Internet of Things (IoT). Electronic advances are enhancing accuracy of weapons, efficiency of engines, all-weather surveillance, and situational awareness. Areas of interest are:

(a) High-powered microwaves, electro-magnetic pulses, directed energy weapons, precision-guided munitions, and kinetic and non-kinetic measures against unmanned aerial vehicles (UAV). For example, high-power microwaves and electro-magnetic pulses could provide the ability to destroy electronic systems whereas high-energy lasers could engage more targets than conventional munitions.

(b) Power source and engine technologies are classical areas where greater efficiencies through high temperature combustion, advance heat exchange process, and hybrid power packs are being aimed. For us, the challenge still remains to develop basic foundational capabilities in design.

(c) Advances in electronics and computing will greatly impact surveillance, electronic warfare (EW) and situational awareness. Intelligence (Human or Humint, Signal or Sigint, Machine or Machint, Geographic or Geoint) and its quick dissemination are areas where strong capabilities need to be created.

(d) Electro-optical systems reflect the increasing importance of improved sensing capabilities during adverse weather. These systems will offer greater abilities using new detector materials and networking. Communications and radar surveillance have also improved through integration of related technologies. 3-D search radars have matured due to advances in signal processing, waveform generation, electronic scanning, etc.

(e) The soldier is fast transforming into a wired command, control and information node using devices mounted on helmets, watches, tablets and mobile phones. There is a need to expand this concept as in our context human centric warfare will continue in the foreseeable future.

(f) Game changing technologies like nano materials, autonomous systems, data fusion and mining, and quantum computing could transform the nature of warfare.

(g) Cyber technologies can have devastating effects in the connected world. The Stuxnet attack against Iranian nuclear facilities provided an early example of this potential. The lack of retaliation to this form of attack is a constraining factor. Internet connectivity also provides the means for hijacking large systems to create asymmetric advantages to adversaries.

(h) Space-based low-cost assets like low earth observation satellites and advances in multi and hyper-spectral imaging will augment all-weather battlefield transparency. These can provide high speed data connectivity, satellite communications, electronic and communications intelligence (ELINT & COMINT) capability and early warning of missile launches. A constellation of 4x CubeSats (miniaturised satellites) can enable daily surveillance of the Line of Actual Control (LAC) and stymie any surprise.

Strategy of Self Reliance

In order to achieve an objective of such massive dimensions, i.e., self-reliance in military systems and near-technological parity with the prime adversary, a long-term view encompassing two to three decades needs to be taken. It should aim to achieve comprehensive technology security and technological parity in the region by 2050. Technological dominance of the kind the USA has enjoyed over the years is far off, as there is a lot to be still achieved in foundational technologies.

Israel and China were dependent on imported technology just after the Yom Kippur war. Israel was dependent mainly on Western weapons and China on vintage equipment that was being manufactured as a sequel to technology transfer from the Soviet Union. Post-Yom Kippur war, Israel made the shift by adopting the human capital intensive growth strategy, focussing on creating a knowledge and skill base in universities and government laboratories. The Chinese adopted the development strategy of IDAR (introduce, digest, absorb and re-innovate) by on-boarding current technologies into Soviet era systems and later developing weapons *de novo*. Technology gaps were filled through import and recruitment of designers from abroad.

We too need to build strengths in areas where capability gaps are identified. All these activities have to take place under an overarching national strategy of self-reliance in order to optimise resources. The tremendous potential of game-changing technologies requires long-term investment and consistent support by higher defence management with a robust collaboration between the military and leading-edge innovators. The following action plan could help channelize our strengths to achieve technological parity:

Short-Term Measures (up to 2035)

- **Technology Insertion.** *Commence with on-boarding of technologies on legacy systems with the aim of making them future ready so as to cover risks for the next two decades.* This will also help develop peoples‘ competencies and local industrial capabilities, besides enabling upgrades of similar platforms in other countries.

- **Indigenization.** Large-scale *indigenization of spare parts* will address hollowness and plug in the MSMEs into the defence industrial eco-system. Assurance of guaranteed buy-back over periods up to 10 years will provide the much needed economy of scale and also boost exports of components.
- **Sub-Systems.** Focus on *indigenization and upgrade of vital sub-systems of indigenously crafted and manufactured weapon platforms* like Arjun, Dhanush, etc., by designating a few numbers as experimental platforms. This would open up avenues for export of affordable systems.
- **Private Sector R&D.** *Commission government-supported, module level R&D in the private sector for futuristic combat vehicles, warships, and aircraft with the aim of integrating them into next generation platforms.* Projects addressing critical capability gaps in fire power, survivability, propulsion and stealth counter-measures could be provided up to 75 per cent funding with little or no repayment requirements.

Long-Term (up to 2050)

- **IDDM Projects.** *Launch de novo design and development* (Indigenously designed, developed and manufactured or IDDM projects related to land, marine, aerial and high-altitude platforms with the stipulation that they be integrated with a minimum of 75 per cent indigenously developed critical sub-systems, while the remaining 25 per cent could be acquired and manufactured in India.
- **Innovation.** *Develop in our universities, technical institutions and private industry, with government support, a versatile eco-system for innovation in disruptive and game changing technologies* so as to provide the military a battle winning edge.
- **Promising Technologies.** *Invest in promising, unproven technologies with the aim of taking a technological lead over the rest of the world.* Battle space management, cyber weapons, high grade intelligence, surveillance and reconnaissance (ISR), track-and-engage capabilities, tactical data links, internet of things, and counters against lab-incubated viruses are some areas of interest.
- **System Design and Integration.** *Consolidate indigenous design and system-*

integration capabilities primarily with government institutions, and augment it by working together with industry.

- **Skill Development.** In order to develop requisite leadership with desired acquisition management and technical skills, there is a need to invest in specific competency development, after identification of science and engineering skill gaps. *We need to utilize the demographic dividend to develop human capital that can create, design, and innovate ahead of other countries.*
- **R&D Budget.** Progressively increase R&D budget to 1.5 per cent of the Gross Domestic Product (GDP) in the short term and 2 per cent in the long term.

Conclusion

In any military stand-off with China, India is likely to be on its own, as events in early 2020 have shown when India found itself isolated among the comity of democratic nations. The emerging threats in the subcontinent may require our military to be ready for operations over longer durations. That will be feasible only if major platforms are designed and developed within the country to provide the desired battle endurance. The approach could centre around acquisition of large numbers of lower cost, operationally effective weapon platforms, duly augmented with game changing technologies that can operate, fly, and fire on a daily basis. We have to look for a fine balance between combat usefulness, cost, and complexity instead of just low or high technology. Local technologies will provide strategic assurance and influence, civilian spin offs, a strong industrial base, and new capabilities to counter an adversary.

One cannot expect indigenous designs to meet all performance requirements in the first iteration, as most attributes are picked up from foreign platforms where they have been misapplied to create ever-increasing complexities. Many nations have relied on operation of less than perfect military hardware systems to help stabilize the system maturity. In the Indian context, being flanked by two incorrigibly antagonist aggressors, adoption of that kind of options would be a formidable challenge. With the Government's sights firmly set on Aatmanirbhar Bharat, the military needs to take charge of that challenge to the extent practicable, and elevate this national effort to trail blaze towards gaining technology security.

19

Emergence of Strategic Challenges from India's Friendly Neighbours

Vinod Anand

Overview

It is axiomatic that strategic challenges emerging in India's neighbourhood cannot be but part of what is happening at the larger global and regional levels. Moreover, the global order has been adversely impacted by the two profound events of the COVID-19 pandemic and Russia's special military operation in Ukraine that have unleashed their own dynamics resulting in the worsening of economic, food and energy security situations not only in South Asia but also elsewhere in the world. India, being the largest nation in South Asia, and with its considerable military and economic heft, is viewed by its smaller neighbours in a variety of ways from being a Big Brother (in both the positive and negative senses) that can help its smaller neighbours in their developmental paths, to a country that can be overbearing in its dealings with the smaller neighbours. The sheer size of India creates apprehensions among its smaller neighbours and they become inclined to play balance-of-power games by inviting external powers in ways that challenge the strategic and security interests of India.

It is also well known that China favours a strategic stance that confines India to South Asia and prevents it from emerging as a strategic competitor to China in Asia or on the larger global stage. India's other neighbour, Pakistan, gets its identity from always being hostile and inimical to India's interests, and that outlook has strengthened its relationship with China and a few other countries that might help it in some way against India. This essay will cover

India's other neighbours that are friendly with India but nevertheless have the potential to create strategic challenges for India. As is evident from the historical context, most of India's neighbours have had, over a time, varying degrees of conflictual relationship with India due to a variety of factors and therefore there is a need for India to evolve ways to address such a situation.

Like India, its neighbours are multi-lingual, multi ethnic, multi religious and multi-cultural societies with cross-border linkages and socio-economic complementarities with India. In the post-colonial period, the economic, social, and other connectivities came under strain which had its negative impact on development of the region. Further, India has borders with all its neighbours whereas most of these countries do not have borders with each other. Therefore, largely, they are prone to having more problems with India rather than amongst themselves. Internal political dynamics in these countries affect to a large extent their relationship with India whereas in the case of India it is not so. Additionally, the region is afflicted with insurgencies, terrorism, extremism, and fundamentalism with wide income disparities and a Low Human Development Index which is compounded by problems of mis-governance and corruption. Thus, political, economic, or social instability in India's neighbourhood could create an environment that would impact India's strategic and security stance adversely. In the following paragraphs, each of India's neighbours, except Afghanistan, Pakistan, and China, would be discussed.

Bangladesh

The liberation of Bangladesh in 1971 through an operation by the Indian armed forces with the support of the Mukti Bahini had created an environment that was conducive to the emergence of a healthy bilateral relationship. With the assassination of Bangabandhu Mujibur Rehman in 1975 and thereafter the establishment of military rule there was a rise of Islamist and pro-Pakistan elements in Bangladesh. In Bangladesh (as in many South Asian nations) there are sections of population who traditionally harbour anti-Indian sentiments and domestic politics are impacted by such an outlook. Later, the Bangladesh National Party (BNP) formed a coalition government with the Jamaat-e-Islami (JeI), a radical Islamist party that was against the country's liberation and was pro-Pakistan. It was in the period from 2001 to 2006 that Sheikh Hasina was able to come to power through democratic elections. However, it was again a coalition wherein the JeI had some MPs who exercised more power. It was only in 2009 and thereafter that Sheikh Hasina, as leader of the Awami League, came back with a resounding majority and transformed Bangladesh's bilateral relationship with India.

During the years of rule by the military dispensations and the BNP, India faced challenges on the strategic security front as several anti-Indian insurgent groups from North-Eastern states found shelter and succour in Bangladesh with the active connivance of Pakistan's and Bangladesh's intelligence agencies. Radical Islamist groups were also instrumental in sending their members to India for terrorist activities. After Sheikh Hasina's arrival on the scene, steps were taken by the Bangladesh government to put a stop to such activities and address India's concerns. India, in conformity with its 'Neighbourhood First Policy' which was based on the Gujral Doctrine enunciated many years ago, went out of the way to resolve a number of outstanding issues with Bangladesh like straightening the land border with the exchange of enclaves and accepting the delineation of maritime boundaries by the Permanent Court of Arbitration at The Hague which went in favour of Bangladesh. Many other milestones in infrastructure development and connectivity have been achieved since through mutual cooperation.

Recent developments in the political and socio-economic fields indicate that Sheikh Hasina is facing protests not only from the major opposition party, the BNP, but also from radical elements. Further, there are sections of the bureaucracy and certain other elements in Bangladesh that have traditionally harboured anti-India proclivities. There have been a number of cases of anti-India rhetoric and attacks on minorities; as the next elections get closer such sentiments against India are bound to rise. The elections in 2023 are going to be the fourth since Sheikh Hasina came to power. Apparently, some reports indicate that the BNP seems to be gaining ground and there are even chances for either party to win. If the BNP comes to power next year, then the challenges for India are likely to become more acute.

In so far as the economic situation is concerned, Bangladesh is facing some headwinds due to COVID and the Ukraine conflict which has led to energy and food crises as well as dwindling of Bangladesh's exports to the European Union; remittances have also been adversely impacted. Therefore, Bangladesh has asked for a package from the IMF. Though Bangladesh has some projects funded by China, it has been careful not to fall into the Chinese debt trap like Sri Lanka. However, military cooperation with China has been on the upward path.

Bangladesh has purchased some major military weapon systems from China including a used Kilo-class submarine. Now China is looking to establish a facility in Bangladesh sea coast to service submarines which is an excuse for expanding its surveillance and strategic presence in the Indian Ocean region. Bangladesh has a Letter of Credit worth USD 500 million for purchase of defence equipment, etc., from India but it has hardly utilised it. Pakistan is also attempting to ride on the coat-tails of China to stage a comeback in Bangladesh to restart its anti-India activities. With the possible change of political leadership in Bangladesh next year, the strategic and security environment for India may be impacted negatively. Both India and Bangladesh need to continue their dialogue and need to address some of the festering issues like migration, sharing of river waters and other bilateral matters.

Nepal

India and Nepal have had very close political, social, economic, and military relationships. Further, the bilateral relationship has been governed to a large extent by the Treaty of Friendship and Peace of 1950, though, of late, there have been calls for revision of some provisions of the Treaty. However, with the abolition of monarchy and the rise of communist parties, instability in the political firmament of Nepal has become almost a permanent feature. Recent elections held in November 2022 were the second after the promulgation of the Republican Constitution that came into force in 2015. About 16 years have elapsed since the Communist revolution. The outcome of elections is highly polarised and divided though the incumbent Prime Minister, Sher Bahadur Deuba, of the Nepali Congress was expected to cobble up a coalition with the Maoist Centre led by 'Prachanda'. However, with the help of the Communist Party of Nepal (United Marxist-Leninist) or UML-L lead by K.P. Oli and after changing sides, Prachanda has formed a government with the prime ministership being shared by both the leaders half and half. It is quite possible that the new government may not be able to last its complete tenure. A point to note is that this will be the 11th government since 2008 which reflects the state of political instability in Nepal. While the Nepali Congress and Deuba have been well disposed towards India, Communist Parties like the UMI-L led by Oli have a pro-China inclination.

To realise its strategic ambitions, the Chinese Ambassador to Nepal had been at pains to forge a coalition of Nepal's communist parties. Apparently, she has been successful in doing so. Further, so far there has not been much progress in China's Belt and Road Initiative (BRI) projects in Nepal as Kathmandu is becoming careful in order to avoid getting entangled in China's debt trap diplomacy. Instead, Nepal is looking for soft loans and grants from China without hidden conditions. Approval by Deuba's government for utilisation of US agency Millennium Challenge Corporation (MCC) grant of 500 million USD, despite objections from China, for developing a power transmission line to India for supply of electricity was a good step. Further, China has laid stress on strengthening military-to-military cooperation with Nepal that had made considerable progress during the tenure of former PM Oli as well as the earlier governments. The Kalapani boundary issue between Nepal and India had acquired more stridency during K. P. Sharma Oli's tenure as prime minister. Therefore, the new government and its policies might further complicate India's strategic challenges.

Additionally, Pakistan has been exploiting the Nepal route for carrying out subversive and inimical activities against India besides settling Muslim populations along the Indo-Nepal border, smuggling of fake Indian currency (FICN) which has often been used by Pakistan to foment terrorism and to carry out various anti-India activities.

As Nepal borders both Tibet and India, it will continue to face a variety of pressures from Beijing and New Delhi. The strategic challenge for India will be to continue to maintain its traditional salience in Nepal despite the rising political, military, and economic presence of China in Nepal. It is quite evident that India has to go out of its way to address some of Nepal's concerns while Kathmandu needs to appreciate the multiple benefits it derives from the type of close socio-economic, defence and people-to-people ties it has with India.

Sri Lanka

The worsening of socio-economic conditions led to large-scale protests in Sri Lanka in April 2022 which resulted in the Rajapaksas, the ruling family, getting thrown out of power. While Ranil Wickremesinghe was installed as the president, it cannot be said that political stability has been achieved. The left-leaning parties like Janatha Vimukti Peramuna (JVP) were able to mobilise the common people against the mis-governance of the Rajapakse family and are also strongly opposed to the current President, Ranil Wickremesinghe. However, the electoral strength of left parties appears to be very limited. In any case, it was the rise in food prices, and fuel and electricity shortages, compounded by dwindling of foreign exchange reserves and unwise socio-economic policies, that led to the turbulent situation.

The Rajapakses were heavily influenced by China and had been keen to take more loans from China, rather than the International Monetary Fund (IMF), because of their nationalist concerns. China's debt trap strategy, though well-known, was overlooked by the Rajapaksas, and thus Sri Lanka became the first victim of such a trap when it had to hand over Hambantota port to China on a 99-year lease. During the crisis, the response from China to provide some funds to help Sri Lanka was somewhat tepid and it came with conditions unfavourable to Sri Lanka. On the other hand, India was more forthcoming in providing succour in terms of provisioning the required fuel and other commodities. India has provided an aid of USD 3.8 billion and a Line of Credit of one billon USD to Sri Lanka to address its economic crisis. The aid is in terms of sending fuel, medicines, and fertilisers as also through currency swap arrangements. It has also helped Sri Lanka in obtaining IMF funds. However, a section of the political class has attributed it to India's motives in helping out the Rajapakses, despite the fact that they have been more pro-China than pro-India. Even India's investment in the Trincomalee oil tank farm was not viewed positively by that political class.

From an Indian perspective, the rising profile of China in Sri Lanka despite India's endeavours to protect its strategic and security interests will continue to be challenging. Sri Lanka has become an important staging post for China to expand its presence in the Indian Ocean in ways which are detrimental to India's security. The docking and replenishment of PLA submarines in Colombo in 2015 and India's objections to the same are well known. While India has been instrumental in creating a number of joint and multilateral mechanisms in the Indian Ocean Region, China has been at work to influence the elites and leaderships of the small island nations through economic inducements and developmental projects that lead to debt traps. In July 2022, India held the sixth meeting of Deputy National Security Advisors of The Maldives, Mauritius, and Sri Lanka for ensuring maritime security, and fighting terrorism, radicalisation, and crime, besides illegal and unregulated fishing.

Further, in August 2022, the Wickremesinghe government approved the docking of the People's Liberation Army Navy's satellite surveillance research ship, *Yuan Wang-5,* at Hambantota port whereas earlier it was not permitted to berth due to objections from India. As the economic situation in Sri Lanka remains precarious, Colombo has been hard put to navigate between China's overwhelming influence and India's strategic and security concerns. Moreover, a section of Sri Lanka's strategic and political community looks at Indian and US influence in the India Ocean differently from how New Delhi and Washington view the same, especially the PLA Navy's ever-increasing presence.

Despite close bilateral relations there is a need for both India and Sri Lanka to understand each other's security concerns. There are a number of existing bilateral and trilateral mechanisms to address security issues including defence cooperation. There are also several joint programmes for improving connectivity, trade, and investment. Therefore, enhanced bilateral cooperation with Sri Lanka on security and strategic issues in the face of China's increasing pressure on Colombo is imperative.

Bhutan

In recent years, the bilateral relationship between Bhutan and India has been undergoing a change because of various domestic and external factors despite the fact that both share a special relationship which in many ways has stood the test of time. Bhutan is strategically important to India because of its geographical location especially as it borders Tibet. China for long has been trying to make inroads into Bhutan through both its political and economic heft and has been attempting to lure Bhutan into its orbit by offering economic benefits and through offers of settling the boundary issue which may or may not be of benefit to Bhutan. The Treaty of 1949 was replaced by the Bhutan-India Treaty of Friendship of 2007 which enabled Bhutan to adopt foreign policies without necessarily following India's advice or through consultation.

Bhutan's transition to democracy in 2008 and thereafter also indicated that there is a section of the population/elite there that is in favour of development and growth through cooperation with China and some other countries. For instance, the Druk Phuensum Tshogpa (DPT) Party led by Jigmi Thinley, whose tenure was from 2008 to 2013, was in favour of taking advantage of China's economic growth, and consequently reduce its dependence on India. However, Prime Minister Modi in June 2014 as part of India's Neighbourhood First Policy, chose Bhutan as his first foreign country to be visited after taking over in May 2014 thus indicating his priorities and the strategic importance of Bhutan for India. The Doklam incident of August

2017 shows that China attempted to capture areas of Bhutan near India-Tibet-Bhutan border trijunction from where China could have gained easy access to India's Siliguri Corridor with the possibility of severing the North-East from the mainland.

India has been aiming at increasing trade volumes and developing infrastructure projects, especially hydro power sector projects, in Bhutan. There is a need to speed up such projects and expand the scope of export of power from Bhutan to India and Bangladesh as well through the sub-regional mechanisms of the Bangladesh-Bhutan-India and Nepal (BBIN) framework.

In so far as the Bhutan-China boundary issue is concerned, there have been 24 rounds of talks since 1984 without any tangible results. Meanwhile, China has also raised claims over Bhutan's Sakteng Sanctuary which can be viewed as a coercive tactic by Beijing. The Chinese Ambassador to India travelled to Thimpu in October 2022 to influence Bhutan to expedite boundary talks. During the COVID-19 pandemic Beijing had also provided medical aid and made offers of increasing people-to-people contacts. However, as is well known, China uses its carrot-and-stick policy to soften its target. However, so far Bhutan has maintained its equipoise; it has not agreed to settle its boundary as the Chinese want it, i.e., exchange of disputed areas in the north with that of the west (i.e., Doklam trijunction area). Thimpu has maintained that the trijunction area dispute has to be settled between the three stakeholders. Beijing has been using all kinds of intimidating tactics in the border areas of Bhutan to pressurise it to conform to China's demands. It is also worth noting that Bhutan does not have diplomatic relations with China.

For India, China's continued attempts to mould Bhutan into seeing its way over the boundary issue as well as diluting its special relationship with India would continue to present a challenge. India, on its part, has kept up its defence cooperation and special relationship with Bhutan. India should continue to forge strong military-to-military linkages and accommodate Bhutan's interests in a meaningful way. The visit of the Indian Army Chief to Bhutan and the visit of the King of Bhutan to India in 2022 was part of the strategic communication between the two sides. It should also be remembered that Bhutan is the only South-Asian neighbour that has not joined China's BRI, as also, it has always addressed India's security concerns.

The Maldives

While the ruling government led by Maldivian President Ibu Solih, since his election in 2018, has been following policies that emphasise on stronger cooperation with India, his predecessor, Abdulla Yameen, who was president from 2013 to 2018 had followed very distinctive pro-China policies. During his period, China had gained strategic advantage by pursuing its BRI projects and developing other dual-use facilities to expand the PLA Navy's presence in the Indian Ocean region. Abdullah Yameen had a very acrimonious relationship with India. However, India had gone out of its way to provide The Maldives with credit lines and developmental funds for infrastructure projects in the shape of the Greater Male Connectivity Project, Hanimaadhoo airport, Hulhumale cricket stadium, Gulhifalhu port, etc. which are highly visible. The bilateral defence cooperation has also gained momentum during President Ibu Solih's tenure.

However, like other South Asian neighbours, domestic politics and its outcome have great a bearing on The Maldives relationship with India. For some time, Abdullah Yameen has been ratcheting up an "India Out" campaign which has acquired some degree of resonance in some sections of the population. President Solih has rejected Yameen's allegations, etc., and has taken measures to stop the campaign. There are also indications of a split in the ruling Maldivian Democratic Party (MDP), wherein former president and the speaker of Parliament, Nasheed, is trying to stage a comeback. The inner wrangling of the MDP could adversely impact the outcome of the elections due in 2023 which in turn might return pro-China Yameen to power, thus posing challenges for India.

During his August 2022 visit to India, President Solih reiterated its 'India First' policy while India underlined its 'Neighbourhood First' policy. The visit came at a time when there was great turmoil and crisis in South Asian countries like Sri Lanka. India has provided 2.8 billion USD worth of financial assistance to Male as against China's debt trap-driven policies with the ulterior aim of realising its hegemonistic proclivities in The Maldives. The joint statement issued after the visit also mentioned that both countries are mindful of each other's security concerns and would not allow their respective territories to be used for inimical activities.

Another trend in The Maldives which presents a challenge to India and the neighbourhood is the growth of Islamic radicalization. This undercurrent of radicalization has been on the upward trajectory since 2008 when several Maldivian fighters went to Afghanistan and later joined the ISIS. Pakistan and some Arabic nations have been sending their religious preachers to The Maldives for radicalization purposes. Opposition parties have blamed MDP for not adhering to Islamic values, thus giving it a political undertone. The latest example was in June 2022 when Islamists attacked an event arranged by the Indian High Commission on International Yoga day. It is believed that the attack was organised by Yameen's men saying that Yoga was against Islamic teachings. Thus, Yameen is using the Islamic card and anti-India rhetoric for attaining his political objectives. Though in end-December 2022, Abdullah Yameen was indicted for corruption and money laundering and awarded 11 years imprisonment, making him ineligible for elections, it is difficult to say whether the 'India Out' campaign would die with his incarceration.

India needs to address the challenges arising in The Maldives in an adroit manner through provision of financial and other types of aid, strengthening people-to-people connections which are quite robust in many ways and be watchful of political, economic, and security developments.

Myanmar

Myanmar is a geo-strategically important neighbour of India that is viewed as a strategic land bridge between India and South-East Asia. Both share a land border of 1,643 km and a maritime boundary of over 740 km. Despite the changing internal political situation and dominance of the military in Myanmar, India has preferred to maintain a constructive dialogue with the ruling dispensations in Myanmar. New Delhi's continual engagement with Myanmar enables it to realise the objectives of its 'Act East' policy enunciated in 2014 which was a progressive step on the earlier Look East policy initiated in 1991. Connectivity with Myanmar also ensures that India can better address its policy objectives in the Association of Southeast Asian Nations (ASEAN), Bay of Bengal Initiative for Multi-Sectoral Technical and Economic Cooperation (BIMSTEC) and Mekong Ganga Cooperation initiative. Peace, security and stability in India's North-East are also important aspects for the development of this region. Several insurgent groups have been operating across the shared borders with an inimical agenda against India. Smuggling of drugs, gun running, human trafficking, etc., are some of the other areas of security concerns.

Myanmar underwent a transition to democracy in some measured manner since 2010 with a military drafted Constitution having been framed in 2008 and the Aung San Suu Kyi-led National League for Democracy (NLD) having again won elections in November 2020 (the previous one being in November 2015). This transition came to an abrupt halt when the Myanmar military staged a coup d'état on 1 February 2021 and took over the reins of power declaring the election result as illegal due to certain irregularities. However, these were only trumped up charges without much basis and as of January 2023, Aung San Suu Kyi has been awarded 33 years of imprisonment. In the last two years, the military has resorted to brutal repression of pro-democracy elements and even resorted to air attacks.

During the turbulence and turmoil in Myanmar, India has sought to protect its interests through sustained engagements with the ruling military regime. India's Army Chief and Foreign Secretary had paid a joint visit to Myanmar in October 2020 before the military took over. After the military takeover, India's then Foreign Secretary visited Myanmar in December 2021 when, in some of his interactions, there was an allusion to Myanmar returning to democracy. However, during the Indian Foreign Secretary visit to Myanmar in November 2022 that issue was avoided. Bilateral discussions revolved around stability and security in the border regions, infrastructure developments and strengthening of bilateral cooperation. There was no discussion on transition to democracy or connected issues; the emphasis was on completion of infrastructure projects like the Kaladan Multimodal Transit Transport Project and the Trilateral Highway between India, Myanmar, and Thailand.

It is quite evident that in India's strategic calculations, the China factor and its rising influence in Myanmar, especially after the Tatmadaw's takeover, looms large. The military Junta has become increasingly dependent economically and militarily on China as the USA and the West have placed a variety of sanctions on Myanmar. Even while Myanmar had been careful in restricting the scope of BRI projects, the military putsch has made Myanmar more amenable to China's demands for expansion of its presence in the country. China has also provided weapons and armaments to the ethnic armed organisations (EAOs) in Myanmar while, at the same time, it has offered itself to be a mediator between the Myanmar government and the EAOs. There is also a history of China helping out some of the Indian insurgent groups in the shape of arms, training, shelter, etc. For example, some United Liberation

Front of Asom (ULFA-I) elements are believed to be camping along the Sino-Myanmar border at Ruili.

In the last few years, Pakistan has also been ramping up its presence in Myanmar through the supply of JF-17 fighter jets in 2018; in fact, since November/December 2022 a Pakistan Air Force team is in Myanmar for training Myanmar Air Force pilots in air operations and precision targeting. There is talk of supply of other weapons and armaments by Pakistan to Myanmar even while there have been differences between the two on the Rohingya issue.

India needs to continue with its pragmatic and constructive approach in engaging Myanmar while maintaining a delicate balance between the ruling dispensation and the democratic forces of Myanmar. The overall objective of India has been to prevent a further slide of Myanmar into the arms of China. Besides, Indian infrastructure projects need to be completed at a fast pace. New Delhi also needs to accommodate Myanmar's demands on easing control over import of some agricultural products like pulses, etc. Border trading and diversification in sectors of trading need to be further encouraged; for example, hydropower surplus in the North-East could be exported to Myanmar.

Conclusion

India has taken several steps to secure its interests in the neighbourhood including pursuing its 'Neighbourhood First' policy. During the COVID pandemic, it provided vaccines and other medical aid to its neighbours to address their health concerns. It has also provided economic and financial aid to countries like Sri Lanka that is mired in a debt crisis. India has also been helping out The Maldives through developmental and project aid as also by addressing its concerns in multiple ways. Similarly, the equation with Bhutan is also on an even keel through development of its hydropower potential and supply of power to India and possibly the same being transmitted to Bangladesh. There has also been good progress in addressing the concerns of Bangladesh regarding boundary settlement and other issues.

With Myanmar, India has always pursued a policy of constructive engagement keeping its security and strategic challenges in mind. The return of the pro-China communist party alliance in Nepal could throw up some challenges for India.

However, the unstable political climate in most of the neighbours remains a cause of concern for India. Most of these countries have sections of the polity that are not favourably disposed towards India. Such elements feel that by bringing in China or some other extra-regional actors they would be better able to look after their interests. Though such expectations have been belied many times, yet the allure of balancing India by inviting outside powers remains. As elections in some of these countries are due, India needs to keep a continual watch over political and economical developments in the region. There is no gainsaying the fact India should go out of its way without expecting any reciprocity to help countries in the neighbourhood as long as its security concerns are not compromised.

20

India's Military Security Imperatives in 2047

Gautam Banerjee

PREAMBLE

The Mission Ahead

At the time of independence from British rule in 1947, while large parts of the civilisational expanse of *Bharatvarsha* was vivisected, the rest of the Indian territory had been well integrated into an independent Union of India. But even then, parts of Indian territories remained in forcible occupation of covetous, revisionist, and militarily aggressive neighbouring powers. Further, our benign and egalitarian dispensation has not prevented various home-grown anarchist groups, under the influence of poisoned notions, from their sabotaging pretentions. At the milestone of the nation's 75 years of independence, therefore, *it is time to visualise, with realist rather than idealist forbearance, as to how the Indian State might proceed towards its destined sovereignty, integrity, stability, and progress while approaching its Centenary of Independence*.

Modern India aspires to harness her innate potentials to emerge as a reckonable powerhouse, a benign one, in the global arena. To secure that objective in the coming decades, India is obliged to enlarge her horizon of strategic interests and prepare to contend with a larger ambit of complex and competing factors that need to be negotiated with due fortitude. As observed from the traditions of global order, robust capability for *national defence* would have to be a prime instrument of that process. In that context, India's future will be influenced by certain '*facts*' to imbibe, '*inevitabilities*' to manage and '*imperatives*' to invest on.

The Theme

This paper discusses the concerns related to India's *national defence* and *military security* that have to be surmounted during the run-up to the Centenary of India's independence—2047—in order to achieve our nationalist *mission.*[1] The discussion is anchored in two inter-related parts, as follows:

PART 1: The *strategic environment* that India would be obliged to contend with during the coming 25 years; and

PART 2: *Strategies, policies* and *procedures* that would facilitate India in building-up the requisite military prowess during the next 25 years.

PART 1: TRAVAILS OF INDIA'S MILITARY SECURITY

Onus of Military Security

The Ambit. India's *military security* is severely burdened by the fundamentally adversarial ideologies of our immediate and powerful neighbours—China and Pakistan. Besides, there are strategically inimical aspects of India's relationships with the rest of her otherwise friendly neighbours, particularly when externally instigated, which have to be built into the nation's futurist scheme of military security.

Adversarial Neighbours. India stands flanked by two innately adversarial neighbours. The northern one wields enormous economic, technological, and military resources and is a major power. The other, though afflicted by severe social, political, and economic woes, is, nevertheless, a robust military power. Both are innately militarist in culture, expansionist in ideology and politically committed to satiate their revisionist agendas by means of various forms of military aggression. Both consider the emergence of a peaceful, democratic, and developed Indian nationhood—notwithstanding that certainty—as a threat to their hegemonic dreams. Joined in a patron-legatee relationship, the duo has thus joined in their relentless mission to destabilise the Indian nationhood. Apart from various kinds of hostile machinations, aggressive use of military power would therefore continue to be their purpose in the future.

Strategic Inclinations of Smaller Neighbours. The irresistible pull of developmental prospects leaves the field open to exploitation by the People's Republic of China (PRC), with its deep pockets to seed discord among our traditionally Indo-centric, friendly neighbours. At another end, by its religion-centric nexuses as well as instigation of anti-India manipulations in any way it can, Pakistan has been relentless in its efforts to alienate India among the neighbouring nations. In the coming years, therefore, India will have to contend with possible upswings in anti-India animus, instigated either externally or by domestic politics, among our neighbours. As a geographic situation, irrespective of size and military capability, becomes highly significant in modern war strategies, neighbourhood antipathy would be one more factor to be considered in India's future matrix of military security.

Indigenous Insurgencies. Instigated by externally-aided unconstitutional ideologies, insurgencies would continue to pose grave dangers to the nation's progressive path. These would need to be controlled by long-periods of military interventions. That must also be India's future military security concerns.

Inferences. The country's political dispensation has apparently been rid itself of its past inhibitions against the hoary principles of national defence, but it is to be seen as to how best a right balance is achieved in good time. Accordingly, India's pledge for the coming 25 years would be to recuse herself from wishful hopes of finding amenability from our ever-hostile neighbouring powers. Preparations to raise India's *military capabilities,* and by implication, the level of her *military deterrence* in line with the hostility of India's habitual enemies, would thus be the key imperative of *national defence* for the coming decades.

Facts and Inevitabilities of Military Security

Since a build-up of national defence is shaped by the sources and causes of conflicts of interests, a realist overview of regional inter-relations is called for at this stage.

The People's Republic of China (PRC) is India Averse

The PRC's claims against India go well beyond just some swathes of territory or changing border alignments in its favour. Even without an iota of provenance of an ethnic, cultural, religious, or terrestrial commonality, the PRC *claims 'historical sovereignty' over two of India's integral provinces* ! That is a most serious concern that drives home the understanding that no matter what the PRC maintains, it will continue to cast India as a spoiler of its sovereignty game plan—the 'Chinese Dream', so to say. To that end, certain *ineradicable facts and inevitabilities* that impinge upon India's national defence need to be reiterated to indicate that the Han-Chinese would never moderate their innate urge for hegemonic usurpations:

1. **Culture of Incurable Covetousness.** In its insatiable quest for an expansionist grab of other nations' territories, their natural resources and capture of their markets, Communist China's culture is committed to the infliction of overwhelming military-economic power to usurp what it, by no stretch of logic, has any right to claim. Indeed, all the three purposes are interlinked, with the capture of water and mineral resources as the enabler of its hegemonic covetousness. Not even a regime change or a liberal dispensation would moderate that predatory ideology.[2] Of course, the Xi Jinping-led regime is the current face of that. It would be wise to shape policies in cognisance of that fact.
2. **Consolidation of Hegemonic Grand Designs.** The Communist Party of China (CPC) is committed not to compromise over what it claims to be China's 'historical territorial rights over lost territories'.[3] In the decades leading to the 2050s, it is therefore more or less certain that the PRC would come to wield formidable maritime and air space control over the China Seas besides gaining an impactful strategic-economic leverage over the Indian Ocean and its littoral community. In the terrestrial context, the PRC's design of arbitrarily redrawing of land boundaries is nearing completion pending entrapment of India and Bhutan. Meanwhile, the process of gaining unilateral control over the lower-riparian flow of multi-national river waters is going on at a brisk pace. All this while, incessant misinformation is broadcast in attempts to make the stakeholders-at-large to accept China's terms and reconcile to new norms of their abridged nationalism.[4] In effect, even if remaining circumspect against testing the USA' superior economic-political-military power, the PRC would, to much extent, succeed in 'normalising' its hegemonic manners over the region. Indeed, the fulfilment of the 'Chinese Dream' would be a nightmare for the entire regional community.
3. **PRC's India Strategy.** In Chinese eyes, India is a nation of pompous pretentions that deserves to be kept in its place. India's geographic centrality, human potential, stable polity, and deep cross-border ties,

besides an unwillingness to submit to a tributary role, is viewed as a major impediment against its dream of regional overlordship. The CPC seeks to steamroll over that impediment with its territorial arrogations, appropriation of common river water rights, diplomatic brazenness, and massive military build-up.[5] Accordingly, the regime is attempting to re-align the Indo-Tibet Line of Actual Control (LAC) through surreptitious encroachments which are then secured against eviction by the threats of 'counter-attack in self-defence'. As for the common river water lifelines, the PRC has gained reckonable control over the Sutlej River and is well on its way to divert the Brahmaputra River. As India's reaction to such attempts hardens, escalation to skirmish, multi-point and multi-sectoral military contestations would be a strong likelihood.

4 **Subversion of India's Security.** India's strategic adversity is further aggravated by the cementing of the Sino-Pakistan alliance and the consequent emboldening of Pakistan's high-pitch anti-India campaigns, both military and diplomatic, while continuing with active sponsorship of terrorist groups into India. Further, the cap on PRC's instigation of insurgencies in India's North-East could be removed, once the native Tibetan culture is subsumed and its grip over the rest of the IOR community is consolidated. According to the regime's timelines, that end is to be met by 2050 or so.

Inferences

The CPC believes that military strength is the source of all forms, including economic power. Having built up its military power, it will not desist from using that power for the furtherance of its expansionist culture. The nations on China's target had therefore pinned hopes of a 'rising China' maturing to the norms of international behaviour and shun its brazen ways. Even the USA-led Western powers, attracted by commercial prospects, fell for that hope. China's post-2011 regime has squarely repudiated that hope. It has found that persistence with military intimidation while keeping short of breaching the targeted nation's threshold of strategic stoicism, yields good results—even against the global super power and its allies. Nations in the PRC's target could deter, but never cure, that inevitability if only by coming together to gather adequate military weight.

In the foreseeable future,. China would continue to regard India as an 'intransigent' challenger to its hegemony, to be disabled howsoever possible. As a consequence, India's strategic situation would remain alienated by China's build-up of disproportionate military power, escalating aggressiveness along the Indo-Tibetan border, arbitrary control over India's share of river waters, force-projections in the Indian Ocean Region (IOR) and incessant political-economic subversion of our hoary Indic neighbourhood ties.

Disrupting India is Pakistan's Survival Kit

Having misled the native, mostly poor, illiterate, and gullible Indian Muslim converts to divide India on religious lines, Pakistan's oligarchy of West Asian origin Muslims has to peg its nationalist identity to the ideology of India animosity. With that ideology, Pakistan cannot help being India's sworn enemy; its compulsive belligerence will continue to rise as India progresses.

Pakistan is a redoubtable adversary. Its significant geography, Islamist pretentions, and deceptively choreographed postures are liable to sway usually empathic global opinion-makers to its cause, notwithstanding its dismal record of despotic, genocidal, and terrorist conduct. Having vivisected India's natural geography, Pakistan now sits blocking India's hoary connections with Central and West Asia. Like the PRC, Pakistan too *contests India's sovereignty over one of the Indian States* (now segregated into a Union Territory). In the future too, it is liable to enter into India-baiting alliances, offer bases to inimical powers, instigate internal disturbances, and get down to aggression in various forms, as indeed it has been doing so far. Lastly, as the inheritor of a heritage of aggressive military culture, the Pakistani polity will remain a daunting threat to Indian nationhood. It is needless to state that in the foreseeable future, Indian defence planners will have to endure Pakistan as a redoubtable assailer.[6]

Wavering, Dithering Neighbours are Liable to Invite Trouble

Strategic salience of neighbouring countries has already been highlighted. These are elaborated herein.

1. Chequered Times with Bangladesh

Though the current Indo-Bangladesh relations are as good as it could be between good neighbours, however, Bangladesh has been through many phases of vicious anti-India activities, recurrence of which in future could be plausible. Besides joining China and Pakistan in compromising India's external security, particularly in the Siliguri Corridor, it could also provoke internal destabilisation by sponsorship terrorist-insurgency activities. In the contemporary hues of power-play, emergence of such situations could be many times more dangerous.

Geography positions Bangladesh to act as a bomb inside India's gut. Friendly relations with Bangladesh backed by recessed deterrence against strategic subversion must be India's priority.

2. *Nepal: A Detractor Kin*

India, over her purported efforts to dominate, has been a regular object of the Nepali polity's contrived 'wolf cries'.[7] In its 'balance of power' gamble, Nepal has been staking dangerously on its 'China Card', even bonhomie with Pakistan, all ostensibly to keep India bound to Nepal's self-interests. Nepal's kow-towing has led to the PRC unilaterally 'realigning' its 'settled' borders with Nepal and to play the kingmaker's role in domestic politics, all that Nepal's Communist Government is obliged to downplay.

Nepal's disavowal of India's strategic compulsions would be a reckonable possibility in the coming days. Indeed, there are seeds of China's southward expansion that could open up another sector of the PRC's aggressive conduct against India. India needs to consider that as one more military test.

3. *Strategic Template in the Rest of the Neighbourhood*

The multi-dimensional nature of modern-day warfare offers much larger scope for smaller neighbours to assume higher degrees of strategic salience, active or passive, in big power posturing, confrontation and warfare. Herein, geographic smallness matters little, strategic location and proclivity to harness it in one way or the other does.[8] The Big Powers' casting influence over smaller countries in the region—Solomon, Fiji, Sri Lanka, The Maldives, Djibouti—exemplifies this fact.[9]

The fact is testified by our recent experiences with many of our traditionally amenable neighbours—Nepal, Sri Lanka, The Maldives, to wit.[10] Economic aspirations remain a high-point of inflection in these democracies, aspirations that cannot be met without looking beyond their cerebral friendship with India. The neighbours' India-averse decisions should therefore be expected in the future, particularly when there are instigating forces lurking around. Strategic locations of each of these nations give them significant capabilities in posing a second-line military threat to India. The optimisation of India's defence preparedness has to be measured in that context.

4. USA's Power-play

For their interests and presence, the USA and its allies are India's strategic neighbours and that will be the case till 2047 and beyond into the foreseeable future. Though this power-group assumes influence over the Indo-Pacific affairs in their self-interest, that also brings many benefits to the regional environment, especially in matters of sovereignty and security. The USA's recent interest lies in restricting such surreptitious advantages that the PRC had been reaping in its quest to equal, if not exceed, the super power itself.

In forging strategic partnerships with India, there are past lessons to be cautious of the US-led power group's interests. It is conceivable that this show is aimed more at making the PRC reconciled to the Western power group's primacy before reverting to profitable re-engagement—profits of technological and commercial engagements are too enticing to be held back for long. High-level US-PRC dialogues over their defence strategies and various other policies related to trade, technology, sanctions, human rights, navigation, etc., are but pointers to that fact that sooner or later, their self-interest would drive another US-PRC rapprochement. That could deprioritise the rest of the regional members' interests. Strategic partnership with India could therefore remain stuck at being a handy counterweight to Chinese ambitions.

In a realist assessment, the amelioration of India's military security concerns could remain capped at the USA-West power group's selective diplomatic solidarity, sales of military hardware and sharing intelligence.

Sum up

In this part, we have scanned the strategic environment in which India will be obliged to progress while preserving her sovereignty and integrity. In so doing, we have jettisoned our repeatedly failed distractions towards such idealist notions of neighbourhood camaraderie that have aggravated the concerns of India's military security. In that, the major concern would emanate from India's unrelenting detractor—the PRC. *Strategic realism infers that as India's progressive interests gather salience, there would be more to India's national defence and defence preparedness than just the commonplace barricading against China's and Pakistan's aggressive designs;* The PRC's instigation of friction points among India's other neighbours should also be expected. Finally, the bonhomie of Indo-US partnership is no less determined by the dynamics of US-PRC relations; with efforts ongoing over their big power détente; that relationship cannot be expected to remain promising for long.

India's military security would therefore have to be pivoted on deterring, on her own, the PRC from attempting to secure its objectives by military force. Indeed, such a China-specific discourse on national defence would more or less cover all other distractions of India's military security.

PART 2: FORTIFYING INDIA'S MILITARY SECURITY

PRC-specificity of India's Security Concerns

The PRC has taken advantage of the multiplicities of global concerns to expand its control over much of the China Sea waters and land features therein. It has also done that, in incremental steps, across the Indo-Tibet border. These usurpations have been secured by surreptitious measures and covered by military intimidation, without having to resort to serious military confrontation. In another front, the PRC is deploying overwhelming economic, military, and political heft to draw the IOR community to its dependency. The formula has succeeded so far. The over-arching effect is to the detriment of India's strategic autonomy and regional influence.

Meanwhile, the PRC is fast building up its military power to rather disproportionate levels. It is also engaged in aggressive military posturing. Obviously, the PRC's war-dance is in anticipation of an eventual rise of reactions against its expansionist agenda. Having committed to recover every inch of its territorial claims and make no compromises on that account, the PRC has left itself with no other benign option.

In the Sino-Indian context, the PRC continues to ratchet up its lead in military power. Brisk Indo-Tibet terrain-specific training, massive scale of military modernisation and re-equipping, out-of-proportion build-up of military logistic infrastructure all along the Indo-Tibet border, besides a steady rise in military activities across Pakistan Occupied Kashmir (PoK) and the Indian Ocean emphasise that fact. Such overwhelming build-up allows the PRC to be poised to strike at India at will, and at its time and place of choosing. All that emboldens Pakistan and India's other distracting neighbours—even distant entities like Turkiye and Malaysia—to raise their levels of India-baiting acrimony.

Of late, the Indian state is seen to have learnt her lesson. Alleviation of adverse inclinations among the regional polity is therefore India's priority, just as her enterprise in strengthening defence preparedness is. However, even while such measures take some years to gain momentum, our principal antagonist remains unrelenting, un-assuaged.

Fortifying against the PRC's Arrogations

It is under this strategic environment that the pledge to fortify India's military security and defence preparedness in the coming 25 years have to be fulfilled. Accordingly, the discussion hereafter is sequenced as follows:

1. Shaping India's Military Security Environment;
2. Capitalising Potentials into Reality of Military Prowess; and
3. Multiplication of Deterrent Military Prowess.

Shaping India's Military Security Environment

India is presently doing all possible political espousing to assuage the aggressiveness in her security environment. To keep the arrogant dragon from being provoked with another urge for direct military aggression, she has made concessions to the extent of vacating the domineering heights of Ladakh's Kailash range features along the LAC, and continues to endure the PLA's persisting attempts of territorial encroachments in various other sectors of the Indo-Tibet border. That stoicism continues even when the aggressor continues to deny, in brazen contradiction of bilateral border stability agreements, to specify the extent of its territorial claims. Short of compromising her sovereignty, there is little more that India can do to stem the tide of China's incessant belligerence.[11] The only way to deal with the situation is to elevate India's defence preparedness, while resisting the PRC's arrogations with due fortitude.

In India's larger ambit of national security, the Indo-Pacific region has gained the strategic focus of big power rivalry. Other members of the regional comity of nations, small and large, have also been drawn into that power politics in order to protect their economic and political interests. Thus, we have one grouping of the USA, the United Kingdom, France, Japan, and Australia and another consisting of revisionist powers like China, Russia, Iran, and Pakistan. Besides, as discussed in the preceding part, the strategic salience of the rest of the South and East Asian nations—Vietnam, South Korea, the

Philippines, Indonesia and Malaysia, for example, cannot be overlooked in the Indo-Pacific calculations. These nations, being intent on nurturing their sovereign aspirations, could become significant in the shaping of military postures one way or the other.[12] Lastly, there are India's immediate neighbours who, as discussed, carry reckonable strategic salience, independent of their size. India's military security is inexorably tied up with the dynamics of military postures adopted by such Indo-Pacific stakeholders. India's defence policies and military preparedness need to be construed accordingly; imprecise 'strategic partnerships' would not be enough to stall the Goliath's belligerence.

The situation enjoins India to further develop effective strategic partnerships with like-minded nations at regional and global levels, of which political-military-industrial partnerships is one aspect. To that purpose, there are security strengthening initiatives such as the various versions of joint military exercises including the Malabar naval exercises, the QUAD (Quadrilateral Dialogue) initiative and its bilateral derivatives, various reciprocal agreements with the USA, Australia, France, South Korea, Singapore, Japan and some others on military Geospatial Information System (GIS), surveillance, logistics and joint training, and establishment of the Sabang Link and CORPAT (Coordinate Patrols) with Indonesia.[13] Inter-operability with advanced militaries furthers the process of military modernisation and diplomatic understanding.

Simultaneously, sustained efforts are underway to modernise and empower the Indian military by means of structural reforms as well as modernisation of in-service weapons and equipment inventories through indigenised and foreign partnership-aided industrialisation. The effort is further being sustained by selective acquisitions of the latest military hardware through defence cooperation agreements as well as cooperative production arrangements like the Indo-US defence technology & trade initiative (DTTI). Above all, raising security consciousness among India's policy-makers has accelerated the build-up of military logistic infrastructure, development of border area connectivity and Nicobar military base, for example.

One effective way of shaping a favourable defence environment is to tap on military-to military relationships. Such relationships within the region have traditionally been very robust, much to each party's informal benefit. It is time to formally sanctify that kind of military intimacy.

Favourably-shaped strategic environment promotes the causes of military security. Backed up with astute policy-making and realist rather than idealist diplomacy in the coming 25 years, the abovementioned initiatives may see a favourable shaping of India's security environment.

Capitalising Potentials into Reality of Military Prowess

It is no news that there are many structural voids as well as resource deficiencies in India's planning and preparedness for national defence. In the matter of India's build-up to the requisite level of military prowess, therefore, the future course of our defence planning needs to be re-oriented to be freed from such long unattended military debilities. India's defence preparedness has to be tested through the foreseeable political context, raised complexities of military and diplomatic professionalism, quantum uplift of defence technology and manufacture, and complement all these with due economic balancing. The purpose is to reap the benefits of realised operational prowess to project effective military deterrence against an increasing militarised environment to the accrual of a due 'peace dividend'.

To reiterate, such a re-orientation of the nation's military security system would have to be rooted at a coalesced political, military, diplomatic, fiscal and technological fundamental within the attainable parameters of cost-effectiveness. It would therefore be in order to consider certain representative examples of those systemic as well as material initiatives which would address the current debilities of our defence preparedness. These initiatives require political 'will' and focused whole-of-government approach to germinate—the trend that has been observed in the recent years—and unremittingly nurtured hereafter as a priority function of the government of the day.

1. **Mandating the Military Forces and the Rest of the Defence Establishments.** The thrust of India's political-military strategic confabulations have so far ended at preventing any territorial loss. That kind of apportioning of open-ended responsibility pushes the military leadership to plan for a somewhat fail-safe force-structure, and hope that the Government would see to the build-up of corresponding resources and its fiscal viability. Defence planning and preparedness then turns into a disjoined affair, while the chasm between the defined and actual force-capabilities remains irreconcilable. In that kind of imprecise arrangement, the foundations of the nation's defence capability—namely, a politically defined and resource-linked

national security strategy, astute nurture of the military organisation and its spirit of military enterprise, upgrade of defence research, and promotion of indigenous defence industry—get marginalised. This systemic debility needs early resolution through *formal articulation of a National Security Strategy (NSS) and following up with a National Defence Strategy (NDS) for military planners to work in the right direction while avoiding redundancies and divergences.*

2. **NSS and NDS.** It is needless to emphasise that the scope of the *NSS and NDS must cover all possible security situations, involving the committed aggressors, possible detractors, and even possible about-turn of neighbourhood friendships*—neighbourhood equations have been known to somersault, after all. Propositions of formally enunciated *'red lines' of national security issues* could be a part of the said NSS. Even if all adverse situations might not lead to an outbreak of military confrontation, it is wise to be prepared for that kind of eventuality. In fact, such propositions could attenuate the occurrence of that situation in the first place. India's national defence establishment is well sensitised to the issue, but formulation of such strategies has to sail through a complex, confounding and contested process which requires the government's firm steering.
3. **Rationalisation of Military's Mandated War-preparedness and Resource Allocation.** There is, of course, a 'government directive', to mandate a particular level of the nation's war-preparedness. That leads professionals to recommend and the government to sanction, necessary inventories and stocks of weaponry, ammunition and combat equipment to be maintained. However, successive governments have been found unable to provide for their sanctioned level of war inventories. Such disconnect between the military's mandate and resource allocation for national defence is harmful to the cause of own military deterrence and encourages ever-lurking detractors to resort to aggressive behaviour. Therefore, *the nation's purpose in the run-up to the year 2047 must be to bridge the said disconnect by accelerated build-up of its fiscal resources and military technology-industry capacities.* The process needs to be sustained through long-term political commitments, particularly so when successor governments come face to face with other compelling and competing demands of democratic governance. Having committed to comprehensive defence

preparedness, it is to be seen as to how the national leadership carries that intent into the coming years.

4. **Systemic Measures in Military Modernisation.** Restructure of infantry and mechanised forces in the 1980s was a well-conceived and articulated measure in answer to the call of the times. Even then, it took over two decades to proceed beyond the first phase of its implementation, while certain layers of support and logistic measures had to remain unattended. A similar fate has befallen subsequent attempts to modernise, even incrementally, the equipment, organisation and manpower of the Indian military force-structure. Such systematic debilities in the governing processes associated with the current military restructure and modernisation *will have to be overcome in our run-up to the goal of strengthening India's military security in an increasingly contentious regional order.*
5. **Acceleration of Organisational Integration.** Integration of tri-service strategising across the entire spectrum of modern warfare as well as operationalisation of joint tri-force force-structuring are yet to progress beyond the tentative stage. *Organisational integration aims at singular processes of military planning and field forces' command, service-specific mechanisms for exercise of control, and joint chains of logistic support.* It therefore nullifies autonomous duplication and redundancies. Having been commenced, this process requires to be progressed, with the government's lead participation, within an accelerated time frame without being bogged down by diversions and distractions. Indeed, there would be hold-ups and hurdles but these have to be resolved, even pushed away if necessary.
6. **Optimisation of Systems and Procedures of Joint-Forces' Warfare.** As exemplified in all the wars and operations fought by independent India, the system of joint-forces warfare has been in practice in various forms, and its record of successes has been commendable. Modern war-fighting machinery requires frequent upgrades of war-waging concepts, expertise in distinct disciplines of military technology and assimilation of complex joint battle procedures. *These require service-specific re-organisation, equipping, training and operational logistics, while simultaneously being attuned to employment in joint-services operational environment.* The duality of this process makes it expensive and time consuming to master, and requires the government's policy and

budgetary support. Once organisational integration is set on course, the concepts and procedures of joint forces' war-fighting would get boosted and would result in projection of formidable military deterrence against our persistent aggressors. That should be the path to our Centenary of Independence goals.

7. **Cogency of Defence Budget.** Over the past decades, India's defence budgeting has remained just about adequate to maintain an operationally recessed military force-structure. As a fallout, all the three services have remained in conditions of '*hollowness*' in terms of deficiencies in war-waging capabilities and obsolescence of military hardware. Consequently, while internal anti-national forces and insurgencies are adequately restrained, and skirmish actions against territorial encroachments by external enemies are vigorously executed, when the time of reckoning arrives, a good part of our military forces could be found in a state of want in their regular battle-worthiness. *The illogic of maintaining a robust military establishment and then more or less confining it to the level of a skirmish and low-intensity combat force should be a matter of serious concern.* The Centenary of our Independence would be an appropriate milestone to resolve that disconnect in national defence.

8. **Bolstering the Foundations of National Defence.** National agencies chartered for *defence-specific technology development, military-industrial production and creation of dual-use defence logistic infrastructure*—transportation, communications, habitat, etc.—have, over the years, been set more or less free from military lien in the name of autonomy and civil control, leaving such agencies to set their convenient objectives and priorities. Resultantly, in many instances, India's foundational defence establishments have distracted from their focus of equipping the forces with modern and customised war-fighting hardware and providing for their unique logistic solutions. Meanwhile, the private sector had been kept, till recently, out of defence manufacturing under the ideals of non-proliferation. The foundation, over which rises a nation's military capability, has been pushed into dilapidation thus, a folly unthinkable in any strategically encumbered country. The Indian military has then to be intent on deterring strong and virulent enemies while operating with military hardware, a good part of which fall in the dated category, and emergent imports of limited numbers of

advanced military hardware. The coming decades have therefore to be dedicated to strengthening the basic foundations of our national defence. In that, *besides re-orientation of policy, fiscal and technology initiatives, there is also the need to re-institutionalise the hoary principles of 'military necessity' and 'military oversight' of defence projects.* Just as the global powers have been ever-intent on observing that principle, India too has to streamline her foundational defence policies if she wishes to manage her national defence from within the limitations of her resources.

9. **Build-up of Operational Logistic Infrastructure.** Logistic inadequacies hamper battle manoeuvrability and that exacerbates the strategic and tactical limitations imposed by shortages of weapons, equipment and manpower—a double whammy, so to say. Border infrastructural projects, besides securing remote territories against surprise and forcible occupation, go on to bring economic uplift among the border habitants, which in turn promotes territorial consolidation. So far, however, our build-up of military logistic infrastructure along the contested border areas has progressed, but haltingly. The priority has finally been registered. However, it will take humungous amounts of fiscal investments and significant uplift of the nation's construction capabilities to meet these requirements and close the window of border area vulnerability. *The imperative here is to keep engaged in brisk border development works and give time for economic and security-related returns to find fruition.* So progressed with conducive policy articulations, it is certain that by 2047, India's border areas would be fairly developed, secure and well populated.

Multiplication of Deterrent Military Prowess

A nation's strategic goals have to be reconciled according to its capability to build up a corresponding level of military power. The Indian state's realisation of its warranted military prowess notwithstanding, our economic and technological limitations could take 15-20 years, possibly more, to see to the fruition of India's slated defence modernisation, including upgrade of logistic and industrial infrastructure, to be at par with her security needs.[14] Moreover, in a resource constrained nation of competing priorities, it is quite possible to visualise a return of the political expediency in lowering the fiscal precedence of military necessities.

From its continued military build-up all across the Indo-Tibet border, frequent conduct of large-scale high-altitude training exercises, and incessant border and sea intrusions, it is also certain that the present state of the India-China border stalemate is but a temporary political pause for the PLA to prepare for the next round of territorial encroachments, 'capture' actually, and resort to its standard subterfuge of 'counter-attack in self-defence' should its expansionism be resisted. Admittedly, such a situation might be diverted by other global developments, but past experiences rule that staking the nation's integrity on that hope would invite peril, once again, which an aspirational India must avoid. Besides, robust defence preparedness itself would deter the adversary's inimical adventurism, besides advancing the nation's overall economic interests.

Here is a confounding situation that calls for interim resolution till India's military modernisation bears optimal fruition at the field level. That call necessitates invocation of innovative *strategic wisdom that would cover, to the extent feasible, the current limitations of India's military's power, and do so within such means and methods which are readily marshalled within our indigenous capacities, both current and those that might be available in the short term.* These are the realities the custodians of our national defence ought to consider. As a corollary, it would be logical to highlight certain strategies which would amplify the nation's military deterrence, and cover, to a great extent, the time needed to build up the nation's requisite military prowess. Obviously, these measures have to be of a political-military construct.

1. **Projection of Credible Deterrence.** Achievement of credible military deterrence is determined by such factors as the state of defence preparedness with built-in offensive capability, quantity and quality of military arsenal, and the 'will' to safeguard national sovereignty. Being relative to what capabilities are achievable in the time frame of 2047, the *goal of military security could be set at acquiring comparatively moderated levels of deterrence*—i.e., capabilities to rupture the looming aggressors' endurable levels of political face-loss and military upsets which could upset their leadership ambitions. To a specified extent, the purpose would also be served by fostering strategic partnerships.
2. **Rationalisation of Military Structure.** As a corollary to the above consideration, our quantitative requirements of formations, fleets and squadrons could be moderated with qualitative upgrades, rather than

expecting the ever-elusive 'manna' to fall. Thus, while proceeding with brisk and demonstrative military modernisation and restructure, build-up of defence logistic infrastructure and industry, the nation's *military force-structure may not be fixated at such services-sponsored targets that are unachievable* in the time frame of 2047, and cover shortfalls by alternative and subsidiary means as discussed herein.

3. **Organisational Integration.** While carrying the cross of their military pledge, the current generation of military leaders would have to accept that beyond a few trickles, not much of modern war-wherewithal is likely to materialise at the battlefield level any time soon. Therefore, the inadequacies of front-line war wherewithal and its effect on battle performance of the field forces would have to be covered with, if partially, by *optimum convergence of tri-service force-capabilities, shedding duplications and redundancies borne out of inter- and intra-service compartmentalisation, and* determined pursuit of *rationalisation and restructure schemes for the defence organisation* as a whole.

4. **Enhancement of Combat Support.** Enhancement of operational flexibility of field forces by elevating the class and quality of battle field intelligence, engineering support and logistic flexibility is a proven recourse to cover, to a certain extent, the shortfall of main combat inventories. That offers *flexible and timely options to field commanders to achieve multiplication of the forces at their disposal, as well as the follow-up battle echelons, by dynamic assembly, deployment and redeployments to various points of decision.* In that endeavour, the nation's robust foundations in the domains of engineering, manufacturing and construction, information, surveillance, communications and data processing technology, besides the vast transportation networks, have to be harnessed as parallel undertakings of military modernisation.

5. **Full Spectrum Regular-Irregular Operations.** The adversity of India's situation calls upon our military leadership's adaption to innovative strategies to stalemate the giant adversary's and collaborators' persistent territorial usurpations and other destabilising efforts which they back with threats of military offensives, nuclear attacks, etc. In that call, adaptation to various forms of *irregular warfare* —in asymmetric, special, grey zone, guerrilla or hybrid modes—should be a matter of our solemn political-military recourse. Furthermore, to stalemate a stronger military power, such adaptations have to go beyond the ambit

of localised special operations that are usually undertaken to reinforce regular tactical and operational flexibilities and their effects, and which the three services are more or less already capable of. The option here is to elevate irregular warfare to the status of a distinct 'operation of war' in its own right. *Professionally prosecuted irregular warfare is long sustainable through articulation of tempo and intensity that could bring a stronger adversary to its point of exhaustion.* Military history is replete with examples of professional prosecution of irregular warfare, in parallel with regular conventional warfare, to achieve singular successes at the strategic levels. Indeed, all the three services of the Indian military have to deliberately prepare for prosecution of irregular operations to disable the persistent enemy.[15]

6. **Trumping over Dated Mindsets.** Lastly, even if the Indian military has been quite efficient in adapting to changing tactical situations in the field, many of its present-day concerns are rooted in its hierarchy's reluctance to emerge from archaic operational convictions that have outlived their purpose. Overcoming that kind of orthodoxy, however, is not simple in an unforgiving organisation that must stand firm upon excruciating demands of tradition, rigour and modernity. To wit, initial rebuffs against revision of military training curricula, development of indigenous weaponry, strengthening of combat support capabilities and build-up of logistic infrastructure came from those who were to be the beneficiaries—the operational hierarchy! *To crystallise our recessed potentials into military prowess and translate them into higher levels of defence preparedness, it would be necessary for military professionals to repudiate the inevitable alarms that would be raised against the defence transformational processes by the prejudices of fixated naysayers.* That must be a key stipulation.

THE WAY TO 2047

In the context of the Sino-Indian dispute, the foregone conclusion is that the PLA's massive build-up across the Indo-Tibet border is meant to prepare the ground to:

(a) Smother the eventual hardening of India's military response to the PLA's future attempts to seize, not just more of Indian territory, but more seriously, two of her constitutional states that are integral to the Indian nation.

(b) Bring the north-western parts of Kashmir State—Ladakh, Siachen, Gilgit-Baltistan and PoK—into the PRC's *de jure or de facto* domain to sustain its geo-economic strategy.

(c) Alienate the new generations of Tibetans from their Indian connection by laying claim over the so-called 'Southern Tibet'. The Communist regime suffers from a banal expectation that such attempts would pull the Tibetan people into its fold.

(d) Subvert India's progress to global significance and keep her destabilised, directly and through its flunkies. The purpose is to barricade India's sphere between the Himalayan foothills and its peninsular waters of the Indian Ocean, leaving the realm to the PRC's dominance.

Under the circumstances, it is obvious that India is destined for long to the inevitability of being subject to China's overbearing military inflictions. Thus, the only practical way of thwarting the PRC's aggressive ways is to demonstrate a credible ability to repudiate domineering impositions and evict encroachments, by force if necessary, and be prepared, demonstratively, to stand up to escalation in hostilities. It is no brainer to understand that neither of these options is achievable for some years to come. In the interim, the purpose of India's defence preparedness is to find, within own limitations, ingenuous ways of keeping the nation's enemies deterred, and if needed, deny them the fruits of their military aggression. This paper looks into that kind of paradoxical endeavour when our resources do not match our tasks, and discusses the possible means of managing that paradox, the underlying principle being that *there is more to warfare than just manpower and hardware and that funding larger forces do not necessarily translate into victory.*[16]

ENDNOTES

1. By convention, the term 'national defence' is defined as a subset of 'national security' whereas 'military security' is a subset of 'national defence'.
2. In so doing, the Chinese regime selectively falsifies 'historical' precedence and brandishes itself as a 'humiliated victim' who is ordained to be allowed, gracefully, to be the regional hegemon among a diffident tributary neighbourhood. Then, having preached peace, friendliness, mutual accommodation, respect and such nobilities with a straight face, it proceeds, 'when the time is ripe', to defile the established norms of international conduct and arm-twist peaceable nations into deferring to its arrogations. A recent instance of China's obduracy in falsehood: The Ministry of Foreign Affairs, People's Republic of China, Xi Jinping's Keynote Speech at the Boao Forum Asia Conference, 21 April 2022.
3. Violation of the four Sino-India border management agreements, deceptive assurances over river-water (Brahmaputra, Mekong, and Salween) security of downstream nations, non-

adherence of the Codes of Conduct in the South China Sea and arbitrary rejection of the International Court of Arbitration's ruling on Filipino islands are some cases in point.

4. To some extent, that is already the case considering that the exercise of 'freedom of navigation' remains tenuous at best, and many times the regional community would rather avoid trouble and reconcile to occupation of various disputed China Sea islands and outcrops, observance of China's air defence identification zone stipulations, reconciliation to China's sea-fishing and mining activities, and even sequester many of their sovereign rights to avoid provoking China's wrath.
5. Some of the PRC's outrageous anti-India acts relate to its Kashmir subterfuge, subversion of neighbours, the nuclear energy issue, discriminating visa rules and shielding of globally-proclaimed terrorist entities.
6. Pakistan military-political influence has been displayed by global condoning of its misadventures of the 1948, 1965 and Kargil wars. Her servility to the Western powers, Islamic nations, and China gets her much indulgence.

INDEX